THE TŪZUK-I-JAHĀNGĪRĪ
OR
MEMOIRS OF JAHĀNGIR

THE TŪZUK-I-JAHĀNGĪRĪ
OR
MEMOIRS OF JAHĀNGIR

FROM THE FIRST TO THE TWELFTH YEAR OF HIS REIGN

Volume–1

Translated by
Alexander Rogers

Edited by
Henry Beveridge

ATLANTIC
PUBLISHERS & DISTRIBUTORS (P) LTD

ATLANTIC
PUBLISHERS & DISTRIBUTORS (P) LTD

7/22, Ansari Road, Darya Ganj, New Delhi
Tel.: +91-11-4077 5252, 2327 3880
E-mail: orders@atlanticbooks.com
Web: www.atlanticbooks.com

Published by Atlantic Publishers & Distributors (P) Ltd.

Reprinted in 22015, 2018, 2021, 2023, 2025

First Published 1909

Printed & bound in India by Atlantic Print Services

PREFACE

MR. ROGERS translated the Memoirs of Jahāngīr several years ago from the edition which Sayyid Aḥmad printed at Ghazipur in 1863 and at Allyghur in 1864. Orientalists are greatly indebted to the Sayyid for his disinterested labours, but his text seems to have been made from a single and defective MS. and is often incorrect, especially in the case of proper names. I have collated it with the excellent MSS. in the India Office and the British Museum, and have thus been able to make numerous corrections. I have also consulted the MS. in the Library of the R.A.S., but it is not a good one. I have, with Mr. Rogers's permission, revised the translation, and I have added many notes.

There is an account of the Memoirs in the sixth volume of Elliot & Dowson's "History of India," and there the subject of the various recensions is discussed. There is also a valuable note by Dr. Rieu in his "Catalogue of Persian MSS.," i, 253. It is there pointed out that there is a manuscript translation of the first nine years of the Memoirs by William Erskine in the British Museum. I have consulted this translation and found it helpful. The MS. is numbered Add. 26,611. The translation is, of course, excellent, and it was made from a good MS.

A translation of what Dr. Rieu calls the garbled Memoirs of Jahāngīr was made by Major David Price and published by the Oriental Translation Committee of the Royal Asiatic Society in 1829. The author of this work is unknown, and its history is an unsolved problem. It is occasionally fuller than the genuine Memoirs, and it contains some picturesque touches, such as the account of Akbar's deathbed. But it is certain that it is, in part at least, a fabrication, and that it contains statements which Jahāngīr could never have made. Compare, for instance, the account of the death of Sohrāb, the son of Mīrzā Rustam, near the end of Price's translation, pp. 138–9, with that given in the genuine Memoirs in the narrative of the fifteenth year of the reign, p. 293, and also in the Iqbāl-nāma, p. 139. Besides being inaccurate, the garbled or spurious Memoirs are much shorter than the genuine work, and do not go beyond the fifteenth year. Price's translation, too, was made from a single and badly written MS.[1] which is now in the R.A.S. Library. Dr. Rieu remarks that it is to be regretted that so poor a fabrication as the garbled Memoirs should have been given to the world as a genuine production of Jahāngīr. This being so, it is appropriate that the present translation of the genuine Memoirs should be published by the Royal Asiatic Society.

When Jahāngīr had written his Memoirs for the first twelve years of his reign he made them into a volume, and had a number of copies made and distributed (Elliot, vi, 360). The first of these he gave to Shāh Jahān, who was then in high favour. The present publication is a translation of the first volume of the Memoirs, but the translation of the whole Memoirs, together with the additions of Mu'tamad Khān and Muḥammad Hādī, has been completed, and it is to be hoped that its publication will follow in due course.

Jahāngīr reigned for twenty-two years, but ill-health and sorrow made him give up the writing of his Memoirs in the seventeenth year of his reign (see Elliot, vi, 280). He then entrusted the task to Mu'tamad Khān, the author of the Iqbāl-nāma, who continued the Memoirs to the beginning of the nineteenth year. He then dropped writing the Memoirs in the name of the emperor, but he continued the narrative of the reign, to Jahāngīr's death, in his own work, the Iqbāl-nāma. Muḥammad Hādī afterwards continued the Memoirs down to Jahāngīr's death, but his work is little more than an abridgment

[1] It is owing to the crabbed writing of Price's MS. that at p. 21 Jahāngīr is made to say that the Prince of Kashmir belonged to the society of Jogis. The real statement is that the prince belonged to the Chak family.

of the Iqbāl-nāma. Sayyid Aḥmad's edition contains the continuations of the Memoirs by Mu'tamad and Muḥammad Hādī, and also Muḥammad Hādī's preface and introduction. But this preface and introduction have not been translated by Mr. Rogers, and I do not think that a translation is necessary. Muḥammad Hādī is a late writer (see Elliot, vi, 392), his date being the first quarter of the eighteenth century, and his introduction seems to be almost wholly derived from the Ma'ā ṣ ir-i-Jahāngīrī of Kāmgār Ḥusainī (Elliot, vi, 257). It consists mainly of an account of Jahāngīr's life from his birth up to his accession.

It is perhaps unnecessary to say anything about the importance of Jahāngīr's Memoirs. They give a lively picture of India in the early decades of the seventeenth century, and are a valuable supplement to the Akbar-nāma. I may be allowed, however, to end this preface with the following remarks which I contributed to the *Indian Magazine* for May, 1907:—

"The Royal authors of the East had more blood in them than those kings whose works have been catalogued by Horace Walpole. To find a parallel to them we must go back to Julius Cæsar, and even then the advantage is not upon the side of Europe. After all, the commentaries of the famous Roman are a little disappointing, and certainly the Memoirs of Bābar and Jahāngīr are far more human and fuller of matter than the story of the Gallic Wars. All Muhammadans have a fancy for writing chronicles and autobiographies, and several Muhammadan kings have yielded to the common impulse. Central Asia has given us the Memoirs of Tamarlane, Bābar, and Ḥaidar, and the chronicle of Abu-l-ghazi; Persia has given us the Memoirs of Shah Tahmasp, and India the Memoirs of the Princess Gulbadan and Jahāngīr. In modern times we see the same impulse at work, for we have the biography of the late Ameer of Afghanistan and the diary of the Shah of Persia.

"The contributions to literature by Royal authors which come to us from the East form a department by themselves, and one which is of great value. Nearly all Eastern histories are disfigured by adulation. Even when the author has had no special reason for flattery and for suppression of truth, he has been dazzled by the greatness of his subject, and gives us a picture which no more reveals the real king than does a telescope the real constitution of the Morning Star. But when Eastern monarchs give us chronicles, the case is different. They have no occasion for fear or favour, and mercilessly expose the failings of their contemporaries. Not that they are to be trusted any more than other Orientals when speaking of themselves. Bābar has suppressed the story of his vassalage to Shah Isma'īl, of his defeat at Ghajdawān, and his treatment of 'Ālam Lodi; and Jahāngīr has glossed over his rebellion against his father, and the circumstances of Shīr-āfgan's death. But when they have to speak of others—whether kings or nobles—they give us the whole truth, and perhaps a little more. An amiable Princess like Gulbadan Begam may veil the faults and weaknesses of her brothers Humāyūn and Hindāl; but Bābar strips the gilt off nearly every one whom he mentions, and spares no one—not even his own father.

"The Memoirs of Bābar, Ḥaidar, and Gulbadan have been translated into English, and those of Ṯahmasp have been translated into German; but unfortunately Jahāngīr's have never been fully translated,[1] though there are extracts in Elliot & Dowson's History, and Major Price many years ago gave us from an imperfect manuscript a garbled account of a few years of his Memoirs. Yet in reality Jahāngīr's Memoirs are not inferior in interest to those of Bābar. Indeed, we may go further and say there is twice as much matter in them as in Bābar's Memoirs, and that they are by far the most entertaining of the two works. Not

[1] A translation was begun by the Rev. Mr. Lowe for the Asiatic Society of Bengal, but only one fasciculus was published. This was in 1889.

that Jahāngīr was by any means as remarkable a man as his great-grandfather. He was a most faulty human being, and his own account of himself often excites our disgust and contempt. But he had the sense not to confine his narrative to an account of himself, and he has given us a picture of his father, the great Akbar, which is a bigger 'plum' than anything in Bābar's Memoirs. But his account of himself has also its charm, for it reveals the real man, and so he lives for us in his Memoirs just as James VI—to whom, and to the Emperor Claudius, he bears a strange and even ludicrous resemblance—lives in the 'Fortunes of Nigel' or Claudius in Suetonius and Tacitus. Jahāngīr was indeed a strange mixture. The man who could stand by and see men flayed alive, and who, as he himself tells us, put one man to death and had two others hamstrung because they showed themselves inopportunely and frightened away his game, could yet be a lover of justice and could spend his Thursday evenings in holding high converse. He could quote Firdūsi's verse against cruelty to animals—

> 'Ah! spare you emmet, rich in hoarded grain—
> He lives with pleasure, and he dies with pain';

and be soft-hearted enough to wish that his father were alive to share with him the delicious mangoes of India. He could procure the murder of Abu-l-faẓl and avow the fact without remorse, and also pity the royal elephants because they shivered in winter when they sprinkled themselves with cold water. 'I observed this,' he says, 'and so I ordered that the water should be heated to the temperature of luke-warm milk.' And he adds: 'This was entirely my own idea; nobody had ever thought of it before.' One good trait in Jahāngīr was his hearty enjoyment of Nature and his love for flowers. Bābar had this also, but he was old, or at least worn out, when he came to India, and he was disgusted by an Indian attempt to poison him, and so his description of India is meagre and splenetic. Jahāngīr, on the other hand, is a true Indian, and dwells delightedly on the charms of Indian flowers, particularises the palās, the bokūl, and the champa, and avows that no fruit of Afghanistan or Central Asia is equal to the mango. He loved, too, to converse with pandits and Hindu ascetics, though he is contemptuous of their avatars, and causes the image of Vishnu as the boar avatar to be broken and flung into the Pushkar lake.

"It is a remark of Hallam's that the best attribute of Muhammadan princes is a rigorous justice in chastising the offences of others. Of this quality Jahāngīr, in spite of all his weaknesses, had a large share, and even to this day he is spoken of with respect by Muhammadans on account of his love of justice. It is a pathetic circumstance that it was this princely quality which was to some extent the cause of the great affront put upon him by Mahābat Khan. Many complaints had been made to Jahāngīr of the oppressions of Mahābat in Bengal, and crowds of suppliants had come to Jahāngīr's camp. It was his desire to give them redress and to punish Mahābat for his exactions, together with his physical and mental weakness, which led to his capture on the banks of the Jhilam.

"One of the many interesting observations in his Memoirs is his account of an inscription he saw at Hindaun. He says that in the thirteenth year of his reign, as he was marching back to Agra, he found a verse by someone inscribed on the pillar of a pleasure-house on an islet in the lake at Hindaun. He then proceeds to quote it, and it turns out to be one of Omar Khayyam's! This is FitzGerald's paraphrase:—

'For some we loved, the loveliest and the best
That from his vintage Time hath prest,
Have drunk their Cup a Round or two before,
And one by one crept silently to rest.'

"The same quatrain has also been quoted by Badayūnī in his history, and the interesting thing about Jahāngīr's quotation of it is that he could see the beauty of the verse and at the same time did not know who was the author. There is also an interest in the fact that the third line contains a different reading from that given in Whinfield's edition of the text. Hindaun is in the Jaipur territory, and one would like to know if the inscription still exists.

"Among other things in Jahāngīr's Memoirs there is the description of the outbreak of the Plague, given to him by a lady of his court [which has been quoted by Dr. Simpson in his book upon Plague], and there is a very full account of Kashmir, which is considerably superior to that in the Ayin Akbarī, which Sir Walter Lawrence has praised."

With reference to the portrait of Jahāngīr prefixed to this volume, it may be interesting to note that it appears from Mr. E. B. Havell's "Indian Sculpture," p. 203, that the British Museum possesses a drawing by Rembrandt which was copied from a Moghul miniature, and which has been pronounced by Mr. Rouffaer to be a portrait of Jahāngīr. Coryat (Purchas, reprint, iv, 473) thus describes Jahāngīr's personal appearance:—"He is fifty and three years of age, his nativity-day having been celebrated with wonderful pomp since my arrival here. On that day he weighed himself in a pair of golden scales, which by great chance I saw the same day; a custom he observes most inviolably every year. He is of complexion neither white nor black, but of a middle betwixt them. I know not how to express it with a more expressive and significant epitheton than olive. An olive colour his face presenteth. He is of a seemly composition of body, of a stature little unequal (as I guess not without grounds of probability) to mine, but much more corpulent than myself."

As regards the bibliography of the Tūzuk-i-Jahāngīrī, I have to note that there is an Urdu translation by Munshī Aḥmad 'Alī Sīmāb of Rāmpūra, that is, Aligarh in Tonk. It was made from Muḥammad Hādī's edition under the patronage of Muḥammad Ibrāhīm 'Alī Khān Nawāb of Tonk, and was published by Newal Kishor in 1291 (1874). There is also a Hindi translation by Munshī Debī Prasād which was published in 1905 at Calcutta by the Bhārat Mitra Press. The Urdu translation referred to by

Mr. Blumhardt in his Catalogue of Hindustani MSS., p. 61, and noticed by Elliot, vi, 401, and Garcin de Tassy, iii, 301, is, as the two latter writers have remarked, a translation of the Iqbāl-nāma. The MS. referred to by Elliot, vi, 277, as having been in the possession of General Thomas Paterson Smith, and which is described in Ethé's Catalogue of the India Office MSS., No. 2833, p. 1533, was made by Sayyid Muḥammad, the elder brother of Sayyid Aḥmad. As the end of the MS. the copyist gives some account of himself and of his family. He made the copy from copies in the Royal Library and in the possession of Rajah Roghū Nāth Singh *alias* Lāl Singh Jālpūr. He finished it in October, 1843. Sayyid Muḥammad was Munsif of Hutgām in the Fatḥpūr district. He died young in 1845. My friend Mr. T. W. Arnold, of the India Office, informs me that Sayyid Aḥmad told him that he found a valuable illustrated MS. of the Tūzuk in the débris of the Delhi Royal Library, and took it home, but that it was lost when his house was plundered by the mutineers. There is in the Bodleian a copy in Sayyid Aḥmad's own handwriting. He states that he made use of ten good MSS. The Englishman at whose request he made the copy was John Panton Gubbins, who was once Sessions Judge of Delhi. This copy is described in the Bodleian Catalogue, p. 117, No. 221. The MS. No. 220 described on the same page was brought home by Fraser, and is a good one, but only goes down to the end of the 14th year.

H. BEVERIDGE

March, 1909

POSTSCRIPT—Since writing this Preface I have been enabled by the kindness of Mr. Irvine to examine the Hindi Jahāngīr-nāma of Debī Prasād. It is not a translation, but an abstract, and I do not think it is of much value. Being a Jodhpūr man he has been able, perhaps, to correct some spellings of places, but he does not seem to have consulted any MSS., and when he comes to a difficulty he shirks it. The most valuable adjunct to the Tūzuk, after the Iqbāl-nāma, is the Ma'āṣir-i-Jahāngīrī of

Kāmgār Ḥusainī. It is important as giving the early history of Jahāngīr, that is, of the time when he was Prince Selīm. There are three copies of his work in the British Museum, but the so-called Maāthir-i-Jahāngīrī of the India Office Library, No. 3098, or 324 of the new Catalogue, is only a copy of the Iqbāl-nāma.

I regret that the number of Errata and Addenda is so large, but when I began the revision I did not know that Sayyid Aḥmad's text was so incorrect. It will be seen that at pp. 158 and 162 I have made two erroneous notes.

H. BEVERIDGE

JAHĀNGĪR'S MEMOIRS.

In the Name of God, the Merciful, the Clement.

CHAPTER I.

By the boundless favour of Allah, when one sidereal hour of Thursday, Jumādā-s̤-s̤ānī 20th, A.H. 1014 (October 24th, 1605), had passed, I ascended the royal throne in the capital of Agra, in the 38th year of my age.[1]

Till he was 28 years old, no child of my father had lived, and he was continually praying for the survival of a son to dervishes and recluses, by whom spiritual approach to the throne of Allah is obtained. As the great master, Khwāja Mu'īnu-d-dīn Chishtī, was the fountain-head of most of the saints of India, he considered that in order to obtain this object he should have recourse to his blessed threshold, and resolved within himself that if Almighty God should bestow a son on him he would, by way of complete humility, go on foot from Agra to his blessed mausoleum, a distance of 140 *kos.* In A.H. 977, on Wednesday, 17th Rabī'u-l-awwal (August 31st, 1569), when seven *gharī* of the aforesaid day had passed, when Libra (Mīzān) had risen to the 24th degree, God Almighty brought me into existence from the hiding-place of nothingness. At the time when my venerated father was on the outlook for a son, a dervish of the name of Shaikh Salīm, a man of ecstatic condition, who had traversed many of the stages of life, had his abode on a hill near Sīkrī, one of the villages of Agra, and the people of that neighbourhood

---

[1] That is, he was 37 years 3 months by the lunar calendar, and 36 years 1 month by solar reckoning (Pādshāhnāma, i, 69). Elliot and all the MSS. have 8th Jumādā-s̤-s̤ānī as the date of the accession, but this is clearly wrong, as Akbar did not die till 13th Jumādā-s-sānī. Evidently the copyists have, as is so often the case, misread *bistam* as has h̄ tam. See Blochmann's remark, p. 454, note 3. That Jahāngīr was not at this time 38 is shown by his stating at p. 37 that he celebrated his 38th birthday at Lahore after the capture of Khusrau.

had complete trust in him. As my father was very submissive to dervishes, he also visited him. One day, when waiting on him and in a state of distraction, he asked him how many sons he should have. The Shaikh replied, " The Giver who gives without being asked will bestow three sons on you." My father said, " I have made a vow that, casting my first son on the skirt of your favour, I will make your friendship and kindness his protector and preserver." The Shaikh accepted this idea, and said, "I congratulate you, and I will give him my own name." When my mother came near the time of her delivery, he (Akbar) sent her to the Shaikh's house that I might be born there. After my birth they gave me the name of Sultan Salīm, but I never heard my father, whether in his cups or in his sober moments, call me Muḥammad Salīm or Sultan Salīm, but always *Shaikhū Bābā.* My revered father, considering the village of Sīkrī, which was the place of my birth, lucky for him, made it his capital. In the course of fourteen or fifteen years that hill, full of wild beasts, became a city containing all kinds of gardens and buildings, and lofty, elegant edifices and pleasant places, attractive to the heart. After the conquest of Gujarāt this village was named Fatḥpūr. When I became king it occurred to me to change my name, because this resembled that of the Emperor of Rūm. An inspiration from the hidden world brought it into my mind that, inasmuch as the business of kings is the controlling of the world, I should give myself the name of Jahāngīr (World-seizer) and make my title of honour (*laqab*) Nūru-d-dīn, inasmuch as my sitting on the throne coincided with the rising and shining on the earth of the great light (the Sun). I had also heard, in the days when I was a prince, from Indian sages, that after the expiration of the reign and life of King Jalālu-d-dīn Akbar one named Nūru-d-dīn would be administrator of the affairs of the State. Therefore I gave myself the name and appellation of Nūru-d-dīn Jahāngīr Pādshāh. As this great event took place in Agra, it is necessary that some account of that city should be given.

Agra is one of the grand old cities of Hindustan. It had formerly an old fort on the bank of the Jumna, but this my father threw down before my birth, and he founded a fort of cut red stone, the like of which those who have travelled over the world cannot point out. It was completed in the space of fifteen or sixteen years. It had four gates and two sally-ports, and its cost was 35 lakhs of rupees, equal to 115,000 *tomān* of current Persian coinage and to 10,500,000 *khānī* according to the Tūrān reckoning. The habitable part of the city extends on both sides of the river. On its west side, which has the greater population, its circumference is seven kos and its breadth is one kos. The circumference of the inhabited part on the other side of the water, the side towards the east, is $2\frac{1}{2}$ kos, its length being one kos and its breadth half a kos. But in the number of its buildings it is equal to several cities of 'Irāq, Khurāsān, and Māwarā'a-n-nahr (Transoxiana) put together. Many persons have erected buildings of three or four storeys in it. The mass of people is so great, that moving about in the lanes and bazars is difficult. It is on the boundary of the second climate. On its east is the province of Qanauj; on the west, Nāgor; on the north, Sambhal; and on the south, Chanderī.

It is written in the books of the Hindus that the source of the Jumna is in a hill of the name of Kalind,[2] which men cannot reach because of the excessive cold. The apparent source is a hill near the pargana of Khiẓrābād.

The air of Agra is warm and dry; physicians say that it depresses the spirits (*rūḥrā ba taḥlīl mībarad*) and induces weakness. It is unsuited to most temperaments, except to the phlegmatic and melancholy, which are safe from its bad effects. For this reason animals of this constitution and temperament, such as the elephant, the buffalo, and others, thrive in its climate.

---

[2] The Sanskrit Kalinda.

Before the rule of the Lodī Afghans, Agra was a great and populous place, and had a castle described by Mas'ūd b. Sa'd b. Salmān in the ode (*qaṣīda*) which he wrote in praise of Maḥmūd, son of Sultan Ibrāhīm, son of Mas'ūd, son of Sultan Maḥmūd of Ghaznī, on the capture of the castle—

"The fort of Agra appeared in the midst of the dust
Like a mountain, and its battlements like peaks."[3]

When Sikandar Lodī designed to take Gwalior he came to Agra from Delhi, which was the capital of the Sultans of India, and settled down there. From that date the population and prosperity of Agra increased, and it became the capital of the Sultans of Delhi. When God Almighty bestowed the rule of India on this illustrious family, the late king, Bābar, after the defeat of Ibrāhīm, the son of Sikandar Lodī, and his being killed, and after his victory over Rānā Sāngā, who was the chief of the Rajas of Hindustan, established on the east side of the Jumna, on improved land, a garden (*chārbāgh*) which few places equal in beauty. He gave it the name of Gul-afshān (Flower-scatterer), and erected in it a small building of cut red stone, and having completed a mosque on one side of it he intended to make a lofty building, but time failed him and his design was never carried into execution.

In these Memoirs, whenever *Ṣāḥib qirānī* is written it refers to Amīr Tīmūr Gūrgān; and whenever *Firdūs-makānī* is mentioned, to Bābar Pādshāh; when *Jannat-āshyānī* is used, to Humāyūn Pādshāh; and when *'Arsh-āshyānī* is employed, to my revered father, Jalālu-d-dīn Muḥammad Akbar Pādshāh Ghāzī.

Melons, mangoes, and other fruits grow well in Agra and its neighbourhood. Of all fruits I am very fond of mangoes. In the reign of my father (*'Arsh-āshyānī*) many fruits of other countries,

---

[3] The couplet appears in Mas'ūd's divan, B.M. MS. Egerton, 701, p. 142*a*, line 4. The preceding lines show that the dust *(gard)* referred to in the first line means the dust caused by the invading army. I take the words *barū bārhāī* to mean the battlements or pinnacles of the fortress, the ī at the end of *bārhā* being intensive.

which till then were not to be had in India, were obtained there. Several sorts of grapes, such as the *ṣāḥibī* and the *ḥabshī*[4] and the *kishmishī,* became common in several towns; for instance, in the bazars of Lahore every kind and variety that may be desired can be had in the grape season. Among fruits, one which they call *ananās* (pineapple), which is grown in the Frank ports,[5] is of excessive fragrance and fine flavour. Many thousands are produced every year now in the Gul-afshān garden at Agra.

From the excellencies of its sweet-scented flowers one may prefer the fragrances of India to those of the flowers of the whole world. It has many such that nothing in the whole world can be compared to them. The first is the *champa* (*Michelia champaca*), which is a flower of exceedingly sweet fragrance; it has the shape of the saffron-flower, but is yellow inclining to white. The tree is very symmetrical and large, full of branches and leaves, and is shady. When in flower one tree will perfume a garden. Surpassing this is the *keoṛā*[6] flower (*Pandanus odoratissimus*). Its shape and appearance are singular, and its scent is so strong and penetrating that it does not yield to the odour of musk. Another is the *rāe bel,*[7] which in scent resembles white jessamine. Its

---

[4] Erskine's manuscript translation of the Tūzuk-i-Jahāngīrī, B.M. MS. Add. 26,611, and the B.M. MS. have *chīnī,* not *habshī.* But I.O. MS. No. 181 and the R.A.S. MS. have *ḥusaḥnī,* and this seems right. See Memoirs, Leyden & Erskine, p. 326, and the Haidarabad Turkī text, p. 284. The *kīshmishī* is a small grape like that of which currants are made.

[5] Cf. *infra* the account of the 11th year, p. 173.

[6] See Memoirs L. & E., p. 330.

[7] The name *rāe bel* is not given in Clarke's Roxburgh, but perhaps it is one of the jessamines, and may be the *bela* of Clarke (p. 30). The *rāe bel* is described by Abu-l-faẓl (Blochmann, pp. 76 and 82). The statement about its flowers being double and treble is obscure. Erskine renders the passage "The leaves are generally two and three fold." The Persian word is *ṭahaqa,* which apparently is equivalent to the tūī or fold of the *Āyīn-i-Akbarī,* Persian text, i, 96. The reference may be to the flowers growing in umbels.

flowers are double and treble (?). Another is the *mūlṣarī*[8] (*Mimusops Elengi*). This tree, too, is very graceful and symmetrical, and is shady. The scent of its flowers is very pleasant. Another is the *ketakī*[9] (*Pandanus*?), which is of the nature of the *keoṛā,* but the latter is thorny, whereas the *ketkī* has no thorns. Moreover, the *ketkī* is yellowish, whereas the *keoṛā* is white. From these two flowers and also from the *chambelī*[10] (*Jasminum grandiflorum*), which is the white jessamine of *wilāyat* (Persia or Afghanistan), they extract sweet-scented oils. There are other flowers too numerous to mention. Of trees there are the cypress (*sarw*), the pine (*sanūbar*), the *chanr* (*Platanus orientalis*), the white poplar (*safidār, Populus alba*), and the *bīd mūllā* (willow), which they had formerly never thought of in Hindustan, but are now plentiful. The sandal-tree, which once was peculiar to the islands (i.e., Java, Sumatra, etc.), also flourishes in the gardens.

The inhabitants of Agra exert themselves greatly in the acquirement of crafts and the search after learning. Various professors of every religion and creed have taken up their abode in the city.

After my accession, the first order that I gave was for the fastening up of the Chain of Justice, so that if those engaged in the administration of justice should delay or practise hypocrisy in the matter of those seeking justice, the oppressed might come

---

8. This is the *bokul* of Indian gardens (Clarke, p. 313), and well deserves Jahāngīr's praise. It is probably the *bholsārī* mentioned in the Āyīn (Blochmann, No. 10, p. 83. Blochmann gives *bholsārī* (p. 70) as the name of a fruit-tree, and the *bholsārī* of p. 83 may be a mistake for *miileari*.

9. The text has *sewtī,* but the *sewtī* seems to be the *Rosa glandulifera* of Roxburgh (Clarke, p. 407) and has no resemblance to the *Pandanus*. See also the description of the *sewtī,* Blochmann, p. 82. (Perhaps there are two *sewt,* one famous for fragrance, the other for beauty. See I.c., pp. 76 and 82.) What is meant in the text is evidently a *Pandanus* and the *ketkī* of Blochmann, p. 83. I have followed, therefore, I.O. MS. 181, and have substituted ketkī for *sewtī*. The *ketkī* may be *Pandanus inermis,* which has no thorns (Clarke, p. 708). Erskine also has *ketkī.*

10. L.c. p. 33 et seq.

to this chain and shake it so that its noise might attract attention. Its fashion was this: I ordered them to make a chain of pure gold,[11] 30 *gaz* in length and containing 60 bells. Its weight was 4 Indian maunds, equal to 42 'Irāqī maunds. One end of it they made fast to the battlements of the Shāh Burj of the fort at Agra and the other to a stone post fixed on the bank of the river. I also gave twelve orders to be observed as rules of conduct (*dastūru-l-'amal*) in all my dominions—

(1) Forbidding the levy of cesses under the names of *tamghā* and *mīr baḥrī* (river tolls), and other burdens which the *jāgīrdārs* of every province and district had imposed for their own profit.

(2) On roads where thefts and robberies took place, which roads might be at a little distance from habitations, the *jāgīrdārs* of the neighbourhood should build *sarā'īs* (public rest-houses), mosques, and dig wells, which might stimulate population, and people might settle down in those *sarā'īs*. If these should be near a *khāliṣa* estate (under direct State management), the administrator (*mutaṣaddī*) of that place should execute the work.

[12](3) The bales of merchants should not be opened on the roads without informing them and obtaining their leave.

[13](4) In my dominions if anyone, whether unbeliever or Musalman, should die, his property and effects should be left for his heirs, and no one should interfere with them. If he should have no heir, they should appoint inspectors and separate guardians to guard the property, so that its value might be expended in lawful expenditure, such as the building of

---

[11] Du Jarric, who gob his information from missionary reports, seems to imply that the chain was of silver, and says that Jahāngīr was following the idea of an old Persian king. It is mentioned in the Siyar al-muta'akhkhirīn (reprint, i, 230) that Muḥammad Shāh in 1721 revived this, and hung a long chain with a bell attached to it from the octagon tower which looked towards the river.

[12] In text this is wrongly made part of regulation 2.

[13] Gladwin and the MSS. have *dilbahra* (exhilarating drink), and this is probably correct. Jahāngīr would know little about rice-spirit.

mosques and *sarā'īs,* the repair of broken bridges, and the digging of tanks and wells.

(5) They should not make wine or rice-spirit (*darbahra*)[13] or any kind of intoxicating drug, or sell them; although I myself drink wine, and from the age of 18 years up till now, when I am 38, have persisted in it. When I first took a liking to drinking I sometimes took as much as twenty cups of double-distilled spirit; when by degrees it acquired a great influence over me I endeavoured to lessen the quantity, and in the period of seven years I have brought myself from fifteen cups to five or six. My times for drinking were varied; sometimes when three or four sidereal hours of the day remained I would begin to drink, and sometimes at night and partly by day. This went on till I was 30 years old. After that I took to drinking always at night. Now I drink only to digest my food.

[14](6) They should not take possession of any person's house.

(7) I forbade the cutting off the nose or ears of any person, and I myself made a vow by the throne of God that I would not blemish anyone by this punishment.

(8) I gave an order that the officials of the Crown lands and the *jāgīrdārs* should not forcibly take the ryots' lands and cultivate them on their own account.

(9) A government collector or a *jāgīrdār* should not without permission intermarry with the people of the *pargana* in which he might be.

(10) They should found hospitals in the great cities, and appoint physicians for the healing of the sick; whatever the expenditure might be, should be given from the *khāliṣa* establishment.

---

[14] This regulation is more fully expounded in Price, p. 7.

(11) In accordance with the regulations of my revered father, I ordered that each year from the 18th[15] of Rabī'u-l-awwal, which is my birthday, for a number of days corresponding to the years of my life, they should not slaughter animals (for food). Two days in each week were also forbidden, one of them Thursday, the day of my accession, and the other Sunday, the day of my father's birth. He held this day in great esteem on this account, and because it was dedicated to the Sun, and also because it was the day on which the Creation began. Therefore it was one of the days on which there was no killing in his dominions.[16]

(12) I gave a general order that the offices and *jāgīrs* of my father's servants should remain as they were. Later, the *manṣabs* (ranks or offices) were increased according to each one's circumstances by not less than 20 per cent. to 300 or 400 per cent. The subsistence money of the *aḥadīs* was increased by 50 per cent., and I raised the pay of all domestics by 20 per cent. I increased the allowances of all the veiled ladies of my father's harem from 20 per cent. to 100 per cent., according to their condition and relationship. By one stroke of the pen I confirmed the subsistence lands[17] of the holders of *aimas* (charity lands) within the dominions, who form the army of prayer, according to the deeds in their possession. I gave an order to Mīrān Ṣadr Jahān, who is one of the genuine Sayyids of India, and who for a long time held the high office of *ṣadr* (ecclesiastical officer) under

---

[15] It is curious that Jahāngīr should give the 18th Rabī'u-l-awwal as his birthday, while the authorities give it as the 17th. Probably the mistake has arisen from Jahāngīr's writing Rabī'u-l-awwal instead of Shahrīwar. His birthday was Rashn the 18th day of Shahrīwar (see Akbarnāma, ii, 344), but it was the 17th Rabī'u-l-awwal. See Muḥammad Hādī's preface, p. 2, and Beale, and Jahāngīr's own statement a few lines above. Possibly Jahāngīr wished to make out that he was born on the 18th Rabī'u-l-awwal and a Thursday, because he regarded Thursday as a blessed day (*mubārak shamba*), whilst he regarded Wednesday as peculiarly unlucky, and called it *kam*, or *gam*, *shamba*.

[16] Cf. Elliot's translation, vi, 513, and note 2.

[17] The MSS. have " the subsistence lands of people in general (*ahāli*) and the *aimas*"

my father, that he should every day produce before me deserving people (worthy of charity).[18] I released all criminals who had been confined and imprisoned for a long time in the forts and prisons.[19]

At a propitious hour I ordered that they should coin gold and silver of different weights. To each coin I gave a separate name, viz., to the *muhr* of 100 *tola,* that of *nūr-shāhī;* to that of 50 *tola,* that of *nūr-sulṭānī;* to that of 20 *tola, nūr-daulat;* to that of 10 *tola, nūr-karam;* to that of 5 *tola, nūr-mihr;* and to that of 1 *tola, nūr-jahānī.* The half of this I called *nūrānī,* and the quarter, *rawājī.* With regard to the silver coins (*sikkas*). I gave to the coin of 100 *tola* the name of *kaukab-i-ṭāli'* (star of horoscope); to that of 50 *tola,* the name of *kaukab-i-iqbāl* (star of fortune); to that of 20 *tola,* the name of *kaukab-i-murād* (star of desire); to that of 10 *tola,* the name of *kaukab-i-bakht* (star of good luck); to that of 5 *tola,* the name of *kaukab-i-sa'd* (star of auspiciousness); to that of 1 *tola,* the name of *jahāngīrī.* The half *jahāngīrī* I called *sulṭānī;* the quarter, *nisārī*[20] (showering money); the dime, *khair-i-qabūl* (the acceptable). Copper, also, I coined in the same proportions, and gave each division a particular name. I ordered that on the gold *muhr* of 100, 50, 20, and 10 *tola* the following verse by Āṣaf

[18] In the text and in Elliot, vi, 515, this is made a separate order, but it is not so in the MSS. If it were, we should have thirteen instead of twelve regulations. This is avoided in text and in Elliot by putting the 6th and 7th regulations into one ordinance. With regard to the regulation about releasing the prisoners, Sir Henry Elliot is somewhat unjust to Jahāngīr in his commentary at p. 515. It was only those who had been *long* imprisoned whom Jahāngīr released, and his proceedings at Ranthambhor in the 13th year (Tūzuk, p. 256) show that he exercised discrimination in releasing prisoners. The account in Price, p. 10, may also be consulted. There Jahāngīr says he released 7,000 men from Gwalior alone. It may be remembered that most of these were political offenders. Private criminals were for the most part put to death, or mutilated, or fined. There were no regular jails.

[19] The above translation of the Institutes should be compared with Sir Henry Elliot's translation and his commentary : History of India, E. & D., vol. vi, Appendix, p. 493.

[20] Erskine's MS. has *īṣārī* for *nīṣārī,* and *akhtar-i-qabūl* instead of *khair-i-qabūl.*

Khān[21] should be impressed—namely, on the obverse was this couplet:—

> " Fate's pen wrote on the coin in letters of light,
> The Shāh Nūru-d-dīn Jahāngīr ";

and between the lines of the verse the Creed (*Kalima*) was impressed. On the reverse was this couplet, in which the date of coinage was signified:—

> " Through this coin is the world brightened as by the sun,
> And the date thereof is 'Sun of Dominion' (Āftāb-i-Mamlakat)."[22]

Between the lines of the verse, the mint, the Hijra year, and the regnal year were impressed. On the *nūr-jahānī,* which is in the place of the ordinary gold *muhr* and exceeds it in weight by 20 per cent. (as 12 to 10), is impressed this couplet of the Amīru-l-umarā:—

> " Shāh Nūru-d-dīn Jahāngīr ibn Akbar Pādshāh
> Made gold's face bright with **the** sheen of sun and moon."

Accordingly, a hemistich was impressed on each face, and also the mint, and the Hijra and regnal year. The *jahāngīrī sikka,* also, which is greater in weight by 20 per cent., was reckoned as equal to a rupee, its weight being fixed in the same manner as that of the *nūr-jahānī* (each was a *tola* in weight, but one was in gold and the other was in silver). The weight of a *tola* is $2\frac{1}{2}$ *misqāls* of Persia and Tūrān.[23]

---

21 This is Blochmann's Āṣaf Khān No. iii, viz. Mīrzā Ja'far Beg. See pp. 368 and 411.

22. The words Āftāb-i-Mamlakat yield, according to the numeration by *abjad*, the date 1014 A.H. (1605).

23. Page 4 of the text is followed by engravings of the coins of Jahāngīr and the inscriptions thereon, for which the editor, Saiyid Ahmad, says he is indebted to Mr. Thornhill, the Judge of Meerut. They do not show the lines of poetry. There is an interesting article on the couplets on Jahāngīr's coins by Mr. C. J. Rodgers, J.A.S.B. for 1888, p. 18.

It would not be good to give all the versified chronograms which were made for my accession. I therefore content myself with the one which Maktūb Khān, the superintendent of the library and picture gallery, and one of my old servants, composed—

> "The second lord of conjunction, Shāhinshāh Jahāngīr,
> With justice and equity sat on the throne of happiness.
> Prosperity, Good Fortune, Wealth, Dignity, and Victory,
> With loins girt in his service, stood rejoicing before him.
> It became the date of the accession when Prosperity
> Placed his head at the feet of the Ṣāḥib-Qirān-i-S̤ānī."[24]

To my son Khusrau a lakh of rupees was presented that he might build up for himself the house of Mun'im Khān[25] the (former) Khānkhānān, outside the fort. The administration and government of the Panjab was bestowed on Sa'īd Khān,[26] who was one of the confidential nobles and connected with my father by marriage. His origin was from the Moghul tribe, and his ancestors were in the service of my forefathers. At the time of his taking leave, as it was said that his eunuchs oppressed and tyrannized over the weak and the poor, I sent a message to him that my justice would not put up with oppression from anyone, and that in the scales of equity neither smallness nor greatness was regarded. If after this any cruelty or harshness should be

---

24 The chronogram is ingenious. The words Sāhib-Qirān-i-Sānī yield only 1013 according to *ahjad*, and this is a year too little. But the verse states that Prosperity (or Fortune), Iqbāl, laid his head at the second lord of conjunction's feet, and the head of Iqbal, according to the parlance of chronogram-composers, is the first letter of the word, that is, alif, which stands for one 1 in *ahjad*, and so the date 1014 is made up. Sāhib-Qirān-i-Sānī means 'the second lord of conjunction,' and is a title generally applied to Shāh Jahān ; the first lord of conjunction (i.e. the conjunction of Jupiter and Venus) was Tīmūr.

25 A great officer under Humāyūn and Akbar. See Āyīn, Blochmann, p. 317.

26 Blochmann, p. 331. He had 1,200 eunuchs. He is generally styled Sa'id Chaghatai. The exact nature of his relationship does not appear. It is not mentioned in his biography in the Ma'āṣir, ii, 403. Perhaps the word (*nisbat*) does not here mean affinity by marriage.

observed on the part of his people, he would receive punishment without favour.[27]

Again, having previously bestowed on Shaikh Farīd Bukhārī, who had been *Mīr Bakhshī* in my father's service, a dress of honour, a jewelled sword, a jewelled inkstand and pen, I confirmed him in the same post, and in order to exalt him I said to him, "I regard thee as *Ṣāḥibu-s-saif-wa-l-qalam* " ("Captain Sword and Captain Pen"). Muqīm,[28] to whom my father had given at the end of his reign the title of W azīr Khān and the viziership of his dominions, I selected for the same title, rank, and service. I also gave Khwājagī Fatḥu-llah a dress of honour, and made him a bakhshi, as formerly. 'Abdu-r-Razzāq Ma'mūrī, although when I was prince he had left my service without cause or reason and had gone over to my father, I made bakhshi as formerly, and I gave him a dress of honour. To Amīnu-d-daula, who when I was prince had the post of bakhshi, and without my leave had run away and taken service with my revered father, not looking to his offences I gave the office of *Ātish-i-begī*[29] (Head of the Artillery), which he had held under my father. I left all those who were in possession of posts, both inside and outside, in the positions which they had with my father. Sharīf Khān[30]

[27] According to the account in Price, p. 16, and in the Ma' āṣir, ii, 405, Sa'id Khān gave a bond that if his people were oppressive he would forfeit his head.

[28] He does not seem to have had any real power, and he was soon superseded. See Ma'āṣir, iii, 932.

[29] It appears from Erskine and from I.O. MS. that this is a mistake for Yātish-begī,' Captain of the Watch,' and that the name is Amīnu-d-dīn, and not Amīnu-d-daula. See Akbarnāma, iii, 474, etc.

[30] Sharīf Khān had been sent by Akbar to recall Jahāngīr to his duty, but instead of coming back he stayed on. He did not accompany Jahāngīr when the latter went off the second time to wait upon his father. Probably he was afraid to do so. Jahāngīr appointed him to Bihar before he left Allahabad to visit his father for the second time. Jahāngīr says Sharīf waited upon him fifteen days after his accession, and on 4th Rajab. This is another proof, if proof were needed, that the copyists have misread the opening sentence of the Tūzuk and have written *hashtam* instead of *bistam*, for 4th Rajab is fifteen days after 20th Jumādā-*l*-ākhir.

had lived with me from his early years. When I was prince I had given him the title of *khān,* and when I left Allahabad to wait upon my honoured father I presented him with a drum and the *tūmān-togh* (standard of *yāk* tails). I had also promoted him to the rank of 2,500 and given him the government of the province of Bihar. I gave him complete control over the province, and sent him off there. On the 4th of Rajab, being fifteen days after my accession, he waited upon me. I was exceedingly pleased at his coming, for his connection with me is such that I look upon him as a brother, a son, a friend, and a companion. As I had perfect confidence in his friendship, intelligence, learning, and acquaintance with affairs, having made him Grand Vizier, I promoted him to the rank of 5,000 with 5,000 horse and the lofty title of *Amīru-l-umarā,* to which no title of my servants is superior. Though his position might have warranted a higher rank, he himself represented to me that until some notable service on his part had become perceptible to me he would not accept a higher grade than that mentioned (5,000).

As the reality of the loyalty of my father's servants had not yet become apparent, and certain faults and errors and unbecoming intentions which were not approved at the throne of the Creator or pleasing to His creatures had shown themselves, they of themselves became ashamed. Though on the day of my accession I had forgiven all offences and determined with myself that I would exact no retribution for past deeds, yet on account of the suspicion that had been aroused in my mind about them I considered the Amīru-l-umarā my guardian and protector; although God Almighty is the guardian of all His servants, and is especially so of kings, because their existence is the cause of the contentment of the world. His father, 'Abdu-ṣ-Ṣamad, who in the art of painting had no equal in the age, had

---

The Pādshāhnāma and Khāfi Khān have 20th, and Price and Price's original say that Sharīf arrived sixteen days after the accession.

obtained from the late king (*Jannat-āshyānī*) Humāyūn the title of *Shīrīn-qalam* (Sweet pen), and in his council had attained a great dignity and was on intimate terms with him (the king). He was one of the chief men of Shīrāz. My honoured father, on account of his former services, paid him great honour and reverence. I made Raja Mān Singh—who was one of the greatest and most trusted noblemen of my father, and had obtained alliances with this illustrious family, inasmuch as his aunt had been in my father's house (i.e. was his wife)[31], and I had married his sister, and Khusrau and his sister Sulṭānu-n-nisā Begam, the latter of whom is my eldest child, were born of her—as before, ruler of the province of Bengal. Though as in consequence of certain of his acts he had no expectation of this favour towards himself, I dignified him with a *chārqab* (vest without sleeves) as a robe of honour, a jewelled sword, and one of my own horses, and sent him off to his province, which is a place of (or can keep up) 50,000 horse. His father was Raja Bhagwān Dās. His grandfather, Raja Bihārī Mal, was the first of the Kachwāha Rājpūts to have the honour of entering my father's service, and he excelled his tribe in truth and sincerity of friendship, and in the quality of valour. After my accession, when all the nobles with their retinues presented themselves at my palace, it came into my mind that I should send this body of retainers under my son, Sultan Parwīz, to make a holy war against the Rānā, who was one of evil deeds, and a foul infidel of the country of Hindustan, and in my father's time had had troops sent constantly against him, but had not been driven off. In a fortunate hour I invested my said son with gorgeous robes of honour, a jewelled waist - sword, a jewelled waist-dagger, and a rosary of pearls

[31] I.O. MS. 181 and Muhammad Hādī have Sulṭān Niṣār Begam. Khāfī Khān, i, 245, has Sulṭān Begam, and says she was born in 994. Price's Jahāngīr, p. 20, says she was born a year before Khusrau. She built a tomb for herself in the Khusrau Bāgh, Allahabad, but she is not buried there (see J.R.A.S. for July, 1907, p. 607). She died on 4th Sha'bān, 1056 (5th September, 1646), and was at her own request buried in her grandfather's tomb at Sikandra (Pādshāhnāma, ii, 603-4).

intermixed with rubies of great price of the value of 72,000 rupees, 'Irāq and Turkmān horses and famous elephants, and dismissed him. About 20,000 horsemen with nobles and chief leaders were appointed to this service. The first was Āṣaf Khān, who in my father's time was one of his confidential servants, and for a long time had been confirmed in the post of bakhshi and afterwards became *dīwān ba istiqlāl* (Chancellor with full powers); him I advanced from the rank of an Amīr to that of Vizier, and promoting him from the command of 2,500 horse to that of 5,000 made him guardian to Parwīz. Having honoured him with a robe of honour, jewelled waist-sword, a horse and an elephant, I ordered that all the *manṣabdārs* (commanders), small and great, should not depart from such orders as he thought proper to give them. I made 'Abdu-r-Razzāq Ma'mūrī his bakhshi and Mukhtār Beg, Āṣaf Khān's paternal uncle, diwan to Parwīz. I also presented to Raja Jagannāth, son of Raja Bihārī Mal, who had the rank of 5,000, a robe of honour and a jewelled waist-sword.

Again, I gave Rānā Shankar, cousin of the Rānā—to whom my father had given the title of Rānā, proposing to send him with Khusrau against the Rānā, but at that time he (Akbar) became a *shanqar* (a falcon, i.e. he died)—a robe of honour and a jewelled sword, and sent him with him.

I presented Mādho Singh, brother's son of Raja Mān Singh, and Rāwal Sāl Darbārī with flags, from this consideration, that they were always present at Court and belonged to the Sekhāwaṭ[32] Rājpūts, and were confidential servants of my father. Each received also the rank of 3,000.

I promoted Shaikh Ruknu-d-dīn the Afghan, to whom when I was prince I had given the title of Shīr Khān, from the grade of 500 to that of 3,500. Shīr Khān is the head of his clan and a very valiant man. He lost his arm by the sword in service against the

[32] Should be Shaikhāwat.

Uzbegs.[33] 'Abdu-r-Raḥman, son of Shaikh Abu-l-faẓl, Mahā Singh, grandson of Rāja Mān Singh, Zāhid Khān, son of Ṣādiq Khān, Wazīr Jamīl, and Qarā Khān Turkmān were exalted to the rank of 2,000; all these obtained robes of honour and horses, and were dismissed. Manohar also obtained leave to join the expedition. He is of the tribe of the Sekhāwaṭ Kachhwāhas, and on him in his young days my father bestowed many favours. He had learned the Persian language, and, although from him up to Adam the power of understanding cannot be attributed to any one of his tribe, he is not without intelligence. He makes Persian verses, and the following is one of his couplets:—

> "The object of shade in Creation is this:
> That no one place his foot on the light of my Lord, the Sun."[34]

If the details were to be described of all the commanders and servants appointed by me, with the conditions and connections and rank of each, it would be a long business. Many of my immediate attendants and personal followers and nobles' sons, house-born ones (*khānazādān*) and zealous Rajputs, petitioned to accompany this expedition. A thousand ahadis, the meaning of which is single ones (Blochmann, p. 20), were also appointed. In short, a force was collected together such that if reliance on the Friend (God) were vouchsafed, it could have embarked on enmity and conflict with any one of the monarchs of power.

> "Soldiers came up from all sides,
> Seizing life from heroes of the world in battle;
> They had no fear of death from the sharp sword,

---

[33] The R.A.S. and I.O. MSS. have here Umrā instead of Uzbegs. Umrā here stands, I think, for Umr Singh, the Rānā of Udaipūr, and the meaning is that Shīr Khān lost his arm in service against the Rānā.

[34] The point of the verse seems to be that light is regarded as something spread like a carpet on the ground, and that to place the foot upon it is to insult the sun. Compare Price, p. 33 ; but Manohar's verse is wrongly translated there owing to a badly written MS. For Manohar see Akbarnāma, iii, 221, and Badayūnī, iii, 201, also Blochmann, p. 494, and his article in *Calcutta Review* for April, 1871, also the Dabistān, translation, ii, 53.

No terror of water[35] and no flight from fire;
In valour singular, in vigour a crowd,
Anvils in endurance, rocks in attack."

When I was prince I had entrusted, in consequence of my extreme confidence[36] in him, my own *ūzuk* seal[37] to the Amīru-l-umarā (Sharīf), but when he was sent off to the province of Bihar I made it over to Parwīz. Now that Parwīz went off against the Rānā, I made it over, according to the former arrangement, to the Amīru-l-umarā.

Parwīz was born of Ṣāḥib-Jamāl (Mistress of Beauty), the cousin[38] of Zain Khān Koka, who, in point of affinity, was on the same footing[39] as Mīrzā 'Azīz Koka, in the 34th year of my father's reign, in the city of Kabul, two years and two months after the birth of Khusrau. After several other children had been born to me and had been received into God's mercy, a daughter was born of Karamsī,[40] who belonged to the Rāṭhor clan, and the

---

35 Probably here *āb* means both water and the water of the sword. These lines are not in the R.A.S. or I.O. MSS.

36 Text, *iḥtiyāt* (caution) ; the MSS. have *i'tiqād* (confidence), and I adopt this reading.

37 Blochmann, p. 52. It was a small round seal. *Ūzūk* or *ūzuk* is a Tartar word meaning a ring, i.e. a signet-ring.

38 Text, *ṣabiyya* (daughter), and this led Blochmann (p. 477, note 2) to say that if Sayyid Aḥmad's text was correct Jahāngīr must have forgotten, in the number of his wives, which of them was the mother of Parwīz. As a fact, Sayyid Aḥmad's text is not correct, though the R.A.S. MS. agrees with it. The two excellent I.O. MSS. have *khwīsh* (relative), which is here equivalent to cousin. So also has the B.M. MS. used by Erskine. According to Muḥammad Hādī's preface Parwīz's mother was the daughter of Khwāja Ḥasan, the paternal uncle of Zain Khān Koka. His birth was in Muḥarram, 998, or 19th Ābān (November, 1589). See also Akbarnāma, iii, 568.

39 I.e., both were Akbar's foster-brothers.

40 Price, p. 20, has Karmitty, and says the daughter only lived two months. Karamsī appears twice in the Akbarnāma as the name of a man ; see Akbarnāma, ii, 261, and iii, 201. The name may mean ' composed of kindness.' The statement in Price is wrong. Bihār Bānī was married to Ṭahmuraṣs. Prince Dāniyāl in his 20th year (see Tūzuk, M. Hādī's continuation, p. 400). According to M. Hādī's preface, Karamsī was the daughter of Rāja Kesho Dās Rāthor, and her daughter

child received the name of Bihār Bānū Begam. To Jagat Gosā'īn,[41] daughter of the Mota Raja (the fat raja), was born Sulṭān Khurram, in the 36th year of my father's reign, corresponding to A.H. 999,[42] in the city of Lahore. His advent made the world joyous (*khurram*),[43] and gradually, as his years increased, so did his excellencies, and he was more attentive to my father than all (my) other children, who was exceedingly pleased with and grateful for his services, and always recommended him to me and frequently told me there was no comparison between him and my other children. He recognised him as his real child.

After that (Khurram's birth) some other children were born who died in infancy, and then within one month two sons were borne by concubines. One of these I called Jahāndār and the other Shahryār.[44]

About this time there came a petition from Sa'īd Khān with regard to granting leave to Mīrzā Ghāzī, who was a son of the ruler of the province of Thathah (Tattah in Sind).[45] I said that as my father had betrothed his sister to my son Khusrau, please God, when this alliance came into force, I would give him leave to return to Sind.

Bihār Bānū was born on 23rd Shahrīwar, 998 (September, 1590). Kesho Dās Rāthor is probably the Kesho Dās Mārū of the Tūzuk.

41. Best known as Jodh Bāī (Blochmann, p. 619).

42. It is extraordinary that Jahāngīr should have put Shāh-Jahān's birth into A.H. 999. The I.O. MSS. support the text, but the R.A.S. MS. has A. H. 1000, which is without doubt right. Cf. Akbarnāma, Bib. Ind., iii, 603. Later on, a great point was made of his having been born in a millennium. The date is 5th January, 1592.

43. Muhammad Hādī says in his preface, p. 6, that Shāh-Jahān's grandfather Akbar gave him the name of Sultan Khurram, 'Prince Joy,' because his birth made the world glad. It was noted that the child was born in the first millennium, and also that, like his father, he was born in the same month as the Prophet.

44. Gladwin says they were twins, but this seems a mistake. They were both born about the time of Akbar's death.

45. In MS. No. 310 of Ethe's Cat. of I.O. MSS. Sa'īd Khān is described as giving as his reason for asking for M. Ghāzī that he had adopted him as his son. Price's Jahāngīr, p. 21, says the same thing.

A year before I became king I had determined that I would drink no wine on Friday eve, and I hope at the throne of God that He will keep me firm in this resolve as long as I live.

Twenty thousand rupees were given to Mīrzā Muḥammad Riẓā Sabzwārī to divide amongst the faqirs and the needy of Delhi. The viziership of my dominions I gave in the proportions of half and half to Khān Beg,[46] to whom when I was prince I had given the title of Wazīru-l-mulk, and to Wazīr Khān[47] (Muqīm), and I gave to Shaikh Farīd Bukhārī, who held the rank of 4,000, that of 5,000. I promoted Rām Dās Kachhwāha, whom my father had favoured, and who held the rank of 2,000, to that of 3,000. I sent dresses of honour to Mīrzā Rustam, son of Mīrzā Sulṭān Ḥusain and grandson of Shāh Ismā'īl, the ruler of Qandahar, and to 'Abdu-r-Raḥīm Khānkhānān, son of Bairām Khān, and to Īraj and Dārāb, his sons, and to other nobles attached to the Deccan (command). Barkhūrdār, son of 'Abdu-r-Raḥmān, son of Mu'ayyid Beg, as he had come to court without a summons, I ordered back to his jagir. [48]It is not according to good manners to go to the king's banquet without a summons, otherwise there would be no forbidding of the doors and walls to the foot of desire.

A month had elapsed after my auspicious accession when Lāla Beg, who while I was prince had obtained the title of Bāz Bahādur, obtained the blessing of waiting on me. His rank, which had been 1,500, was raised to 4,000. I promoted him to the Subah of Bihar and gave him 2,000 rupees. Bāz Bahādur is of the lineage of the special attendants of our family; his father's name was Niẓām, and he was librarian to Humāyūn. Kesho Dās Mārū, who is a Rājpūt of the province of Mairtha and is greater

---

[46] This should be Jān, and is so in I.O. MS. 181.

[47] See Ma'ā'ṣiru-l-umarā, iii, 932. The meaning of the half and half is that the two men were made coadjutors.

[48] In R.A.S. and I.O. MSS. the following passage is a verse. See also Mr. Lowe's translation, p. 16.

in loyalty than his contemporaries, I promoted to the rank of 1,500. I directed the *'ulamā* and the learned men of Islam to collect those of the distinctive appellations of God which were easy to remember, in order that I might make them into my rosary[49] (*ward*). On Friday eves[50] I associate with learned and pious men, and with dervishes and recluses. When Qilīj Khān, who was one of the old retainers of the State in my revered father's reign, was appointed to the government of the province of Gujarat, I presented him with a lakh of rupees for his expenses. I raised Mīrān Ṣadr Jahān from the rank of 2,000 to that of 4,000. I knew him in my childhood when I read the "Forty Sayings" with Shaikh 'Abdu-n-Nabī,[51] whose history is given in detail in the Akbarnāma. From these early days till now Mīrān Ṣadr Jahān has acted towards me with single-minded loyalty, and I regard him as my preceptor in religious matters (*khalīfa*). Whilst I was prince and before my revered father's illness, and during that time, when the ministers (pillars of the State) and the high nobles had become agitated, and each had conceived some idea of gain for himself and wished to become the originator of some act which could only bring ruin on the State, he had not failed in the activity of his service and devotedness. Having made 'Ināyat Beg,[52] who for a long period in the reign of my father had been Master of Works (*Dīwān-i-buyūtāt*) and held the rank of 700, half-vizier of my dominions in the place of Wazīr Khān, I gave him the high title of I'timādu-d-daula with the rank

[49] *Wird* means 'daily practice,' and may be the word intended here.

[50] Cf. this with the fuller details in Price, p. 22. Following Blochmann, I take Shab-i-jum'a to mean Thursday and not Friday night.

[51] The text has 'Abdu-l-Ghanī, but this, as the MSS. show and Blochmann has pointed out, is a mistake for 'Abdu-n-Nabī. 'Abdu-n-Nabī was strangled, and the common report is that this was done by Abu-l-faẓl. If this be true it is rather surprising that Jahāngīr does not mention it as an excuse for killing Abu-l-faẓl. Cf. the account of Mīrān Ṣadr Jahān in Price, p. 24. The "Forty Sayings is a book by Jāmī. See Rieu, Cat. i, 17, and also Dr. Herbelot s.v. *Arbain*.

[52] This should be Ghiyās̤ Beg. He was father of Nūrjahān. According to the Ma'ās̤iru-l-umarā (i, 129), he was commander of 1,000 under Akbar.

of 1,500, and I appointed Wazīr Khān to the *Dīwānī* of the province of Bengal, and assigned to him the settlement of the revenues thereof. To Patr Dās, who in the time of my father had the title of Rāy Rāyān, I gave the title of Raja Bikramājīt. The latter was one of the great Rajas of India, and it was in his reign that astronomical observatories were established in India. I made Patr Dās Master of Ordnance, and ordered that he should always have light artillery[53] in the arsenal, 50,000 light guns[54] and 3,000 gun-carriages, ready and in efficient order. He was a *khatrī* by caste, and rose in my father's service from being accountant of the elephants' stables to be diwan and an amir. He is not wanting in military qualities and in administrative skill. I made Khurram, the son of Khān A'ẕam ('Azīz Koka), who had had the rank of 2,000, an officer of 2,500.

As it was my desire that many of the Akbarī and Jahāngīrī officers should obtain the fruition of their wishes, I informed the bakhshis that whoever wished to have his birthplace made into his jagir should make a representation to that effect, so that in accordance with the Chingīz canon (*tūra*) the estate might be conveyed to him by *āl tamghā* and become his property, and he might be secured from apprehension of change. Our ancestors and forefathers were in the habit of granting jagirs to everyone

---

53 *Topkhāna-i-rikāb,* lit. stirrup-arsenal. It means light artillery that could accompany royal progresses. See Bernier, and Irvine, A. of M., 134.

54. Text, *topchī,* which seems properly to mean a gunner, but the number is preposterous. Cf. Blochmann, p. 470, and Price, p. 28. Price's original has 6,000 *topchī,* mounted on camels, and has *pāytakhi,* i.e. the capital. Erskine has " To have always in readiness in the arsenal arms and accoutrements for 50,000 matchlock men." This seems reasonable, for even if Jahāngīr ordered 50,000 musketeers, he would not have required them to be kept in the arsenal. It seems to me that though *chī* in Turki is the sign of the agent (*nomen agentis*) it is occasionally used by Indian writers as a diminutive. Thus *topchī,* here probably means a small gun or a musket, and in Hindustani we are familiar with the word *chīlamchī,* which means a small basin. At p. 301 of the Tūzuk, four lines from foot, we have the word *īlchī,* which commonly means an ambassador—an agent of a people—used certainly not in this sense, and apparently to mean a number of horses. It is, however, doubtful if *īlchī,* here be the true reading.

under proprietary title, and adorned the farmans for these with the *āl tamg͟hā* seal, which is an impressed seal made in vermilion (i.e. red ink). I ordered that they should cover the place for the seal with gold-leaf (*ṭilāposh*) and impress the seal thereon, and I called this the *altūn*[55] *tamg͟hā*.

I had selected from the other sons of S͟hāhruk͟h, Mīrzā Sulṭān,[56] son of Mīrzā S͟hāhruk͟h the grandson of Mīrzā Sulaimān, who was a descendant (great-grandson) of Mīrzā Sulṭān Abū Sa'īd and for a long time ruler of Badakhshan, and with consent of my[57] revered father brought him into my service. I count him as a son, and have promoted him to the rank of 1,000. I also promoted Bhāo Singh, son of Raja Mān Singh and the most capable of his sons, from his original rank to that of 1,500. I raised Zamāna Beg,[58] son of G͟hayūr Beg of Kabul, who has served me personally from his childhood, and who, when I was prince, rose from the grade of an ahadi to that of 500, giving him the title of Mahābat K͟hān and the rank of 1,500. He was confirmed as bakhshi of my private establishment (*s͟hāgird-pīs͟ha*).

I promoted Raja Bīr Singh Deo, a Bandela Rajput, who had obtained my favour, and who excels his equals and relatives in valour, personal goodness, and simple-heartedness, to the rank of 3,000. The reason for his advancement and for the regard shown to him was that near the end of my revered father's time, S͟haik͟h Abu-l-faẓl, who excelled the S͟haik͟hzādas of Hindustan in wisdom and learning, had adorned himself outwardly with the jewel of sincerity, and sold it to my father at a heavy price. He had been summoned from the Deccan, and, since his feelings

---

[55] Text, *aknūn* (now), which is a mistake for *altūn* (gold). See Elliot and Dowson, vi, 288. *Āl* is vermilion in Turkī and *altūn*-gold. Jahāngīr means that he changed the name from *āl tamg͟hā* to *altūn tamg͟hā*.

[56] Mīrzā Sulṭān was great-grandson of Sulaimān.

[57] Perhaps the reference is to the boy's own father. He was alive at this time, and Akbar was not.

[58] This is the man who afterwards rebelled and made Jahāngīr his prisoner.

towards me were not honest, he both publicly and privately spoke against me. At this period when, through strife-exciting intriguers, the august feelings of my royal father were entirely embittered against me, it was certain that if he obtained the honour of waiting on him (Akbar) it would be the cause of more confusion, and would preclude me from the favour of union with him (my father). It became necessary to prevent him from coming to Court. As Bīr Singh Deo's country was exactly on his route and he was then a rebel, I sent him a message that if he would stop that sedition-monger and kill him he would receive every kindness from me. By God's grace, when Shaikh Abu-l-faẓl was passing through Bīr Singh Deo's country, the Raja blocked his road, and after a little contest scattered his men and killed him. He sent his head to me in Allahabad. Although this event was a cause of anger in the mind of the late king (Akbar), in the end it enabled me to proceed without disturbance of mind to kiss the threshold of my father's palace, and by degrees the resentment of the king was cleared away.

I made Mīr Ẓiyā'u-d-dīn of Qazwīn, who had done me service in the days of my princehood and had shown loyalty, commander of 1,000 and accountant of the stables. An order was given that every day thirty horses should be produced before me for the purpose of making presents. I honoured Mīrzā 'Alī Akbarshāhī, who is one of the distinguished braves of this family,[59] with the rank of 4,000, and gave him the sarkar of Sambhal as his jagir.

---

59. Text, *ulūs-i-Dihli.* Blochmann (p. 482 n.) points out that this is a very doubtful term, as Mīrzā 'Alī came from Badakhshan. On examining three MSS. of the Tūzuk-i-Jahāngīrī I find no word *Dihli,* but the words *īn ulūs,* ' this tribe or family,' and I think this must be the correct reading, and refers to the Timurides. The same phrase occurs at text, p. 173. Blochmann suggests to read *Dūldāy* for *Dihli,* but I think it more probable that the word *Dihli* should be *'āli. Mīrzā* 'Alī was styled Akbarshāhi, and no doubt this is why Jahāngīr writes in *ulūs* or *ulūs-ī-'alī. Mīrzā* 'Alī is often mentioned in the Akbarnama in connection with the wars in the Deccan, and is generally called Akbarshāhī, e.g. at p. 702. For an account of

One day the Amīru-l-umarā (Sharīf Khān) greatly pleased me by an incidental remark. It was this: "Honesty and dishonesty are not confined to matters of cash and goods; to represent qualities as existing in acquaintances which do not exist, and to conceal the meritorious qualities of strangers, is dishonesty. In truth, honesty of speech consists in making no distinction between intimates and strangers and in describing each man as he really is."

When I sent off Parwīz I had said to him, "If the Rana himself, and his eldest son who is called Karan, should come to wait upon you and proffer service and obedience, you should not do any injury to his territory." My intention in this recommendation was of two kinds; one, that inasmuch as the conquest of Transoxiana was always in the pure mind of my revered father, though every time he determined on it things occurred to prevent it, if this business could be settled, and this danger dismissed from my mind, I would leave Parwīz in Hindustan, and in reliance on Allah, myself start for my hereditary territories, especially as at this time there was no permanent ruler in that region. Bāqī Khān, who, after 'Abdu-llah Khān and 'Abdu-l-Mu'mīn Khān, his son, had acquired complete independence, had died, and the affairs of Walī Muḥammad Khān, his brother, who is now the ruler of that region, had not as yet been brought into proper order. Secondly, to bring about the termination of the war in the Deccan, of which a part in the time of my revered father had been acquired, so that it might come into possession, and be incorporated with the Imperial dominions. My hope is that through the favour of Allah both these undertakings will be accomplished.

> "Though a king should seize the seven climes,[60]
> He still would labour to take others."

---

his pathetic death see Blochmann, I.c., the Ma'āsiru-l-umarā, iii, 357, and the text, p. 163.

[60] The MSS. have a different reading, "If a king seize country and climes," etc.

I promoted Mīrzā Shāhrukh,[61] grandson of Mīrzā Sulaimān, (once) the ruler of Badakhshan, who was nearly related to my family, and held the rank of 5,000 in my father's service, to the rank of 7,000. The Mīrzā is a true Turk in disposition and simple-minded. My father conferred great honour on him, and whenever he bade his own sons sit he gratified him also with this distinction. Notwithstanding the mischievous propensities of the people of Badakhshan, the Mīrzā in this familiarity never left the right road, or undertook anything that might lead to unpleasantness. I confirmed him in the Subah of Malwa just as my father had kindly conferred it on him.

I conferred on Khwāja 'Abdu-llah, who is of the Naqsh-bandī family, and in the commencement of his service was an ahadi, and who had risen by degrees to the command of 1,000, but without reason had gone into my father's service, the rank and jagir my father had conferred on him. Although I considered it best for my own prosperity that my attendants and people should go into his (Akbar's) service, yet this had occurred without my leave, and I was rather annoyed at it. But the fact is that he is a manly and zealous man; if he had not committed this fault he would have been a faultless hero (*jawān*).

Abū-n-nabī,[62]. the Ūzbeg, who is one of the distinguished inhabitants of Māwarā'a-n-nahr and in the time of 'Abdu-l-Mu'mīn Khān was governor of Mashhad, obtained the rank of 1,500.

Shaikh Ḥasan is the son of Shaikh Bahā.[63] From the days of his childhood to this day he has always been in my service and in attendance on me, and when I was prince was distinguished

---

[61] Shāhrukh was married to Jahāngīr's half-sister, Shakaru-n-nisā. He was a Timurid.

[62] The MSS. have Abū-l-walī, and this seems more likely.

[63] The MSS. have Bhinā, and Price's original seems also to have Bhinā. Muqarrab did not return for about seven months, as this entry could not have been made till then. See p. 35 of Persian text of Tūzuk.

by the title of Muqarrab Khān. He was very active and alert in his service, and in hunting would often traverse long distances by my side. He is skilful with the arrow and the gun, and in surgery is the most skilful of his time. His ancestors also had been well practised in this profession. After my accession, in consequence of the perfect confidence I had in him, I sent him to Burhanpur to bring the children and dependants of my brother Dāniyāl to wait on me, and sent a message to the Khānkhānān in low and high words[64] and profitable admonitions. Muqarrab Khān performed this service correctly and in a short time, and, clearing off the suspicions which had entered the minds of the Khānkhānān and the nobles of that place, brought those who had been left behind by my brother in safety and security, together with his establishment and property and effects, to Lahore, and there presented them before me.

I promoted Naqīb Khān,[65] who is one of the genuine Sayyids of Qazwīn and is called Ghiyāṣu-d-dīn 'Alī, to the rank of 1,500. My father had distinguished him with the title of Naqīb Khān, and in his service he had complete intimacy and consideration. Shortly after his accession he (Akbar) had discussed several matters with him, and from this familiarity he called him *ākhūnd.* He has no equal or rival in the science of history and in biographies. There is in this day no chronologist like him in the inhabited world. From the beginning of Creation till the present time, he has by heart the tale of the four quarters of the world. Has Allah granted to any other person such faculty of memory?

---

[64] Text, *Sukhunān-i-past u buland*. Cf. Steingass, s.v. *past*. Words gentle and severe seem meant.

[65] See Blochmann, p. 447. He is mentioned by Du Jarric as disputing with the Catholic priests before Jahāngīr (see J.A.S.B. for 1896, p. 77). According to Badayūnī, iii, 98, it was Naqīb's father, 'Abdu-l-Latīf, with whom Akbar read (see Akbarnāma, ii, 19). 'Abdu-1-Laṭīf and his family arrived in 963 (1556). Erskine understands Jahāngīr's remark to mean that Naqīb was his (Jahāngīr's) teacher, but probably Jahāngīr means that it was Naqīb's father who taught Akbar, or he has confounded the father and son. As Naqīb lived till 1023 (1614), he would probably be too young in 1556 to have been Akbar's teacher.

Shaikh Kabīr, who was of the family of the venerable Shaikh Salīm, I had honoured with the title of Shajā'at Khān when I was prince, on account of his manliness and bravery. I now selected him for the rank of 1,000.

On Sha'bān 27th (28th December, 1605) a strange thing was done by the sons of Akhayrāj, son of Bhagwān Dās, the paternal uncle[66] of Raja Mān Singh. These unlucky ones, who bore the names of Abhay Rām, Bijay Rām, and Shyām Rām, were exceedingly immoderate. Notwithstanding that the aforesaid Abhay Rām had done improper (disproportioned) acts, I had winked at his faults. When at this date it was represented to me that this wretch was desirous of despatching his wives and children without leave to his own country and afterwards of himself running away to the Rāna, who is not loyal to this family, I referred to Rām Dās and other Rajput nobles, and said to them that if any one of them would become security for them, I would confirm the rank and jagir of those wretches, and passing over their offences would forgive them. In consequence of their excessive turbulence and bad disposition no one became security. I told the Amīru-l-umarā that as no one would be bound for them, they must be handed over to the charge of one of the servants of the Court until security was forthcoming. The Amīru-l-umarā gave them over to Ibrāhīm Khān Kākar, who was afterwards dignified with the title of Dilāwar Khān, and Ḥātim,[67] second son of Manglī, who held the title of Shāhnawāz Khān.[68] When these wished to disarm these foolish people, they refused, and, not observing the dues of good manners, began, together with their servants, to quarrel and fight. The Amīru-l-umarā reported the circumstance to me, and I ordered them to be punished according to their deeds. He betook himself to

---

[66] Mān Singh was the adopted son of Bhagwān Dās, and it would appear from this passage that he was his nephew also.

[67] The MSS. have Hātim s. Bābūī Manglī, and this is right. See Blochmann, p. 370, n. i, and p. 473.

[68] The MSS. have Shāhwār.

driving them off, and I sent Shaikh Farīd also after him. One Rajput armed with a sword, and another with a dagger stood up to the Amīru-l-umarā. One of his attendants named Quṭb engaged the man with the dagger and was killed. The Rajput also was cut to pieces. One of the Afghan attendants of the Amīru-l-umarā attacked the one who had the sword and killed him. Dilāwar Khān drew his dagger and turned towards Abhay Rām, who with two others was holding his ground, and after wounding one of these fell down after receiving wounds from the three. Some of the ahadis and the men of the Amīru-l-umarā opposed and slew these doomed men. A Rajput drew his sword and turned to Shaikh Farīd; he was met by a Ḥabshī slave, who brought him down. This disturbance took place in the courtyard of the public palace. That punishment served as a warning to many who had not looked to consequences. Abū-n-nabī[69] represented that if such a deed had been done in the Ūzbeg country the whole family and connections of that band of men would have been destroyed. I replied that as these people had been treated kindly and educated by my revered father I carried on the same benevolence to them, and justice demands that many shall not be chastised for the fault of one.

Shaikh Ḥusain Jāmī, who now sits on the cushion of *darwīshī* and is one of the disciples of the dervish of Shiraz,[70] had written to me from Lahore six months before my accession that he had seen in a dream that saints and pious men had delivered over the affairs of the kingdom to that chosen one of the Court of Allah (Jahāngīr), and that, rejoicing in this good news, he should await the event, and that he hoped that when it had occurred,

---

[69] I.O. MSS. have Abū-l-walī. He was an Ūzbeg, and received the title of Bahādur Khān. See Ma'āsiru-l-umarā, i, 400, and Akbarnāma, iii, 820 and 839, where he is called Abū-l-Baqā. The real name seems to be Abūl Be or Bey, and this is how Erskine writes the name.

[70] The text seems corrupt. The I.O. MSS. say nothing about Shiraz, but merely that Ḥusain Jāmī was a disciple who had a dervish character (*sīrat*) ; nor does the R.A.S. MS. mention Shiraz.

the faults of Khwāja Zakariyyā, who was one of the Aḥrāriyya,[71] would be pardoned.[72]

I conferred on Tāsh Beg Furjī,[73] who was one of the old servants of the State, and whom my father had honoured with the title of Tāj Khān, and who had the rank of 2,000, that of 3,000, and I raised Tukhta[74] Beg Kābulī from the rank of 2,500 to that of 3,000. He is a brave and active man, and was greatly trusted in the service of my uncle, Mīrzā Muḥammad Ḥakīm. I promoted Abū-l-Qāsim Tamkīn,[75] who was one of my father's old servants, to the rank of 1,500. There are few men such as he for abundance of children; he has thirty sons, and if his daughters do not number so many they must be half that number. I dignified Shaikh 'Alā'u-d-dīn, grandson of Shaikh Salīm, who had strong connections with me, with the title of Islām Khān, and promoted him to the rank of 2,000. He had grown up with me from his childhood, and may be a year younger than I. He is a brave and well-dispositioned youth, and is distinguished in every way above his family. Till now he has never drunk intoxicating

---

[71] That is, descended from the famous Central Asian saint Khwāja Aḥrār.

[72] Something seems to have fallen out of the text and MSS., for this passage is obscure and not connected with the context. It is clearer in Price's version, where it is brought in as part of Jahāngīr's statements about promotions, and where (p. 40) we read as follows :—" I shall now return to the more grateful subject of recording rewards and advancements.....On Khwāja Zakariyyā, the son of Khwāja Muḥammad Yaḥyā, although in disgrace, I conferred the rank of 500. This I was induced to do on the recommendation of the venerated Shaikh Husain Jāmī. Six months previous to my accession," etc. Evidently the statement about Zakariyyā's promotion has been omitted accidentally from the Tūzuk. There is a reference to the Shaikh's dream in Muḥammad Hādī's preface to the Tūzuk (p. 15). He says there that it was the saint Bahā'u-l-ḥaqq who appeared in a dream to Ḥusain Jāmī and told him that Sulṭān Salīm would soon be king.

[73]. I.e. of Furj or Furg in Persia. But Furjī is a mistake for Qūrchī (belonging to the body-guard). He was a Mogul. See Blochmann, p. 457.

[74]. Text has wrongly Pakhta. See Blochmann, p. 469. He received the title of Sardār Khān.

[75]. Should be Namakīn. See Blochmann, p. 199.

drinks, and his sincerity towards me is such that I have honoured him with the title of son.

I have bestowed on 'Alī Aṣghar Bārha, who has not a rival in bravery and zeal, and is the son of Sayyid Maḥmūd Khān Bārha, one of my father's old nobles, the title of Saif Khān, and thus distinguished him amongst his equals and connections. He is evidently a brave youth. He was always one of the confidential men who went with me to hunt and to other places. He has never in his life drunk anything intoxicating, and as he has abstained in his youth he probably will attain high dignities. I granted him the rank of 3,000.

I promoted Farīdūn, son of Muḥammad Qulī Khān Barlās, who held the rank of 1,000, to that of 2,000. Farīdūn is one of the tribe of Chaghatāy, and is not devoid of manliness and courage.

I promoted Shaikh Bāyazīd, grandson of Shaikh Salīm, who held the rank of 2,000, to that of 3,000. The first person who gave me milk, but for not more than a day, was the mother of Shaikh Bāyazīd.

[76]One day I observed to the Pandits, that is, the wise men of the Hindus, "If the doctrines of your religion are based on the incarnation of the Holy Person of God Almighty in ten different forms by the process of metempsychosis, they are virtually rejected by the intelligent. This pernicious idea requires that the Sublime Cause, who is void of all limitations, should be possessed of length, breadth, and thickness. If the purpose is the manifestation of the Light of God in these bodies, that of itself is existent equally in all created things, and is not peculiar to these ten forms. If the idea is to establish some one of God's attributes, even then there is no right notion, for in every faith and code there are masters of wonders and miracles distinguished beyond

---

[76] This passage has been translated by Elliot (vi, 289). See also Price (p. 44), where the discussion is fuller.

the other men of their age for wisdom and eloquence."[77] After much argument and endless controversy, they acknowledged a God of Gods, devoid of a body or accidents,[78] and said, "As our imagination fails to conceive a formless personality (*z̲āt-i-mujarrad*), we do not find any way to know Him without the aid of a form. We have therefore made these ten forms the means of conceiving of and knowing Him." Then said I, "How can these forms be a means of your approaching the Deity?"

My father always associated with the learned of every creed and religion, especially with Pandits and the learned of India, and although he was illiterate, so much became clear to him through constant intercourse with the learned and wise, in his conversations with them, that no one knew him to be illiterate, and he was so acquainted with the niceties of verse and prose compositions that his deficiency was not thought of.

In his august personal appearance he was of middle height, but inclining to be tall; he was of the hue of wheat; his eyes and eyebrows were black, and his complexion rather dark than fair; he was lion-bodied,[79] with a broad chest, and his hands and arms long. On the left side of his nose he had a fleshy mole, very agreeable in appearance, of the size of half a pea. Those skilled in the science of physiognomy considered this mole a sign of great prosperity and exceeding good fortune. His august voice was very loud, and in speaking and explaining had a peculiar richness. In his actions and movements he was not like the

---

[77] Jahāngīr's idea is somewhat vaguely expressed, but his meaning seems to be that the ten incarnations do not illustrate any attribute of God, for there have been men who performed similar wonders. The corresponding passage in the text used by Major Price is differently rendered by him, but his version is avowedly a paraphrase, and it appears incorrect in this passage.

[78] Literally, "of the How and the Why."

[79] Text, *s̲h̲īr-andām*, 'tiger-shaped,' which I think means thin in the flank (see Steingass, s.v.). I have taken the translation of the words *malāḥat* and *ṣabāḥat* from Elliot. See his note vi, 376, where the two words seem wrongly spelt.

people of the world, and the glory of God manifested itself in him.

> "Greatness in his manner, kingship in his lineage,
> As if Solomon would have put the ring on his finger."[80]

Three months after my birth my sister, Shāhzāda Khānam, was born to one of the royal concubines; they gave her over to his (Akbar's) mother, Maryam Makānī. After her a son was born to one of the concubines, and received the name of Shāh Murād. As his birth occurred in the hill country of Fatḥpūr, he was nicknamed *Pahārī*. When my revered father sent him to conquer the Deccan, he had taken to excessive drinking through associating with unworthy persons, so that he died in his 30th year, in the neighbourhood of Jālnāpūr, in the province of Berar. His personal appearance was fresh-coloured; he was thin in body and tall of stature. Dignity and authority were evident in his movements, and manliness and bravery manifested themselves in his ways. On the night of Jumādā-l-awwal 10th, A.H. 979 (September, 1572), another son was born to one of the concubines. As his birth took place at Ajmīr in the house of one of the attendants of the blessed shrine of the reverend Khwāja Mu'īnu-d-dīn Chishtī, whose name was Shaikh Dāniyāl, this child was called Dāniyāl.

After the death of my brother Shāh Murād, he (Akbar), towards the end of his reign, sent Dāniyāl to conquer the Deccan and followed him himself. When my revered father was besieging Āsīr (Āsīrgarh) he, with a large body of nobles such as the Khānkhānān and his sons, and Mīrzā Yūsuf Khān, invested the fort of Ahmadnagar and it came into the possession of the victorious officers about the time that Āsīr was taken. After my father 'Arsh-āshyānī had returned in prosperity and victory from Burhanpur towards his capital, he gave the province to Dāniyāl and left him in possession of that territory. Dāniyāl took

---

[80] Erskine has " Let Sulaimān place his ring on his finger."

to improper ways, like his brother Shāh Murād, and soon died from excessive drinking, in the 33rd year of his age. His death occurred in a peculiar way. He was very fond of guns and of hunting with the gun. He named one of his guns *yaka u janāza,* 'the same as the bier,' and himself composed this couplet and had it engraved on the gun:—

> "From the joy of the chase with thee, life is fresh and new;
> To everyone whom thy dart strikes, 't is the same as his bier."[81]

When his drinking of wine was carried to excess, and the circumstance was reported to my father, farmans of reproach were sent to the Khānkhānān. Of course he forbade it, and placed cautious people to look after him properly. When the road to bring wine was completely closed, he began to weep and to importune some of his servants, and said: "Let them bring me wine in any possible way." He said to Murshid Qulī Khān, a musketeer who was in his immediate service: "Pour some wine into this *yaka u janāza,* and bring it to me." That wretch, in hope of favour, undertook to do this, and poured double-distilled spirit into the gun, which had long been nourished on gunpowder and the scent thereof, and brought it. The rust of the iron was dissolved by the strength of the spirit and mingled with it, and the prince no sooner drank of it than he fell down.

> "No one should draw a bad omen:[82]
> If he does, he draws it for himself."

Dāniyāl was of pleasing figure, of exceedingly agreeable manners and appearance; he was very fond of elephants and horses. It was impossible for him to hear of anyone as having a good horse or elephant and not take it from him. He was fond of Hindi songs, and would occasionally compose verses with

---

[81] Price translates—
" In pleasure of the chase with thee, my soul breathes fresh and clear ; But who receives thy fatal dart, sinks lifeless on his bier."

[82] Perhaps referring to the name which Dāniyāl gave to his gun, and which recoiled on himself, but the MSS. and text have *nagīrad,* and not *bagīrad.*

correct idiom in the language of the people of India, which were not bad.

After the birth of Dāniyāl a daughter was born to Bībī Daulat-Shād whom they named Shakaru-n-nisā Begam.[83] As she was brought up in the skirt of my revered father's care, she turned out very well. She is of good disposition and naturally compassionate towards all people. From infancy and childhood she has been extremely fond of me, and there can be few such relationships between brother and sister. The first time when, according to the custom of pressing the breast of a child and a drop of milk is perceptible, they pressed my sister's breast and milk appeared, my revered father said to me: "Bābā! drink this milk, that in truth this sister may be to thee as a mother." God, the knower of secrets, knows that from that day forward, after I drank that drop of milk, I have felt love for my sister such as children have for their mothers.

After some time another girl was born to this same Bībī Daulat-Shād, and he (Akbar) called her Ārām Bānū Begam.[84] Her disposition was on the whole inclined to excitement and heat. My father was very fond of her, so much so that he described her impolitenesses as politenesses, and in his august sight they, from his great love, did not appear bad. Repeatedly he honoured me by addressing me, and said: "Bābā! for my sake be as kind as I am, after me, to t' is sister, who in Hindi phrase is my darling (that is, dearly cherished). Be affectionate to her and pass over her little impolitenesses and impudences."

The good qualities of my revered father are beyond the limit of approval and the bounds of praise. If books were composed with regard to his commendable dispositions, without suspicion

---

[83] The MSS. have Shakar-niṣ̤ār,'sugar-sprinkling.' She lived into Shāh-Jahān's reign.

[84] She died unmarried in Jahāngīr's reign.

of extravagance, and he be not looked at as a father would be by his son, even then but a little out of much could be said.

Notwithstanding his kingship and his treasures and his buried wealth, which were beyond the scope of counting and imagination, his fighting elephants and Arab horses, he never by a hair's breadth placed his foot beyond the base of humility before the throne of God, but considered himself the lowest of created beings, and never for one moment forgot God.

> "Always, everywhere, with everyone, and in every circumstance,
> Keep the eye of thy heart secretly fixed on the Beloved."

The professors of various faiths had room in the broad expanse of his incomparable sway. This was different from the practice in other realms, for in Persia[85] there is room for Shias only, and in Turkey, India, and Tūrān there is room for Sunnis only.

As in the wide expanse of the Divine compassion there is room for all classes and the followers of all creeds, so, on the principle that the Shadow[86] must have the same properties as the Light, in his dominions, which on all sides were limited only by the salt sea, there was room for the professors of opposite religions, and for beliefs good and bad, and the road to altercation was closed. Sunnis and Shias met in one mosque, and Franks and Jews in one church, and observed their own forms of worship.

He associated with the good of every race and creed and persuasion, and was gracious to all in accordance with their condition and understanding. He passed his nights in wakefulness, and slept little in the day; the length of his sleep

---

[85] This must, I think, be the meaning, though according to the wording the statement would seem to be that there is no room for Shias except in Persia. Erskine has "None but Shias are tolerated in Persia, Sunnis in Rūm and Tūrān, and Hindus in Hindustan."

[86] Kings are regarded as shadows of God.

during a whole night and day (*nycthemeron*) was not more than a watch and a half. He counted his wakefulness at night as so much added to his life. His courage and boldness were such that he could mount raging, rutting elephants, and subdue to obedience murderous elephants which would not allow their own females near them—although even when an elephant is bad-tempered he does no harm to the female or his driver—and which were in a state in which they might have killed their drivers or the females, or not have allowed their approach. He would place himself on a wall or tree near which an elephant was passing that had killed its mahout and broken loose from restraint, and, putting his trust in God's favour, would throw himself on its back and thus, by merely mounting, would bring it under control and tame it. This was repeatedly seen.

He ascended the throne in his 14th year. Hemū, the infidel whom the Afghan ruler had raised to high station, collected a wonderful force after King Humāyūn's death, with a stud of elephants such as no ruler of Hindustan had at that time, and he went towards Delhi. Humāyūn had appointed Akbar to drive off some of the Afghans from the foot-hills of the Panjab, but just then he exemplified the hemistich which is a description of the accident and the chronogram of his death—

> "The august monarch (Humāyūn) fell from the roof. The news (of the death) was conveyed to my father by Naẓar-jīvī."[87]

Bairām Khān, who was then his tutor, having collected the nobles who were in the province, chose an auspicious hour and seated him on the throne of rule in pargana Kalānūr, near Lahore.

When Hemū reached the neighbourhood of Delhi, Tardī Beg Khān and a large force that was in the city drew up to oppose him. When the preparations for the combat had been made the armies attacked one another, and, after considerable endeavours

[87] The chronogram is one year short, yielding 962 instead of 963.

and strife, defeat fell on Tradī Beg Khān and the Moguls, and the army of darkness overcame the army of light.

> "All things and battles and fights are of God,
> He knows whose will be the victory.
> From the blood of the brave and the dust of the troops,
> The earth grew red and the heavens black."

Tardī Beg Khān and the other defeated ones took the road to my revered father's camp. As Bairām Khān disliked Tardī Beg, he made this defeat an excuse to put him to death.

A second time, through the pride engendered in the mind of this accursed infidel by his victory, he came out of Delhi with his force and elephants and advanced, while the glorious standards of His Majesty (Akbar) proceeded from Kalānūr for the purpose of driving him away. The armies of darkness and light met in the neighbourhood of Panipat, and on Thursday, Muḥarram 2nd, A.H. 964 (November 5th, 1556), a fight took place. In the army of Hemū were 30,000 brave fighting horsemen, while the *ghāzīs* of the victorious army were not more than 4,000 or 5,000. On that day Hemū was riding an elephant named Hawā'ī. Suddenly an arrow struck the eye of that infidel and came out at the back of his head. His army, on seeing this, took to flight. By chance Shāh Qulī Khān Maḥram with a few brave men came up to the elephant on which was the wounded Hemū, and would have shot an arrow at the driver, but he cried "Do not kill me; Hemū is on this elephant." A number of men immediately conveyed Hemū as he was to the king (Akbar). Bairām Khān represented that it would be proper if the king with his own hand should strike the infidel with a sword, so that obtaining the reward of a ghāzī (warrior of the Faith) he might use this title on the imperial farmans. The king answered, "I have cut him in pieces before this," and explained: "One day, in Kabul, I was copying a picture in presence of Khwāja'Abdu-ṣ-Ṣamad Shīrīn Qalam, when a form appeared from my brush, the parts of which were separate and divided from each other. One of those near asked, 'Whose picture is this?' It came to my tongue to say that it was the likeness of Hemū." Not defiling his hand with his (Hemū's) blood, he told one of his servants to cut off his head. Those killed in the defeated army numbered 5,000 in addition to those who fell in various places round about.

Another of the well-known deeds of Akbar was the victorious expedition against Gujarat, and his rapid march there, at the time when Mīrzā Ibrāhīm Ḥusain, Muḥammad Ḥusain Mīrzā, and Shāh Mīrzā revolted from this State and went towards Gujarat, and all the nobles of that province, combining with the turbulent of those parts, besieged the fort of Ahmadabad in which was Mīrzā 'Azīz Koka with the royal army. His Majesty, in consequence of the distracted state of Jījī Angā, the mother of the last-named Mīrzā, started for Gujarat with a body of royal troops without delay from the capital of Fathpur. Having covered in the space of nine days the long road which it should take two months to accomplish, sometimes on horseback, sometimes on a camel or in a bullock-cart, he arrived at Sarnāl.

When, on 5th Jumādā-l-awwal, 980 (September 15th, 1572), he reached the neighbourhood of the enemy's camp, he consulted with those who were loyal to him. Some said he should make a night attack on the camp. His Majesty, however, said that a night attack was the resort of the faint-hearted and the way of the deceitful, and immediately gave orders to beat the drums and set the horsemen at them. When the river Sābar Mahī (Sābarmatī) was reached, he ordered his men to cross it in order. Muḥammad Ḥusain Mīrzā was agitated by the noise of the army of victory, and himself came forward to reconnoitre. Subḥān Qulī Turk, also with a troop of brave men, went to the river's bank to enquire into the enemy's position. The Mīrzā asked what troops these were. Subḥān Qulī replied that they were of the army of King Jalālu-d-dīn Akbar. That ill-fated one would not believe this, and said his spies had seen the king fourteen days before in Fathpur, and that it was clear Subḥān Qulī was lying.

To this Subḥān Qulī rejoined, "Nine days ago the king with this expedition started from Fathpur." "How could elephants have come?"[88] asked the Mīrzā. "What need was there of elephants?" answered Subḥān Qulī. "Young men and heroes who cleave rocks, and are better than famous and raging elephants, have come; the difference between loyalty and sedition will now become known." The Mīrzā, after this conversation, turned aside and began to marshal his troops. The king waited until his advanced guard sent word that the enemy had put on their armour. He then moved forward, and although he sent several times to order the Khān A' ẓam to advance, the latter stood still. It was said to Akbar that, as the enemy was in force, it would be well to remain on his side of the river until the army of Gujarat arrived from within the fort. His Majesty answered: "Always, and especially in this affair, I have put my trust in God. If I had considered routine, I should not have come in this rapid manner. Now that our foe is ready for the fight, we ought not to delay." With these words, and with his innate reliance on God as his shield, he put his horse into the river with a few chosen men whom he had appointed to ride with him. Though it was not supposed that there was a ford, he crossed in safety. He had called for his helmet, but in the agitation of bringing it his armour-bearer dropped the face-guard (*buffe*). His comrades did not regard this as a good omen, but he said at once, "It is an excellent omen, for it has revealed my face."[89] Meantime the wretched Mīrzā arrayed his ranks to fight his benefactor.

"If thou come out (to fight) with thy benefactor,
If thou wert the sphere, thou wouldest be reversed."

---

[88] According to the Ṭabaqāt, Elliot, v, 366, what the Mīrzā said was " Where are the elephants ?"

[89] The word for 'face-guard' is *pīsh-rūy* (front-face), and Jahāngīr makes his father pun upon the word, saying," It has loosed (opened) my front-face." Cf. Price, p. 54.

The Khān A'ẓam had had no idea that the king would cast the shadow of his compassion on these regions with such speed and eagerness, and he believed no one who gave him news of that arrival, until convinced by visible proof. Then, arraying the army of Gujarat, he prepared to march. Meanwhile Āṣaf Khān also sent news to him. Before his army issued from the fort the enemy had appeared from amongst the trees. The king, taking the Divine aid as the security of his courage, started off. Muḥammad Qulī Khān Turk and Tardī Khān Dīwāna came forward with a band of brave followers, and after a little fighting turned rein. On this His Majesty said to Bhagwān Dās, "The enemy are unnumbered and we are few; we must attack with one face and one heart; for a clenched fist is more useful than an open hand." With these words he drew his sword, and with shout of *Allahu-akbar* and *Yā Mu'īn*[90] charged with those devoted to him.

> "The sense of the age evaporated with the clamour,
> The ear of the heavens was split with the shouts."

The royal right and left wings and a band of brave men in the centre fought with valour. Stars (*kaukabā'ī*), which are a kind of firework, were lighted by the enemy; they twisted about among the thorn-bushes, and created such confusion that a noted elephant of the enemy began to move and threw their troops into disarray. With this the royal centre came up and dispersed Muḥammad Ḥusain and his force. Mān Singh Darbārī overcame his foe under the king's eyes, and Rāgho Dās Kachhwāha sacrificed his life. Muḥammad Wafā, who was of the house-born of the State, behaving very bravely, fell wounded from his horse. By the favour of the Creator who cherishes His servants, and simply through the courage and good fortune of the exalted king, the enemy were scattered and defeated. In gratitude for

[90] 'The helper.' This is an allusion to Akbar's patron saint, Mu'īnu-d-dīn Chishtī, whose name he adopted as his battle-cry.

this great victory the king turned his face in supplication to the throne of his merciful Maker, and poured forth his thanks.

One of the kalāwants (musicians) represented to His Majesty that Saif Khān Kokaltāsh had offered the coin of his life in loyalty to the State, and on enquiry it appeared that when Muḥammad Ḥusain Mīrzā with some of his riffraff was attacking the centre Saif Khān met him and fighting valiantly became a martyr. The Mīrzā himself was wounded by the hands of the brave men of the main body. The Kokaltāsh mentioned is the elder brother of Zain Khān Koka.

A strange circumstance was this: on the day before the battle, when the king was eating, he asked Hazāra, who was learned in the science of looking at the shoulder-blades (a kind of divination), to see on whose side the victory would be. Hazāra said: "The victory will be on your side, but one of the chiefs of your army will become a martyr." Whereupon Saif Khān Koka said, "Would that this blessing might fall to my lot!"

"Many an omen that we have treated as jest[91]
Became true when the star passed by."

In short, Mīrzā Muḥammad Ḥusain turned his reins, but his horse's feet became entangled in the thorn-brake and he fell. An ahadi of the king, Gadā 'Alī by name, found him, and having mounted him before him on his horse took him to the king. As two or three claimed a share in his capture, His Majesty asked who had made him prisoner. "The king's salt," he answered. The king ordered his hands, that had been fastened behind him, to be tied in front. Meanwhile he asked for water. Farḥat Khān, who was one of the confidential slaves, struck him on the head, but the king, disapproving of this, sent for his private drinking water and satisfied his thirst. Up to this time Mīrzā 'Azīz Koka and the garrison of the fort had not come out. After the capture of the

---

[91] The reading in the lithograph seems wrong ; the MSS. have *az bāzīcha*, 'in jest'.

Mīrzā, His Majesty was proceeding slowly towards Ahmadabad. He had delivered the Mīrzā to Rāy Rāy Singh Rāṭhor, one of the Rajput chiefs, to be put on an elephant and brought with him. Meanwhile Ikhtiyāru-l-mulk, who was one of the influential Gujarati leaders, made his appearance with an army of nearly 5,000 men. Complete confusion fell upon the royal troops. The king, as his natural valour and lofty disposition required, ordered the drums to be beaten, and Shajā'at Khān, Rāja Bhagwān Dās, and some others charged on in front to fight this force. Fearing that the enemy might get possession of Mīrzā Muḥammad Ḥusain, Rāy Rāy Singh's men, by the advice and plan of the aforesaid Raja (Bhagwān Dās), cut off his head. My father did not want to kill him. The forces of Ikhtiyāru-l-mulk also were dispersed, and he was thrown from his horse into the thorn thicket. Suhrāb Beg Turkmān cut off his head and brought it in. It was only by the grace and power of God that such a victory was won by a small number of men.

In the same way are beyond all reckoning the conquest of the province of Bengal, the capture of well-known and celebrated forts in Hindustan such as Chitor and Rantambhor, the subjection of the province of Khandesh, and the taking of the fort of Āsīr and of other provinces which by the exertions of the royal armies came into the possession of the servants of the State. If these were related in detail it would be a long story.

In the fight at Chitor, the king with his own hand killed Jitmal, the leader of the men in the fort. He had no rival in shooting with a gun, and with the one with which he killed Jitmal, and which was called Sangrām, he killed some 3,000 or 4,000 birds and beasts.[92] I may be reckoned a true pupil of his. Of all sports I am most disposed to that with the gun, and in one day have shot eighteen deer.

---

[92] Abū-l-faẓl is more moderate ; he says (Blochmann, p. 116) that Akbar killed 1,019 animals with Sangrām.

Of the austerities practised by my revered father, one was the not eating the flesh of animals. During three months of the year he ate meat, and for the remaining nine contented himself with Ṣūfī food, and was no way pleased with the slaughter of animals. On many days and in many months this was forbidden to the people. The days and months on which he did not eat flesh are detailed in the Akbarnāma.

On the day I made I'timādu-l-mulk diwan, I put Mu'izzu-l-mulk in charge of the *dīwānī-i-buyūtāt* (care of buildings). The latter is a Sayyid of Bākharz,[93] and under my revered father was accountant of the *kurkarāq* department.[94]

On one of my accession days, a hundred of the Akbarī and Jahāngīrī servants were promoted to higher rank and jagirs. At the commencement of the Ramaẓān 'Īd, as it was the first after my accession, I came down to the 'Īdgāh from my auspicious throne. There was a great crowd, and having performed the dues of thanksgiving and praise I returned to the palace, where according to the verse "From the table of kings favours come to beggars," I commanded a sum of money to be spent in alms and charity. Some lakhs of dāms of this were entrusted to Dūst Muḥammad (afterwards Khwāja Jahān), who divided them amongst faqirs and those who were in want, and a lakh of dāms each was given to Jamālu-d-dīn Ḥusain Anjū (the lexicographer), Mīrzā Ṣadr Jahān, and Mīr Muḥammad Riẓā Sabzawārī to dispose of in charity in different quarters of the city. I sent 5,000 rupees to the dervishes of Shaikh Muḥammad Ḥusain Jāmī, and gave directions that each day one of the officers of the watch[95] should give 50,000 dāms to faqirs. I sent a jewelled sword to the Khānkhānān, and promoted Jamālu-d-dīn Anjū to the rank of 3,000. The office of *Ṣadr* was entrusted to Mīrān Ṣadr Jahān, and I

---

[93] Blochmann says, of Mashhad, p. 381.

[94] The furriery. See Blochmann, pp. 87 n. and 616. *Kurk* means ' fur ' in Turki.

[95] The word *yātish* is omitted in text, but occurs in the MSS.

ordered Ḥājī Koka, who was one of my father's foster-sisters, [96]to bring before me in the palace such women as were worthy to be presented with land and money. I promoted Zāhid Khān, son of Muḥammad Ṣādiq Khān, from the rank of 1,500 to that of 2,000.

It had been the custom[97] that when the gift of an elephant or horse was made to anyone, the naqibs and the Masters of the Horse (*Mīr Ākhūrān*) took from him a sum of money as *jilawāna* (bridle-money). I gave orders that this money should be paid by the government, so that people might be freed from the importunities and demands of that set of men.

At this time Sālbāhan arrived from Burhanpur and produced before me the horses and elephants of my deceased brother Dāniyāl. Of the elephants, one male named Mast Alast appeared to me the best, and I gave him the name of Nūr Gaj. A wonderful thing showed itself in this elephant; on the sides of his ears small lumps had grown about the size of melons, and from them came fluid such as drops from an elephant in the rutting season; moreover, the top of his forehead was more prominent than in other elephants. It was a splendid and imposing animal.[98]

I gave to my son Khurram (Shāh-Jahān) a rosary of jewels, with the hope that he might obtain fulfilment of all his desires, both in visible and in spiritual things.

As I had remitted in my dominions customs duties amounting to krors, I abolished also all the transit dues (*sā'ir-jihāt*) in Kabul, which is one of the noted towns on the road to Hindustan. These brought in 1 kror and 23 lakhs of dams. From

---

[96] Hājī Koka was sister of Sa'ādat Yār Koka (Akbar-nāma, iii, 856). According to Price this passage refers to a widows' fund.

[97] This was one of Akbar's regulations (Blochmann, p. 142). The amount was ten dams on each muhr of the horse's value, calculated on an increase of 50 per cent. See also Price, p. 61.

[98] This passage is not clear, but the peculiarity to which attention is drawn seems rather the prominent forehead than the oozing fluid. Price (p. 62) has a fuller account of this elephant.

the provinces of Kabul and Qandahar large sums used to be derived every year from customs (*zakā't*), which were in fact the chief revenue of those places. I remitted these ancient dues, a proceeding that greatly benefited the people of Iran and Turan.

Āṣaf Khān's jagir in the subah of Bihār had been given to Bāz Bahādur; I therefore ordered that a jagir in the Panjab should be given to him. As it was represented to me that a large sum was in arrears in his jagir, and now that the order for exchange had been given its collection would be difficult, I directed that a lakh of rupees should be given to him from the Treasury and the arrears recovered from Bāz Bahādur for the royal revenues.

I promoted Sharīf Āmulī to the rank of 2,500, original and increase. He is a pure-hearted, lively-spirited man. Though he has no tincture of current sciences, lofty words and exalted knowledge often manifest themselves in him. In the dress of a faqir he made many journeys, and he has friendship with many saints and recites the maxims of those who profess mysticism. This is his conversation, not his practice (*qāli-ū ast na ḥālī*). In the time of my revered father he relinquished the garments of poverty and asceticism, and attained to amirship and chiefship. His utterance is exceedingly powerful, and his conversation is remarkably eloquent and pure, although he is without Arabic. His compositions also are not devoid of verve.[99]

A garden in Agra had been left by Shāh Qulī Khān Maḥram, and as he had no heirs I handed it over to Ruqayya Sulṭān Begam, the daughter of Hindāl Mīrzā, who had been the honoured wife of my father.[100] My father had given my son Khurram into her charge, and she loved him a thousand times more than if he had been her own.

---

[99] See Blochmann, pp. 176, 452, and the very full account of him in the Ma'āṣir, iii, 285. Amul is an old city south of the Caspian and west of Astrabad.

[100] She was Akbar's first and principal wife, but bore him no children. She long survived him.

THE GREAT FEAST OF NAURŪZ

On the night of Tuesday, Z̲ī-l-qa'da 11th, A.H. 1014 (March 11th or 12th, 1606), in the morning, which is the time of the blessing of light, his Eminence the Great Luminary passed from the constellation of the Fish to the House of Honour in the constellation of the Ram. As this was the first New Year's Day after my auspicious accession I ordered them to decorate the porticoes of the private and public halls of the palace, as in the time of my revered father, with delicate stuffs, and to adorn them handsomely. From the first day of the Naurūz to the 19th degree of the Ram (Aries), which is the day of culmination, the people gave themselves over to enjoyment and happiness. Players and singers of all bands and castes were gathered together. Dancing lulis and charmers of India whose caresses would captivate the hearts of angels kept up the excitement of the assemblies. I gave orders that whoever might wish for intoxicating drinks and exhilarating drugs should not be debarred from using them.

> "Cupbearer! brighten my cup with the light of wine;
> Sing, minstrel, for the world has ordered itself as I desire."[101]

In my father's time it had become established that one of the great nobles should prepare an entertainment on each of the 17 or 18 days of the festival, and should present His Majesty the king with choice gifts of all kinds of jewels and jewelled things, precious stuffs, and elephants and horses, and should invite him to take the trouble to come to his assembly. By way of exalting his servants, he would deign to be present, and having looked at the presents would take what he approved of and bestow the remainder on the giver of the entertainment. As my mind was inclined to the comfort and ease of the army and subjects, I this

---

[101] These are the opening lines of an ode of Hāfiz.

year let them off their gifts with the exception of a few from my immediate retainers, which I accepted in order to gratify them. In those same days many servants of the State obtained higher rank. Amongst them I raised Dilāwar Khān Afghān to 1,500, and I raised Rāja Bāso, who was a landholder of the hill country of the Panjab, and who from the time I was prince till now has kept the way of service and sincerity towards me and held the rank of 1,500, to 3,500. Shāh Beg Khān, the governor of Qandahar, I promoted to 5,000, and Rāy Rāy Singh, a Rājpūt noble, obtained the same rank. I gave 12,000 rupees for expenses to Rānā Shankar.

At the beginning of my reign, a son of that Muẓaffar Gujarātī who claimed to be descended from the rulers of that country lifted up the head of disturbance and attacked and plundered the environs of the city of Ahmadabad. Some sardars such as Pīm[102] Bahādur Ūzbeg and Rāy 'Alī Bhatī, who were amongst the distinguished and brave men there, became martyrs in that outbreak. At length Rāja Bikramājīt and many mansabdars were provided by me with 6,000 or 7,000 horse, and appointed to assist the army of Gujarat. It was decided that when things had quieted down, by the driving off of those seditious people, Rāja Bikramājīt should be Subahdar of Gujarat. Qilīj Khān, who had been previously nominated to this office, should come to Court. After the arrival of the royal troops the thread of the rebels' union was severed; they took refuge in different jungles, and the country was reduced to order. The news of this victory reached the ear of my state and dignity in the most acceptable of hours (New Year time).

About this time there came a representation from my son Parwīz that the Rānā had left *thāna* Mandal, which is about 30[103] or 40 *kos* from Ajmīr, and had run away, and that a force had

---

[102] Ma'āṣiru-l-umarā, *Yatīm* instead of Pīm or Bīm. See Blochmann, p. 470. Erskine has Saīn Bahādur.

[103] MS. 181 has 34.

been appointed to pursue him; and that it was to be hoped the good fortune of Jahāngīr would cause him to become non-existent.

On the last day of the feast of the New Year, many servants of the State were honoured with favours and increase of rank. Pīshrau Khān was an old retainer and had come from Persia (*wilāyat*) with Humāyūn; indeed, he was one of the men whom Shāh Tahmāsp had sent with Humāyūn. His name was Mihtar Sa'ādat. As under my father he was superintendent (*dārogha*) and head (*mihtar*) of the *farrāsh-khāna* (store department), and had no equal in this service, he had given him the title of Pīshrau Khān (the active Khān). Though he was a subordinate (?) servant and had an artificer's disposition (*qalaqchī mashrab*), I looked to his claims of service and gave him the rank of 2,000.[104]

THE FLIGHT OF KHUSRAU IN THE MIDDLE OF THE FIRST YEAR OF MY REIGN.

Futile[105] ideas had entered the mind of Khusrau in consequence of his youth and the pride youths have, and the lack of experience and the lack of foresight of worthless companions, especially at the time of my revered father's illness. Some of these short-sighted ones, through the multitude of their crimes and offences, had become hopeless of pardon and indulgence, and imagined that by making Khusrau a tool they might conduct the affairs of State through him. They overlooked the truth that acts of sovereignty and world rule are not things to be arranged by the worthless endeavours of defective intellects. The just

[104] I think Jahāngīr means that though the Khān was an excellent servant in his own line, he was hardly fit for the command of 2,000 or for the title of Khān. Cf. his praise of him at p. 71 (Blochmann, p. 498). He was called Pishrau probably from his going on ahead with the advance camp, as being in charge of the carpets, etc., as well as because of his personal activity.

[105] In Price's Jahāngīr, p. 15, Jahāngīr states that he had imprisoned Khusrau in the upper part of the royal tower in the castle of Agra. It was from this confinement that Khusrau escaped.

Creator bestows them on him whom he considers fit for this glorious and exalted duty, and on such a person doth He fit the robe of honour.

> "He who is seized of Fortune cannot be deprived of it;
> Throne and diadem are not things of purchase;
> It is not right to wrest crown and dominion
> From the head which God, the Crown-cherisher, has indicated."

As the futile imaginations of the seditious and shortsighted had no result but disgrace and regret, the affairs of the kingdom were confirmed in the hands of this suppliant at the throne of Allah. I invariably found Khusrau preoccupied and distracted. However much, in favour and affection for him, I wished to drive from his mind some of his fears and alarms, nothing was gained until, at last, by the advice of those whose fortune was reversed, on the night of Sunday, Zī-l-ḥijja 8th, of the year mentioned (April 6th, 1605), when two gharis had passed, he made a pretence[106] of going to visit the tomb of His Majesty (Akbar), and went off with 350 horsemen, who were his adherents, from within the fort of Agra. Shortly after, one of the lamp attendants who was acquainted with the Wazīru-l-mulk gave him the news of Khusrau's flight. The Vizier took him to the Amīru-l-umarā, who, as the news seemed true, came in a distracted state of mind to the door of the private apartments and said to one of the eunuchs, "Take in my request and say that I have a necessary representation to make, and let the king honour me by coming out." As such an affair had not entered my thoughts, I supposed that news had come from the Deccan or Gujarat. When I came out and heard what the news was, I asked, "W hat must be done? Shall I mount myself, or shall I send Khurram?" The Amīru-l-umarā submitted that he would go if I ordered it. "Let it be so," I said. Afterwards he said, "If he

---

[106] Du Jarric says it was in this way that he was allowed to pass the sentinols. Du Jarric gives the date of Khusrau's flight as 15th April, 1606 (this would be New Style). By Sunday night is meant Saturday evening. Sunday was Akbar's birthday.

will not turn back on my advice, and takes up arms, what must be done?" Then I said, "If he will go in no way on the right road, do not consider a crime anything that results from your action. Kingship regards neither son nor son-in-law. No one is a relation to a king."

When I had said these words and other things, and had dismissed him, it occurred to me that Khusrau was very much annoyed with him, and that in consequence of the dignity and nearness (to me) which he (the Amīr) enjoyed, he was an object of envy to his equals and contemporaries.[107] Perhaps they might devise treachery and destroy him. I therefore ordered Mu'izzu-l-mulk to recall him, and selecting in his place Shaikh Farīd Bakhshī-begī commanded him to start off at once, and to take with him the mansabdars and ahadis who were on guard. Ihtimām Khān the *kotwāl* was made scout and intelligence officer. I determined, God willing, to start off myself when it was day. Mu'izzu-l-mulk brought back the Amīru-l-umarā.

About this time, Aḥmad Beg Khān and Dūst Muḥammad Khān had been sent off to Kabul,[108] and had got as far as Sikandra, which was on Khusrau's route. On his arrival they came out of their tents with some of their people, and returned and waited on me with the news that Khusrau had taken the Panjab road and was hastening on. It occurred to me that he might change his route and go somewhere else. As his maternal uncle, Mān Singh, was in Bengal, it occurred to many of the servants of the State that he might go in that direction. I sent out

---

107 Elliot (vii, 292) makes the Amīru-l-umarā envious of his peers, and Jahāngīr apprehensive lest he should destroy Khusrau, but he had just told him that nothing he did against Khusrau would be wrong. Clearly Jahāngīr's fear was that his favourite should be destroyed by Khusrau, or perhaps by the Amīr's treacherous associates.

108. The text has a curious mistake here : instead of *ba Kābul* it has *bakāwal* ('superintendent of the kitchen') as part of Dūst Muḥammad's name. Dūst was not *bakāwal*, but held higher office, and was later put in charge of the fort of Agra and given the title of Kḥwāja Jahān.

on every side, and ascertained that he was making for the Panjab. Meantime day dawned, and in reliance on the grace and favour of God Almighty, and with clear resolve, I mounted, withheld by nothing and no one.

> "In truth, he who is pursued by sorrow
> Knows not how the road is or how he may travel it.
> This he knows, that horror drives him on:
> He knows not with whom he goes nor whom he leaves behind."

When I reached the venerable mausoleum of my revered father, which is three kos from the city, I begged for aid to my courage from the spirit of that honoured one. About this time they captured and brought in[109] Mīrzā Ḥasan, son of Mīrzā Shāhrukh, who had proposed to accompany Khusrau. He could not deny it when I questioned him, and I ordered them to tie his hands and mount him on an elephant.[110] This was the first good omen manifested through the kindness and blessing of that venerable one. At midday, as it had become exceedingly hot, having rested awhile under the shade of a tree, I said to the Khān A'ẕam that we, with all our composure, were in such a state that we had not taken till now our regular allowance of opium, which it was the practice to take the first thing in the morning, and no one had reminded us of the omission. We might imagine from this what was now the condition of that graceless one (Khusrau).[111]

My trouble was this, that my son without any cause or reason should become an opponent and an enemy. If I should make no endeavour to capture him, the fractious or rebellious would have an instrument, or else he would take his own way and go for an asylum to the Ūzbegs or the Persians, and contempt would fall

---

[109] Price, p. 6, note.

[110] According to Khāfī Khān (i, 250) he was put to death, unless the expression "claws of death" is merely rhetorical. The Ma'āṣir (iii, 334) says he was imprisoned.

[111] The above obscure passage is explained in Price, p. 69.

upon my government. On this account, having made a special point of capturing him, I went on after a short rest two or three kos beyond pargana Mathura, which is 20 kos from Agra, and I alighted at one of the villages of that pargana where there is a tank.

When Khusrau arrived at Mathura, he met Ḥusain Beg Badakhshī, who was of those who had received favours from my revered father and was coming from Kabul to wait on me. As it is the temperament of the Badakhshīs to be seditious and turbulent, Khusrau regarded[112] this meeting as a godsend, and made Ḥusain Beg the captain and guide of 200 or 300 Badakhshan Aimāqs, who were with him.

Anyone whom they met, they plundered of horses and goods. Merchants and conveyers of goods were plundered by these rascals, and wheresoever they went men's wives and children were not safe from the calamity of these wretches. With his own eyes Khusrau was witnessing the oppression practised in the hereditary dominions of his ancestors, and after being a witness of the improper deeds of these rascals he a thousand times every moment wished death for himself. Finally, he had no remedy but to temporize with and support those dogs. If good luck and fortune had assisted him in his affairs, he would have made repentance and regret his voucher, and come without any deceit to wait on me. God, who knows the world of secrets, knows that I should have passed over his offences entirely and shown him such favour and affection that to the extent of a hair's point no estrangement or fear would have remained upon his mind. Inasmuch as during the lifetime of the late king (Akbar) an intention of joining in the sedition of some of the rebels had manifested itself in his mind, and he knew that this had come to my knowledge, he placed no reliance on my kindness and affection. His mother, while I was prince, in grief at his ways and

[112] Elliot (vi, 293) observes that this is a very involved and obscure passage.

behaviour and the misconduct of her brother Mādho Singh,[113] killed herself by swallowing opium (*tiryāq*).[114] What shall I write of her excellences and goodness? She had perfect intelligence, and her devotion to me was such that she would have sacrificed a thousand sons and brothers for one hair of mine. She constantly wrote to Khusrau and urged him to be sincere and affectionate to me. When she saw that it was of no use and that it was unknown how far he would be led away, she from the indignation and high spirit which are inherent in the Rajput character determined upon death. Her mind was several times disturbed, for such feelings were hereditary, and her ancestors and her brothers had occasionally showed signs of madness, but after a time had recovered. At a time when I had gone hunting, on Zī-l-ḥijja 26th, 1013[115] (May 6th, 1605), she in her agitation swallowed a quantity of opium, and quickly passed away. It was as if she had foreseen this behaviour of her unworthy son.

My first marriage and that at the commencement of my adolescence was with her. After Khusrau's birth I gave her the title of Shāh Begam. When she could not endure the bad conduct of her son and brother towards me she became disgusted with life and died, thereby escaping the present grief and sorrow. In consequence of her death, from the attachment I had for her, I passed some days without any kind of pleasure in life or existence, and for four days, which amount to 32 watches, I took nothing in the shape of food or drink. When this tale was told to my revered father, a letter of condolence of excessive kindness and affection reached this devoted disciple, and he sent me a robe of honour and the auspicious turban tied just as he had taken it off his head. This favour threw water on the flame of my grief and afforded complete quiet and repose to my unquietude

[113] Blochmann, p. 418.

[114] The word *tiryāq* means both opium and antidote.

[115] Blochmann, relying on Khāfi Khān, puts her death in 1011, and the Akbār-nāma (iii, 826) puts it in 1012. The chronogram in the Khusrau Bāgh yields 1012. See J.R.A.S. for July, 1907, p. 604.

and disturbance. My intention in relating these circumstances is to point out that no evil fortune is greater than when a son, through the impropriety of his conduct and his unapproved methods of behaviour, causes the death of his mother and becomes contumacious and rebellious to his father, without cause or reason, but simply through his own imaginations and futile ideas, and chooses to avoid the blessing of waiting upon him. Inasmuch as the Almighty Avenger lays a proper punishment on each action, of necessity his condition finally came to this, that he was caught under the worst circumstances, and falling from a position of trust became captive to perpetual incarceration.

> "When the man of sense behaves as if drunk,
> He puts his foot in a snare, his head in a noose."

To sum up, on Tuesday, Zī-l-ḥijja 10th, I alighted at the station of Hoḍal.[116] Shaikh Farīd Bakhshī and a band of valiant men were chosen to pursue Khusrau and became the vanguard of the victorious army. I sent back Dūst Muḥammad, who was in attendance on me, on account of his previous service and his white beard, to take charge of the fort of Agra and of the zanāna and the treasuries. When leaving Agra, I had placed the city in the charge of I'timādu-d-daula and Wazīru-l-mulk. I now said to Dūst Muḥammad, "As we are going to the Panjab, and that province is in the diwani of I'timādu-d-daula, you will despatch him to us, and will imprison and keep watch over the sons[117] of Mīrzā Muḥammad Ḥakīm who are in Agra; as when such proceedings manifest themselves in the son of one's loins what may one expect from nephews and cousins?" After the dispatch of Dūst Muḥammad, Mu'izzu-l-mulk became bakhshi.

On Wednesday I alighted at Palwal, and on Thursday at Farīdābād; on Friday, the 13th, I reached Delhi. From the dust of

---

[116] Where Lord Bellomont died in 1656. See Manucci (Irvine), i, 71.

[117] Probably this means the grandsons. At p. 329 it is mentioned that the grandsons had been confined in Gwalior up to the 16th year.

the road (i.e. immediately) I hastened to the venerated tomb of Humāyūn, and there besought help in my purpose, and with my own hand distributed money to poor persons and dervishes. Thence turning to the shrine of the venerable saint Shaikh Niẓ̤āmu-d-dīn Auliyā, I performed the dues of pilgrimage. After this I gave a portion[118] of money to Jamālu-d-dīn Ḥusain Anjū and another portion to Ḥakīm Muẓ̤affar that they might divide it amongst the poor and dervishes. On Saturday the 14th I stayed in Sarāy Narela.[119] This rest-house (*sarāy*) Khusrau had burned as he went.

The rank of Āqā Mullā, brother of Āṣaf Khān, who had been exalted by becoming my servant, was fixed in original and increase at 1,000 with 300 horse. He was in close attendance during this journey. Considering that some of the Aimāqs attached to the royal army were in league with Khusrau, and fearing that consequently some fraud or sedition might enter their minds, 2,000 rupees were given to their leaders to distribute amongst their men and make them hopeful of the Jahāngīrī favour. I gave money to Shaikh Faẓlu-llah and Rāja Dhīrdhar to distribute to faquirs and brahmans on the road. I gave orders that to Rānā Shankar in Ajmir should be given 30,000 rupees by way of assistance for his expenditure.

On Monday, the 16th, I reached the pargana of Pānīpat.[120] This station and place used to be very propitious to my gracious father and honoured ancestors, and two great victories had been gained in it. One was the defeat of Ibrāhīm Lodī, which was won by the might of the victorious hosts of His Majesty Firdūs - makānī. The story of this has been written in the histories of the time. The second victory was over the wicked Hemū, and was

---

118. *Pāra*, qu. 'a heap'

119. Narela is said to be $15\frac{1}{2}$ miles north-west of Delhi. William Finch, in his itinerary, mentions the stage as Nalera, a name that corresponds with Jahāngīr's.

120. 53 miles north of Delhi.

manifested from the world of fortune in the beginning of the reign of my revered father, as has been described by me in detail.

At the time that Khusrau had left Delhi and was proceeding to Panipat, it happened that Dilāwar Khān had arrived there. When shortly before Khusrau's arrival he heard of this affair, he sent his children across the Jumna and bravely determined to hasten on and throw himself into the fort of Lahore before Khusrau should arrive. About this time 'Abdu-r-Raḥīm also reached Panipat from Lahore, and Dilāwar Khān suggested to him that he too should send his children across the river, and should stand aside and await the victorious standards of Jahāngīr. As he was lethargic and timid, he could not make up his mind to do this, and delayed so much that Khusrau arrived. He went out and waited on him, and either voluntarily or in a state of agitation agreed to accompany him. He obtained the title of Malik Anwar and the position of vizier. Dilāwar Khān, like a brave man, turned towards Lahore, and on his road informed everyone and everybody of the servants of the court and the *karoriyān,* and the merchants whom he came across, of the exodus of Khusrau. Some he took with him, and others he told to stand aside out of the way. After that, the servants of God were relieved of the plundering by robbers and oppressors. Most probably, if Sayyid Kamāl in Delhi, and Dilāwar Khān at Panipat, had shown courage and determination, and had blocked Khusrau's path, his disorderly force would not have been able to resist and would have scattered, and he himself would have been captured. The fact is that their talents (*himmat*) were not equal to this, but afterwards each made amends for his fault, viz., Dilāwar Khān, by his rapid march, entered the fort of Lahore before Khusrau reached it, and by this notable service made amends for his earlier shortcoming, and Sayyid Kamāl manfully exerted himself in the engagement with Khusrau, as will be described in its own place.

On Zī-l-ḥijja 17th the royal standards were set up in the pargana of Karnāl. Here I raised 'Ābidīn Khwāja, son of Khwāja Kalān Jūybārī and *pīrzāda* (spiritual adviser), son of 'Abdu-llah Khān Ūzbeg, who had come in the time of my revered father, to the rank of 1,000. Shaikh Niẓām Thaneswarī, who was one of the notorious impostors (*shayyādān*) of the age, waited on Khusrau, and having gratified him with pleasant news, again[121] led him out of the (right) path, and then came to wait on me. As I had heard of these transactions, I gave him his road expenses and told him to depart for the auspicious place of pilgrimage (Mecca). On the 19th the halt was in pargana Shāhābād. Here there was very little water, but it happened that heavy rain fell, so that all were rejoiced.

I promoted Shaikh Aḥmad Lāhorī, who from my princehood had filled the relationship of service and discipleship and the position of a house-born one (*khānazāda*) to the office of Mīr-i-'Adl (Chief Justice). Disciples[122] and sincere followers were presented on his introduction, and to each it was necessary to give the token[123] and the likeness (*shast u shabah*). They were given on his recommendation (?). At the time of initiation some words of advice were given to the disciple: he must not confuse or darken his years with sectarian quarrels, but must follow the

---

121 Instead of *tāza* the MSS. have *pāra*, and the meaning seems to be that he accompanied Khusrau for some distance. In Price's Jahāngīr (p. 81) it is said that Niẓām received 6,000 rupees.

122 This is an interesting passage, because it is Jahāngīr's account of his father's 'Divine Faith.' But it is obscure, and copyists seem to have made mistakes. It is explained somewhat by the MS. used by Price (trans., pp. 82, 83), where more details are given than in the text. It is there stated that Aḥmad was Mīr-i-'Adl of Jahāngīr before the latter's accession.

123. The text has *dast u sīna* (hand and bosom), but the correct words, as is shown in the I.O. MS., No. 181, are *shast u shabiha* or *shabah*, and these refer to the ring or token and the portrait given by Akbar to the followers of the ' Divine Faith. 'See Blochmann, pp. 166 n. and 203 ; and Badayūnī, ii, 338. Aḥmad appears to be the Aḥmad Sūfī of Blochmann, pp. 208, 209, and of Badayūnī, ii, 404, and Lowe, p. 418. He was a member of the ' Divine Faith.'

rule of universal peace with regard to religions; he must not kill any living creature with his own hand, and must not flay anything. The only exceptions are in battle and the chase.

> "Be not the practiser of making lifeless any living thing,
> Save in the battlefield or in the time of hunting."

Honour the luminaries (the Sun, Moon, etc.), which are manifesters of God's light, according to the degree of each, and recognize the power and existence of Almighty God at all times and seasons. Be careful indeed that whether in private or in public you never for a moment forget Him.

> "Lame or low[124] or crooked or unrefined,
> Be amorous of Him and seek after Him."

My revered father became possessed of these principles, and was rarely void of such thoughts.

At the stage of Alūwa (?)[125] I appointed Abū-n-nabī (?)[126] Ūzbeg with fifty-seven other mansabdars to assist Shaikh Farīd, and gave the force 40,000 rupees for its expenses. To Jamīl Beg were given 7,000 rupees to divide among the Aimāqs (cavalry). I also presented Mīr Sharīf Āmulī[127] with 2,000 rupees.

On Tuesday the 24th of the same month they captured five of the attendants and comrades of Khusrau. Two of these, who confessed to his service, I ordered to be thrown under the feet of elephants, and three who denied were placed in custody that enquiry might be made. On Farwardīn 12th of the first year of my reign, Mīrzā Ḥusain and Nūru-d-dīn Qulī the *kotwāl* entered Lahore, and on the 24th of the same month a messenger of Dilāwar Khān arrived (there) with news that Khusrau was moving on Lahore and that they should be on their guard. On

---

124 Text, *pūj* or *pūch*, but the manuscript reading *lūk* is preferable. Erskine's MS. has *lūj*, naked.

125 Price (p. 83) has Anand or Anwand. Apparently Alūwa is right ; it is a place 18 miles north-west of Umballa. Cf. "India under Aurangzib," by J. N. Sarkar.

126 Abū-l-Bey, the Abū-l-Baqā of Akbar-nāma, iii, 820.

127 A member of the 'Divine Faith' (Blochmann, p. 452, etc.).

the same day the city gates were guarded and strengthened, and two days later Dilāwar Khān entered the fort with a few men and began to strengthen the towers and walls. Wherever these were broken and thrown down he repaired them, and, placing cannon and swivel guns on the citadel, he prepared for battle. Assembling the small number of the royal servants who were in the fort, they were assigned their several duties, and the people of the city also with loyalty gave their assistance. Two days later, and when all was ready, Khusrau arrived, and, having fixed a place for his camp, gave orders to invest[128] the city and to prepare for battle, and to burn one of the gates on any side where one could be got at. "After taking the fort," he said to his wicked crew, "I will give orders to plunder the city for seven days and to make captive the women and children."

This doomed lot set fire to a gate, and Dilāwar Beg Khān, Ḥusain Beg the dīwān, and Nūru-d-dīn Qulī the kotwal built a wall inside opposite the gateway.

Meantime Sa'īd Khān, who was one of those appointed to Kashmir and was now encamped on the Chenāb, having heard the news, started rapidly for Lahore. When he reached the Ravi he sent word to the garrison of the fort that he came with a loyal intention and that they should admit him. They sent someone at night and conducted him and some of his men inside. When the siege had lasted nine days, news of the approach of the royal army came repeatedly to Khusrau and his adherents. They became helpless (*bī pā*), and made up their minds that they must face the victorious army.

As Lahore is one of the greatest places in Hindustan, a great number of people gathered in six or seven days. It was reported on good authority that 10,000 or 12,000 horse were collected, and had left the city with the view of making a night attack on the royal vanguard. This news was brought to me at the *sarāy* of

---

[128] The text has *qatl* by mistake for *qabl*.

Qāẓī 'Alī on the night of Thursday the 16th. Although it rained heavily in the night I beat the drum of march and mounted. Arriving in Sulṭānpūr at dawn I remained there till noon. By chance, at this place and hour the victorious army encountered that ill-fated band. Mu'izzu-l-mulk had brought a dish of roast meat,[129] and I was turning towards it with zest when the news of the battle was brought to me. Though I had a longing to eat the roast meat, I immediately took a mouthful by way of augury and mounted, and without waiting for the coming up of men and without regard to the smallness of my force I went off in all haste. However much I demanded my *chiltah* (wadded coat), they did not produce it. My only arms were a spear and sword, but I committed myself to the favour of God and started off without hesitation. At first my escort did not number more than fifty horsemen; no one had expected a fight that day. In fine, when I reached the head of the bridge of Gobindwāl,[130] 400 or 500 horse, good and bad, had come together. When I had crossed the bridge the news of a victory was brought to me. The bearer of the good news was Shamsī, *tūshakchī* (wardrobe man), and for his good news he obtained the title of Khūsh-khabar Khān. Mīr Jamālu-d-dīn Ḥusain, whom I had sent previously to advise Khusrau, came up at the same time and said such things about the number and bravery of Khusrau's men as frightened his hearers. Though news of the victory came continuously, this simple-minded Sayyid would not believe it, and expressed incredulity that such an army as he had seen could be defeated by Shaikh Farīd's force, which was small and not properly equipped. When they brought Khusrau's litter[131] with two of his eunuchs, the Mīr admitted what had happened. Then, alighting from his horse, he placed his head at my feet and professed

[129] *Bīryānī*. See Blochmann, p. 60.

[130] The Gundvāl of Tiefenthaler, i, 113. Cunningham, in his history of the Sikhs, spells it Goïndwāl. It is on the Beas.

[131] The text has *singhāsan* instead of *sukhāsan*. Kāmgār Ḥusainī has *sukhpāl*.

every kind of humility and submission, and said that there could be no higher or more lofty fortune than this.

In this command Shaikh Farīd behaved with sincerity and devotion. The Sayyids of Bārha, who are of the brave ones of the age, and who have held this place in every fight in which they have been, formed the van. Saif Khān, son of Sayyid Maḥmūd Khān Bārha, the head of the tribe, had shown great bravery and had received seventeen wounds. Sayyid Jalāl, also of the brethren of this band, received an arrow in his temple and died a few days later. At the time when the Sayyids of Bārha, who were not more than fifty or sixty in number, having received wounds from 1,500 Badakhshī horsemen, had been cut to pieces, Sayyid Kamāl, who, with his brothers, had been appointed to support the van, came up on the flank and fought with wondrous bravery and manliness. After that the men of the right wing raised the cry of *Pādshāh salāmat* ("Long live the King") and charged, and the rebels hearing the words, gave up and scattered abroad to various hiding-places. About 400 Aimāqs became crushed on the plain of anger and overcome by the victorious army. Khusrau's box of jewels and precious things which he had always with him, fell into our hands.

"Who thought that this boy of few years
Would behave so badly to his sire?
At the first taste of the cup he brings up the lees.
He melts away my glory and his own modesty.
He sets on fire[132] the throne of Khūrshīd,
He longs for the place of Jamshīd."

Short-sighted men in Allahabad had urged me also to rebel against my father. Their words were extremely unacceptable and disapproved by me. I know what sort of endurance a kingdom would have, the foundations of which were laid on hostility to a father, and was not moved by the evil counsels of such worthless

---

[132] Instead of the *basūzānād* of the text, the MSS. have *bashūrānad*, he defiles. In the last line they have *jāy* instead of *takht*.

men, but acting according to the dictates of reason and knowledge I waited on my father, my guide, my *qibla,*[133] and my visible God, and as a result of this good purpose it went well with me.

In the evening of the day of Khusrau's flight I gave Rāja Bāso, who is a trusty zamindar of the hill-country of Lahore, leave to go to that frontier, and, wherever he heard news or trace of Khusrau, to make every effort to capture him. I also appointed Mahābat Khān and Mīrzā 'Alī Akbarshāhī to a large force, which was to pursue Khusrau in whatever direction he might go. I resolved with myself that if Khusrau went to Kabul, I would follow him and not turn back till he was captured. If not delaying in Kabul he should go on to Badakhshan and those regions, I would leave Mahābat Khān in Kabul and return myself (to India). My reason for not going to Badakhshan was that that wretch would (in that case) certainly ally himself with the Ūzbegs, and the disgrace would attach to this State.

On the day on which the royal troops were ordered to pursue Khusrau, 15,000 rupees were given to Mahābat Khān and 20,000 to the ahadis, and 10,000 more were sent with the army to be given to whom it might be necessary to give it on the way.

On Saturday, the 28th, the victorious camp was pitched at Jaipāl,[134] which lies seven kos from Lahore. On the same day Khusrau arrived with a few men on the bank of the Chenāb. The brief account of what had happened is that after his defeat those who had escaped with him from the battle became divided in opinion. The Afghans and Indians, who were mostly his old retainers, wished to double back like foxes into Hindustan, and to become a source of rebellion and trouble there. Ḥusain Beg, whose people and family and treasure were in the direction of Kabul, suggested going to Kabul. In the end, as action was taken

---

133 I.e. the place to which to turn in prayer.

134 Elliot (vi, 299) has Jahān, and the word in the MSS. does not look like Jaipāl.

according to the wish of Ḥusain Beg, the Hindustanis and the Afghans decided to separate themselves from him. On arriving at the Chenāb, he proposed to cross at the ferry of Shāhpūr, which is one of the recognized crossings, but as he could find no boats there he made for the ferry of Sodharah, where his people got one boat without boatmen and another full of firewood and grass.

The ferries over the rivers had been stopped because before Khusrau's defeat orders had been given to all the jagirdars and the superintendents of roads and crossings in the subah of the Panjab that as this kind of dispute had arisen they must all be on the alert. Ḥusain Beg wished to transfer the men from the boat with firewood and grass to the other, so that they might convey Khusrau across. At this juncture arrived Kīlan,[135] son-in-law of Kamāl Chaudharī of Sodharah, and saw a body of men about to cross in the night. He cried out to the boatmen that there was an order from the king Jahāngīr forbidding unknown men from crossing in the night, and that they must be careful. Owing to the noise and uproar, the people of the neighbourhood gathered together, and Kamāl's son-in-law took from the boatmen the pole with which they propel the boat, and which in Hindustani is called *ballī,* and thus made the boat unmanageable. Although money was offered to the boatmen, not one would ferry them over. News went to Abū-l-Qāsim Namakīn, who was at Gujarat, near the Chenāb, that a body of men were wanting to cross the river by night, and he at once came to the ferry in the night with his sons and some horsemen. Things went to such a length that Ḥusain Beg shot arrows at the boatmen,[136] and Kamāl's son-in-law also took to shooting arrows from the river-bank. For four kos the boat took its own way down the river, until at the end of the night it grounded, and try as they would they could not get

[135] This word appears to be a mistake ; it is not in the MSS.

[136] When the boat stuck, the boatmen swam ashore, and it was probably then that Ḥusain shot at them. See Blochmann, p. 414, n. 2.

it off. Meantime it became day. Abū-l-Qāsim and Khwāja Khiẓr Khān, who by the efforts of Hilāl Khān had assembled on this (? the west) side of the river, fortified its west bank, and the zamindars fortified it on the east.

Before this affair of Khusrau's, I had sent Hilāl Khān as *sazāwal* to the army appointed for Kashmīr under Sa'īd Khān, and by chance he arrived in the neighbourhood (of the ferry) that same night; he came in the nick of time, and his efforts had great effect in bringing together Abū-l-Qāsim Khān Namakīn, and Khwāja Khiẓr Khān in the capture of Khusrau.

On the morning of Sunday, the 24th of the aforesaid month, people on elephants and in boats captured Khusrau, and on Monday, the last day of the month, news of this reached me in the garden of Mīrzā Kāmrān. I immediately ordered the Amīru-l-umarā to go to Gujarat and to bring Khusrau to wait on me.

In counsels on State affairs and government it often happens that I act according to my own judgment and prefer my own counsel to that of others. In the first instance I had elected to wait on my revered father from Allahabad in opposition to the advice of my faithful servants, and I obtained the blessing of serving him, and this was for my spiritual and temporal good. By the same course of conduct I had become king. The second instance was the pursuit of Khusrau, from which I was not held back by taking time to ascertain the (auspicious) hour, etc., and from which I took no rest until I captured him. It is a strange thing that after I had started I asked Ḥakīm 'Alī, who is learned in mathematics, how the hour of my departure had been (i.e. whether propitious or not), and he replied that in order to obtain my object if I had wished to select an hour, there could not have been for years one selected better than that in which I mounted.

On Thursday, Muḥarram 3rd, 1015, in Mīrzā Kāmrān's garden, they brought Khusrau before me with his hands tied and chains on his legs from the left side[137] after the manner and custom of Chingīz Khān. They made Ḥusain Beg stand on his right hand and 'Abdu-r-Raḥīm on his left. Khusrau stood weeping and trembling between them. Ḥusain Beg, with the idea that it might profit him, began to speak wildly. When his purport became apparent to me I did not allow him to continue talking, but handed over Khusrau in chains, and ordered these two villains to be put in the skins of an ox and an ass, and that they should be mounted on asses with their faces to the tail[138] and thus taken round the city. As the ox-hide dried more quickly than that of the ass, Ḥusain Beg remained alive for four watches and died from suffocation. 'Abdu-r-Raḥīm, who was in the ass's skin and to whom they gave some refreshment from outside, remained alive.

From Monday, the last day of Zī-l-ḥijja, until the 9th of Muḥarram of the aforesaid year, I remained in Mīrzā Kāmrān's garden because the time was unpropitious.[139] I bestowed Bhairawal,[140] where the battle had taken place, on Shaikh Farīd, and rewarded him with the high title of Murtaẓā Khān. For the sake of good government I ordered posts to be set up on both sides of the road from the garden to the city, and ordered them to hang up and impale the seditious Aimāqs and others who had taken part in the rebellion. Thus each one of them received an extraordinary punishment. I gave headship to those landholders who had shown loyalty, and to every one of the Chaudharīs

---

137 " With a chain fastened from his left hand to his left foot, according to the law of Chingīz Khān" (Gladwin's Jahāngīr, quoted by Elliot, vi, 507). But apparently what is meant is that Khusrau was led up from the left side of the emperor.

138 Du Jarric, in his history of the Jesuit Missions, gives some details about the punishment. The bullock and ass were slaughtered on the spot and their skins were sewed on the bodies of the unhappy men. Horns and ears were left on the skins.

139 Perhaps the meaning is that the weather was bad.

140 The proper form seems to be Bhaironwāl, the Bhyrowal of the maps. It is on the right bank of the Bīāh (Beas) on the road from Jalandhar to Amritsar. See Blochmann, p. 414, note.

between the Jhelam and the Chenāb I gave lands for their support.

Of Ḥusain Beg's property there were obtained from the house of Mīr Muḥammad Bāqī nearly seven lakhs of rupees. This was exclusive of what he had made over to other places and of what he had with him. After this, whenever his name is mentioned, the words[141] *gāwān u kharān* (bullocks and asses) will be used. When he came to this Court in company with Mīrzā Shāhrukh he had one horse. By degrees his affairs flourished so that he became possessed of treasure both visible and buried, and projects of this kind entered his mind.

While Khusrau's affair was still in the will of God, as there was no actual governor between Afghanistan and Agra, which is a source of sedition and mischief, and, fearing that Khusrau's affair might be prolonged, I ordered my son Parwīz to leave some of the sardars to look after the Rānā and to come to Agra with Āṣaf Khān and a body of those nearly connected with him in the service. He was to consider the protection and management of that region his special charge. But by the blessed favour of Allah, Khusrau's affair was settled before Parwīz arrived in Agra; I accordingly ordered my aforesaid son to come and wait on me.

On Wednesday, Muḥarram 8th, I auspiciously entered the fort of Lahore. A number of loyalists represented to me that my return to Agra would be for the good of the State at this time when much was going amiss in Gujarat, in the Deccan, and in Bengal. This counsel did not meet with my approval, for the reports of Shāh Beg Khān, the governor of Qandahar, showed that the officers of the Persian border were meditating an attack on that fortress. They had been moved thereto by the

---

141 The words are omitted in the text. Erskine read in his MS. *gāu jizwan,* which I do not understand. The I.O. MSS. and B.M. MS. Or 3276 have *gāwān u kharān*. Ḥusain Beg, whose proper name was Ḥasan, was a brave soldier, and did good service under Akbar. See his biography in Blochmann, p. 454.

machinations of the residuum of the Mirzas of Qandahar's army, which was always shaking the chain of contention. The Persian officers had written letters to these malcontents, and there was likelihood of a disturbance. It occurred to me that the death of His Majesty Akbar and the unreasonable outbreak of Khusrau might put an edge on their design, and that they might attack Qandahar. What had occurred to my mind became a realized fact. The governor of Farāh, the Malik of Sīstan, and the jagirdars of that neighbourhood, with the assistance of Ḥusain Khān, the governor of Herat, invaded Qandahar. Praise is due to the manliness and courage of Shāh Beg Khān, who planted his foot firmly like a man, and strengthened the fort, and seated himself on the top of the third (?) citadel of the aforesaid fort in such a manner that outsiders could see his entertainments. During the siege he girded not his loins, but with bare head and feet arranged parties of pleasure; yet no day passed that he did not send a force from the fort to meet the foe and did not make manly efforts. This went on as long as he was in the fort. The Qizilbāsh army had invested on three sides. When news of this reached Lahore it was clearly advisable to remain in that neighbourhood. A large force was immediately appointed under the leadership of Mīrzā Ghāzī, who was accompanied by a number of men of rank and servants of the Court, such as Qarā Beg and Tukhta Beg, who had been promoted with the titles of Qarā Khān and Sardār Khān. I appointed Mīrzā Ghāzī to a mansab of 5,000 personal, and horsemen, and bestowed drums on him. Mīrzā Ghāzī was the son of Mīrzā Jānī Tarkhān, king of Thathah (Sind), and by the efforts of 'Abdu-r-Raḥīm Khānkhānān that country had been conquered in the reign of the late king. The country of Thathah was included in his jagir, and he held the rank with personality and horsemen of 5,000. After his death his son Mīrzā Ghāzī was raised to his rank and service. Their ancestors were among the amirs of Sulṭān Ḥusain Mirza Bāy-qarā, the ruler of Khurasan, and they were originally descended from the amirs of Tīmūr (*Ṣāḥib-qirānī*). Khwāja 'Āqil was appointed bakhshi of this army; 43,000 rupees were given to Qarā Khān for road expenses, and 15,000 to Naqdī Beg and Qilīj Beg, who were to accompany Mīrzā Ghāzī. I determined to stay at Lahore in order to settle this matter and with the intention of a tour to Kabul. About this time the rank of Ḥakīm Fatḥu-llah was fixed, original and increased, at 1,000 personality and 300 horse. As Shaikh Ḥusain Jāmī had dreams about me which had come true, I gave him twenty lakhs of dams, equivalent to 30,000 or 40,000 rupees, for the expenses of himself and his monastery and the dervishes who were with him. On the 22nd I promoted 'Abdu-llah Khān to the rank of 2,500 personal and 500 horse, original and increased. I ordered to be given to the ahadis two lakhs of rupees to be paid in advance and deducted by degrees from their monthly pay. I bestowed 6,000 rupees on Qāsim Beg Khān, the son-in-law of Shāh Beg Khān, and 3,000 rupees on Sayyid Bahādur Khān.

In Gobindwāl, which is on the river Bīyāh (Beas), there was a Hindu named Arjun,[142] in the garments of sainthood and sanctity, so much so that he had captured many of the simple-hearted of the Hindus, and even of the ignorant and foolish followers of Islam, by his ways and manners, and they had loudly sounded the drum of his holiness. They called him *Gūrū,* and from all sides stupid people crowded to worship and manifest complete faith in him. For three or four generations (of spiritual successors) they had kept this shop warm. Many times it occurred to me to put a stop to this vain affair or to bring him into the assembly of the people of Islam.

At last when Khusrau passed along this road this insignificant fellow proposed to wait upon him. Khusrau happened to halt at the place where he was, and he came out and did homage to him. He behaved to Khusrau in certain

[142] The fifth Gūrū of the Sikhs and the compiler of the Granth. He was the father of Har Govind. See Sayyid Muhammad Laṭīf's history of the Panjāb, p. 253. Arjun's tomb is in Lahore.

special ways, and made on his forehead a fingermark in saffron, which the Indians (Hinduwān) call *qashqa*,[143] and is considered propitious. When this came to my ears and I clearly understood his folly, I ordered them to produce him and handed over his houses, dwelling-places, and children to Murtaẓā Khān, and having confiscated his property commanded that he should be put to death.

There were two men named Rājū and Ambā, who, under the shadow of the protection of the eunuch Daulat Khān, made their livelihood by oppression and tyranny, and had done many acts of oppression in the few days that Khusrau was before Lahore. I ordered Rājū to the gallows and a fine to be taken from Ambā, who was reputed to be wealthy. In short, 15,000 rupees were collected from him, which sum I ordered them to expend on *bulghur-khānas* (refectories) and in charity.

Sa'du-llah Khān, son of Sa'd Khān, was promoted to the rank of 2,000 personal and 1,000 horse.

In his great desire to wait upon me, Parwīz traversed long distances in a short time, in the rainy season and incessant rain, and on Thursday, the 29th, when two watches and three *gharī* of day had passed, obtained the blessing of seeing me. With exceeding kindness and affection, I took him into the embrace of favour and kissed his forehead.

When this disgraceful conduct showed itself in Khusrau, I had resolved not to delay in any place till I had captured him. There was a probability that he might turn back towards Hindustan, so it appeared impolitic to leave Agra empty, as it was the centre of the State, the abode of the ladies of the holy harem, and the depository of the world's treasures. On these accounts I had written when leaving Agra to Parwīz, saying that his loyalty had had this result, that Khusrau had fled and that Fortune had turned her face toward himself; that I had started in

---

143 But qashqa is a Turkish word. The Hindi phrase seems to be *ṭīkā*.

pursuit of Khusrau, and that he should consequently dispose of the affairs of the Rānā in some way according to the necessity of the time, and for the benefit of the kingdom should himself come quickly to Agra. I had delivered into his charge the capital and treasury, which was equal to the wealth of Qārūn,[144] and I had commended him to the God of power. Before this letter reached Parwīz, the Rānā had been so humbled that he had sent to Āṣaf Khān to say that as by his own acts he had come to shame and disgrace, he hoped that he would intercede for him in such a way that the prince would be content with his sending Bāgha,[145] who was one of his sons. Parwīz had not agreed to this, and said that either the Rānā himself should come or that he should send Karan. Meantime the news of Khusrau's disturbance arrived, and on its account Āṣaf Khān and other loyalists agreed to the coming of Bāgha, who obtained the blessing of waiting on the prince near Mandalgaṛh.

Parwīz, leaving Rāja Jagannāth and most of the chiefs of his army, started for Agra with Āṣaf Khān and some of those near to him and his own attendants, and with him brought Bāgha to the Court. When he came near Agra he heard the news of the victory over Khusrau and his capture, and after resting two days an order reached him that as matters appeared settled in all quarters he should betake himself to me, in order that on the prescribed date he might obtain the good fortune of waiting on me. I bestowed on him the parasol (*āftāb-gīr*),[146] which is one of the signs of royalty, and I gave him the rank of 10,000 and sent an order to the officials to grant him a *tankhwāh* jagir. At this time I sent Mīrzā 'Alī Beg to Kashmir; 10,000 rupees were delivered to Qāẓī 'Izzatu-llah to divide amongst faqirs and the poor of Kabul. Aḥmad Beg Khān was promoted to the rank of 2,000 personal and 1,250 horse, original and extra. At the same

---

144 The cousin of Moses, famous for his wealth ; the Korah of the Bible.

145 Gladwin has Nāgh.

146 Blochmann, p. 50.

time Muqarrab Khān, who had been sent to Burhanpur to bring the children of Dāniyāl, returned after an absence of 6 months 22 days and had the honour of an audience, and related in detail what had occurred in those regions.

Saif Khān was promoted to the rank of 2,000 personal and 1,000 horse. Shaikh 'Abdu-l-Wahhāb[147] of the Bukhara sayyids, who was governor of Delhi under the late king, was dismissed from the post (by me) for certain ill-deeds done by his men, and was entered amongst the holders of subsistence lands and the *arbāb-i-sa'ādat.*

In the whole of the hereditary dominions, both the crown lands and the jagirs, I ordered the preparation of *bulghur-khānas* (free eating-houses), where cooked food might be provided for the poor according to their condition, and so that residents and travellers both might reap the benefit.

Amba[148] Khān Kashmīrī, who was of the stock of the rulers of Kashmir, was selected for the rank of 1,000 personal and 300 horse. On Monday, Rabī'u-l-ākhir 9th, I gave Parwīz a special sword; and jewelled swords were presented also to Quṭbu-d-dīn Khān Koka and the Amīru-l-umarā. I saw Dāniyāl's children, whom Muqarrab Khān had brought; there were three sons and four daughters. The boys bore the names Ṭahmūraṣ,[149] Bāysughar, and Hūshang. Such kindness and affection were shown by me to these children as no one thought possible. I resolved that ṭahmūraṣ, who was the eldest, should always be in waiting on me, and the others were handed over to the charge of my own sisters.

---

147 Akbar-nāma, iii, 748, and Blochmann, p. 546. He was a man of piety and learning, and Jahāngīr means that he restored him to his former quiet life. The *arbāb-i-sa'ādat,* or auspicious persons, were those who offered up prayers for the king's prosperity and other blessings.

148 Amba was killed later by Nūr-Jahān's husband, Shīr Afgan (Tūzuk, pp. 54, 55).

149 Blochmann, p. 310.

A special dress of honour was sent to Rāja Mān Singh in Bengal. I ordered a reward of 30 lakhs of dams to Mīrzā Ghāzī. I bestowed on Shaikh Ibrāhīm, son of Quṭbu-d-dīn Khān Koka, the rank of 1,000 personal and 300 horse, and dignified him with the title of Kishwar Khān.

As when I started in pursuit of Khusrau I had left my son Khurram in charge of the palaces and treasury, I now, when that affair had been settled, ordered the said son to attend upon Haẓrat Maryam-zamānī and the other ladies, and to escort them to me. When they reached the neighbourhood of Lahore, on Friday the 12th of the month mentioned, I embarked in a boat and went to a village named Dahr to meet my mother, and I had the good fortune to be received by her. After the performance of obeisance and prostration and greeting which is due from the young to the old according to the custom of Chingīz, the rules of Tīmūr and common usage, and after worship of the King of the World (God), and after finishing this business, I obtained leave to return, and re-entered the fort of Lahore.

On the 17th, having appointed Mu'izzu-l-mulk bakhshi of the army against the Rānā, I dismissed him to it. As news had come of the rebellion of Rāy Rāy Singh and his son, Dulīp, in the neighbourhood of Nāgor, I ordered Rāja Jagannāth to proceed against them with others of the servants of the State and Mu'izzu-l-mulk, and to put a stop to this disturbance. I gave 50,000 rupees to Sardār Khān, who had been appointed to the place of Shāh Beg Khān as Governor of Qandahar, and I promoted him to the rank of 3,000 personal and 2,500 horse. To Khiẓr Khān, the late ruler of Khandesh, were given 3,000 rupees, and to his brother, Aḥmad Khān,[150] who is one of the khānazādas of the State. Hāshim Khān, son of Qāsim Khān, who is one of the house-born of the State, and worthy of

[150] These words are not in the MSS., and they seem to have crept into the text by mistake and to be a premature entry of words relating to Hāshim, etc. The brother of the former ruler (or king) of Khandesh could hardly be a *khānazād*.

advancement, I promoted to the rank of 2,500 personal and 1,500 horse. I gave him also one of my own horses. I sent robes of honour to eight individuals amongst the nobles of the army of the Deccan.[151] Five thousand rupees were given to Niẓām of Shiraz, the storyteller. Three thousand rupees were given for the expenses of the *bulghūr-khāna* of Kashmir to the *wakīl* of Mīrzā 'Alī Beg, the governor of that place, to send to Srinagar. I presented a jewelled dagger of the value of 6,000 rupees to Quṭbu-d-dīn Khān.

News reached me that Shaikh Ibrāhīm Bābā, the Afghan, had opened a religious establishment (lit. one of being a shaikh and having disciples) in one of the parganas[152] of Lahore, and as his doings were disreputable and foolish a considerable number of Afghans had collected round him. I ordered him to be brought and handed over to Parwīz to be kept in the fort of Chunar; so this vain disturbance was put an end to.

On Sunday, 7th Jumādā-l-awwal, many of the mansabdars and ahadis were promoted: Mahābat Khān obtained the rank of 2,000 personal and 1,300 horse, Dilāwar Khān 2,000 personal and 1,400 horse, Wazīru-l-mulk 1,300 personal and 550 horse, Qayyām Khān 1,000 personal and horse, Shyām Singh 1,500 personal and 1,200 horse; in the same way forty-two mansabdars were promoted. On most days the same observances occur. I presented Parwīz with a ruby of the value of 25,000 rupees. On W dnesday the 9th of the aforesaid month, the 21st of Shahrīwar,[153] after three watches and four gharis, the feast for my solar weighing, which is the commencement of the 38th year of my age, took place. According to custom they got ready the weighing apparatus and the scales in the house of Maryam-

---

[151] This should be, according to the MSS., "army against the Rānā," not army of the Deccan.

[152] The MSS. have " in the neighbourhood of Lahore." Parwīz had then charge of Bihar.

[153] Text, wrongly, Bahman. Jahāngīr was born on the 21st of *Sh*ahrīwar.

zamānī (his mother). At the moment appointed blessings were invoked and I sate in the scales. Each suspending rope was held by an elderly person who offered up prayers. The first time the weight in gold came to three Hindustani maunds and ten seers. After this I was weighed against several metals, perfumes, and essences, up to twelve weighings, the details of which will be given hereafter. Twice a year I weigh myself against gold and silver and other metals, and against all sorts of silks and cloths, and various grains, etc., once at the beginning of the solar year and once at that of the lunar. The weight of the money of the two weighings I hand over to the different treasurers for faqirs and those in want. On the same auspicious day I promoted Quṭbu-d-dīn Khān Koka, who for many years had expected such a day,[154] with various favours. First, I gave him the rank of 5,000 personal and horse, and with this a special robe of honour, a jewelled sword, and one of my own horses, with a jewelled saddle, and I gave him leave to go to the subahdarship of the province of Bengal and Orissa, which is a place for 50,000 horse. As a mark of honour he set off accompanied by a large force, and two lakhs of rupees were given him as a sumptuary allowance. My connection with his mother is such that as in my childhood I was under her guardianship and care, I have not so much affection for my own mother as for her. She is to me my gracious mother, and I do not hold him less dear than my own brothers and children. Quṭbu-d-dīn is the foster-brother who is most fit for fosterage. I gave 300,000 rupees to his auxiliaries. On this day I sent 130,000 as a marriage present (*sāchiq*) for the daughter of Pahārī (his brother Murād), who had been betrothed to Parwīz.

On the 22nd, Bāz Bahādur Qalmāq, who had long been guilty of evil practices in Bengal, by the guidance of fortune obtained the honour of kissing my threshold. I gave him a jewelled dagger, 8,000 rupees, and promoted him to the rank of 1,000

[154] Apparently, had long looked forward to the happy day when Jahāngīr should be weighed as a king.

personal and horse. One lakh of rupees and cash and jewels were bestowed on Parwīz. Kesho Dās Mārū was promoted to the grade of 1,500 personal and horse. Abū-l-ḥasan, who had been the diwan and factotum of my brother Dāniyāl, together with his children,[155] had the honour of an audience, and was raised to the rank of 1,000 personal and 500 horse. On the 1st of the second Jumādā Shaikh Bāyazīd,[156] who was one of the shaikhzādas of Sīkrī, well known for brilliance of understanding and knowledge, and the connection of old service,[157] was honoured with the title of Mu'aẕẕam Khān, and to him I gave the government of Delhi. On the 21st of the same month I presented Parwīz with a necklace composed of four rubies and one hundred pearls. The rank of Ḥakīm Muẕaffar was fixed at 3,000 personal and 1,000 horse, original and extra. I gave 5,000 rupees to Nathu Māl (?), Rāja of Manjholi.[158]

A remarkable occurrence was the discovery of a letter from Mīrzā 'Azīz Koka to 'Alī Khān, the ruler of Khandesh. I had had an impression that he had a particular enmity to me on Khusrau's account, who was his son-in-law. From the discovery of this writing it became clear that he had never given up his innate treachery, and had adopted this unbecoming attitude towards my revered father also. In short, this letter which he had written at some time to Rāja 'Alī Khān was from beginning to end full of abuse and disapprobation, and said things which no enemy even could have written and such as could not be attributed to anyone, and far less to one like His Majesty, *'Arsh-āshyānī,* a king and an appreciative sovereign, who from childhood had educated him and brought him up because of what was due for services rendered by his mother, and raised

[155] Perhaps the meaning is that he was introduced along with Dāniyāl's children.

[156] Blochmann, p. 492.

[157] This refers to his parentage.

[158] In the MSS. this name seems to be Bhīm Mal. Manjholi is written Manjholah in Blochmann, p. 175.

the standard of reliance on him to such a high degree as no other person possessed. This letter fell into the hands of Khwāja Abū-l-ḥasan in Burhanpur amongst the property of Rāja 'Alī Khān. He brought and laid it before me. In reading and seeing it the hair on my limbs stood on end. But for the consideration and due recognition of the fact that his mother had given her milk to my father I could have killed him with my own hand. Having procured his attendance I gave the letter into his hand and told him to read it with a loud voice to those present. When he saw the letter I thought his body would have parted from his soul, but with shamelessness and impudence he read it as though he had not written it and was reading it by order. Those present in that paradise-like assembly of the servants of Akbar and Jahāngīr and heard the letter read, loosened the tongue of reproach and of curses and abuse. I put the question to him, "Leaving aside the treacheries which in reliance on your worthless self you contrived against *my* fortune, what was done to you by my father, who raised you and your family from the dust of the road to such wealth and dignity as to make you the envy of your contemporaries, that you should write these things to the enemies of his Empire? W hy did you enrol yourself amongst the wicked and disloyal? Truly, what can one make of an original nature and innate disposition? Since your temperament has been nourished by the water of treachery, what else can spring up but such actions? Passing over what you did to myself, I gave you the rank you had held before, thinking that your treachery was directed against me only. Since it has become known that you behaved in a similar way to your benefactor and visible Deity, I leave you to the thoughts and actions which you formerly had and still have." After these remarks his lips closed, and he was unable to make any reply. What could he have said in the presence of such disgrace? I gave an order to deprive him of his jagir. Although what this ingrate had done was unpardonable, yet in the end, from certain considerations, I passed it over.

On Sunday the 26th of the above-mentioned month was held the marriage feast of Parwīz and the daughter of Prince Murād. The ceremony was performed in the house of Her Highness Maryam-zamānī. The entertainment was arranged in the house of Parwīz, and all who were present were exalted with all kinds of honour and civilities. Nine thousand rupees were handed over to Sharif Āmulī and other nobles, to be given in alms to faqirs and other poor people.

On Sunday the 10th Rajab I left the city to hunt in Girjhak and Nandana,[159] and took up my quarters in the garden of Rām Dās, where I remained four days.

On Wednesday the 13th the solar weighing of Parwīz took place. They weighed him twelve times against various metals and other things, and each weighing came to two maunds and eighteen seers. I ordered the whole to be distributed amongst faqirs. At this time the rank of Shajā'at Khān was fixed at 1,500 personal and 700 horse, original and extra.

After the march of Mīrzā Ghāzī and his force it occurred to me to send a second contingent after him. Having bestowed on Bahādur[160] Khān Qūrbegī the rank of 1,500 personal and 800 horse, original and extra, I started off a body of cavalry,[161] which came to about 3,000, with him under the leadership of Shāh Beg and Muḥammad Amīn. For the expenses of this force 200,000 rupees were given and 1,000 musketeers were also appointed.

I left Āṣaf Khān to guard Khusrau and defend Lahore. The Amīru-l-umarā was deprived of the honour of waiting on me, as he had a severe illness and remained in the city. 'Abdu-r-Razzāq Ma'mūrī, who had been summoned from the Rānā's country,

---

[159] ? Nandanpur. These places are in Sindsagār, near Multān.

[160] MS. 181 has Bahār, and it has 600 instead of 800 horse.

[161] Text, *Ūymāq pūrī* (?). MS. 181 has *būrī*, and 305 seems to have the same. Can it mean 'red cavalry'? As Blochmann has pointed out, 371, n. 2, the word Ūymāq does not always mean the tribe, but was used to denote a superior kind of cavalry.

was promoted to be bakhshi at headquarters, and it was ordered that in company with 'Abū-l-ḥasan he should perform this service permanently. Following my father's rule, I appoint two men in association in the discharge of the chief offices, not from want of confidence in them, but because, as they are mortal and no man is safe from accidents or illness, if any confusion or obstacle should present itself to one the other is there so that the affairs of the servants of God may not come to ruin.

At this time also news came that at the Dasahrā, which is one of the fixed feast days of the Hindus, 'Abdu-llah Khān had made an incursion from Kālpī, which is his jagir, into the province of Bandīlah, and displaying great valour made prisoner Rām Chand, son of Madhūkar, who for a long time had made a centre of disturbance in that difficult country and taken him to Kālpī. For this service he was presented with a standard and raised to 3,000 personal and 2,000 horse.

Petitions from the subah of Bihar represented that Jahāngīr Qulī Khān had had a battle with Sangrām, one of the chief zamindars of Bihar, who had about 4,000 horse and innumerable foot, on account of certain opposition and disloyalty on rough land, and that on the field the aforesaid Khān had exerted himself manfully. In the end Sangrām died of a gunshot wound; many of his men fell in the battle, and those saved from the sword took to flight. Since this distinguished affair had been brought about by Jahāngīr Qulī Khān, I promoted him to the rank of 4,500 personal and 3,500 horse.

Three months and six days passed by in hunting; 581 animals were captured with the gun, hunting leopards and nets, and a *qamargāh;* of these 158 were killed by my own gun. The qamargah was held twice; on one occasion in Girjhāk, when the ladies were present, 155 animals were killed; and the second time, in Nandīna, 110.[162] The details of the animals killed are as follows: mountain sheep, 180; mountain goats, 29; wild asses, 10; Nilgai, 9; antelope, etc., 348.

On Wednesday the 16th Shawwāl I returned safe from my hunting, and when one watch and six gharis of day had passed I entered Lahore on the day named. During this hunting a strange affair was witnessed At Chandwālah, where a minaret had been erected, I had wounded in the belly a black antelope. When wounded, a sound proceeded from him such as I have never heard from any antelope, except in the rutting season. Old hunters and those with me were astonished, and said they never remembered nor had they heard from their fathers that such a voice issued from an antelope except at rutting time. This has been written down because it is not void of strangeness. I found the flesh of thc mountain goat more delicious than that of all wild animals, although its skin is exceedingly ill-odoured, so much so that even when tanned the scent is not destroyed. I ordered one of the largest of the he-goats to be weighed; it was 2 maunds and 24 seers, equal to 21 foreign maunds (Persian). I ordered a large ram to be weighed, and it came to 2 maunds and 3 seers *Akbarī*, equal to 17 Persian (*wilāyatī*) maunds. The largest and strongest of the wild asses weighed 9 maunds and 16 seers, equal to 76 Persian (wilayati) maunds. I have frequently heard from hunters and those fond of the chase that at a certain regular time a worm develops in the horns of the mountain ram, and that this worm causes an irritation which induces the ram to fight with his hind, and that if he finds no rival he strikes his head against a tree or a rock to allay the irritation. After enquiry it seems that the same worm appears in the horn of the female sheep, and since the female does not fight the statement is clearly untrue. Though the flesh of the wild ass is lawful food and most men like to eat it, it was in no way suited to my taste.

---

[162] The *qamargāh* or ring-hunt produced 265 head of game ; the rest were shot at other times ; the total of the list should be apparently 576.

Inasmuch as before this time the punishment of Dulīp and of his father, Rāy Rāy Singh, had been ordered, there now came news that Zāhid Khān, the son of Ṣādiq Khān, and 'Abdu-r-Raḥīm, son of Shaikh Abū-l-faẓl, and Rānā Sankar and Mu'izzu-l-mulk, with another force of mansabdars and followers of the Court, had heard news of Dulīp in the neighbourhood of Nāgor, which is in the subah of Ajmir, and having moved against him had found him. As he could find no way of escape, of necessity he planted a firm foot and came to blows with the royal army. After a short encounter he was badly beaten and gave over many to slaughter, and himself, taking with him his own effects, fled into the vale of ruin.

"With broken arms and loosened belt,
No power to fight and no care for head."

In spite of his old age, I continued Qilīj Khān in his mansab because of his service under my father, and I ordered that he should get a jagir in the sarkar of Kālpī.

In the month Zī-l-qa'da the mother of Quṭbu-d-dīn Khān Koka, who had given me her milk and was as a mother to me or even kinder than my own kind mother, and in whose lap I had been brought up from infancy, was committed to the mercy of God. I placed the feet of her corpse on my shoulders and carried her a part of the way (to her grave). Through extreme grief and sorrow I had no inclination for some days to eat, and I did not change my clothes.

FEAST OF THE SECOND NEW YEAR.

On Wednesday the 22nd Zī-l-qa'da, 1015 (10th March, 1607), when $3\frac{1}{2}$ gharis of the day had passed, the sun rose to his House of Honour. They decorated the palace after the usual fashion: a great entertainment was prepared, and having seated myself at an auspicious hour on the throne of accession I exalted the nobles and courtiers with kindness and favour. On this same auspicious day it was learned from the reports sent from

Qandahar that the army sent under Mīrzä Ghāzī, son of Mīrzā Jānī, to succour (which had been appointed to assist) Shāh Beg Khān, had entered the city of Qandahar on the 12th of Shawwāl. When the Persians heard of the arrival of the victorious army at the last stage before the aforesaid city,[163] they became surprised and wretched and repentant, and did not draw rein until they had reached the Helmand, fifty or sixty kos distant.

In the second place it became known that the governor of Farāh and a number of the officers of that neighbourhood had taken it into their heads, after the death of the late king, that in this confusion Qandahar might easily fall into their hands, and without waiting for an order from Shāh 'Abbās had collected together and won over the Chief of Sewistān (Sīstān). Sending someone to Ḥusain Khān, the governor of Herat, they asked for support from him. He also sent a force. After that they turned to attack Qandahar. Shāh Beg Khān, the governor of that place, seeing that battle has two heads, and that if (which God forbid!) he should be defeated he would lose possession of Qandahar, thought that to confine himself in a fort would be better than to fight. He therefore determined to hold the fort, and sent quick messengers to the Court. It happened that at this time the royal standards had started from Agra in pursuit of Khusrau, and had arrived at Lahore. Immediately on hearing this news (from Shāh Beg Khān), a large force was sent off of amirs and mansabdars under Mīrzā Ghāzī. Before the Mīrzā reached Qandahar the news had been carried to the Shāh (of Persia) that the governor of Farāh, with some of the jagirdars of that neighbourhood, had proceeded towards the province of Qandahar. Considering this an improper proceeding, he sent Ḥusain Beg, a well-known man and one of his own intimates, to make enquiries. He also sent a farman in their names that they should move away from the vicinity of Qandahar and go to their own places and abodes, because the friendship and amity of his ancestors with the

[163] The MSS. have the 6th stage instead of "last."

dignified family of Jahāngīr Pādshāh were of old standing. That body, before the arrival of Ḥusain Beg and the King's order, not being able to oppose the royal army, considered the opportunity of returning a favourable one. The said Ḥusain Beg censured the men and started off to wait on me, which he had the honour to do at Lahore. He explained that the ill-fated army which had attacked Qandahar had acted without the order of Shāh 'Abbās. God forbid (he said) that in consequence of this any unpleasantness should remain in my mind. In short, after the victorious troops reached Qandahar, they, according to orders, delivered the fort over to Sardār Khān, and Shāh Beg Khān returned to Court with the relieving force.

On the 27th Zī-l-qa'da, 'Abdu-llah Khān, having brought Rām Chand Bandīlah into captivity and chains, brought him before me. I ordered them to take the fetters from his legs, and bestowed on him a robe of honour, and handed him over to Rāja Bāso that he might take security and release him and a number of his relations who had been captured with him. This through my clemency and kindness came to pass. He had never imagined such clemency and kindness as I showed to him.

On the 2nd Zī-l-ḥijja I gave my son Khurram a *tūmān u tūgh*, a flag and drums, and bestowed on him the rank of 8,000 personal and 5,000 horse, and gave an order for a jagir. On the same day, having exalted Pīr Khān,[164] son of Daulat Khān Lodī, who had come from Khandesh with the children of Dāniyāl, with the title of Ṣalābat Khān and honoured him with the rank of 3,000 personal and 1,500 horse, and presented him with a standard and drums, I promoted him to the distinction of sonship (*farzandī*) beyond his fellows and equals. The ancestors and uncles of Ṣalābat Khān's grandfather had been great and honourable among the tribe of Lodī. An earlier Daulat Khān, uncle of Ṣalābat Khān's grandfather, when Ibrāhīm after his father Sikandar's death, began to behave ill to his father's amirs

[164] This is the famous Khān Jahān Lodī of Shāh Jahān's reign.

and destroyed many, became apprehensive, and sent his younger son, Dilāwar Khān, to wait upon H.M. Bābar in Kabul, and suggested to him the acquisition of Hindustan. As Bābar also had this enterprise in mind, he at once proceeded in that direction, and did not turn his rein till he reached the neighbourhood of Lahore. Daulat Khān with his followers obtained the good fortune to wait upon him, and performed loyal service. As he was an old man, adorned with inward and outward excellencies, he did much good service. He (Bābar) generally called him "father," and entrusting to him as before[165] the government of the Panjab placed its amirs and jagirdars under his jurisdiction. Taking Dilāwar Khān with him he (Bābar) returned to Kabul. When he (Bābar) came a second time into the Panjab with intent to invade Hindustan, Daulat Khān waited on him, and about the same time died. Dilāwar Khān was honoured with the title of Khānkhānān, and was with Bābar in the battle he had with Ibrāhīm. In the same way he was permanently in waiting on the late king Humāyūn. In the *thānā* of Mungir, at the time of his (Humāyūn's) return from Bengal, he fought bravely against Shīr Khān Afghān, and was made prisoner on the field of battle. Although Shīr Khān urged him to take service with him, he refused and said, "Thy ancestors were always the servants of mine: how, then, could I do this?" Shīr Khān was enraged, and ordered him to be shut up in a wall.[166]

'Umar Khān, the grandfather of Ṣalābat Khān Farzand, who was cousin of Dilāwar Khān, had been treated with respect in the time of Salīm Khān. After Salīm Khān's death and the slaughter of Fīrūz, his son, at the hand of Muḥammad Khān, 'Umar Khān and his brethren became suspicious of Muḥammad Khān and went to Gujarat, where 'Umar Khān died. Daulat Khān, his son, who was a brave young man of pleasant appearance, and good at all things, chose the companionship of

[165] Text, *ba dastūr*.

[166] I.e. built him up in it.

'Abdu-r-Raḥīm, son of Bairām Khān, who had been dignified with the title of Khān-khānān in the reign of Akbar, and performed excellent service. The Khānkhānān regarded him as his own brother, or even a thousand times better than his brother, and dearer. Most of the Khānkhānān's victories were gained through Daulat Khān's valour and manliness.[167] When my revered father, having taken the province of Khandesh and the fort of Āsīr, returned to Agra, he left Dāniyāl in charge of that province and of all the provinces acquired from the rulers of the Deccan. At this time Dāniyāl had separated Daulat Khān from the Khānkhānān, and was keeping him in attendance on himself and handing over to him for disposal all the business of the State. He showed him much favour and perfect affection until he died in his service. He left two sons, one Muḥammad Khān, and the other Pīr Khān; Muḥammad Khān, who was the elder, died a short time after his father. Dāniyāl, too, wore himself out with drinking. After my accession I summoned Pīr Khān to Court. As I discovered in him a good disposition and natural abilities, I raised the pedestal of regard for him to the point that has been described. To-day there is not in my government any person of greater influence than he, so much so that on his representation I pass over faults which are not pardoned at the intercession of any of the other servants of the Court. In short, he is a young man of good disposition, brave, and worthy of favour, and what I have done for him has been done rightly, and he will be exalted by further favours.[168]

As I had made up my exalted mind to the conquest of Māwarā'a-n-nahr (Transoxiana), which was the hereditary kingdom of my ancestors, I desired to free the face of Hindustan from the rubbish of the factious and rebellious, and leaving one of my sons in that country, to go myself with a valiant army in

---

[167] Jahāngīr did not like the Khānkhānān, and so here belittles his services.

[168] During Shāh Jahān's reign, Khān Jahān Lodī fled from Court, was pursued, and killed.

due array, with elephants of mountainous dignity and of lightning speed, and taking ample treasure with me, to undertake the conquest of my ancestral dominions. In accordance with this idea, I despatched Parwīz to drive back the Rānā, and intended to go myself to the Deccan, when just at that moment the improper action of Khusrau took place, and it became necessary to pursue him and put an end to that disturbance. For the same reason, the undertaking of Parwīz did not assume a promising appearance, and regarding the exigency of the time he gave a respite to the Rānā. Bringing with him one of the Rānā's sons, he came to wait on me, and had the bliss of attending me in Lahore. When I was at ease about Khusrau's disturbance, and the repulse of the Qizilbāshes, who had invested Qandahar, had been brought about in a facile way, it came into my mind to make a hunting tour to Kabul, which is like my native land. After that I would return to Hindustan, when the purposes of my mind would pass from design to action. In pursuance of these steps, on the 7th Zī-l-ḥijja, at an auspicious hour, I left the fort of Lahore and took up my quarters in the Dil-āmīz Garden, which is on the other side of the Ravi, and stayed there four days. Sunday, the 19th Farwardīn, which is the culmination of His Majesty the Sun, I passed in the garden, and some of the servants of the Court were favourably and kindly honoured with increased rank. Ten thousand rupees were bestowed on Ḥasan Beg, the envoy of the ruler of Persia (Shāh ‘Abbās). Leaving Qilīj Khān, Mīrān Ṣadr Jahān, and Mīr Sharīf Āmulī in Lahore, I ordered them to settle in consultation any matters that might present themselves. On Monday I marched from the garden mentioned, and encamped at the village of Harhar, 3 $\frac{1}{2}$ kos distant from the city. On Tuesday the royal standards alighted at Jahāngīrpūr, which is one of my fixed hunting-places. In this neighbourhood had been erected by my order a *manār* at the head of the grave of an antelope called

Mansarāj,[169] which was without equal in fights with tame antelopes and in hunting wild ones. On a stone of that manar was carved this prose composition, written by Mullā Muḥammad Ḥusain of Kashmir, who was the chief of the elegant writers of the day: "In this enchanting place an antelope came into the world-holding (*jahān-gīrī*) net of the God-knowing ruler Nūru-d-dīn Jahāngīr Pādshāh. In the space of one month, having overcome his desert fierceness, he became the head of the special antelopes." On account of the rare quality of this antelope, I commanded that no person should hunt the deer of this plain, and that their flesh should be to Hindus and Muhammadans as is the flesh of cows and pigs. They made the gravestone in the shape of an antelope. I ordered Sikandar Mu'īn, the jagirdar of the aforesaid pargana, to build a strong fort in the village of Jahangirpur.

On Thursday, the 14th, I encamped in the pargana of Chandāla.[170] Thence on Saturday, the 16th, making one stage in the middle, I came to Ḥāfi ẓ ābād.[171] I stayed in the station which had been erected by the exertions of the *karorī* of that place, Mīr Qiyāmu-d-dīn. Having reached the Chenāb in two marches on Thursday, the 21st Zī-l-ḥijja, I crossed the river by a bridge which had been built there, and my camp was pitched in the neighbourhood of the pargana of Gujrat. At the time when His Majesty Akbar went to Kashmir, a fort had been built on that bank of the river. Having brought to this fort a body of Gujars who had passed their time in the neighbourhood in thieving and highway robbery, he established them here. As it had become the abode of Gujars, he made it a separate pargana, and gave it the name of Gujrat. They call Gujars a caste which does little manual work and subsists on milk and curds. On Friday I

169 Perhaps the antelope's name was Rāj, and the syllable *man* the pronoun 'my,' when the translation would be 'my antelope Rāj.' See Elliot, vi, 302, and R.A.S. MS., No. 124.

170 Perhaps the Jandiāla of the Indian Gazetteer, vii, 137.

171 Indian Gazetteer, v, 239.

pitched at Khawāṣṣpūr, five kos from Gujrat, founded by Khawāṣṣ Khān, a slave of Shīr Khān Afghān. Thence, with two halts in the middle, I pitched on the bank of the Bihaṭ (Jhelam). On that night a great wind blew and a black cloud hid the face of the sky. The rain was of such violence that old men remembered none such. It turned to hail, and every hailstone was the size of a hen's egg. From the flooding of the river and the force of the wind and rain, the bridge broke. I, with the inmates of the harem, crossed in a boat. As there were few boats, I ordered the men not[172] to cross in these, but to rebuild the bridge. It was finished in a week, and the whole army crossed with ease. The source of the Bihaṭ is a spring in Kashmir called the Vīr-nāg; in the language of India a snake is *vīr-nāg*. Clearly there had been a large snake at that place. I went twice to the spring in my father's lifetime; it is 20 kos from the city of Kashmir. It is an octagonal reservoir about 20 yards by 20. Near it are the remains of a place of worship for recluses; cells cut out of the rock and numerous caves. The water is exceedingly pure. Although I could not guess its depth, a grain of poppy-seed is visible until it touches the bottom. There were many fish to be seen in it. As I had heard that it was unfathomable, I ordered them to throw in a cord with a stone attached, and when this cord was measured in *gaz* it became evident that the depth was not more than once and a half the height of a man. After my accession I ordered them to build the sides of the spring round with stone, and they made a garden round it with a canal; and built halls and houses about it, and made a place such that travellers over the world can point out few like it. When the river reaches the village of Pāmpūr, at a distance of ten kos from the city, it increases, and all the saffron of Kashmir is obtained in this village. I do not know if there is so much saffron in any other place in the world. The annual crop is 500 maunds by Hindustan weight, equal to 5,000 *wilāyat* (Persian) maunds. In attendance on my revered father, I went to

---

[172] Text omits the negative.

this place at the season when the saffron was in flower. On other plants of the world, first the branches (stems) shoot out and then the leaves and flowers. On the contrary, when the saffron stem is four fingers breadth from the dry ground, its flowers shoot out, of the colour of the iris,[173] with four petals, and in the middle are four threads (*rīs͟ha*) of an orange colour like that of the flower, and of the length of a finger-joint. This is the saffron. The land is not ploughed[174] or irrigated, the plant springs up amongst the clods. In some places its cultivation extends for a kos, and in others for half a kos. It looks better from a distance. At the time of plucking, all my attendants got headache from its sharp scent. Though I drank wine and took a cup, I too got headache. I asked the animal-like Kashmiris, who were employed in picking the flowers, how they felt. I ascertained that they had never experienced headache in their lives.

The waters from the spring Vīr-nāg and of other streams and nullahs that join from right and left form the river Bihat, which passes through the heart of the city. Its breadth in most places is not more than a bowshot.[175] No one drinks its water, because of its heaviness and indigestibility. All the people of Kashmir drink the water of a lake that is near the city, and is called Dall. The river Bihat enters this lake and flows through to the Panjab by the Bārāmūla Pass, Paklī, and Dantūr.

In Kashmir there is plenty of water from streams and springs. By far the best is that of the Lār valley, which joins the Bihat in the village of S͟hihābu-d-dīn-pūr. This village is one of the celebrated places of Kashmir, and is on the Bihat. About a hundred plane-trees (*chanār*) of graceful form clustered[176]

---

[173] Text, *sūsanī* ; apparently a blue iris.

[174] The text has *s͟humār* wrongly for *s͟hiyār*, and it seems that the negative of the text is wrong, since it does not occur in the MSS. Abū-l-faẓl gives the number of petals and stamens more correctly than Jahāngīr.

[175] *Az tikka andāzī* ; perhaps 'the cast of a javelīn.'

[176] Lit. ' have joined hands. '

together on one plot of ground, pleasant and green, join each other so as to shade the whole plot, and the whole surface of the ground is grass and trefoil[177] ; so much so that to lay a carpet on it would be superfluous and in bad taste. The village was founded by Sulṭān Zainu-l-'ābidīn, who for 52 years ruled Kashmir with absolute sway. They speak of him as the great Pādshāh. They tell many strange customs of his. There are many remains and traces of buildings of his in Kashmir. One of these is in the midst of a lake called Wulūr, and of which the length and breadth are more than three or four kos. It is called Zain-lankā, and in making it they have exerted themselves greatly. The springs of this lake are very deep. The first time they brought a large quantity of stone in boats and poured it on the place where now the building stands it had no result. At last they sank some thousands of boats with stones, and with great labour recovered a piece of ground 100 gaz by 100 gaz out of the water, and made a terrace, and on one side thereof the Sultan erected a temple for the worship of his supreme God. Than this there is no finer place.[178] He often came to the spot by boat and engaged in worship of the King of Wisdom. They say he spent many "forty days" in that place. One day a wicked son of his came to that place to kill him, and finding him alone, drew a sword and went in. When his eye fell on the Sultan, however, on account of his venerable dignity and the might of his virtues, he became confused and bewildered and turned away. The Sultan shortly after came out and seated himself in the boat with this same son, and started for the city. On the way he said to his son, "I have forgotten my rosary; get into a canoe and fetch it for me." The son having gone into the temple sees his father in the same place, and the graceless man with complete shame of face falls at his father's feet and asks pardon for his fault. They have told

---

[177] *Sih-barga;* but this reading seems doubtful ; perhaps it is *sīr-i-barga,* full of leaves. Jahāngīr says that to lay a carpet on the grass would be *bī-dardī,* unfeeling, unsympathetic, and *kam salīqagī.*

[178] The text has *naqsh bar jāy,* but the true reading seems to be *nafīztar.*

many tales of such miracles as this of him, and they say also that he had well practised the science of *khala'*.[179] When, from the ways and methods of his sons, he perceived in them signs of haste in seeking for rule and government, he would say to them, "To me it is very easy to abandon rule, and even to pass away from life, but when I am gone you will do nothing, and the time of your prosperity will not endure long, but in a short time you will obtain the recompense of your evil deeds and your own dispositions." Having spoken thus, he gave up eating and drinking, and passed forty days in this manner. He made not his eye acquainted with sleep, and employed himself after the manner of men of piety and austerity in the worship of God Almighty. On the fortieth day he gave up the deposit of his existence, and entered into the mercy of God. He left three sons—Ādam Khān, Ḥājī Khān, and Bahrām Khān. They quarrelled with each other, and all three were ruined. The government of Kashmir was transferred to the tribe of the Chaks, who belonged to the class of the common soldiers of the country. During their dynasty three of the rulers constructed buildings on three sides of the terrace formed by Zainu-l-'ābidīn in the Wulur Lake, but none of these is as strong as his.

Autumn and Spring in Kashmir are things worthy to be seen. I witnessed the Autumn season, and it appeared to me to be better than what I had heard of it. I have never seen Spring in that province, but hope to do so some day. On Saturday the 1st of Muḥarram (18th April, 1607) I left the bank of the Bihat, and with one day between reached the fort of Rohtās, which was built by Shīr Khān Afghān. This fort was founded in a cleft of the ground, and the strength of it cannot be imagined. As the place is near the Ghakhar territory, and they are a proud and rebellious people, he had looked to this fort specially as a means of punishing and defeating them. When a little of the building had been done Shīr Khān died and his son, Salīm Khān, obtained

[179] *'Ilm-i-khala'-i-badan,* 'withdrawal of the soul from the body' (Erskine).

the grace to complete it. On each of the gates[180] they have carved on a stone the cost of erecting the fort; 16 krors, 10 lakhs of dams, and more were expended, equal in Hindustan reckoning to 4,025,000 rupees, and according to the currency of Iran to 120,000 *tūman,* and in the currency of Turan to 1 *arb,* 21 lakhs and 75,000 *khānī,* that are now current.[181]

On Tuesday the 4th of the month, having travelled four kos and three-quarters, I encamped at Tīla.[182] Thence I came down to the village of Bhakra. In the Ghakhar tongue *bhakra*[183] is a jungle. The jungle was composed of clusters of flowers, white and scentless. I came the whole way from Tīla to Bhakra in the middle of the river-bed,[184] which had running water in it, with oleander flowers of the colour of peach-blossom. In Hindustan this plant is always in full bloom (*purbār*). There was much of it on the banks of this river. The horsemen and men on foot who were with me were told to put bunches of the flower on their heads, and whoever did not do so had his turban taken off; a wonderful flower-bed was produced.

On Thursday the 6th of the month the halting-place was at Hatyā. On this road many palās - trees (*Butea frondosa*) were in blossom. This flower, too, is peculiar to the jungles of Hindustan;

---

180 So in text, but the MSS. and Elliot, vi, 307, have "on one of the gates."

181. The figures seem wrong, and the MSS. differ. See Elliot, vi, 307. Apparently the correct sum in rupees is 34 lakhs 23,000. At p. 61 the khani of Turan is reckoned at one-third of a rupee. If the dam be taken at its ordinary value of one-fortieth of a rupee, the number of rupees should be 40 lakhs 25,000, and if the khani of Turan be one third of a rupee we should read one kror instead of one arb. Probably Jahāngīr has used arb as meaning kror, and not 100 krors. There is a valuable note on his expedition through the Ghakkar country in Blochmann, p. 486. Blochmann takes the figures for the rupees to be four krors, but probably this is due to wrong pointing.

182 The MSS. and text have Pila or Pila. I adopt Tīla from Blochmann, p. 487, note. Elliot has Tillah, vi, 307, and note.

183 In Tolbort's account of Lūdhiyāna, J.A.S.B. for 1869, p. 86, *bhakhra* is given as the name of a creeping plant *(Pedalium murex).*

184 *Rūd-khāna*; this, according to Blochmann, should be the river Kahan, -*khāna* being a mistake for Kahan. See p. 487 note. But all the MSS. have *khāna*.

it has no scent, but its colour is flaming orange. The base of the flower is black; the flower itself is as big as a red rose. It is so beautiful that one cannot take one's eyes off it. As the air was very sweet and clouds had hidden the sun, and rain was gently sprinkled about, I felt an inclination to drink wine. In short this road was traversed with great enjoyment and pleasure. They call the place Hatyā because it was founded by a Ghakkar named Hāthi (elephant). From Mārgala to Hatyā the country is called Pothūwār.[185] In these regions there are few crows. From Rohtās to Hatyā is the place and abode of the Bhūgyāls,[186] who are related to and of the same ancestry as the Ghakkars.

Marching on Friday the 7th, I travelled 4 1/2 kos and alighted at the station of Pakka.[187] This place is called Pakka because the *sarāy* is of burnt brick, and in the Hindi language what is ripe (that is, not raw material) is called *pakka.* The station was strangely full of dust and earth. The carts reached it with great difficulty owing to the badness of the road. They had brought from Kabul to this place *rīwāj* (rhubarb), which was mostly spoiled.

On Saturday the 8th we marched $4\frac{1}{2}$ kos and encamped at the village of Khar.[188] *Khar* in the Ghakkar language is a rent and breakage. There are few trees in this country. On Sunday the 9th I halted beyond Rāwalpindī. This place was founded by a Hindu named Rāwal, and *pindī* in the Ghakkar tongue means a village. In the valley near this station there was a stream flowing, the waters of which were collected in a pool. As this halting-place was not devoid of freshness I alighted there for a time, and I asked the Ghakkars the depth of the pool. They gave me no precise answer, but said they had heard from their fathers that

---

185 See Elliot, vi, 309 note.

186 Būgyāls ; Elliot, vi, 309. They are descendants of Sultān Būgā.

187 Paka is mentioned in Tiefenthaler, i, 114.

188 Khor ; Elliot, vi, 309 note. Near the Mānikyāla tope.

there were alligators in the pool which wounded animals that came there, and on that account no one had the boldness to go in. I ordered them to throw in a sheep. It swam across the pool and came out. I then ordered a *farrāsh* to go in, and he also came out safe. It thus became clear that there was no foundation for what the Ghakkars had said. The pool was an arrow's flight in width.

On Monday the 10th the village of Kharbūza[189] was our stage. The Ghakkars in earlier times had built a dome here and taken tolls from travellers. As the dome was shaped like a melon it became known by that name. On Tuesday the 11th I halted at Kāla-pānī, which in Hindi means black water. There is a mountain pass (*kotal*) at this place called Mārgalla; in Hindi *mār* means to beat and *galla* is a caravan, the name therefore means the place of the plundering of the caravan. The boundary of the Ghakkar country is here. This tribe are wonderfully like animals; they are always squabbling and fighting with one another. Although I wished to put an end to this fighting, I was unable to do so.

"The soul of the fool is doomed to trouble."[190]

On Wednesday the 12th the camp was at Bābā Hasan Abdāl. One kos to the east of this station there is a waterfall over which the stream rushes with great force. There is no fall like it on the

---

[189] Kharbūza Sarāy is marked on Elphinstone's map.

[190] Mr. Rogers has ' ' The soul of the fool thou canst purchase for little." Perhaps the sense is "God grants life to the fool on hard terms." Erskine has "To serve a fool is hard indeed." Possibly the literal meaning is "You buy the soul of the fool at a high price," that is, it costs a great deal to win him over. Elliot had what is probably the best rendering, "Barbarous characters should be treated with severity"; though in Elliot, vi, 310, the translation is, "The life of fools is held very cheap in troublous times."

way to Kabul. On the road to Kashmir there are two or three like it.[191]

In the middle of the basin, in which is the source of the stream, Rāja Mān Singh has erected a small building. There are many fish in the basin of the length of half a gaz and a quarter gaz. I halted three days at this enchanting place, drinking wine with those who were intimate with me and employing myself in catching fish. Until now I had never thrown a *sufra* net, which is a famous kind of net, and which in Hindi they call *bhanwar*[192] *jāl.* It is not easy to throw. I threw it with my own hand and caught twelve fish, and putting pearls into their noses,[193] let them loose in the water. I enquired into the story of Bābā Ḥasan from the story-tellers and from the inhabitants of the place, but no one could tell me any particulars. The celebrated place at that station is a spring which flows from the foot of a little hill, exceedingly clear, sweet, and nice, as witness this couplet of Amīr Khusrau:—

> "In the bottom of the water, from its clearness, a blind man
> Can count the sand-grains in the heart of the night."

Khwāja Shamsu-d-dīn Muḥammad Khwāfī, who was for long employed as Vizier by my revered father, had made a platform and a reservoir there, into which is led the water from the spring, and thence is used in cultivation and in gardens. On the edge of this terrace he had built a dome for his own burial.

---

191 Apparently this remark must have been written after Jahāngīr's visit to Kashmir by the Bāramūla route in the fourteenth year.

192 *Bhanwar*, as Mr. Lowe has pointed out, means in Hindi an eddy or whirlpool.

193 William Finch says that at Hasan Abdāl there were many fish with gold rings in their noses hung by Akbar, and that the water is so clear that you may see a penny in the bottom. Jahāngīr's informants were apparently not versed in hagiography. Bābā Hasan Abdāl is apparently the saint who was an ancestor of Ma'ṣūm Bhakarī, and is buried at Qandahar. See Beale, and Jarrett's translation of the Āyīn, ii, 324 note. The Sikhs identify the place with their Bābā Nānak. It is not a wife of Akbar who is buried at Ḥasan Abdāl, but Ḥakīm Abū-l-fatḥ and his brother.

By chance his destiny was not there, and (the bodies of) Ḥakīm Abū-l-fatḥ Gīlānī and his brother Ḥakīm Humām, who were close to the person and had the complete confidence of my revered father, were placed in that dome in accordance with his order.

On the 15th the halt was at Amrohī.[194] It is a wonderfully green place, in which no ups and downs were visible. In this village and its neighbourhood there are 7,000 or 8,000 households of Khaturs and Dalāzāks. All kinds of mischief and oppression and highway robbery take place through this tribe. I ordered the government of this region and Attock to be given to Ẓ afar Khān, son of Zain Khān Koka, and that by the time of the return of the royal standards from Kabul they should march all the Dalāzāks to Lahore and capture the head men of the Khaturs and keep them in prison.

On Monday, the 17th, a march was made, and, with one stage in between, the royal standards alighted near the fort of Attock on the bank of the river Nīlāb (Indus). At this stage Mahābat Khān was promoted to the rank of 2,500. This fort was built by the late king Akbar, and was completed by the labours of Khwāja Shamsu-d-dīn Khwāfī. It is a strong fort. At this time the water of the Nīlāb was low,[195] and accordingly a bridge had been made with eighteen boats, and the people crossed over easily. I left the Amīru-l-umarā at Attock on account of weakness of body and illness. An order was given to the bakhshis that, as the province of Kabul could not support a large army, they should only allow the immediate attendants of the Court to cross the river, and until the return of the royal standards the royal camp

---

[194] Elliot has Amardī, but the MSS. have Amrohī. The Ma'āṣir, ii, 755, has Āhrū'ī. See Blochmann, p. 522.

[195] Az *taghyān farūd āmada*. Perhaps the meaning is exactly the opposite, viz. ' had come down in violence. ' But if so, could a bridge have been made, and with eighteen boats ? The time was the 4th or 5th May. Elliot has "the Nīlāb was very full."

should remain at Attock. On Wednesday, the 19th, with the princes and some of the private servants, having mounted on to a raft (with inflated skins underneath), and having crossed the river Nīlāb safely, I alighted on the bank of the river Kāma. The Kāma is a river that flows by the *qaṣba* (fortified town) of Jalālābād. The *jāla* is a structure they make of bamboos and grass and place underneath it skins full of air. In this province they call them *shāl* (or *sāl*). In rivers and streams in which there are rocks they are safer than boats. 12,000 rupees were given to Mīr Sharīf Āmulī and to a number of men, who had been appointed to perform services at Lahore, to divide amongst the faqirs. An order was given to 'Abdu-r-Razzāq Ma'mūrī[196] and to Bihārī Dās, bakhshi of the Ahadis, to complete the force that had been appointed to accompany Ẓafar Khān and send them away. With one stage in between, the camp halted at the saray of Bāra. On the other side of the river Kāma there is a fort which Zain Khān Koka built at the time when he was appointed to subjugate the Yūsufza'e Afghans, and called Naushahr (Newcastle). About 50,000 rupees were spent upon it. They say that Humāyūn used to hunt rhinoceros in this region. I also heard from my father that he had twice or thrice witnessed such a hunt in the company of his father. On Thursday, the 25th, I alighted at the saray of Daulatābād. Aḥmad Beg of Kabul, jagirdar of Peshawar, with the Maliks of the Yūsufza'es and the Ghoriya-khel, came and waited on me. As the service of Aḥmad Beg was not approved, I transferred him from that territory (wilāyat) and conferred it on Shīr Khān, the Afghan. On Wednesday, the 26th, I encamped in the garden of Sardār Khān, which he had made in the neighbourhood of Peshawar. I walked round Ghorkhatrī, which is the worshipping-place of the jogīs in this neighbourhood, with the idea that I might see some faqirs from association with whom I might obtain grace. But that was like looking for the phœnix or the philosopher's stone. A herd without any religious knowledge

---

196 According to the Ma'āṣiru-l-umarā, iii, 376, Ma'mūr is a village in Arabia.

came to my view, from seeing whom I derived nothing but obscurity of mind. On Thursday, the 27th, I arrived at the halting-place of Jamrūd, and on Friday, 28th, at the Khaibar Kotal (Khyber Pass) and encamped at 'Alī Masjid, and on Saturday I traversed the tortuous (*mārpīch,* i.e. snake-twisting) Pass, and alighted at Gharīb-khāna. At this stage Abū-l-qāsim Namakīn, Jagirdar of Jalālābād, brought an apricot, which was not inferior in beauty to good Kashmir apricots. At the stage of Daka they brought from Kabul *gīlās* (cherries), which my revered father had entitled *Shāh-ālū.* As I was much inclined to cat them, inasmuch as I had not (hitherto?) obtained them, I ate them with great zest as a relish to wine. On Tuesday, 2nd Ṣafar, I encamped at Basāwal, which is on the bank of the river. On the other side of the river there is a mountain which has no trees or grass on it, and on that account they call this mountain the hill of Bīdaulat (unfortunate). I heard from my father that in mountains like this there are mines of gold. On the mountain of Āla Būghān, at the time when my revered father went to Kabul, I had had a *qamargāh* hunt, and killed several[197] red deer. As I had handed over the administration of all civil affairs to the Amīru-l-umarā, and his illness increased greatly, and forgetfulness came over his faculties to such an extent that what was settled in one hour he forgot in the next, and his forgetfulness was increasing day by day, on Wednesday, the 3rd Ṣafar, I entrusted the duties of the viziership to Āṣaf Khān, presenting him with a special robe of honour, and inkstand and a jewelled pen. It was a remarkable coincidence that twenty-eight years previously to this, at the same halting-place, my revered father had promoted him[198] to

---

[197] The MSS. have *ṣad* instead of *chand,* i.e. 100.

[198] This Āsaf Khān is Qawāmu-d-din Ja'far Beg and the No. iii of Blochmann, p. 411. Apparently his appointment as Mir Bakhshi was made in 989 (1581), in which year Akbar went to Kabul. Blochmann says Āṣaf Khān was made Mir Bakhshi in the room of Qāzī 'Alī, and we find at p. 372 of A.N. , iii, that Qāzī "Alū Bakhshī was appointed in that year to the Panjab. Twenty-eight years before 1016 (to the beginning of which Jahāngīr is referring) yields 988. Basāwal is on right bank of Kabul River below Jalālābād.

the rank of Mīr Bakhshī (chief paymaster).. A ruby which his brother[199] Abū-l-qāsim had bought for 40,000 rupees and sent him, he presented as an offering on obtaining the viziership. He petitioned that Khwāja Abū-l-ḥasan, who held the offices of bakhshi and the *Qūr,* etc., might go with him. Jalālābād was transferred from Abū-l-qāsim Namakīn to 'Arab Khān. A white rock was present in the river-bed; I ordered them to carve it in the form of an elephant and cut upon its breast this hemistich, which agrees with the date of the Hijra year: "The white stone elephant of Jahāngīr Pādshāh," that is, 1016.

On the same day Kalyān, son of Rāja Bikramājīt, came from Gujarat. Certain extraordinary proceedings on the part of this rebellious rascal had been reported to me. Amongst these was this. He had kept a Musulmān *lūlī* woman in his house, and for fear this affair should become known had killed her father and mother and buried them in his house. I ordered that he should be imprisoned until I could enquire into his proceedings, and after ascertaining the truth I ordered first that they should cut out his tongue and place him in perpetual confinement, and that he should eat his food with dog-keepers and outcasts. On W dnesday I encamped at Surkhāb. Thence I alighted at Jagdalak. At this stage I saw many *ballūt*[200]-trees (oak or chestnut), which are the best wood for burning. Although this stage had neither passes nor declivities there were plenty of rocks. On Friday, the 12th, I encamped at Āb-i-bārīk, and Saturday, the 13th, at Yūrt-i-pādshāh. On Sunday, the 14th, I alighted at Khūrd Kābul (little Kabul). At this stage I entrusted the Chief Justiceship and Qaziship of the city of Kabul to Qāẓī 'Ārif, son of Mullā Ṣādiq Ḥalwā'ī. They brought some ripe *shāh-ālū* (cherries) from the village of Gulbahār to this place; of these I ate with much enjoyment nearly a hundred. Daulat, the head of

---

[199] Text *bautī,* but the MSS. have *lūtī,* i.e. dancing-girl.

[200] Generally spelt *ballūṭ*, either the oak or the chestnut. Cf. Erskine's Baber, p. 145. Sir Alexander Burnes calls the *ballūṭ* the holly.

the village of Jigrī[201] (?), brought some uncommon flowers, such as I had never seen in my life. Thence I alighted at Bikrāmī. At this place they brought to show me a piebald[202] animal, like the flying (i.e. jumping) mouse, which in the Hindi tongue they call *galahrī* (squirrel), and said that mice would not frequent any house in which this animal was. On this account they call this animal the master of mice. As I had never seen one before, I ordered my painters to draw a likeness of it. It is larger than a mongoose. On the whole it is very like a civet cat. Having appointed Aḥmad Beg Khān to punish the Afghans of Bangash, I ordered 'Abdu-r-Razzāq Ma'mūrī, who was in Attock, to take 2,000,000 rupees under the charge of Mohan Dās, son of Rāja Bikramājīt, with him, and divide it among the auxiliaries of the aforesaid army. One thousand musketeers were also ordered to accompany this army.

Shaikh 'Abdu-r-Raḥmān, son of Shaikh Abū-l-faẓl, was promoted to the rank of 2,000 personal and 1,500 horse, and obtained the title of Afẓal Khān. 15,000 rupees were presented to 'Arab Khān, and 20,000 rupees more for the repair of the fort of Pesh Bulāgh.[203] I bestowed Sarkār Khānpūr[204] in fief on Dilāwar Khān Afghān. On Thursday, the 17th, from the Mastān bridge as far as the Shahr-ārā garden, which was the encamping place for the royal standards, scattering rupees, half-rupees, and quarter-rupees to faqirs and indigent persons on both sides of the road, I entered the aforesaid garden. It appeared to be very green and fresh. As it was a Thursday I gave a wine entertainment to my intimates, and on account of hilarity and excitement ordered those who were of equal age to myself and had been my playfellows to jump over the stream that flowed through the middle of the garden and was about four gaz in width. Most of

---

[201] See below, p. 52, where the *Ra'īs* or headman of Chikrī is mentioned.

[202] Cf. Erskine's Baber, p. 145.

[203] The fort of Pesh Bulāq is mentioned in the third volume of the Akbar-nāma, p. 512. It is marked on the map of Afghanistan between Daka and Jalālābād.

[204] *Sic* in text, but should be Jaunpūr as in the MSS.

them could not jump it, and fell on the bank or into the stream. Although I jumped it, yet now that I was 40 years of age I could not jump it with the activity that I had shown in the presence of my revered father when I was 30. On this day I perambulated seven of the famous gardens of Kabul. I do not think that I ever walked so far before.

First of all I walked round the Shahr-ārā (city-adorning), then the Mahtāb (moonlight) garden, then the garden that Bīka Begam, grandmother of my father, had made, then passed through the Ūrta-bāgh (middle garden), then a garden that Maryam-makānī, my own grandmother, had prepared, then the Ṣūrat-khāna garden, which has a large *chanār*-tree, the like of which there is not in the other gardens of Kabul. Then, having seen the Chārbāgh, which is the largest of the city gardens, I returned to my own abode. There were abundance of cherries on the trees, each of which looked as it were a round ruby, hanging like globes on the branches. The Shahr-ārā garden was made by Shahr-bānū[205] Begam, daughter of Mīrzā Abū Sa'īd, who was own aunt to the late king Bābar. From time to time it has been added to, and there is not a garden like it for sweetness in Kabul. It has all sorts of fruits and grapes, and its softness is such that to put one's sandalled[206] feet on it would be far from propriety or good manners. In the neighbourhood of this garden an excellent plot of land came to view, which I ordered to be bought from the owners. I ordered a stream that flows from the *guzargāh* (ferry, also bleaching green) to be diverted into the middle of the ground so that a garden might be made such that in beauty and sweetness there should not be in the inhabited world another like it. I gave it the name of Jahān-ārā (world - adorning). Whilst I was at Kabul I had several entertainments in the Shahr-ārā garden, sometimes with my intimates and courtiers and

[205] There was also a Shahr-bānū who was Bābar's sister. Bika Begam was Bābar's widow and the lady who carried his bones to Kabul.

[206] *Bakafsh-pāy*, which Erskine renders 'with slippers on 'and Elliot' 'with his shoes on. '

sometimes with the ladies of the harem. At nights I ordered the learned and the students of Kabul to hold the cooking entertainment,[207] *bughra,* and the throwing of bughra, together with *arghushtak* dances.

To each of the band of *Bughrā'iyān* I gave a dress of honour, and also gave 1,000 rupees to divide amongst themselves. To twelve of the trustworthy courtiers I ordered 12,000 rupees to be given, to be bestowed every Thursday, as long as I was in Kabul, on the poor and needy. I gave an order that between two plane-trees that were on the canal bank in the middle of the garden—to one of which I had given the name of Farāḥ-bakhsh (joy-giver) and the other Sāya-bakhsh (shade-giver)—they should set up a piece of white stone (marble?) one gaz in length and three-quarters of a gaz in breadth, and engrave my name thereon (and those of my ancestors) up to Tīmūr. It was set forth on the other side that I had done away with the whole of the customs dues and charges of Kabul, and whichever of my descendants and successors should do anything contrary to this would be involved in the wrath and displeasure of God. Up to the time of

---

[207] Bāyazīd Biyāt describes Humāyūn as holding a cooking festival in Badakhshān. See A.N., i, translation, p. 496, n. 2. They cooked *bughra,* which appears to be macaroni. The text wrongly has raqẓ az 'ishq (love-dances). The real word, as the MSS. show, is arghushtaq, which is a kind of dance (not a child's game as in Johnson). It is described in Vullers, s.v., in accordance with the account in the Burhān-i-qāṭi'. It is a dance by girls or young men, and is accompanied with singing and with clapping of hands, etc. Probably it is the dance described by Elphinstone in his account of Kabul, i, 311, where he says : "The great delight of all the western Afghans is to dance the Attun or Ghoomboor. From ten to twenty men or women stand up in a circle (in summer before their houses and tents, and in winter round a fire) ; a person stands within the circle to sing and play on some instrument. The dancers go through a number of attitudes and figures ; shouting, clapping their hands, and snapping their fingers. Every now and then they join hands, and move slow or fast according to the music, all joining in chorus. When I was showed this, a love-song was sung to an extremely pretty tune, very simple, and not unlike a Scottish air." Erskine's translation is : " Custards and confections were presented, and the amusements of dancing girls and arghustak were introduced."

my accession these were fixed and settled, and every year they took large sums on this account from the servants of God (the Muhammadan people in general). The abolition of this oppression was brought about during my reign. On this journey to Kabul complete relief and contentment were brought about in the circumstances of my subjects and the people of that place. The good and leading men of Ghaznīn and that neighbourhood were presented with robes of honour and dealt kindly with, and had their desires excellently gratified.

It is a strange coincidence that (the words) *rūz-i-panjshanba hīzhdaham-i-Ṣafar,*[208] Thursday, 18th Ṣafar, which is the date of my entry into Kabul, give the Hijra date thereof.

I ordered them to inscribe this date on the stone. Near a seat (*takht*) on the slope of a hill to the south of the city of Kabul, and which is known as Takht-i-shāh, they have made a stone terrace where Firdūs-makānī (Bābar) used to sit and drink wine. In one corner of this rock they have excavated a round basin which could contain about two Hindustani maunds of wine. He caused his own blessed name with the date to be carved on the wall of the terrace which is next to the hill. The wording is, "The seat of the king, the asylum of the world, Ẓahīru-ddīn Muḥammad Bābar, son of 'Umar Shaikh Gūrgān, may God perpetuate his kingdom, 914 (1508 – 9)." I also ordered them to cut out of stone another throne parallel to this, and dig another basin of the same fashion on its side, and engrave my name there, together with that of Ṣāḥib-qirānī (Tīmūr). Every day that I sat on that throne I ordered them to fill both of the basins with wine and give it to the servants who were present there. One of the poets of Ghaznin found the date of my coming to Kabul in this

---

208 The words seem to me to yield 1066, but if we read *pajshanba* instead of *panjshanba* we get 1016, which is the Hijra date of Jahāngīr's entry into Kabul and corresponds to 4th June, 1607. A marginal note on I.O.M. 305 makes the chronogram clear by writing *rūz-i-panchanba hizhdah-i-Safar*, thereby getting rid of the *mīm* and the *yā* of *hīzhdaham* and bringing out the figures 1016.

chronogram—"The king of the cities of the seven climes" (1016). I gave him a dress of honour and a present, and ordered them to engrave this date on the wall near the aforesaid seat. Fifty thousand rupees were given to Parwīz; Wazīr-al-mulk was made Mir Bakhshi. A firman was sent to Qilīj Khān to despatch 170,000 rupees from the Lahore treasury for expenses of the army at Qandahar. After visiting the Khiyābān (avenue) of Kabul and the Bībī Māh-rū, I ordered the governor of that city to plant other trees in the place of those cut down by Ḥusain Beg Rū-siyāh (the black-faced). I also visited the Ūlang-yūrt of Chālāk and found it a very pleasant place. The Ra'is of Chikrī (Jigrī?) shot with an arrow a *rang*[209] and brought it to me. Up to this time I had never seen a rang. It is like a mountain goat, and there is a difference only in its horns. The horns of the rang are bent, and those of the goat are straight and convoluted.

In connection with the account of Kabul the commentaries of Bābar[210] passed in view before me. These were in his own handwriting, except four sections (*juz'*[211]) that I wrote myself. At the end of the said sections a sentence was written by me also in the Turkī character, so that it might be known that these four sections were written by me in my own hand. Notwithstanding that I grew up in Hindustan, I am not ignorant of Turkī speech and writing.[212] On the 25th Ṣafar I with the people of the harem

---

[209] Evidently a kind of sheep.

[210] This is a reference to Bābar's Memoirs.

[211] A *juz'* is said to consist of eight leaves or sixteen pages. Does Jahāngīr mean that he wrote sixty-four pages ?

[212] Probably the sections which Jahāngīr wrote were those printed in the Ilminsky edition and which bring the narrative down to Bābar's death. They seem to have been in great measure copied from the Akbar-nāma. Jahāngīr does not say if he wrote them when he was in Kabul or previously. According to Blochmann, J.A.S.B. for 1869, p. 134, one *juz'* = two sheets of paper. The passage is translated in Elliot, vi, 315. Though Jahāngīr does not say when he wrote the four sections, I think that his language implies that these additions were in the manuscript when he was looking at it in Kabul. Perhaps he made them when he was a student in India, and for the sake of practice in Turkī. He may have translated the sections from the Akbar-nāma. All, I think, he did in Kabul was to put the Turkī note,

visited the *julgāh* (plain) of Safīd-sang, a very bright and enjoyable place. On Friday, the 26th, I enjoyed the blessing of a pilgrimage to (the tomb of) H.M. Firdūs-makānī (Bābar). I ordered much money and food, bread, and sweetmeats for the souls of the departed to be distributed to faqirs. Ruqayya Sulṭān Begam, daughter of Mīrzā Hindāl, had not performed a pilgrimage to her father's tomb, and on that day had the honour to do so. On Thursday, 3rd Rabī'u-l-awwal, I ordered them to bring my racehorses (*āspān-i-dawanda*) to the Khiyābān (avenue). The princes and the Amirs raced them. A bay Arab horse, which 'Ādil Khān, the ruler of the Deccan, had sent to me, ran better than all the other horses. At this time the son of Mīrzā Sanjar Hazāra and the son of Mīrzā Māshī, who were the chief leaders of the Hazāras, came to wait on me. The Hazāras of the village of Mīrdād produced before me two rangs[213] that they had killed with arrows. I had never seen a rang of this size; it was larger by 20 per cent. than a large *mārkhūr* (?).

News came that Shāh Beg Khān, the governor of Qandahar, had reached the parganah of Shor,[214] which is his jagir. I determined to give Kabul to him and return to Hindustan. A petition came from Rāja Bīrsing-deo that he had made a prisoner of his nephew, who had been creating a disturbance and had

stating that the sections were his. But possibly even this was done before. Elliot, vi, 315, has the words " to complete the work," but these words do not occur in the MSS. that I have seen. The translation in Elliot, seems to represent Jahāngīr's words as meaning that the work was complete, but that the four sections were not, like the rest, in Bābar's handwriting, and so Jahāngīr re-copied them. But it does not appear that there could be any object in his doing this. There is a valuable article in the Zeitschrift d. Deutschen Morgenl. Gesellsch. for 1883, p. 141, by Dr. Teufel, entitled "Bābur und Abū'l-faẓl," in which the fragments in Ilminsky are discussed. But the passage in the Tūzuk-i-Jahāngīrī is not referred to.

213 The text mentions a horse, but the MSS. have not this, and it seems to be a mistake.

214 Apparently the Shorkot of I.G., xii, 424. In the Rechnau Dūāb (Jarrett, ii, 321). It is north of Multan and in the Jhang district.

killed many of his men. I ordered him to send him to the fort of Gwalior to be imprisoned there. The parganah of Gujrāt[215] in the Panjab Sarkār I bestowed on Shīr Khān, the Afghan. I promoted Chīn Qilīj, son of Qilīj Khān, to the rank of 800 personal and 500 horse. On the 12th I sent for Khusrau and ordered them to take the chains off his legs that he might walk in the Shahr-ārā garden. My fatherly affection would not permit me to exclude him from walking in the aforesaid garden. I transferred the fort of Attock and that neighbourhood from Aḥmad Beg to ẓafar Khān. To Tāj Khān, who was nominated to beat back the Afghans of Bangash, I gave 50,000 rupees. On the 14th I gave 'Alī Khān Kaṛorī,[216] who was one of my revered father's old servants and was the *dārogha* of the Naqārakhāna (drum-house), the title of Naubat Khān, and promoted him to the rank of 500 personal and 200 horse. I made Rām Dās *ātālīq* to Mahā Singh, grandson of Rāja Mān Singh, who had also been nominated to drive back the rebels of Bangash. On Friday, the 18th, the *wazn-i-qamarī* (the weighing according to the lunar year) for my 40th year took place. On that day the assembly was held when two watches of the day had passed. I gave 10,000 rupees of the money of the weighing to ten of my confidential servants to divide amongst those who deserved it and the needy. On this day a petition came from Sardār Khān, governor of Qandahar, by way of Hazāra and Ghaznīn, in twelve days; its purport was that the ambassador of Shāh 'Abbās, who had started for the Court, had entered the Hazāra[217] (country). The Shah had written to his own people: "What seeker of occasion and raiser of strife has come against Qandahar without my order? Perhaps he does not know what is our connection with H.M. Sulṭān Tīmūr, and especially with Humāyūn and his glorious descendants. If they by chance should have taken the country into their possession they should hand it to the friends and servants of my brother Jahāngīr

[215] I.G. v, 188.

[216] Perhaps the 'Alī Dūst Khān of Blochmann, p. 533.

[217] The MSS. have Herat, and this is probably correct.

Pādshāh and return to their own abodes." I determined to tell Shāh Beg Khān to secure the Ghaznin road in such a way that travellers from Qandahar might reach Kabul with ease. At the same time I appointed Qāẓī Nūru-d-dīn to the Ṣadārat of the province of Malwah and Ujjain. The son of Mīrzā Shādmān Hazāra and grandson of Qarācha Khān, who was one of the influential Amirs of Humāyūn, waited on me. Qarācha Khān had married a woman from the Hazāra tribe, and this son[218] had been born by her. On Saturday, the 19th, Rānā Shankar, son of Rānā Ūday Singh, was promoted to the rank of 2,500 personal and 1,000 horse. An order was given for the rank of 1,000 personal and 600 horse for Rāy Manohar. The Shinwārī Afghans brought a mountain ram the two horns of which had become one and had become like a rang's horns. The same Afghans killed and brought a *mārkhūr* (Erskine translates this 'a serpent - eating goat'), the like of which I had never seen or imagined. I ordered my artists to paint him. He weighed four Hindustani maunds; the length of his horns was 1 1/2 gaz.[219] On Sunday, the 27th, I gave the rank of 1,500 personal and 1,000 horse to Shajā'at Khān, and the *ḥawīlī* (district surrounding) of Gwalior was placed in the jagir of I'tibār Khān. I appointed Qāẓī 'Izzatu-llah with his brothers to the Bangash duty. At the end of the same day a petition came to me from Islām Khān from Agra, together with a letter which Jahāngīr Qulī Khān had written to him from Bihar. Its purport was that on the 3rd Ṣafar (30th May, 1607), after the first watch, 'Alī Qulī Istājlū had wounded Quṭbu-d-dīn Khān at Bardwan, in the province of Bengal, and that he had died when two watches of the same night had passed. The details of this matter are that the aforesaid 'Alī Qulī was *sufrachī* (table servant) to Shāh Ismā'īl (the 2nd), ruler of Iran; after his

---

[218] That is, apparently, Mīrzā Shādmān, but perhaps the meaning is that Qarācha had sought a wife for his son among the Hazāras, and not that he had himself married an Hazāra woman.

[219] The MSS. have " less than $1\frac{1}{2}$ gaz by $\frac{1}{8}$ (*nīm-pāo*)."

death he took to flight through his natural wickedness and habit of making mischief, and came to Qandahar, and having met at Multan the Khānkhānān, who had been appointed to the charge of the province of Tulamba,[220] started with him for that province. The Khānkhānān in the field[221] placed him among the servants of the late king (Akbar), and he having performed services in that campaign was promoted to a rank in accordance with his condition, and was a long time in the service of my revered father. At the time when he (Akbar) went in prosperity to the provinces of the Deccan, and I was ordered against the Rānā, he came and became servant to me. I gave him the title of Shīr-afgan (tiger-throwing). When I came from Allahabad to wait on my revered father, on account of the unfriendliness that was shown me, most of my attendants and people were scattered abroad, and he also at that time chose to leave my service. After my accession, out of generosity I overlooked his offences, and gave an order for a jagir for him in the Subah of Bengal. Thence came news that it was not right to leave such mischievous persons there, and an order went to Quṭbu-d-dīn Khān to send him to Court, and if he showed any futile, seditious ideas, to punish him. The aforesaid Khān had reason to know him (his character), and with the men he had present, immediately the order arrived, went hastily to Bardwan, which was his jagir. When he (Shīr-afgan) became aware of the arrival of Quṭbu-d-dīn Khān, he went out to receive him alone with two grooms. After he arrived and entered into the midst of his army (his camp) the aforesaid Khān surrounded him. When from this proceeding on the part of Quṭbu-d-dīn Khān a doubt arose in his mind, he by way of deceiving him said: "What proceeding is this of thine?"[222] The aforesaid Khān, keeping back his own men,

---

[220] Should, I think, be Tattah, i.e. Sind.

[221] *Ghaibāna*, 'secretly.' But the phrase merely means that the appointment was not made in the Emperor's presence.

[222] Text *baryasht*, ' he turned round. ' But the MSS. have *chi rawish-i-tūżukast*, " What kind of arrangement is this ?"

joined him alone in order to explain the purport of the order to him. Seeing his opportunity he immediately drew his sword and inflicted two or three severe wounds upon him. Amba Khān Kashmīrī, who was descended from the rulers of Kashmir and was connected (by marriage?) with the aforesaid Khān, and had a great regard for him by way of loyalty and manliness, rushed forward and struck a heavy blow on 'Alī Qulī's head, and that vicious fellow inflicted a severe wound on Amba Khān with the point of his sword.[223] When they saw Quṭbu-d-dīn Khān in this state, his men attacked him (Shīr-afgan), and cut him in pieces and sent him to hell. It is to be hoped that the place of this black-faced scoundrel will always be there. Amba Khān obtained martyrdom on the spot, and Quṭbu-d-dīn Khān Koka after four watches attained the mercy of God in his quarters. What can I write of this unpleasantness? How grieved and troubled I became! Quṭbu-d-dīn Khān Koka was to me in the place of a dear son, a kind brother, and a congenial friend. What can one do with the decrees of God? Bowing to destiny I adopted an attitude of resignation. After the departure of the late King and the death of that honoured one, no two misfortunes had happened to me like the death of the mother of Quṭbu-d-dīn Khān Koka and his own martyrdom.

On Friday, the 6th Rabī'u-l-ākhir, I came to the quarters of Khurram (Shāh-Jahān), which had been made in the Ūrta Garden. In truth, the building is a delightful and well-proportioned one. Whereas it was the rule of my father to have himself weighed twice every year, (once) according to the solar and (once according to the) lunar year, and to have the princes weighed according to the solar year, and moreover in this year, which was the commencement of my son Khurram's 16th lunar

---

[223] *Shamshīr-i-sīkhakī*, ' pointed sword, poniard'?

year, the astrologers and astronomers[224] represented that a most important epoch according to his horoscope would occur, as the prince's health[225] had not been good, I gave an order that they should weigh him according to the prescribed rule, against gold, silver, and other metals, which should be divided among faqirs and the needy. The whole of that day was passed in enjoyment and pleasure in the house of Bābā Khurram, and many of his presents were approved.

As I had experienced the excellencies of Kabul, and had eaten most of its fruits, in consequence of important considerations and the distance from the capital, on Sunday, the 4th Jumādā-I-awwal, I gave an order that they should send out the advance camp in the direction of Hindustan. After some days I left the city, and the royal standards proceeded to the meadow of Safīd-sang. Although the grapes were not yet fully ripe, I had often before this eaten Kabul grapes. There are many good sorts of grapes, especially the Ṣāḥibī and Kishmishī. The cherry also is a fruit of pleasant flavour, and one can eat more of it than of other fruits; I have in a day eaten up to 150 of them. The term *shāh-ālū* means *gīlās*[226] (cherry), which are obtainable in most places of the country, but since *gīlās* is like *gīlās,* which is one of the names of the *chalpāsa* (lizard), my revered father called it *shāh-ālū*. The *zard-ālū paywandī*[227] is good, and is abundant. There is especially a tree in the Shahr-ārā garden, that Mīrzā Muḥammad Ḥakīm, my uncle, planted, and is known as the Mīrzā'ī. The apricots of this tree are quite unlike the apricots of other trees. The peaches

---

[224] The meaning of two words being used probably is that both Hindu and Persian astrologers are referred to. Blochmann, p. 311, says that Shāh-Jahān's birthday was 30th Rabī'u-l-awwal.

[225] Lit., " His disposition had changed from equability."

[226] *Gīlās* is a cherry in Kashmiri. See Blochmann's Āyīn, p. 616. Abū-l-faẓl mentions in the Āyīn (Blochmann, p. 66) that Akbar called *gilās shāh-ālū*.

[227] *Paywandī* means 'to graft,' and possibly this is the meaning here, but Steingass gives *paywandī* as part of the name of a plum. The text seems to be corrupt, and perhaps what Jahāngīr wrote was "the *zard-ālū* resembles the *khūbānī*."

also are very delicious and plentiful. They had brought some peaches from Istālif. I had them weighed in my presence, and they came exactly in weight to 25 rupees, which is 68 current *miṣqāl*. Notwithstanding the sweetness of the Kabul fruits, not one of them has, to my taste, the flavour of the mango. The parganah of Mahāban was given as jagir to Mahābat Khān. 'Abdu-r-Raḥīm, paymaster of the Ahadis, was promoted to the rank of 700 personal and 200 horse. Mubārak Khān Sarwānī was appointed to the faujdarship of the sarkar of Ḥiṣār. I ordered that Mīrzā Farīdūn Barlās should have a jagir in the Subah of Allahabad. On the 14th of the aforesaid month I gave Irādat Khān, brother of Āṣaf Khān, the rank of 1,000 personal and 500 horse, and presenting him with a special robe of honour and a horse, bestowed on him the paymastership of the Subah of Patna and Ḥājīpūr. As he was my *qūrbegī*, I sent by his hand a jewelled sword for my son (*farzand*) Islām Khān, the governor of the aforesaid Subah. As we were going along I saw near 'Alī Masjid and Gharīb-khāna a large spider of the size of a crab that had seized by the throat a snake of one and a half gaz in length and half strangled it. I delayed a minute to look on at this, and after a moment it died (the snake).

I heard at Kabul that in the time of Maḥmūd of Ghazni a person of the name of Khwāja Tābūt[228] had died in the neighbourhood of Ẓuḥāk and Bāmiyān, and was buried in a

---

228 Text has Yāqūt, but it is clear from the Iqbāl-nāma, p. 25, and from I.O. MS. 181 that the name is Khwāja Tābūt, ' the coffin Khwāja.' The author of the Iqbāl-nāma was the person sent to make the inquiry, and he gives a long account of what he saw. A surgeon was sent with him, as the Khwāja was said to have been martyred, and it was necessary to report on the wounds. The coffin story is mentioned in the Āyīn, i, 194. See Jarrett, ii, 409-10, but the translation is not quite accurate, I think. The punctuation of the text seems to me to be correct. It is characteristic of Jahāngīr and the author of the Iqbāl-nāma that they take no notice of the colossal figures at Bāmiyān, though Abū-l-faẓl does. See Jarrett's note. It is stated in the Iqbāl-nāma that Khwāja Tābūt was said to have been killed in the time of Chingiz Khān. If so, the Sulṭān Maḥmūd mentioned by Jahāngīr must be Sulṭān Maḥmūd Ghorī.

cave, whose limbs had not yet rotted asunder. This appeared very strange, and I sent one of my confidential record writers with a surgeon to go to the cave and, having seen the state of affairs as they were, to make a special report. He represented that half of the body which was next the ground had most of it come asunder, and the other half which had not touched the ground remained in its own condition. The nails of the hands and feet and the hair of the head had not been shed, but the hair of the beard and moustache as far as one side of the nose had been shed. From the date that had been engraved on the door of the cave it appeared that his death had occurred before the time of Sulṭān Maḥmūd. No one knows the exact state of the case.

On Thursday, the 15th Arslān Bī, governor of the fort of Kāhmard, who was one of the servants of middle rank (?) of Walī Muḥammad Khān, ruler of Tūrān, came and waited on me.[229] I had always heard that Mīrzā Ḥusain, son of Shāhrukh Mīrzā, had been killed by the Ūzbegs. At this time a certain person came and presented a petition in his name, and brought a ruby of the colour of an onion, which was worth 100 rupees, as an offering. He prayed that an army might be appointed to assist him, so that he might take Badakhshan out of the Ūzbegs' hands. A jewelled dagger-belt was sent him, and an order given that, as the royal standards had alighted in those regions, if he really was Mīrzā Ḥusain, son of Mīrzā Shāhrukh, he should first hasten into my presence, so that having examined his petitions and claims I might send him to Badakhshan. Two hundred thousand rupees were sent for the army that had been sent with Mahā Singh and Rām Dās against the rebels of Bangash.

On Thursday, the 22nd, having gone to the Bālā Ḥiṣār, I inspected the buildings in that place. As the place was not fit for me I ordered them to destroy these buildings and to prepare a palace and a royal hall of audience. On the same day they

---

[229] He was appointed governor of Sehwān (Iqbāl-nāma, p. 27).

brought a peach from Istālif, *barābar sar-i-buh bakalānī,* "as big as an owl's head" (?).[230] I had not seen a peach of such a size, and ordered it to be weighed, and it came to 63 Akbari rupees, or 60 tolas. When I cut it in half its stone also came into two pieces, and its substance was sweet. I had in Kabul never eaten better fruit from any tree. On the 25th news came from Malwa that Mīrzā Shāhrukh had bid farewell to this transitory world, and God Almighty had submerged him in His mercy. From the day on which he entered the service of my revered father till the time of his departure, from no act of his could dust be brought into the royal mind. He always did his duty with sincerity. The aforesaid Mīrzā apparently had four sons: Ḥasan and Ḥusain were born of the same womb (i.e. they were twins). Ḥusain fled from Burhanpur and went by sea to Iraq, and thence to Badakhshan, where they say he now is, as has been written about his message and his sending some one to me. No one knows for certain whether it is the same Mīrzā Ḥusain, or the people of Badakhshan have raised up this one like other false Mīrzās and given him the name of Mīrzā Ḥusain. From the time when Mīrzā Shāhrukh came from Badakhshan and had the good fortune to wait on my father until now, nearly 25 years have passed. For some time the people of Badakhshan, on account of the oppression and injury they have to undergo from the Ūzbegs, have given notoriety to a Badakhshan boy, who had on his face the marks of nobility, as really the son of Mīrzā Shāhrukh and of the race of Mīrzā Sulaimān. A large number of the scattered Ūymāqs, and the hill-people of Badakhshan, whom they call Gharchal (Georgians?), collected round him, and showing enmity and disputing with the Ūzbegs, took some of the districts of Badakhshan out of their possession. The Ūzbegs

---

230 The MSS. merely have "of a size that I had never seen before." Probably the text is corrupt, and the meaning may be "as big as a head." *Bih* is a quince, and perhaps this is what is meant here. Or the meaning may be "equal to the biggest for size." Or *sar* may be a mistake for *sih* and the meaning be "equal in size to three (ordinary peaches)."

attacked that false Mīrzā and captured him, and placing his head on a spear sent it round to the whole country of Badakhshan. Again the seditious people of Badakhshan quickly produced another Mīrzā. Up to now several Mīrzās have been killed. It appears to me that as long as there is any trace of the people of Badakhshan they will keep up this disturbance. The third son of the Mīrzā is Mīrzā Sulṭān, who excels in appearance and disposition all the other sons of the Mīrzā. I begged him from his revered father, and have kept him in my own service, and having taken great pains with him reckon him as my own child. In disposition and manners he has no likeness to his brothers. After my accession I gave him the rank of 2,000 personal and 1,000 horse, and sent him to the Subah of Malwa, which was his father's place. The fourth son is Badī'u-z-zamān, whom he always had in attendance on himself; he obtained the rank of 1,000 personal and 500 horse.

While I was at Kabul, no *qamargāh* hunt had taken place. As the time for returning to Hindustan had come near, and I was very desirous of hunting red deer, I ordered them to go forward as soon as possible and surround the hill Faraq,[231] which is seven kos from Kabul. On Tuesday, the 4th Jumādā-l-awwal, I went to hunt. Nearly 100 deer had come into the enclosure (qamargah). About a half of these were taken, and a very hot hunt took place. I gave 5,000 rupees in rewards to the ryots who were present at the hunt. On the same day an increase of 500 horse was ordered to the rank of Shaikh 'Abdu-r-Raḥmān, son of Shaikh Abū-l-faẓl, so as to bring it to 2,000 personal and (2,000) horse. On Thursday, the 6th, I went to the throne-place of the late king Bābar. As I was to leave Kabul on the next day I looked on that day as a feast day, and ordered them to arrange a wine-party on the spot, and fill with wine the little reservoir they had cut in the rock. Cups were given to all the courtiers and servants who were present, and few days have passed in such enjoyment and

---

[231] I.O. MS. 181 has Qarqara mountains. There is also the reading Kharaq.

pleasure. On Friday, the 7th, when a watch of day had passed, leaving the city auspiciously and with pleasure, a halt was made at the *julgāh* (meadow) of the Safīd-sang. From the Shahr-ārā as far as the julgah I scattered to faqirs and poor people *darb* and *charan,* that is, half and quarter rupees.[232] On that day, when I mounted my elephant for the purpose of leaving Kabul, the news arrived of the recovery of the Amīru-l-umarā and Shāh Beg Khān. The news of the good health of these two chief servants of mine I took as an auspicious omen for myself. From the julgah of the Safīd-sang, marching one kos on Tuesday, the 11th, I halted at Bikrām. I left Tāsh Beg Khān at Kabul to take proper care of Kabul and neighbourhood until the coming of Shāh Beg Khān. On Tuesday, the 18th, I marched two and a half kos from the halting-place of Būtkhāk by the road Dū'āba,[233] and encamped at a spring on the bank of which there are four plane-trees. No one till now had looked to the preparation of this halting-place, and they were ignorant of its condition and suitability. It is in truth a most excellent spot, and one fit to have a building erected in it. At this halting-place another qamargah hunt took place, when about 112 deer, etc., were taken. Twenty-four rang antelope and 50 red antelope and 16 mountain goats were taken. I had never till now seen a rang antelope alive.[234] It is in truth a wonderful animal of a beautiful shape. Although the black buck of Hindustan looks very finely made, the shape and fashion and appearance of this antelope is quite a different thing. They weighed a ram and a rang; the ram came to a maund and 33 seers and the rang to two maunds and 10 seers. The rang, although of this size, ran so that ten or twelve swift dogs were worn out and seized it with a hundred thousand difficulties. The flesh of the sheep of the Barbary goat in flavour does not surpass that of the rang. In the same village kulangs (demoiselle crane) were also caught.

---

232 Blochmann, p. 31.

233 Du' āba is mentioned as a stage by W. Finch.

234 The text omits the word *zinda,* ' alive. '

Although Khusrau had repeatedly done evil actions and deserved a thousand kinds of punishment, my fatherly affection did not permit me to take his life. Although in the laws of government and the ways of empire one should take notice of such disapproved deeds, I averted my eyes from his faults, and kept him in excessive comfort and ease. It became known that he was in the habit of sending men to scoundrels who did not consider consequences, and of inciting them to give trouble and attempt my life, and making them hopeful with promises. A band of these ill-fated ones of little foresight having joined together, desired to attack me in the hunts that took place in Kabul and those parts. As the grace and protection of God Almighty are the guardians and keepers of this sublime dynasty, they did not attain to their end. On the day when the halt was at the Surkhāb, one of that band went at the risk of his life to Khwāja Waisī, the Dīwān of my son Khurram, and revealed that nearly 500 men at Khusrau's instigation had conspired with Fatḥu-llah, son of Ḥakīm Abū-l-fatḥ, Nūru-d-dīn, son of Ghiyāṣu-d-dīn 'Alī Āṣaf-khān, and Sharīf, son of I'timādu-d-daulah (Nūr-Jahān's father), and were awaiting an opportunity to carry out the designs of the enemies and evil-wishers of the king. Khwāja Waisī told this to Khurram, and he in great perturbation immediately told me. I gave Khurram the blessing of felicity, and prepared to get hold of the whole set of those short-sighted ones and punish them with various kinds of punishment. Again, it came to my mind, as I was on the march, and the seizure of these people would create a disturbance and confusion in the camp,[235] to order the leaders of the disturbance and mischief to be apprehended. I handed over Fatḥu-llah in confinement to certain trusty men, and ordered capital punishment for the other two wretches, with three or four of the

---

[235] The *urdū* or camp was probably not with Jahāngīr then, and he thought that if he sent to it for the capture of 500 there would be confusion. He therefore contented himself at the time with arresting the ringleaders. There is a full account of the conspiracy in the Iqbāl-nāma, p. 27, etc.

chief among the black-faced (conspirators). I had dignified Qāsim 'Alī, who was one of the servants of the late king Akbar, after my accession with the title of Dayānat Khān. He always accused Fatḥu-llah of a want of loyalty, and said things about him. One day he said to Fatḥu-llah: "At the time when Khusrau fled and the king pursued him, you said to me: 'The Panjab should be given to Khusrau and this quarrel cut short.'" Fatḥu-llah denied this, and both resorted to oaths and curses (on themselves). Ten or fifteen days had not passed after this altercation when that hypocritical wretch was arrested, and his false oath did its business.

On Saturday, the 22nd Jumādā-l-awwal, the news came of the death of the Ḥakīm Jalālu-d-dīn Muẓaffar Ardistānī, who was of a family of skill and medicine and claimed to be a descendant of Galen. At all events he was an unequalled healer. His experience added to his knowledge.[236] As he was very handsome and well-made in the days of his youth (*sāda-rū'īhā*)[237] he frequented the assemblies of Shāh Ṭahmāsp, and the king recited this hemistich about him:—

"We have a pleasant physician: come, let us all be ill."

Ḥakīm 'Alī, who was his contemporary, exceeded him in skill. In short, in medical skill and auspiciousness and rectitude and purity of method and disposition he was perfect. Other physicians of the age could not compare with him. In addition to his medical skill he had many excellencies. He had perfect loyalty towards me. He built at Lahore a house of great pleasantness and purity, and repeatedly asked me to honour it (with my presence). As I was very fond of pleasing him I consented. In short, the aforesaid Ḥakīm, from his connection with me and being my physician, had great skill in the management of affairs and business of the world, so that for

[236] Possibly the meaning is "his experience was greater than his skill."

[237] Lit., when he was smooth-faced, i.e. beardless.

some time at Allahabad I made him Diwan of my establishment. On account of his great honesty he was very exacting in important business, and people were vexed at this method of proceeding. For about twenty years he had ulcerated lungs, and by his wisdom preserved in some measure his health. When he was talking he mostly coughed so much that his cheek and eyes became red, and by degrees his colour became blue. I often said to him: "Thou art a learned physician: why dost thou not cure thy own wounds?" He represented that wounds in the lungs were not of such a nature that they could be cured. During his illness one of his confidential servants put poison into some medicine he was in the habit of taking every day and gave it to him. When he perceived this he took remedies for it. He objected very much to be bled, although this was necessary. It happened that he was going to the privy when his cough overcame him and opened the wounds in his lungs. So much blood poured out of his mouth and brain that he became insensible and fell, and made a fearful cry. An *āftābachī* (ewer-bearer) becoming aware of this, came into the assembly-room, and seeing him smeared with blood cried out: "They have killed the ḥakīm." After examining him it was seen that there was no sign of wounds on his body, and that it was the same wound in the lungs that had begun to flow. They informed Qilīj Khān, who was the Governor of Lahore, and he, having ascertained the true state of the affair, buried him. He left no capable son.

On the 24th, between the garden of Wafā and Nīmlah, a hunt took place, and nearly forty red antelope were killed. A female panther (*yūz*) fell into our hands in this hunt. The zamindars of that place, Laghmānīs, Shālī, and Afghans, came and said that they did not remember nor had they heard from their fathers that a panther had been seen in that region for 120 years. A halt was made on the 2nd Jumādā-l-ākhir, at the Wafā Garden, and the assembly for the solar weighing was held. On the same day Arslān Bī, an Ūzbeg who was one of the Sardars and nobles of 'Abdu-l-Mūmin Khān, and was at that time governor of the fort of Kāhmard, having left his fort, had the blessing of waiting on me. As he had come from friendship and sincerity, I exalted him with a special robe of honour. He is a simple Ūzbeg, and is fit to be educated and honoured. On the 4th of the month an order was given that 'Izzat Khān, the governor[238] of Jalālābād, should make the hunting-ground of the Arzina plain into a qamargah (ring-hunting ground). Nearly 300 animals were captured, namely, 35 *qūch* (rams?), 25 *qūshqī* (?), 90 *arghalī* (wild sheep), 55 *tūghlī* (yaks?), 95 antelope (*safīda*).

As it was the middle of the day when I arrived at the hunting-place and the air was very hot, the (*tāzī*) Arabian dogs had been exhausted.[239] The time for running dogs is in the morning or at the end of the day. On Saturday, the 12th, the halt was at Akūra Saray (?). At this stage Shāh Beg Khān,[240] with a good force, came and waited on me. He was one who had been brought up by my father, the late king Akbar. In himself he is a very brave man and energetic, so much so that constantly in the time of my father he fought several single combats, and in my own reign defended the fort of Qandahar from the hosts of the ruler of Iran. It was besieged for a year before the royal army arrived to his assistance. His manners towards his soldiers are those of an Amir (nobleman, *umarāyāna*), and not according to discipline (*qudrat*), especially towards those who have helped him in battles or are with him in campaigns. He jokes much with his servants, and this gives him an undignified appearance.[241] I

---

238 The I.O. MSS. do not call him governor, and the names of the animals captured differ in the MSS. from those given in the text. The latter are obviously wrong, and I have discarded them. The Iqbāl-nāma, p. 30, has Arzana as the name of the hunting-ground. Erskine has Arzina.

239 Erskine has "many of the hounds were destroyed." *Sagān-i-tāzī* probably means greyhounds, whether bred in Arabia or elsewhere.

240 Blochmann, p. 377, and Ma'a ṣiru-l-umarā, ii, 642. He was an Arghūn.

241 The passage is obscure and the text is corrupt. Erskine's translation is: "His manners towards the soldiers is frank and gallant, but not according to the rules of discipline, especially towards those who have been or are in the wars with him. He is much flattered by his servants, which gives him a light appearance."

have repeatedly warned him about this, but as it is in his nature my remonstrances have had no effect.

On Monday, the 14th, I promoted Hāshim Khān, who is one of the household, born ones of our dynasty, to the rank of 3,000 with 2,000 horse, and I made him governor of the province of Orissa. On the same day news came that Badī'u-z-zamān, son of Mīrzā Shāhrukh, who was in the province of Malwa, through folly and youth had started with a body of rebels to go to the province of the Rānā and join him. 'Abdu-llah Khān, the governor of that place, being informed of this event went after him, and having made him prisoner on the way, slew several of the wretches who had joined with him. An order was given that Ihtimām Khān should start from Agra and bring the Mīrzā to the court. On the 25th of the aforesaid month news came that Imām Qulī Khān, nephew of Walī Khan, ruler of Māwarā'a-n-nahr, had killed him who was called Mīrzā Ḥusain, who had been reported to be the son of Mīrzā Shāhrukh. In truth, the killing of the sons of Mīrzā Shāhrukh is like the killing of the demons, as they say that from every drop of their blood demons are produced. In the station of Dhaka, Shīr Khān, the Afghan, whom when I left I had placed at Peshawar to guard the Khaibar Pass, came and waited on me. He had made no default in preserving and guarding the road. Ẓafar Khān, son of Zain Khān Koka, had been appointed to move on the Dalāzāk Afghans and the tribe of Khatur, who had perpetrated all kinds of misdeeds in the neighbourhood of Attock and the Beas and that vicinity. After performing that service and the conquest of those rebels, who numbered about 100,000 houses, and sending them off towards Lahore, he came and waited upon me at the same halting-place, and it was evident that he had performed that service as it ought to have

---

Evidently Erskine read *nāzī* or *nāz* instead of *bāz* as in the text, and the MSS. support his reading. I think, however, that *nāz kashīdan* means 'to jest.' Instead of the *tā bamāndand* of text the MSS. have *yā namāyand*, the meaning being those soldiers who have served him well, or are doing so. We learn from Blochmann, p. 378, that Shāh Beg was "a frank Turk."

been done. As the month of Rajab, corresponding with the Ilāhī month of Ābān, had arrived,[242] and it was known that this was one of the months fixed for the lunar weighing (*wazn-i-qamarī*) of my father, I determined that the value of all the articles which he used to order for his own weighing in the solar and lunar years should be estimated, and that what this came to should be sent to the large cities for the repose of the soul of that enlightened one, and be divided amongst the necessitous and the faqirs. The total came to 100,000 rupees, equal to 300 Irāq tumāns, and 300,000 of the currency of the people of Māwarā'a-n-nahr.

Trustworthy men divided that sum among the twelve chief cities, such as Agra, Delhi, Lahore, Gujarat (Ahmadabad), etc. On Thursday, the 3rd Rajab, I favoured with the title of Khān-jahān my son (*farzand*) Ṣalābat Khān, who is not less to me than my own sons, and ordered that they should in all firmans and orders write of him as Khān-jahān. A special robe of honour and a jewelled sword were also given him. Also, having entitled Shāh Beg Khān Khān-daurān, I presented him with a jewelled waist-dagger, a male elephant, and a special horse. The whole of the sarkars of Tīrah, Kabul, Bangash, and the province of Sawād (Swat) Bajaur, with the (task of) beating back the Afghans of those regions, and a jagir and the faujdarship were confirmed to him. He took leave from Bābā Ḥasan Abdāl. I also ordered Rām Dās Kachhwāha to receive a jagir in this province and to be enrolled among the auxiliaries of this Subah. I conferred on Kishan Chand, son of the Mota (fat) Rāja, the rank of 1,000 personal and 500 horse. A firman was written to Murtaẓā Khān (Sayyid Farīd), governor of Gujarat, that as the good conduct and excellence and abstemiousness of the son of Miyān Wajīhu-d-dīn[243] had been reported to me, he should hand over to him from me a sum of money, and that he should write and send me

[242] The peculiarity of this year was that the lunar month and the solar month of Akbar's birth, viz. Rajab and Ābān, coincided, so that there was a double celebration.

[243] Wajīhu-d-dīn was a famous Gujarat saint. He died in 998.

some of the names of God which had been tested. If the grace of God should be with me I would continually repeat[244] them. Before this I had given leave to Zafar Khān to go to Bābā Ḥasan Abdāl to collect together game for sport. He had made a *shākhband* (literally a tying together of horns or branches). Twenty-seven red deer and 68 white ones came into the *shākhband*. I myself struck with arrows 29 antelope, and Parwīz and Khurram also killed some others with arrows. Afterwards orders were given to the servants and courtiers to shoot. Khān Jahān was the best shot, and in every case of his striking an antelope the arrow penetrated through and through.[245] Again, on the 14th of the month of Rajab, Zafar Khān had arranged a qamargah at Rawalpindi. I struck with an arrow a red deer at a long distance, and was highly delighted at the arrow striking him and his falling down. Thirty-four red deer and 35 *qarā-qūyrūgh* (black-tailed) antelope, which in the Hindi language theycall *chikāra,* and two pigs were also killed. On the 21st another qamargah had been arranged within three kos of the fort of Rohtas by the efforts and exertions of Hilāl Khān. I had taken with me to this hunt those who were screened by the curtains of honour (the members of the zanānah). The hunt was a good one and came off with great *éclat.* Two hundred red and white antelope were killed. Passing on from Rohtas, the hills of which contain these antelope, there are in no place in the whole of Hindustan, with the exception of Girjhāk and Nandanah, red deer of this description. I ordered them to catch and keep some of them alive, in order that possibly some of them might reach Hindustan for breeding purposes. On the 25th another hunt took place in the neighbourhood of Rohtas. In this hunt also my

---

[244] The word used by Jahāngīr, and which has been translated 'repeat continually,' is *mudāwamat*, and Erskine understood it to mean that Jahāngīr hoped to prolong his life by this exercise.

[245] *Har ahū'ī kih zad bar sar-i-tīr raft.* The literal rendering apparently is : "whenever an antelope was struck by him the arrow entered up to its (the arrow's) head." Perhaps the meaning simply is every arrow (or bullet) that he shot went home.

sisters and the other ladies were with me, and nearly 100 red deer were killed. It was told me that Shams Khān, uncle of Jalāl Khān[246] Gakkhar, who was in that neighbourhood, notwithstanding his great age took much delight in hunting, such that young men had not so much enjoyment in it. When I heard that he was well-disposed towards faqirs and dervishes I went to his house, and his disposition and manners pleased me. I bestowed on him 2,000 rupees, and the same sum on his wives and children, with five other villages with large receipts by way of livelihood for them, that they might pass their days in comfort and contentment. On the 6th Sha'ban, at the halting-place of Chandālah, the Amīru-l-umarā came and waited on me. I was greatly pleased at obtaining his society again, for all the physicians, Hindu and Musulman, had made up their minds that he would die. Almighty God in His grace and mercy granted him the honour of recovery, in order that it might be known to such as do not recognize His will that for every difficult ill, which those who look on the outside of causes only may have given up as hopeless, there is One who is powerful to provide a cure and remedy out of His own kindness and compassion. On the same day Rāy Rāy Singh,[247] one of the most considerable of the Rajput Amirs, ashamed on account of the fault he had committed in the matter of Khusrau, and who was living at his home, came, and under the patronage of the Amīru-l-umarā obtained the good fortune of waiting on me; his offences were pardoned. At the time that I left Agra in pursuit of Khusrau I had in full confidence left him in charge of Agra, so that when the ladies (*maḥalhā*)[248] should be sent for he might come with them. After the ladies were sent for he went for two or three stages with them, and in the village of Mathura, on merely hearing foolish tales, separated from them, and went to his

---

[246] Jalāl Khān was a grandson of Sultān Ādam (Blochmann, pp. 455 and 486).

[247] See *infra* for another notice of him in the chapter on Gujrat.

[248] One of Jahāngīr's wives was a daughter of Rāy Rāy Singh (of Bikanir). See Blochmann, p. 310.

native place (Bikanir). He thought that as a commotion had arisen he would see where the right road was. The merciful God, who cherishes His servants, in a short time having arranged that affair broke the rope of the alliance of those rebels, and this betrayal of his salt remained a burden on his neck. In order to please the Amīru-l-umarā I ordered the rank which he formerly held to be confirmed to him, and his jagir to remain as it was. I promoted Sulaimān Beg, who was one of my attendants from the time when I was prince, to the title of Fidā'ī Khān. On Monday, the 12th, a halt was made at the garden of Dil-āmīz, which is on the bank of the river Ravi. I waited on my mother in this garden. Mīrzā Ghāzī, who had done approved service in command of the army at Qandahar, waited on me, and I bestowed great favour on him.

On Tuesday, the 13th, I auspiciously entered Lahore. The next day Mīr Khalīlu-llah, son of Ghiyāṣu-d-dīn Muḥammad, Mīrmīrān, who was of the descendants of Shāh Ni'matu-llah Walī, paid his respects.[249] In the reign of Shāh Ṭahmāsp there was no family of such greatness in the whole country, for the sister of the Shah, by name Jānish Begam, was in the house of (married to) Mīr Ni'matu-llah, the father of the Mīrmīrān. A daughter who was born to them, the Shah gave in marriage to his own son Isma'īl Mīrzā, and making the sons of that Mīrmīrān sons-in-law, gave his younger daughter to his eldest son, who had the same name as his grandfather, and connected (in marriage) the daughter of Isma'īl Mīrzā, who was born of the niece of the Shah, to another son, Mīr Khalīlu-llah. After the death of the Shah, by degrees the family went to decay, until in the reign of Shāh 'Abbās they became all at once extirpated, and they lost the property and effects that they had and could no longer remain in their own place. Mīr Khalīlu-llah came to wait upon me. As he had undergone trouble on the road, and the signs of sincerity were apparent from his circumstances, having

[249] See Rieu, Cat. ii, p. 634.

made him a sharer of my unstinted favours I gave him 12,000 rupees in cash, and promoted him to the rank of 1,000 personal and 200 horse, and gave an order for a jagir.

An order was given to the civil department (*dīwāniyān*) to confer the rank of 8,000 personal and 5,000 horse on my son Khurram, and to provide a jagir for him in the neighbourhood of Ujjain, and to assign the Sarkar of Ḥiṣār Fīrūza to him. On Thursday, the 22nd, on the invitation of Āṣaf Khān, I went with my ladies to his house and passed the night there. The next day he presented before me his own offerings, of the value of ten lacs of rupees, in jewels and jewelled things, robes, elephants, and horses. Some single rubies and jacinths and some pearls, also silk cloths with some pieces of porcelain from China and Tartary, were accepted, and I made a present of the rest to him. Murtaẓā Khān from Gujarat sent by way of offering a ring made of a single ruby of good colour, substance, and water, the stone, the socket, and the ring being all of one piece. They weighed 1 1/2 tanks and one surkh, which is equal to one misqal and 15 surkh. This was sent to me and much approved. Till that day no one had ever heard of such a ring having come to the hands of any sovereign. A single ruby weighing six surkhs or two tanks and 15 surkhs,[250] and of which the value was stated to be £25,000, was also sent. The ring was valued at the same figure.

On the same day the envoy of the Sharif of Mecca came to wait on me with a letter and the curtain of the door of the Ka'bah. He showed great friendship towards me. The said envoy had bestowed on him 500,000 *dām*, equal to 7,000 or 8,000 rupees,

---

250. There is evidently something wrong in the text, for a ruby weighing 6 surkhs could not weigh 2 tanks and 15 surkhs. I.O. MS. 181 has *barja* instead of surkh, but I do not know what this means. Perhaps *shash-gūsha*,' hexagonal,' was intended. This view is confirmed by the Iqbāl-nāma, p. 31, which has *shash pahlū*, 'six-sided.' Erskine's MS. also had 'six-sided,' and he translates "a six-sided ruby which weighed two *tangs* fifteen *surkhs*." I.O. MS. 305.") has *shash pārchn*, and it is evident that this word, as also the *barja* of No. 181, is the *pārche* of Steingass, which means a segment or facet.

and I resolved to send the Sharif the equivalent of 100,000 rupees of the precious things of Hindustan. On Thursday, the 10th of the month, a piece of the Subah of Multan was added to the jagir of Mīrzā Ghāzī, though the whole of the province of Thattah had been given to him in jagir. He was also promoted to the rank of 5,000 personalty and 5,000 horse. The government of Qandahar and the protection of that region, which is the frontier of Hindustan, were assigned to his excellent administration. Conferring on him a robe of honour and a jewelled sword I gave him his leave. In fine, Mīrzā Ghāzī possessed perfection,[251] and he made also good verses. He used Waqārī as his *takhalluṣ*, or poetic name (Rūz-i-rūshan, Bhopal 1297, p. 455; also Ma'āṣiru-l-umarā, vol. iii, p. 347). This is one of his couplets:—

> "If my weeping should cause her to smile, what wonder?
> Though the cloud weep, the cheek of the rose-bush smiles."

On the 15th the offering of the Khankhanan was presented to me: 40 elephants, some jewelled and decorated vessels, some Persian robes, and cloth that they make in the Deccan and those parts, had been sent by him, altogether of the value of 150,000 rupees. Mīrzā Rustam and most of the office-holders of that Subah had also sent good offerings. Some of the elephants were approved. News of the death of Rāy Durgā,[252] who was one of those who had been brought up by my revered father, arrived on the 18th of the month. He had been in attendance for forty years and more in the position of an Amir on my revered father, until, by degrees, he had risen in rank to 4,000. Before he obtained the good fortune of waiting on my father, he was one of the trusted servants of Rānā Ūday Singh. He died on the 29th. He was a good military man. Sulṭān Shāh, the Afghan, whose disposition was turbulent and mischievous, passed his time in the service of Khusrau, and had his complete intimacy, so much

---

[251] This remark about Mīrzā Ghāzī, and also the quotation, do not occur in the two I.O. MSS.

[252] Blochmann, p. 417.

so that this rebel was the cause of the running away of that unfortunate one. After the defeat and capture of Khusrau he went off alone (?)[253] into the skirts of the hills of Khiẓrābād and that region. At last he was made prisoner by Mīr Mughal, the *karorī* of that place. As he had been the cause of the destruction and ruin of such a son, I ordered them to shoot him with arrows on the plain of Lahore. The aforesaid karori was promoted to higher rank, and was dignified with a grand dress of honour. On the 29th Shīr Khān, the Afghan, who was one of my old servants, died. One might say that he took his own life, because he was continually drinking wine, to the extent that in every watch he used to drink four brimming cups of arrack of double strength. He had broken the fast of the Ramaẓān of the past year, and took it into his head this year that he would fast in the month of Sha'bān on account of his having broken the fast of Ramaẓān, and would fast for two months together. In abandoning his usual custom, which is a second nature, he became weak and his appetite left him, and becoming very weak he passed away in his 57th year. Patronising his children and brothers according to their circumstances, I bestowed on them a portion of his rank and jagir.

On the 1st of the month of Shawwāl I went to visit Maulānā Muḥammad Amīn, who was one of the disciples of Shaikh Maḥmūd Kamāngar (the bow-maker). The Shaikh Maḥmūd[254] mentioned was one of the great men of his age, and H.M. Humāyūn had entire reliance on him, so much so that he once poured water on his hands. The aforesaid Maulānā is a man of good disposition, and is free, notwithstanding the attachments and accidents (of the world), a faqir in manner and ways, and acquainted with brokenness of spirit. His company pleased me exceedingly. I explained to him some of the griefs that had

---

[253] *Bayaktā*, but the I. O. MSS. have *batagpāy*, 'rapidly.'

[254] Properly Zainu-d-dīn Maḥmūd. See the story in Badayūnī, Ranking, p. 589; also Akbar-nāma translation, i, 611, and Blochmann, p. 539 and note.

entangled themselves in my mind and heard from him good advice and agreeable words, and found myself greatly consoled at heart. Having presented him with 1,000 *bīghā* and 1,000 rupees in cash by way of maintenance, I took leave. One watch of day had passed on Sunday when I left Lahore on my way to the capital of Agra. Having made Qilīj Khān governor, Mīr Qawāmu-d-dīn diwan, Shaikh Yūsuf bakhshi, and Jamālu-d-dīn kotwal, and presented each according to his circumstances with dresses of honour, I turned towards my desired way. On the 25th, having passed over the river at Sultanpur, I proceeded two kos and halted at Nakodar. My revered father had given Shaikh Abū-l-faẓl[255] gold of the weight of 20,000 rupees to build an embankment between these two parganahs and prepare a waterfall, and in truth I found a halting-place exceedingly pleasant and fresh. I ordered Mu'izzu-l-mulk, the jagirdar of Nakodar, to erect a building and prepare a garden on one side of this embankment, so that wayfarers seeing it might be pleased. On Saturday, 10th Zī-l-qa'da, Wazīru-l-mulk, who before my ascension had the good fortune to serve me, and was Diwan of my establishment, died of diarrhœa. At the end of his life a son of evil fortune (lit. footsteps) had been born in his house, who in the space of forty days ruined[256] (Erskine has 'ate') both his father and mother, and who himself died when he was two or three years old. It occurred to me that the house of Wazīru-l-mulk must not all at once be ruined, and patronising Manṣūr, his brother's son, I gave him rank. Indeed,[257] he showed no love to me (the scent of love did not come from him). On Monday, the

---

[255] I do not know if this is the author. There appears to be no mention of the construction in the Akbar-nāma. Nakodar is in the Jalandhar district (I.G., x, 180, and Jarrett, ii, 317). Perhaps the two tombs at Nakodar mentioned in I.G. as of Jahāngīr's time are those of Muqīm the Wazīru-l-mulk and his wife. See Tūzuk, pp. 6 and 64.

[256] *Khwurd*, lit. 'devoured.' Apparently he refers to the fact of the birth as a misfortune. I.O. MS. 181 has *sar-i-mādar u pidar rā khwurd*, and the A.S. 124 has *shīr-i-mādar u pidar-i-khūd*, 'the milk of his own mother and father'!

[257] This is given as a quotation in No. 181.

14th, I heard on the road that between Panipat and Karnal there were two tigers that were giving much trouble to wayfarers. I collected the elephants and sent them off. When I arrived at their (the tigers') place I mounted a female elephant, and ordered them to place the elephants round them after the manner of a qamargah (enclosure), and by the favour of Allah killed both with a gun, and thus got rid of the raging tigers that had closed the road to the servants of God. On Thursday, the 18th,[258] I halted at Delhi and alighted at the residence which Salīm Khān, the Afghan, had made in the days of his rule in the middle of the river Jumna and called Salīmgaḍh. My revered father had given the place to Murtaẓā Khan, who was originally an inhabitant of Delhi. The aforesaid Khan had built on the margin of the river a terrace of stone excessively pleasant and bright. Below that building[259] near the water there was made a square *chaukandī* with glazed tiles by the order of H.M. Humāyūn, and there are few places with such air. In the days when the late king Humāyūn honoured Delhi with his presence, he often sat there with his intimates, and associated with the members of his assemblies. I passed four days in that place, and with my courtiers and intimates enjoyed myself with wine parties. Mu'aẓẓam Khān, who was governor of Delhi, presented offerings. The jagirdars and citizens also made offerings and presents, each according to his circumstances. I was desirous to employ some days in a qamargah hunt in the parganah of Pālam, which is one of the places near the aforesaid city and one of the fixed hunting-grounds. As it was represented to me that the (fortunate) hour for approaching Agra had come very near, and another proper hour was not to be obtained at all near that time, I gave up the intention, and embarking on board a boat went on by water. On the 20th of the month of Ẕī-l-qa'da four boys and three girls, children of Mīrzā Shāhrukh, whom he had

[258] This should be the 17th if Monday was the 14th.

[259] The MSS. seem to have *mutaṣṣil-i-māb-i-chaukandī*, 'in shape like a chaukandī(?).' It was from the roof of this building that Humāyūn fell.

not mentioned to my father, were brought. I placed the boys among my confidential servants, and made over the girls to the attendants of the ladies of the harem in order that they might look after them. On the 21st of the same month Rājā Mān Singh came and waited on me from the fort of Rohtas, which is in the province of Patna and Behar, after orders had been sent to him six or seven times. He also, like Khān A'ẓam, is one of the hypocrites and old wolves of this State. What they have done to me, and what has happened to them from me, God the knower of secrets knows; possibly no one could mention such another case (?). The aforesaid Raja produced as offerings 100 elephants, male and female, not one of which was fit to be included among my private elephants. As he was one of those who had been favoured by my father, I did not parade his offences before his face, but with royal condescension promoted him.

On this day they brought a talking *jal* (lark) which distinctly said "Miyān Ṭūṭī." It was very strange and wonderful. In Turki they call this bird *turghai.*[260]

THE THIRD NEW YEAR'S FEAST FROM MY ACCESSION.

On Thursday, the 2nd Zī-l-ḥijja, corresponding with the 1st Farwardīn (19th March, 1608), the Sun, which enlightens and heats the world with its splendour, changed from the constellation of Pisces to the joyful mansion of Aries, the abode of pleasure and rejoicing. It gave the world fresh brightness, and being aided by the Spring clothed those who had been plundered by the cold season, and tyrannised over by the Autumn, with the robes of honour of the New Year and the

---

[260] *Turghai* or *turghei* is a thrush according to Vambéry, and was the name of Timur's father. Perhaps the bird was the large *mainā*, the Bhīmrāj or Bhringraj (?) of the Āyīn, Jarrett, ii, p. 125 and note. In Scully's Glossary, *turghai* is said to be the lark. The text arranges the words differently from the MSS. They have *mushakhkhas Miyān Tūṭi gufta*, and Erskine translates 'which said clearly Miyān Tuti.' But possibly Jahāngīr meant that it spoke clearly like a parrot.

garments of emerald green, and gave them compensation and recuperation.

> "Again to Not-Being came the world's lord's order,
> 'Restore what thou hast devoured.'"

The feast of the New Year was held in the village of Rankatta,[261] which is five kos off (from Agra), and at the time of transit (of the sun) I seated myself on the throne with glory and gladness. The nobles and courtiers and all the servants came forward with their congratulations. In the same assembly I bestowed on K͟hānjahān the rank of 5,000 personal and horse. I selected K͟hwāja Jahān for the post of bakhshi. Dismissing Wazīr K͟hān from the Viziership of the province of Bengal, I sent in his place Abū-l-ḥasan S͟hihābk͟hānī; and Nūru-d-dīn Qulī became kotwal of Agra. As the glorious mausoleum of the late king Akbar was on the road, it entered my mind that if in passing by I should have the good fortune of a pilgrimage to it, it might occur to those who were shortsighted that I visited it because it was the place where my road crossed. I accordingly had determined that this time I would enter Agra, and after that would go on foot on this pilgrimage to the shrine, which is two and a half kos off, in the same way that the Ḥaẓrat (my father), on account of my birth, had gone from Agra to Ajmir. Would that I might also traverse the same on my head! When two watches of day had passed of Saturday, the 5th[262] of the month, at an auspicious hour, I returned towards Agra, and scattering with two hands 5000 rupees in small coins on the way, entered the august palace

---

[261] Blochmann, p. 332. Sikandra, Akbar's tomb, lies half-way between Rankattah and Agra. Tiefenthaler, i, 206, gives the name as Runcta, and says it is a famous place, as Rām there took the figure of Paras Rām. Jarrett, ii, 180, has Rangtah, and it is there described as a village on the Jumna, near the city, and a much frequented place of worship. The Agra volume of the N.W.P. Gazetteer, p. 764, spells it Runkutta, and says it is 9 miles north-west of Agra. See also Ma'ā ṣ ir, ii, 407, art. Sa'ād K͟hān, where mention is made of Rankatta, and Hilālābād, and Blochmann, p. 332.

[262] If Thursday was the 2nd, Saturday would be the 4th. He went first to Agra from Rangta, apparently.

which was inside the fort. On this day Rāja Bīr Singh Deo brought a white cheeta to show me. Although other sorts of creatures, both birds and beasts, have white varieties, which they call *ṭūyghān,*[263] I had never seen a white cheeta. Its spots, which are (usually) black, were of a blue colour, and the whiteness of the body was also inclined to bluishness. Of the albino animals that I have seen there are falcons, sparrow-hawks, hawks (*shikara*) that they call *bīgū*[264] in the Persian language, sparrows, crows, partridges, florican, *podna*[265] (*Sylvia olivacea*), and peacocks. Many hawks in aviaries are albinos. I have also seen white flying mice (flying squirrels) and some albinos among the black antelope, which is a species found only in Hindustan. Among the *chikāra* (gazelle), which they call *safida* in Persia, I have frequently seen albinos. At this time Ratan, son of Bhoj-hāra, who is one of the chief Rajput nobles, came to the camp and waited on me, bringing three elephants as an offering. One of these was much approved, and they valued it in the office at 15,000 rupees. It was entered among my private elephants, and I gave it the name of Ratangaj. The value of elephants of the former great Rajas of India was not more than 25,000 rupees, but they have now become very dear. I dignified Ratan with the title of Sarbuland Rāy. I promoted Mīrān Ṣadr Jahān to the rank of 5,000 personal and 1,500 horse and Mu'aẓẓam Khān to 4,000 personal and 2,000 horse. 'Abdu-llah Khān was promoted to 3,000 and 500 horse. Muẓaffar Khān and Bhāo Singh each obtained the rank of 2,000 personal and 1,000 horse. Abū-l-ḥasan diwan had 1,000 and 500 horse. I'timādu-d-daulah that of 1,000 personal and 250 horse. On the 25th Rāja Sūraj Singh, the maternal uncle of my son Khurram, came and paid his respects to me. He brought with him Shyām, the cousin of the turbulent

---

263 *Ṭūyghun* or *ṭūyghūn* is given in Zenker as Turkī for the white falcon. See Elliot, vi, 317.

264. *Bīghū*, which is given in Zenker, is Turkī. The text has *līfū*. The I.O. MSS. have *bīgū*.

265. Should be *būdana*, 'quail.'

Umrā. In truth he possesses some skill and understands well how to ride elephants. Rāja Sūraj Singh had brought with him a poet who wrote verse in the Hindi tongue. He laid before me a poem in my praise to the purport that if the Sun had a son it would be always day and never would be night, because after his setting that son would sit in his place and keep the world in light. Praise and thanksgiving to God that God gave your father such a son that after his death men should not wear mourning which is like the night. The Sun had envy on this account, saying, "Would I might also have a son who, taking my place, should not allow night to approach the world, for from the light of your rising and the illumination of your justice, notwithstanding such a misfortune, the spheres are so bright that one might say 'night had neither name nor sign.'" Few Hindi verses of such freshness of purport have ever reached my ear. As a reward for this eulogy I gave him an elephant. The Rajputs call a poet Chāran (name of a caste who are many of them poets). One of the poets of the age has turned[266] these sentiments into (Persian) verse—

> "If the world-illuminator had a son,
> There would be no night; it would be always day;
> For when his gold-crowned head was hidden
> His son would display his tiara peak.
> Thanks that after such a father
> Such a son sits in his place.
> For from the demise of that king
> No one made black robes for mourning."

On Thursday, the 8th Muḥarram, 1017[267] (24th April, 1608), Jalālu-d-dīn Mas'ūd, who held the rank of 400 personal and was not wanting in bravery, and who in several battles had done great deeds, died at about the age of 50 or 60 years of diarrhœa. He was an opium-eater, and used to eat opium after breaking it in pieces, like cheese, and it is notorious that he frequently ate

---

[266] Apparently this is a translation from the Hindi.

[267] Text wrongly has 1014.

opium from the hand of his own mother. When his disease became violent and there was a prospect of his death, his mother from excessive love for him ate more opium than was right out of that which she used to give her son, and two or three hours after his death she also died. I have never heard of such affection on the part of a mother for her son. It is the custom among the Hindus that after the death of their husbands women burn themselves, whether from love, or to save the honour of their fathers, or from being ashamed before their sons-in-law, but nothing like this was ever manifested on the part of mothers, Musulman or Hindu. On the 15th of the same month I presented my best horse by way of favour to Rāja Mān Singh. Shāh 'Abbās had sent this horse with some other horses and fitting gifts by Minūchihr, one of his confidential slaves, to the late king Akbar. From being presented with this horse the Raja was so delighted that if I had given him a kingdom I do not think he would have shown such joy. At the time they brought the horse it was three or four years old. It grew up in Hindustan. The whole of the servants of the Court, Moghul and Rajput together, represented that no horse like this had ever come from Iraq to Hindustan. When my revered father gave the province of Khandesh and the Subah of the Deccan to my brother Dāniyāl, and was returning to Agra, he by way of kindness told Dāniyāl to ask of him whatever he desired. Seizing the opportunity, he asked for this horse, and he accordingly gave it to him. On Tuesday, the 20th, a report came from Islām Khān with the news of the death of Jahāngīr Qulī Khān, the governor of the Subah of Bengal, who was my special slave. On account of his natural excellence and innate merit he had been enrolled in the list of the great Amirs. I was much grieved at his death. I bestowed the rule of Bengal and the tutorship to Prince Jahāndār on my *farzand*[268] Islām Khān, and in his place gave the government of the Subah of Behar to Afẓal Khān (son of Abū-l-faẓl). The son of Ḥakīm 'Alī,

[268] Jahāngīr calls Islām *farzand* because he was the son of his foster-brother. Jahāngīr Qulī means 'slave of Jahāngīr.'

whom I had sent on some duties to Burhanpur, came and brought with him some Karnatic jugglers who had no rivals or equals; for instance, one of them played with ten balls, each of which was equal to an orange and one to a citron, and one to a *surkh*,[269] in such a way that notwithstanding some were small and some large he never missed one, and did so many kinds of tricks that one's wits became bewildered. At the same time a dervish from Ceylon came and brought a strange animal called a *deonak*[270] (or *devang*). Its face was exactly like a large bat, and the whole shape was like that of a monkey, but it had no tail. Its movements were like those of the black tailless monkey which they call *ban mānush* (jungle man) in the Hindi language. Its body was like that of a young monkey two or three months old. It had been with the dervish for five years.[271] It appeared that the animal would never grow larger. Its food is milk and it also eats plantains. As the creature appeared very strange, I ordered the artists to take a likeness of it in various kinds of movement. It looked very ugly.

On the same day Mīrzā Farīdūn Barlās was promoted to the rank of 1,500 personal and 1,300 horse. An order was given that Pāyanda[272] Khān Moghul, as he had reached old age after exerting himself as a soldier, should receive a jagir equal to 2,000 personal. Ilf Khān was promoted to the rank of 700 personal and 500 horse. The rank of Islām Khān, my son (*farzand*), the governor of the Subah of Bengal, was fixed at 4,000 personal and 3,000 horse. The guardianship of the fort of Rohtas was bestowed on Kishwar Khān, son of Quṭbu-d-dīn Khān Koka. Ihtimām Khān was raised to the rank of 1,000 personal and 300 horse, and made *mīr baḥr* (admiral) and was appointed to the charge of the *nawāra* (fleet) of Bengal. On the 1st Ṣafar Shamsu-d-

---

269 The seed of *Abrus precatorius*.

270 Or *devtaq*. Qu, *devanāyak?* The MSS. have *yūnk* and *wabūnk*. The text is corrupt and has converted the word for 'bat' into a 'lamb.'

271 The text is corrupt.

272 Blochmann, p. 387.

dīn Khān, son of Khān A'ẓam, made an offering of ten elephants, and, receiving the rank of 2,000 personal and 1,500 horse, was selected for the title of Jahāngīr Qulī Khān, and ẓafar Khān received the rank of 2,000 personal and 1,000 horse. As I had demanded in marriage the daughter of Jagat Singh, eldest son of Rāja Mān Singh, I on the 16th sent 80,000 rupees for the *sāchaq* (a marriage present) to the house of the aforesaid Raja in order to dignify him. Muqarrab Khān sent from the port of Cambay a European curtain (tapestry), the like of which in beauty no other work of the Frank painters had ever been seen. On the same day my aunt, Najību-n-nisā Begam,[273] died in the 61st year of her age of the disease of consumption and hectic fever. I promoted her son, Mīrzā Wālī, to the rank of 1,000 personal and 200 horse. A man of Māwarā'a-n-nahr, of the name of Aqam Ḥājī, who for a long time had been in Turkey and was not without reasonableness and religious knowledge, and who called himself the ambassador of the Turkish Emperor, waited upon me at Agra. He had an unknown writing (? illegible letter). Looking to his circumstances and his proceedings none of the servants of the Court believed in his being an ambassador. When Tīmūr conquered Turkey, and Yildirīm Bāyazīd, the ruler of that place, fell alive into his hands, he, after levying tribute and taking one year's revenue, determined to hand back into his possession the whole of the country of Turkey. Just at that time Yildirīm Bāyazīd died, and (Tīmūr), having handed over the kingdom to his son Mūsā Chelebī, returned. From that time until now, notwithstanding such favours, no one had come on the part of the emperors, nor has any ambassador been sent: how, then, can it now be believed that this person from Māwarā'a-n-nahr should have been sent by the emperor? I could in no way understand the affair, and no one could bear witness to the accuracy of his claim: I therefore told him to go wherever he

[273] Sister of Mirzā Ḥakīm, also known as Fakhru-n-nisā (Blochmann, p. 322). The MSS. have Bakhtu-n-nisā, and it would seem that the Najibu-n-nisā of the text is a wrong reading. See Gulbadan Begam's Memoirs, p. 214.

might wish. On the 4th Rabī'u-l-awwal the daughter of Jagat Singh entered the harem, and the marriage ceremony was performed in the house of Her Highness Maryam-zamānī. Amongst the things sent with her by Rāja Mān Singh were 60 elephants.

As I had determined to conquer the Rānā, it occurred to me that I should send Mahābat Khān. I appointed 12,000 fully armed cavalry under able officers to go with him, and in addition 500 ahadis, 2,000 musketeers on foot, with artillery made up of 70 to 80 guns mounted on elephants and camels; 60 elephants were appointed to this duty. Two million rupees of treasure were ordered to be sent with this army. On the 16th of the said month Mīr Khalīlu-llah, grandson of Mīr Ni'matu-llah Yazdī, the whole of whose circumstances and family history has already been written, died of diarrhœa. In his appearance the traces of sincerity and dervishhood were manifest. If he had lived and passed a long time in my service he would have risen to high rank. The bakhshi of Burhanpur had sent some mangoes, one of which I ordered to be weighed; it came to 52 1/2 tolas. On Wednesday, the 18th, in the house of Maryam-zamānī, the feast of the lunar weighing of my 40th year was held. I ordered the money used in weighing to be divided amongst women and needy persons. On Thursday, the 4th Rabī'u-l-ākhir, Ṭāhir Beg, the bakhshi of the Ahadis, was given the title of Mukhliṣ Khān, and Mullā-i-Taqiyyā Shūstarī,[274] who was adorned with excellencies and perfections, and was well acquainted with the science of history and genealogy, that of Mu'arrikh Khān. On the 10th of the same month, having given Barkhūrdār, the brother of 'Abdu-llah Khān, the title of Bahādur Khān, I dignified him among his fellows. Mūnis Khān, son of Mihtar Khān, presented me with a jug of jasper (jade), which had been made in the reign of Mīrzā Ulugh Beg Gūrgān, in the honoured name of that

274 Text wrongly has Shamshīrī. The MSS. have Shūstarī, and this is right. See Blochmann, pp. 208, 209, and 518.

prince. It was a very delicate rarity and of a beautiful shape. Its stone was exceedingly white and pure. Around the neck of the jar they had carved the auspicious name of the Mīrzā and the Hijra year in *riqā'*[275] characters. I ordered them to inscribe my name and the auspicious name of Akbar on the edge of the lip of the jar. Mihtar[276] Khān was one of the ancient slaves of this State. He had the honour of serving the late king Humāyūn, and during the reign of my revered father had attained the rank of nobility. He regarded him as one of his confidential servants. On the 16th a firman was issued that the country of Sangrām,[277] which had been given for a year by way of reward to my son (*farzand*) Islām Khān, should be handed over for the same purpose for a year to Afẓal Khān, the governor of the Subah of Behar. On this day I promoted Mahābat Khān to the rank of 3,000 personal and 2,500 horse, and Yūsuf Khān, son of Ḥusain Khān Tukriyah, obtained that of 2,000 personal and 800 horse. On the 24th I gave leave to Mahābat Khān and the Amirs and men who had been appointed to subdue the Rānā. The aforesaid Khan was honoured with a robe of honour, a horse, a special elephant, and a jewelled sword. Ẓafar Khān, having been honoured with a standard, was presented with a private robe of honour and a jewelled dagger. Shajā'at Khān also was presented with a standard, and I gave him a robe of honour and a special elephant. Rāja Bīr Singh Deo received a robe of honour and a special horse, and Manglī Khān a horse and jewelled dagger. Narāyan Dās Kachhwāhah, 'Alī Qulī Darman, and Hizabr Khān Tahamtan obtained leave. On Bahādur Khān and Mu'izzu-l-mulk the bakhshi jewelled daggers were conferred, and in the same manner all the Amirs and leaders, each one according to his degree, were honoured with royal gifts. A watch of the day had passed when the Khankhanan, who had been selected for

---

[275] *Riqā'* is a kind of writing (Blochmann, pp. 99, 100).

[276] Blochmann, p. 417. His name was Anīsu-d-dīn.

[277] This must be Rāja Sangrām of Kharakpur, who had been a rebel. See Blochmann, p. 446 and note.

the high honour of my Ātālīq (guardian), came from Burhanpur and waited on me. Delight and happiness had so overpowered him that he did not know whether he came on his head or his feet. He threw himself bewildered at my feet. By way of favour and kindness I lifted up his head and held it in an embrace of kindliness and affection, and kissed his face. He brought me as offerings two strings of pearls and some rubies and emeralds. The value of the jewels was 300,000 rupees. Besides these he laid before me many valuable things. On the 17th Jumādā-l-awwal Wazīr Khān, the Diwan of Bengal, came and waited on me, and offered 60 elephants, male and female, and one Egyptian[278] ruby. As he was one of the old servants and he performed every duty, I ordered him to remain in attendance on me. As Qāsim Khān and his elder brother, Islām Khān, could in no way keep the peace together, I had sent for the former to my own presence; and he yesterday came and waited on me. On the 22nd, Āṣaf Khān, made me an offering of a ruby of the weight of seven *ṭānk,* which Abū-l-qāsim, his brother, had bought in the port of Cambay for 75,000 rupees. It is of a beautiful colour and well-shaped, but to my belief is not worth more than 60,000 rupees. Great faults had been committed by Dulīp Rāy, son of Rāy Rāy Singh, but as he took refuge with my *farzand* Khān Jāhān his offences were pardoned, and I knowingly and purposely passed over his delinquencies. On the 24th the sons of Khānkhānān, who had followed after him, arrived and waited on me and produced as an offering the sum of 25,000 rupees. On the same day the said Khan offered 90 elephants. On Thursday, the 1st Jumādā-s̤-s̤ānī, the feast of my solar year was celebrated in the house of Maryam-zamānī. Some of the money I divided among the women, and an order was given that the balance should be distributed to the poor of the hereditary kingdoms. On the 4th of the month I ordered the Diwans to give a jagir, according to his rank, of 7,000 rupees to Khān A'z̤am.

---

[278] Text Qutbī, but I think the word is Qibṭī, 'Egyptian.'

On this day a female antelope in milk was brought that allowed itself to be milked with ease, and gave every day four seers of milk. I had never seen or heard of anything of the kind before. The milk of the antelope, of the cow, and the buffalo in no way differs. They say it is of great use in asthma. On the 11th of the month Rāja Mān Singh asked for leave to complete the army of the Deccan to which he had been appointed, as well as to visit Amber, his native place. I gave him a male elephant of my own called Hushyār-mast, and gave him leave. On Monday, the 12th, as it was the anniversary of the death of the late king Akbar, in addition to the expenses of that entertainment, which are fixed separately, I sent 4,000 rupees more to be divided among the faqirs and dervishes who are present in the enlightened mausoleum of the venerated one. On that day I exalted 'Abdu-llah, the son of Khān A'z̤am, with the title of Sarfarāz Khān, and 'Abdu-r-Raḥīm, son of Qāsim Khān, with that of Tarbiyat Khān. On Tuesday, the 13th, I sent for Khusrau's daughter, and saw a child so like her father as no one can remember to have seen. The astrologers used to say that her advent would not be auspicious to her father, but would be auspicious to me. At last it became known that they had augured rightly. They said that I should see her after three years. I saw her when she had passed this age. On the 21st of the month Khānkhānān determined to clear out the province of the Nizāmu-l-mulk, into which, after the death of the late king Akbar, some disturbances had found their way, and stated in writing that "If I do not complete this service in the course of two years, I shall be guilty (of a fault), on the condition that in addition to the force that had been allotted to that Subah 12,000 more horse with 1,000,000 rupees should be sent with me." I ordered that materials for the army and the treasure should be quickly prepared, and he should be despatched. On the 26th Mukhliṣ Khān, bakhshi of the ahadis, was appointed bakhshi of the Subah of the Deccan, and I bestowed his place on Ibrāhīm Ḥusain Khān, the Mīr Baḥr. On the 1st Rajab, Pīshrau Khān and

Kamāl Khān, who belonged to the servants who were in constant attendance on me (*rū-shinās*), died. Shāh Tahmāsp had given Pīshrau Khān as a slave to my grandfather, and he was called Sa'ādat. When he was promoted in the service of the late king Akbar to the daroghahship and superintendence of the *farrāshkhāna* (carpet department), he obtained the title of Pīshrau. He was so well acquainted with this service that one might say it was a garment they had sewn on the stature of his capacity. When he was 90 years old he was quicker than lads of 14. He had the good fortune to serve my grandfather, my father, and me. Until he breathed his last he was never for a moment without the intoxication of wine.

> "Besmeared with wine Fighānī[279] went to the dust.
> Alas! if the angels[280] smelt his fresh shroud!'

He left 1,500,000 rupees. He has one very stupid son, called Ri'āyat. On account of his father's claims for services performed, I gave the superintendence of half the farrashkhana to him and the other half to Tukhmāq Khān. Kamāl Khān was one of the slaves sincerely devoted to my service; he is of the caste of the Kalāls of Delhi. On account of the great honesty and trustworthiness that he had shown I made him *bakāwal-begī* (chief of the kitchen). Few such servants are ever met with. He had two sons, to both of whom I showed great kindness, but where are there others like him? On the 2nd of the said month La'l[281] Kalāwant, who from his childhood had grown up in my father's service, who had taught him every breathing and sound that appertains to the Hindi language, died in the 65th or 70th year of his age. One of his girls (concubines) ate opium on this event and

---

279 Fighānī a famous poet and also a drunkard. See Rieu, ii, p. 651, and Sprenger, Oude Cat., p. 403. *Fighānī* also means lamentation, and there is a play in the couplet on the double meaning.

280 In the Elliot MSS., B.M., the second line is translated "Alas! if the angels made his shroud of another kind of odour! "The angels, meant are Nakīr and Munkar.

281 Blochmann, p. 612.

killed herself. Few women among the Musulmans have ever shown such fidelity.

In Hindustan, especially in the province of Sylhet,[282] which is a dependency of Bengal, it was the custom for the people of those parts to make eunuchs of some of their sons and give them to the governor in place of revenue (*māl-wājibī*). This custom by degrees has been adopted in other provinces, and every year some children are thus ruined and cut off from procreation. This practice has become common. At this time I issued an order that hereafter no one should follow this abominable custom, and that the traffic in young eunuchs should be completely done away with. Islām Khān and the other governors of the Subah of Bengal received firmans that whoever should commit such acts should be capitally punished, and that they should seize eunuchs of tender years who might be in anyone's possession. No one of the former kings had obtained this success. Please Almighty God, in a short time this objectionable practice will be completely done away with, and the traffic in eunuchs being forbidden, no one shall venture on this unpleasant and unprofitable proceeding. I presented the Khānkhānān with a bay horse out of those sent me by Shāh 'Abbās; it was the head of the stable of my private horses. He was so rejoiced over it that it would be difficult to describe. In truth a horse of this great size and beauty has hardly come to Hindustan. I also gave him the elephant Futūḥ, that is unrivalled in fighting, with twenty other elephants. As Kishan Singh, who was accompanying Mahābat Khān, performed laudable service, and was wounded in the leg by a spear in the fight with the Rānā's men, so that about twenty noblemen of his were killed and about 3,000 made captive, he was promoted to the rank of 2,000 personal and 1,000 horse. On the 14th of the same month I gave an order for Mīrzā Ghāzī to betake himself to Qandahar. A strange occurrence was that as soon as the aforesaid Mīrzā started from Bakhar for that province the news

---

[282] Cf. Jarrett, ii, p. 122.

of the death of Sardār Khān, the governor of that place, came. Sardār Khān was one of the permanent and intimate attendants of my uncle Muḥammad Ḥakīm, and was known as Tukhta[283] Beg. I gave half his rank (the pay of it) to his sons. On Monday, the 17th, I went on foot on my pilgrimage to the enlightened mausoleum of the late king. If it had been possible, I would have traversed this road with my eyelashes and head. My revered father, on account of my birth, had gone on foot on a pilgrimage to the shrine of Khwāja Mu'īnu-d-dīn Sanjarī Chishtī, from Fatḥpūr to Ajmir, a distance of 120 kos: if I should traverse this road with my head and eyes, what should I have done? When I was dignified with the good fortune of making this pilgrimage, I saw the building that had been erected in the cemetery. It did not come up to my idea of what it ought to be, for that would be approved which the wayfarers of the world should point to as one the like of which was not in the inhabited world. Inasmuch as at the time of erecting the aforesaid building the affair of the ill-starred Khusrau took place, I started for Lahore, and the architects had built it after a design of their own. At last a certain expenditure was made until a large sum was expended, and work went on for three or four years. I ordered that experienced architects should again lay the foundations, in agreement with men of experience, in several places, on a settled plan. By degrees a lofty building was erected, and a very bright garden was arranged round the building of the shrine, and a large and lofty gateway with minarets of white stone was built. On the whole they told me the cost of this lofty edifice was 1,500,000 rupees, equivalent to 50,000 current tumans of Persia and 4,500,000 khanis, according to the currency of Tūrān.

On Sunday, the 23rd, I went with a band of courtiers who had not seen it to look at the reservoir in the house of Ḥakīm 'Alī, like one that had been made at Lahore in the time of my father. The reservoir is 6 gaz by 6 gaz. At its side has been

---

[283] Blochmann, p. 469.

erected a well-lighted room, the entrance to which is through the water, but the water does not get into it. Ten or twelve people could meet in it. He made an offering of some of the cash and jewels that had accumulated[284] in his time. After looking at the room, and the entering of a number of courtiers therein, I raised him to the rank of 2,000, and returned to the palace. On Sunday, the 14th Sha'bān, the Khānkhānān was honoured with a jewelled sword for the waist, a robe of honour, and a special elephant, and was given leave to go to his duty in the Deccan. Rāja Sūraj Singh, who was attached to him in that service, was raised to the rank of 3,000 personal and 2,000 horse. As it was again represented to me that oppression was being committed by the brethren and attendants of Murtaẓā Khān on the ryots and people of Ahmadabad in Gujarat, and that he was unable properly to restrain his relations and people about him, I transferred the Subah from him and gave it to A'ẓam Khān, and it was settled that the latter should attend at court, and that his eldest son Jahāngīr Qulī Khān should go to Gujarat as his deputy. The rank of Jahāngīr Qulī Khān was fixed at 3,000 personal and 2,500 horse. An order was given that in company with Mohan Dās dīwān and Mas'ūd Beg Hamazānī bakhshī he should carry on the business of the province. Mohan Dās was promoted to the rank of 800 with 500 horse, and Mas'ūd Beg to 300 with 150 horse. Tarbiyat Khān, one of the personal servants, was given the rank of 700 with 400 horse, and Naṣru-llah the same. Mihtar Khān, whose circumstances have been related, died at this time, and I promoted his son Mūnis Khān to the rank of 500 personal and 130 horse. On Wednesday, the 4th Zī-l-ḥijja, Khusrau had a son born to him by the daughter of the Khān A'ẓam, and I gave him the name of Buland-akhtar. On the 6th of the same month Muqarrab Khān sent a picture (with a report) that the belief of the Franks was this, that the picture was that of Tīmūr. At the time when Yildirīm Bāyazīd was taken prisoner by

---

[284] "What money and articles be could produce at the time" (Elliot, vi, 320).

his victorious army, a Nazarene, who at that time was ruler[285] of Constantinople, had sent an ambassador with gifts and presents in token of submission and service, and an artist who had been sent with the ambassador took his likeness and brought it away. If this story were true, no better gift could be presented to me. But as the picture had no resemblance to any of his descendants I was not satisfied of the truth of the statement.

THE FOURTH NEW YEAR'S FEAST AFTER THE AUSPICIOUS ACCESSION.

The passing of the great star that illumines the world into the constellation of Aries took place on the night of Saturday, the 14th Z̲ī-l-ḥijja, in Hijra 1017 (21st Ṃarch, 1609), and New Year's Day that made brilliant the world began with good auspices and rejoicing. On Friday, the 5th Muḥarram, in the year 1018, Ḥakīm ʻAlī died. He was an unrivalled physician; he had derived much profit from Arabic sciences. He had written a commentary on the Canon (of Avicenna) in the time of my revered father. He had greater diligence than understanding, just as his appearance was better than his disposition, and his acquirements better than his talents; on the whole he was bad-hearted, and of an evil spirit. On the 20th Ṣafar I dignified Mīrzā Bark̲h̲ūrdār with the title of K̲h̲ān ʻĀlam. They brought from the neighbourhood of Fatḥpūr a watermelon, greater than any I had ever seen. I ordered them to weigh it, and it came to 33 seers. On Monday, the 19th Rabī'u-l-awwal, the feast of my annual lunar weighing was arranged in the palace of my revered mother; a part of the money was divided among the women who had assembled there on that day.

As it had been evident that in order to carry on the affairs of the State in the Subah of the Deccan it was necessary to send one

---

285 Apparently the person spoken of as a Nazarene (Christian) was the Emperor of Constantinople. Can this picture be the original of that prefixed to White & Davey's translation of Timūr's Institutes ?

of the princes there, it came into my mind to send my son Parwīz there. I ordered them to send his equipments and fix the hour for his departure. I summoned to Court Mahābat Khān, who had been nominated to the command of the army against the rebel Rānā to arrange certain matters at headquarters, and appointed in his place 'Abdu-llah Khān, whom I exalted with the title of Fīrūz-jang. I sent 'Abdu-r-Razzāq bakhshī to carry an order to all the mansabdars of that army not to depart from the orders of the aforesaid Khān, and to pay every heed to his thanks and blame. On the 4th Jumādā-l-awwal one of the goatherds, who are a particular tribe, brought before me a gelded goat that had teats like a female, and gave every day sufficient milk to take with a cup of coffee.[286] As milk is one of the favours of Allah, and the source which nourishes many animals, I looked on this strange affair as an omen for good. On the 6th of the same month, having given him the rank of 2,000 personal and 1,500 horse, I sent Khurram, son of Khān A'ẓam, to the government of the province of Sorath, which is known as Jūnagaḍh (in Kaṭhiyawāḍ). I honoured[287] Ḥakīm Ṣadrā with the title of Masīḥu-z-zamān, and gave him the rank of 500 personal and 30 horse. On the 16th a jewelled waist-sword was sent to Rāja Mān Singh. On the 22nd, having handed over 2,000,000 rupees for the expenses of the army of the Deccan, which had been ordered for Parwīz, to a separate treasurer, 500,000 rupees more were given for the private expenses of Parwīz. On the 25th, Wednesday, Jahāndār (his son), who previously to this had been appointed, together with Quṭbu-d-dīn Khān Koka, to Bengal, came and waited on me. In reality it became known to me that he was a born devotee.[288] As my mind was taken up with the preparations for the Deccan, on the 1st Jumādā-l-ākhir I nominated the Amīru-l-umarā as well to that duty. He was honoured with the

[286] Perhaps the meaning is enough milk to till a coffee-cup.

[287] According to the contemporary, but anonymous, author quoted in Elliot, vi, 448, this was in reward for restoring the sight of Khusrau.

[288] *Majẕūh-i-mādar-zād*. Probably the meaning is that he was a born idiot.

favour of a robe of honour and a horse. Having promoted Karam Chand, son of Jagannāth, to the rank of 2,000 personal and 1,500 horse, I sent him in company with Parwīz. On the 4th of the month 370 ahadi horse were appointed with 'Abdu-llah Khān to the assistance of the army employed against the Rānā. One hundred horses were also despatched from the government stables to be given as he thought proper to the mansabdars and ahadis. On the 17th I gave a ruby of the value of 60,000 rupees to Parwīz, and another ruby with two single pearls, worth about 40,000 rupees, to Khurram. On Monday, the 28th, Jagannāth was promoted to the rank of 5,000 personal and 3,000 horse, and on the 8th of Rajab, Rāy Jāy Singh was promoted to that of 4,000 personal and 3,000 horse, and was dismissed for service in the Deccan. On Thursday, the 9th, Prince Shahriyār from Gujarat came and waited on me. On Tuesday, the 4th, I despatched my son Parwīz on the service of conquering the country of the Deccan. He was presented with a robe of honour, a special horse, a special elephant, a sword, and a jewelled dagger. The Sardars and Amirs who were appointed with him each according to his condition received and were made happy with the favour of a horse, a robe of honour, an elephant, a sword, and a jewelled dagger. I appointed 1,000 ahadis to be in attendance on Parwīz for the service of the Deccan. On the same day a representation came from 'Abdu-llah Khān that having pursued the rebel Rānā into the hill country into rough places, he had captured several of his elephants and horses. When night came on he had escaped with difficulty with his life. As he had made things go hard with him, he would soon be taken prisoner or killed. I promoted the said Khān to the rank of 5,000 personal, and a rosary of pearls, worth 10,000 rupees, was given to Parwīz. As I had given the province of Khandesh and Berar to the said son, I also conferred on him the fort of Āsīr, and 300 horses were sent with him to be given to ahadis, mansabdars, and whomever else he might consider worthy of favour. On the 26th, Saif Khān Bārha was given the rank of 2,500 personal and 1,350 horse, and appointed to the faujdarship of the Sarkar of Hisar. On Monday, the 4th Sha'bān, an elephant was given to Wazīr Khān. On Friday, the 22nd, I gave an order that as *bang* and *būza* (rice spirit) were injurious, they should not be sold in the bazars and that gambling should be abolished, and on this subject I issued stringent orders. On the 25th they brought a tiger from my private menagerie to fight with a bull. Many people gathered together to see the show, and a band of Jogis (religious mendicants) with them. One of the Jogis was naked, and the tiger, by way of sport, and not with the idea of rage, turned towards him. It threw him on the ground and began to behave to him as it would to its own female. The next day and on several occasions the same thing took place. As no such thing had ever been seen before and was exceedingly strange, this has been recorded.[289] On the 2nd of the month of Ramaẓān, at the request of Islām Khān, Ghiyās[290] Khān was promoted to the rank of 1,500 personal and 800 horse. Farīdūn Khān Barlās was promoted to the rank of 2,500 with 2,000 horse. One thousand *tolcha* of gold and silver and 1,000 rupees were given in alms on the day of the procession of the sun into the constellation of the Scorpion, which, according to the general acceptation of the Hindoos, is called the Sankrānt. On the 10th of that month an elephant was presented to Shāh Beg Yūzī[291] (? the panther-keeper), and Salāmu-llah, the Arab, who is a distinguished young man and a relative (son-in-law?) of Mubārak, the ruler of Darful.[292] On

---

289 The story is also told in the Iqbāl-nāma, p. 37, where it is said that the tiger was one brought by a calendar as a present. It had the name of La'l Khān and was very tame. It is added that the tiger did no injury to the jogi with his claws or teeth.

290 The MSS. have 'Ināyat.

291 I.O. MS. No. 181, Shāh Beg Khān.

292 Salāmu-llah is mentioned later on (p. 78), and is described as brother's son of Mubārak, who held the country of Jotra (?) and Darful. He is also mentioned in the Iqbāl-nāma, p. 38, where Mubārak is described as ruler (*ḥākim*) of Jūyza and Safūl (?). But a MS. of the Iqbāl-nāma in my possession only mentions Jūyza or Jūyna. I think Jūyza must be Juina or Juanny, which, according to Sir William Jones, is one of the names of the island of Johanna or Hinzuan (one of the

account of some suspicion that Shāh 'Abbās had entertained against him, he came to wait upon me. I patronised him, and gave him the rank of 400 personal and 200 horse. Again, another force, containing 193 mansabdars and 46 ahadis, I sent after Parwīz for service in the Deccan. Fifty horses were also entrusted to one of the servants of the Court to convoy to Parwīz.

On Friday, the 13th, a certain idea came into my mind, and this rhymed *ghazal* was produced:—

"What shall I do, for the arrow of loss of thee has pierced my liver!
So that the (evil) eye not reaching me again may reach another?
Thou movest as if frenzied, and the world is frenzied for thee.
I burn rue lest thy eye should reach me.

I am frenzied at union with my friend, and in despair at her absence.
Alas for the grief that has o'erwhelmed me!
I've grown mad that I may rush on the pathway of meeting:
W e o for the time that brought me the news!
Jahāngīr, the time for humility and prayer is every morning,[293]
I hope that some spark of light may take effect."

On Sunday, the 15th, I sent 50,000 rupees as *sāchaq* to the house of the daughter of Muẓaffar Ḥusain Mīrzā, son of Sulṭān Ḥusain Mīrzā, son of Bahrām Mīrzā, son of Shāh Isma'īl Ṣafawī, who had been demanded in marriage for my son Khurram. On the 17th of the month Mubārak Khān Sarwānī was honoured with the rank of 1,000 personal and 300 horse. Five thousand rupees were also given to him, and 4,000 rupees to Ḥājī Bī Ūzbeg. On the 22nd a ruby and a pearl were given to Shahriyār. One hundred thousand rupees were given for the subsistence of the Ūymāqs (special cavalry) who had been appointed for

---

Comorro Islands), and that Safūl must be Sofala, a town on the east coast of Africa. Sir W. Jones was landed on Johanna, and has a long account of the island (see his works). The Iqbāl-nāma says that Salāmu-llah killed himself with drink. There is a short notice of him in the Ma'āsir, ii, 641, where he is called by his title of Shajā'at Khān.

293 The I.O. MSS. have a different reading here. Instead of 'every morning' they have 'renew (humility).' The word nūr, 'light,' in the last line probably refers to Jahāngīr's name of Nūru-d-dīn.

service in the Deccan. Two thousand rupees were given to Farrukh Beg, the painter, who is unrivalled in the age. Four thousand rupees were sent for expenditure on Bābā Ḥasan Abdāl. One thousand rupees were handed to Mullā 'Alī Aḥmad Muhrkan (engraver) and Mullā Rūzbihān Shīrāzī to expend on the anniversary festival of Ḥaẓrat Shaikh Salīm at his mausoleum. An elephant was given to Muḥammad Ḥusain, the writer, and 1,000 rupees to Khwāja 'Abdu-l-Ḥaqq Anṣārī. I gave orders to the Diwans that having raised the rank of Murtaẓā Khān to 5,000 personal and horse they should give him a jagir. I ordered Bihārī Chand Qānūngū, of the Sarkar of Agra, to take 1,000 footmen and equipment from the Zamindars of Agra, and, fixing their monthly pay, to send them to Parwīz in the Deccan, and 500,000 rupees more were fixed for the expenses of Parwīz. On Thursday, the 4th Shawwāl, Islām Khān was promoted to the rank of 5,000 personal and 5,000 horse, Abū-l-walī Beg Ūzbeg to that of 1,500 and Ẓafar Khān to that of 2,500. Two thousand rupees were given to Badī'u-z-zamān, son of Mīrzā Shāhrukh, and 1,000 rupees to Pathān Miṣr. I ordered that drums should be given to all of them as their rank had been raised to 3,000 and higher. Five thousand rupees more of the money from my weighing were entrusted for the construction of a bridge at Bābā Ḥasan Abdāl and the building that is there to Abū-l-wafā, son of Ḥakīm Abū-l-fatḥ, in order that he might exert himself and put the bridge and the aforesaid building in perfect order. On Saturday, the 13th, when four gharis of day were left, the moon began to be eclipsed. By degrees the whole of its body was obscured, and it continued till five gharis of night had passed. In order to avert the bad omen of this I had myself weighed against gold, silver, cloth, and grain, and gave away in alms all kinds of animals, such as elephants, horses, etc., the cost of all of which was 15,000 rupees. I ordered them to be distributed among the deserving and the poor. On the 25th, at the request of her father, I took the daughter of Rām Chand Bandīlah into my service (i.e. married her). I gave an elephant to Mīr Fāẓil, nephew of Mīr

Sharīf, who had been appointed to the faujdarship of Qabūlah and those regions. 'Ināyat-ullah was dignified with the title of 'Ināyat Khān. On Wednesday, the 1st Zī-l-qa'da, Bihārī Chand was granted the rank of 500 personal and 300 horse. A *khapwa* (dagger), adorned with jewels, was given to my son Bābā Khurram. Mullā Ḥayātī, by whom I had sent a message to the Khānkhānān, with a verbal message containing (expressions of) all kinds of condescension and affection, came and brought before me a ruby and two pearls of the value of about 20,000 rupees, which the Khānkhānān had sent by him. Mīr Jamālu-d-dīn Ḥusain, who was in Burhanpur and whom I had sent for, came and waited on me. I presented Shajā'at Khān Dakhanī with 2,000 rupees. On the 6th of the aforesaid month, before Parwīz arrived at Burhanpur, a petition came from the Khankhanan and the Amirs that the Dakhanis had assembled together and were making disturbances. When I discovered that, notwithstanding the nomination of Parwīz and the army that had proceeded with him and been appointed to his service, they were still in need of support and assistance, it occurred to me that I should go myself, and by Allah's favour satisfy myself with regard to that affair. In the meanwhile a petition came also from Āṣaf Khān that my coming there would be for the advantage of the daily-increasing State. A petition from 'Ādil Khān, from Bijapur, also came, that if one of the trusted ones of the Court could be appointed there to whom he could tell his desires and claims, so that the envoy might convey them to me, he hoped that it might become the means of affording profit to these slaves (i.e. himself). On this account I consulted with the Amirs and loyal men, and told them to represent whatever entered into anyone's mind. My son Khān Jahān represented that inasmuch as so many Amirs had been despatched for the conquest of the Deccan, it was not necessary for me to go in person. If he were ordered, he himself would go and attend on the prince and would, please God, perform this duty while serving him. Those words were approved of by all those who were loyal. I had never contemplated separation from him, but as the affair was an important one I necessarily gave him permission, and ordered that as soon as matters had been arranged he should return without delay, and should not remain more than a year in those regions. On Tuesday, the 17th Z̲ī-l-qa'da, he was free to go. I presented him with a special gold-embroidered robe of honour, a special horse with a jewelled saddle, a jewelled sword, and a special elephant. I also gave him a yak-tail standard (*tūmān ṭūg̲h̲*). I appointed Fidā K̲h̲ān, who was one of my faithful servants, and to whom I gave a robe of honour and a horse and his expenses, promoting him to the rank of 1,000 personal and 400 horse, original and extra, to go with K̲h̲ān Jahān, in order that if it were necessary to send anyone to 'Ādil K̲h̲ān according to his request, he might despatch him. Lankū Pandit, who in the time of the late king Akbar had come with offerings from 'Ādil K̲h̲ān, I also gave leave to go with K̲h̲ān Jahān, bestowing on him a horse, a robe of honour, and money. Of the Amirs and soldiers who had been appointed with 'Abdu-llah K̲h̲ān to the duty of beating back the Rānā, men such as Rāja Bīr Singh Deo, S̲h̲ajā'at K̲h̲ān, Rāja Bikramājīt, and others, with 4,000 or 5,000 horse, were nominated to support K̲h̲ān Jahān. I sent Mu'tamad K̲h̲ān with the announcement that I had made him a *sazāwal* (i.e. one who urges on others), and that he was to act along with K̲h̲ān Jahān in Ujjain. Out of the men of the palace, I sent 6,000 or 7,000 horse with him, such as Saif K̲h̲ān Bārha, Ḥājī Bī Ūzbeg, Salāmullah 'Arab, brother's son of Mubārak 'Arab, who had in his possession the province of Jūtra (?)[294] and Darfūl (?) and that neighbourhood, and other mansabdars and courtiers. At the time of giving them leave I gave each one an increase of rank and robe of honour and money for their expenses. Making Muḥammad Beg paymaster of the army, I provided him with 1,000,000 rupees to take with him. I sent to Parwīz a special

[294] See note above. Jūtra or Jotra is probably a mistake for the island of Johanna, i.e. Hinzuan. Darfūl is Dazfūl in I.O. MS. No. 181.

horse, and to the Khankhanan and other Amirs and officers who were appointed to that Subah dresses of honour.

After carrying out these matters I left the city for the purpose of hunting. One thousand rupees were given to Mīr 'Alī Akbar. As the Rabī' Faṣl (Spring season) had arrived, for fear any damage should happen to the cultivation of the ryots from the passage of the army, and notwithstanding that I had appointed a *qūrīsāwul*[295] (Erskine has Kor, the Yasawal) (probably a kind of provost marshal) with the band of ahadis for the purpose of guarding the fields, I ordered certain men to see what damage had been done to the crops from stage to stage and pay compensation to the ryots. I gave 10,000 rupees to the daughter of the Khankhanan, the wife of Dāniyāl, 1,000 rupees to 'Abdu-r-Raḥīm Khar (i.e. ass) for expenses, and 1,000 to Qāchā the Dakhani. On the 12th, Khānjar Khān, brother of 'Abdu-llah Khān, received the rank of 1,000 personal and 500 horse original and extra, and Bahādur Khān, another brother, that of 600 personal and 300 horse. On this day two antelopes with horns and one doe were taken. On the 13th I bestowed on and sent to Khān Jahān a special horse. Having promoted Badī'u-z-zamān, son of Mīrzā Shāhrukh, to the rank of 1,000 and 500 horse, I gave him 5,000 rupees for expenses, and he was sent off with Khān Jahān for service in the Deccan. On this day two male and three female antelope were killed. On Wednesday, the 10th, I killed a female *nīlgāw* and a black antelope with a gun, and on the 15th a female nilgaw and a *chikāra* (gazelle). On the 17th of the month two rubies and a pearl were brought to me by Jahāngīr Qulī Khān from Gujarat, as well as a jewelled opium box, which Muqarrab Khān had sent from the port of Cambay. On the 20th I killed with a gun a tigress and a nilgaw. There were two cubs with the tigress, but they disappeared from view in consequence of the thickness of the jungle and the number of trees. An order

[295] Possibly *Qūr Yasāwul* is right, but most probably it was a *yasāwul* attached to the *Qūr*, for which see Blochmann, p. 50.

was given that they should search for and bring them. When I reached the halting-place my son Khurram brought me one of the cubs, and the next day Mahābat Khān caught the other and brought it. On the 22nd, when I had got within shot of a nilgaw, suddenly a groom (*jilaudār*) and two *kahār* (bearers) appeared, and the nilgaw escaped. In a great rage I ordered them to kill the groom on the spot, and to hamstring[296] the kahars and mount them on asses and parade them through the camp, so that no one should again have the boldness to do such a thing. After this I mounted a horse and continued hunting with hawks and falcons, and came to the halting-place.

Next day, under the guidance of Iskandar Mu'īn, I shot a large nilgaw, and promoted him to the rank of 600 personal and 500 horse. On Friday, the 24th, Ṣafdar Khān, who had come from the Subah of Behar, had the good fortune to perform his obeisance to me. He presented as offerings a hundred muhrs, a sword, and five female and one male elephant. The male elephant was accepted. On the same day Yādgār Khwāja of Samarkand came from Balkh and paid his respects. He made offerings of an album, some horses, and other presents, and was dignified with a robe of honour. On Wednesday, 6th Zī-l-ḥijja, Mu'izzu-l-mulk, who had been removed from the pay-mastership of the army against the rebel Rānā, ill and miserable, waited on me. On the 14th of the said month, having pardoned all the faults of 'Abdu-r-Raḥīm Khar,[297] I promoted him to the rank of *yūzbāshī* (centurion) and 20 horse, and ordered him to go to Kashmir and in company with the bakhshi of that place hold a

[296] Jahāngīr's conduct was sufficiently brutal, but the text has made it worse than it was by omitting the word *pay* before *pāy*. The back tendons of the bearers' feet were cut. Their feet were not cut off. Erskine translates the passage rightly, and the I. O. MSS. agree with him.

[297] This was the same 'Abdu-r-Rahīm who was a companion of Khusrau, and after his capture was sweated in a skin. As he had life left in him he escaped from that destruction, and, on being released, became one of the personal servants, and served His Majesty till by degrees the latter became gracious to him. (Note of Sayyid Aḥmad.)

muster of the troops of Qilīj Khān and all the jagirdars and Uymaks in the service or not, and to bring the list. Kishwar Khān, son of Quṭbu-d-dīn Khān, came from the fort of Rohtas and had the good fortune to pay his respects to me.

THE FIFTH NEW YEAR'S FEAST FROM THE AUSPICIOUS ACCESSION.

On Sunday, the 24th Zī-l-ḥijja (20th March, 1610), after two watches and three gharis the sun entered into the constellation of Aries, which is the house of honour and good fortune, and at this auspicious hour the New Year's feast was arranged at Bāk Bhal, one of the villages of the parganah of Bārī, and according to the rules of my revered father I mounted the throne. On that morning, which was the New Year's Day that lighted up the world, and coincided with the 1st of Farwardīn of the 5th year from my accession, I held a public reception, and all the nobles and servants of the Court had the good fortune to pay their respects. Some of the nobles' offerings were laid before me. Khān A'ẓam gave a pearl worth 4,000 rupees ; Mīrān Ṣadr Jahān, twenty-eight hawks and falcons, and other gifts ; Mahābat Khān, two European boxes, the sides of which were made with slabs of glass, so that whatever was placed inside could be seen from outside in a way that you might say there was nothing between them ; Kishwar Khān, twenty-two male and female elephants. In the same way each of the servants of the Court laid before me the presents and offerings that they had. Naṣrullah, son of Faṭhu-llah sharbatchī (in charge of the *sharbat*), was placed in charge of the offerings. By Sārang Deo, who had been appointed to carry orders to the victorious army of the Deccan, I sent souvenirs (*tabarruk*) to Parwīz and to each of the officers. I presented Ḥusāmu-d-dīn, son of Ghāzī Khān[298] Badakhshī, who had taken to the ways of a dervish and seclusion, with 1,000

298 Ghāzī Khān was one of the famous officers of Akbar. Husām his son was married to Abū-l-fazl's sister. See Blochmann, p. 440.

rupees and a *fařjī* shawl. The day after the New Year's Day I mounted and started for a tiger-hunt. Two males and a female were killed. I gave rewards to the ahadis who had shown bravery and gone in to the tigers, and increased their monthly pay. On the 26th of the same month I went and busied myself mostly with hunting nilgaw. As the air was hot and the (propitious) hour for re-entering Agra had nearly arrived, I went to Rūpbās, and hunted antelope in that neighbourhood for some days. On Saturday, the 1st Muḥarram, 1019, Rūp Khawāṣṣ, who was the founder of Rūpbās, presented the offering that he had prepared. That which pleased was accepted and what remained was given him back as a reward. At the same time Bāyazīd Mankalī and his brothers, who had come from the Subah of Bengal, were honoured with paying their respects. Sayyid Ādam, son of Sayyid Qāsim Bārha, who had come from Ahmadabad, also had the same good fortune. He presented an elephant as an offering. The faujdarship of the Subah of Multan was given to Walī Bī Ūzbeg in place of Tāj Khān.

On Monday, the 3rd Muḥarram of the 5th year, I halted at the Mandākar Garden, which is in the neighbourhood of the city. On the morning on which was the auspicious hour of entry into the city, after a watch and two gharis had passed I mounted and rode on a horse to the beginning of the inhabited part, and when I came to the immediate neighbourhood mounted on an elephant, so that the people from far and near might see, and scattering money on both sides of the road, at the hour that the astrologers had chosen, after midday had passed, entered with congratulation and happiness the royal palace. In accordance with the usual custom of the New Year I had ordered them to decorate the palace, which is like the courts of heaven. After seeing the decorations, Khwāja Jahān laid before me the offering that he had prepared. Having accepted out of the ornaments and jewels, dresses and goods, whatever I approved of, I gave the rest as a reward to him. I had ordered the clerks of the hunting department to write out (a list of) all the animals that had been killed from the time of my leaving until I re-entered the city. At this time they represented that in 56 days 1,362 animals, quadrupeds, and birds had been killed ; the tigers were 7 in number; nilgaw, male and female, 70 ; black buck, 51; does and mountain goats and antelope (*rojh*), etc., 82 ; *kulang* (cranes), peacocks, *surkhāb*,[299] and other birds, 129; fish, 1,023. On Friday, the 7th, Muqarrab Khān came from the ports of Cambay and Surat, and had the honour of waiting on me. He had brought jewels and jewelled things, and vessels of gold and silver made in Europe, and other beautiful and uncommon presents, male and female Abyssinian slaves, Arab horses, and things of all kinds that came into his mind. Thus his presents were laid before me for two and a half months, and most of them were pleasing to me. On this day Ṣafdar Khān, who held the rank of 1,000 personal and 500 horse, had an increase of 500 personal and 200 horse, and was presented with a standard, and given leave to return to his former jagir. Standards were also given to Kishwar Khān and Farīdūn[300] Khān Barlās. A fighting elephant for Afẓal Khān (Abū-l-faẓl's son) was handed over to his son Bishūtan, to take to his father. I bestowed 1,000 rupees on Khwāja Ḥusain, a descendant of Khwāja Mu'īnu-d-dīn Chishtī, as was usual for the half-year. The Khankhanan had sent as an offering a "Yūsuf and Zulaikhā" in the handwriting of Mullā Mīr 'Alī,[301] with illustrations and in a beautiful gilt binding, worth 1,000 muhrs. This Ma'ṣūm, his Wakil, brought and submitted. Up to the day of culmination, which is the conclusion of the New Year's feast, every day many offerings were laid before me by the Amirs and servants of the Court. Whichever of the rarities was approved of by me I accepted, and gave back what was left.

299 Brahmini ducks.

300 A son of Akbar's officer, Muḥammad Qulī Barlās (Blochmann, pp. 342 and 478).

301 Mir 'Alī was a famous calligrapher. See Rieu, Cat., ii, 531. Can the copy mentioned by Jahāngīr be that in the Bodleian Library, which Sir W . Jones praised so highly ? A writer in the Journal of the Moslem Institute for January-March, 1907, p. 186, suggests that the copy is in the Bankipur Library.

On Thursday, the 13th, corresponding to the 19th Farwardīn, which is the day of culmination of the sun and of gladness and pleasure, I ordered them to prepare an entertainment of different kinds of intoxicating drinks, and an order was given to the Amirs and servants of the Court that everyone might choose the kind of drink he affected. Many took wine and some *mufarriḥ* (exhilarating drinks), whilst some ate what they wished of the preparations of opium. The assembly was successfully held. Jahāngīr Qulī Khān from Gujarat had sent as an offering a throne of silver, inlaid and painted, of a new fashion and shape, which was presented to me. A standard was also conferred on Mahā Singh. In the commencement of my reign I had repeatedly given orders that no one should make eunuchs or buy or sell them, and whoever did so would be answerable as a criminal. At this time Afẓal Khān sent some of these evildoers to Court from the Subah of Behar, who were continually perpetrating this vile offence. I ordered these unthinking ones (*bī-'āqibatān*) to be imprisoned for life.

On the night of the 12th an uncommon and strange event took place. Some Delhi singers (*Qawwālān,* see Jarrett, ii, 236) were singing songs in my presence, and Sayyidī[302] Shāh was, by way of buffoonery, mimicking a religious dance. This verse of Amīr Khusrau was the refrain (*miyān-khāna*) of the song—

> "Each nation has its right road of faith and its shrine (*qibla-gāhī*).
> I've set up my shrine (*qibla*) on the path of him with the cocked cap."

I asked what was the real meaning of the (last) hemistich. Mullā 'Alī Aḥmad,[303] the seal engraver, who in his own craft was one of the first of the age, and had the title of Khalīfa, and was an old servant, and with whose father I had learned when I was little, came forward and said, "I have heard from my father that

---

302 The Iqbāl-nāma, p. 41, has Shayyādī, 'a dervish, a hypocrite,' and the R.A.S. MS. has Sayyidī Shayyād. Shayyād is used at p. 60 to mean an impostor. Here, perhaps, it would mean a buffoon.

303 'Alī Ahmad's father was Shaikh Husain. See Blochmann, p. 53.

one day Shaikh Niẓāmu-d-dīn Auliyā had put his cap on the side of his head, and was sitting on a terraced roof by the bank of the Jumna and watching the devotions[304] of the Hindus. Just then Amīr Khusrau appeared, and the Shaikh turned to him and said, 'Do you see this crowd,' and then he recited this line:—

> 'Each race has its right road of faith and its shrine' (qibla-gāhī).

The Amīr, without hesitating, respectfully did homage to the Shaikh, and addressing him said—

> 'I've set up my shrine in the direction of him with the cocked cap.'"[305]

The aforesaid Mullā, when these words were uttered, and the last words of the second hemistich passed over his tongue, became senseless and fell down. Conceiving a great fear from his falling down, I went to his head. Most of those who were present doubted whether he had not had an epileptic fit. The physicians who were present distractedly made inquiry and felt his pulse and brought medicine. However much they beat their hands and feet and exerted themselves, he did not come to. Immediately he fell he had delivered his soul to the Creator. As his body was quite warm, they thought that possibly some life might be left in him. After a short time it became evident that the thing was all over and he was dead. They carried him away dead to his own house. I had never seen this kind of death, and sent money to his sons for his shroud and burial, and the next morning they sent him to Delhi and buried him in the burial-place of his ancestors.

On Friday, the 21st, Kishwar Khān, who held the rank of 1,500, was promoted to 2,000 personal and horse, and, having been presented with an Iraq horse out of my private stable, a

---

[304] It was the bathing of the Hindus that the saint was watching.

[305] The point of Amir Khusrau's hemistich is that *kaj-kulāh* literally means 'the awry cap,' and so refers to the saint, who had his cap on his ear or on the side of his head. But it also means one who is presumptuous, and has left the true path of religion. It also means, according to Steingass, a beloved person.

robe of honour and a private elephant, named Bakht-jīt,[306] and the Faujdarship of the country of Uch, was dismissed with a view to the punishment of the rebels of that region. Bāyazīd Mankalī, having been honoured with a robe and a horse, was sent off together with his brothers in the company of Kishwar Khān. An elephant from my private stud, by name 'Ālam-gumān, was entrusted to *Ḥabību*-llah for Rāja Mān Singh and sent. A special horse was sent to Bengal for Kesho Dās Mārū,[307] and a female elephant was now given to 'Arab Khān, the jagirdar of Jalalabad. At this time Iftikhār Khān had sent an offering of a rare elephant from Bengal. As I approved of it, it was entered among my private elephants. I raised the rank of Aḥmad[308] Beg Khān, who had been nominated to the command of the army of Bangash on account of his good service and that of his sons, from his original rank of 2,000 personal and 1,500 horse by 500 more personal. I sent a gold throne[309] of jewelled work for Parwīz, and a *sarpīch,* which was of rubies and pearls, and made at a cost of 2,000 rupees, was sent for Khān Jahān by the hand of Ḥabīb, son of Sarbarāh Khān, to Burhanpur. At this time it became known that Kaukab, son of Qamar Khān, had become intimate with a Sanyasi, and by degrees his words, which were all blasphemous and impious, made an impression on that foolish fellow. He had made 'Abdu-l-Laṭīf, son of Naqīb Khān, and Sharīf, his cousins, partners in that error. When this affair was discovered, with only a slight frightening they revealed certain circumstances with regard to themselves, the relation of which would be extremely disgusting. Considering their punishment advisable, I imprisoned Kaukab[310] and Sharīf

---

306 I.O. MS. 181 has *Takht-i-bakht* (Throne of fortune).

307 Kesho Dās was perhaps the father of Karamsī, one of Akbar's wives. See Blochmann, p. 310.

308 Blochmann, p. 465.

309 *Takhtī*, qu. a signet ?

310 Kaukab is mentioned again at the end of the twelfth year. For notice of his father see Blochmann, p. 485.

after giving them a whipping, and ordered 'Abdu-l-Laṯīf a hundred lashes in my presence. This special chastisement (was given) for the purpose of carrying out the Divine law in order that other ignorant persons might not be disposed towards the same actions. On Monday, the 24th, Mu'az̤z̤am K͟hān was despatched to Delhi to punish the rebels and disaffected of that neighbourhood. Two thousand rupees were given to S͟hajā'at K͟hān Dakhanī. I had ordered S͟haik͟h Ḥusain Dars͟hanī to proceed with certain firmans to Bengal and presents to each of the Amirs of that Subah. I now gave him his orders and despatched him. With an eye on his actions and his approved services, I promoted Islām K͟hān to the rank of 5,000 personal and horse, and bestowed on him a special dress of honour. I gave a special dress of honour also to Kis͟hwar K͟hān, and presented Rāja Kalyān with an Iraq horse, and similarly to the other Amirs there were given robes of honour or horses. Farīdūn Barlās, who held the rank of 1,500 personal and 1,300 horse, I promoted to 2,000 personal and 1,500 horse.

On the night of Monday, the 1st Ṣafar, through the carelessness of the servants, a great fire occurred in the house of K͟hwāja Abū-l-ḥasan, and before they became aware of it and the fire could be put out many of his properties were burnt. In order to afford consolation to the mind of the K͟hwāja and to make up for the loss he had sustained, I gave him 40,000 rupees. On Saif K͟hān Bārha, who had been cherished and brought up by me, I bestowed a standard. I increased the rank of Mu'izzu-l-mulk, who had been appointed to the Diwanship of Kabul, from his original of 1,000 personal and 225 horse by 200 personal and 275 horse, and dismissed him. The next day I sent a *phūl-kaṭāra* (dagger) studded with valuable jewels to Burhanpur to K͟hān Jahān.

A widow woman complained that Muqarrab K͟hān had taken her daughter by force in the port of Cambay, and after some while, during which he had kept her in his own house, when she enquired for the girl had said that she had died by an unavoidable death. I ordered an enquiry to be made into the affair. After much search I discovered that one of his attendants had been guilty of this outrage, and had him put to death, and reduced Muqarrab Khān's mansab by one half, and made an allowance to the woman who had been thus injured.

As on Sunday, the 7th of the month, a *qirān-i-naḥsīn* (an unlucky conjunction) had occurred, I gave alms of gold and silver and other metals, and different kinds of cereals, to faqirs and indigent people to be divided in most parts of the dominion. On the night of Monday, the 8th, having sent for Shaikh Ḥusain Sirhindī and Shaikh Muṣṭafā, who were celebrated for the adoption of the ways of dervishdom and the state of poverty, a party was held, and by degrees the assembly engaged warmly in *samā'* and *wajd* (dervish dancing and ecstasy). Hilarity and frenzy were not wanting. After the meeting was over I gave money to each and gave him leave. As Mīrzā Ghāzī Beg Tarkhān repeatedly made representations with regard to provisions for Qandahar and the monthly pay of the musketeers of the said fort, I ordered 200,000 rupees to be sent there from the treasury of Lahore.[311]

On the 19th Urdibihisht, in the fifth year of my reign, corresponding with the 4th Ṣafar, there occurred a strange affair at Patna, which is the seat of government of the province of Behar. Afẓal Khān, the governor of the Subah, went off to the jagir to which he had just been appointed, and which was at a distance of 60 kos from Patna, and handed over the fort and the city to the charge of Shaikh Banārasī and Ghiyāṣ Zain-khānī, the Diwan of the Subah, and to a number of other mansabdars. With the idea that there were no enemies in that region he did not satisfy himself as he should have with regard to the protection of the fort and city. By chance, at that time an unknown man of the

[311] Elliot, vi, 321.

name of Quṭb belonging to the people of Uch, who was a mischievous and seditious fellow, came to the province of Ujjainiyya,[312] which is in the neighbourhood of Patna, with the look of a dervish and the clothes of a beggar, and having made acquaintance with men of that part, who were always seditious, represented to them that he was Khusrau, who had escaped from prison and conveyed himself there ; saying that if they would accompany and assist him, after the affair had been completed they would be the ministers of his State. In short, deceiving those simpletons with foolish words he brought them over to him and persuaded them that he was Khusrau. He showed those deceived ones the parts about his eyes, where at some time he had produced scars, of which the marks were still apparent, and told them that in the prison they had fastened cups (*kaṭorī*) on them and those were the marks.[313] Through these falsehoods and deceit a number of foot- and horsemen had collected round him, and had obtained information that Afẓal Khān was not at Patna. Considering this a great opportunity, they made a raid, and when two or three hours of the day had passed on Sunday came to the city, and being hindered by nothing went for the fort. Shaikh Banārasī, who was in the fort, obtaining news of this, went in a disturbed state to the gate of

[312] Ujjainiyya here means Bhojpūr.

[313] Apparently we may infer from this that Jahāngīr did blind or attempt to blind his son Khusrau, though he says nothing about it. Else why should this impostor pretend that he had marks of the blinding? Tavernier says Khusrau was blinded. Du Jarric also tells us that Jahāngīr blinded Khusrau on his way back from Kabul, when he came to the place where Khusrau had fought the battle. He was blinded by some juice of a plant being poured into his eyes. The juice resembled milk (qu. *Euphorbia*). One of his captains, who was also a judge, was likewise blinded there along with his son. W. Finch, too, speaks of this outbreak. He also says that Khusrau was reported to have been blinded on the battlefield with a glass. Another story was that Jahāngīr merely caused a handkerchief to be tied over his eyes and had it sealed with his own seal. It is mentioned in Whiteway's "Rise of the Portuguese Power in India," p. 165, note, that fifteen relatives of the King of Ormuz had been blinded by red-hot bowls having been passed close to their eyes.

the fort. The enemy, who came on with speed, did not give him time to close the gate of the fort. Together with Ghiyāṣ, he betook himself to the side of the river by a wicket gate, and procuring a boat proposed to go to Afẓal Khān. Those rebels came with ease into the fort and took possession of Afẓal Khān's property and the royal treasury; and some of those wretched creatures who wait on events, who were in the city and its neighbourhood, joined them. This news reached Afẓal Khān at Gorakhpur (Kharakpūr),[314] and Shaikh Banārasī and Ghiyāṣ also came to him there by way of the river. Letters came from the city that this wretch, who called himself Khusrau, was in reality not Khusrau. Afẓal Khān, placing his trust on the grace and mercy of Allah, and through my good fortune, started without delay against those rebels. In five days he reached the neighbourhood of Patna. When the news of Afẓal Khān's coming reached those scoundrels, they entrusted the fort to one of those whom they had confidence in, and the horse and foot arraying themselves went out for four kos to meet Afẓal Khān. A fight took place on the bank of the river Pūn Pūn, and after a slight skirmish the array of those ill-fated ones was broken and they became scattered. In great bewilderment a second time that wretch was coming into the fort with a few men. Afẓal Khān followed him, and did not allow them to close the gate of the fort. Going to Afẓal Khān's house in a state of confusion, they fortified the house and remained there for three watches, and fought. They wounded about thirty people with arrows. After his companions had gone to *jahannam* (hell) he himself became helpless, and asked for quarter, and waited upon Afẓal Khān. In order to put a stop to this affair, Afẓal Khān executed him on the same day, and imprisoned some of his companions who had fallen alive

[314] Kharakpūr. The word is written Gorakhpur in some MSS., but I think it is clear that Kharakpūr is the place meant, for 'Abdu-r-Rahmān had lately got Sangrām's estate of Kharakpūr in jagir. The fact, too, that he fought with the impostor at the Pūn Pūn to the east of Patna shows that he was coming back from down the Ganges.

into his hand. These items of news one after another reached the royal ear. I summoned to Agra Shaikh Banārasī and Ghiyāṣ Zain-khānī and the other mansabdars who had made default in holding the fort and protecting the city, and ordered their hair and beards to be cut off, and that they should be clothed in women's clothes, seated on asses, and paraded round the city of Agra and in the bazars, as a warning and example to others.

At this time representations succeeded each other from Parwīz and the Amirs appointed to the Deccan and those who were well-wishers of the State, that 'Ādil Khān Bījāpūrī prayed that they would send to him Mīr Jamālu-d-dīn Ḥusain Injū, on whose words and acts all the rulers of the Deccan had great reliance, that he might associate himself with them and dispel the fear in their minds, and the affairs of that place might be arranged as it might seem proper to 'Ādil Khān, who had chosen the way of loyalty and service. In any case, he might drive out of their minds the fear that was in them, and soothing them might give him hopes of the royal favour. In order to obtain this end, on the 16th of the same month I despatched the above-mentioned Mīr, giving him a present of 10,000 rupees. I increased the former rank of Qāsim Khān, which was 1,000 personal and 500 horse, by 500 personal and horse, in order that he might go to the support of his brother Islām Khān in Bengal. At the same time, in order to punish Bikramājīt, Zamindar of the province Bāndhū,[315] who had withdrawn his foot from the circle of obedience and service, I appointed Mahā Singh, grandson of Rāja Mān Singh, to proceed to put down the disaffection in that region and at the same time administer the estate of the jagiṛ of the Raja, which was in that neighbourhood.

On the 20th of the month I gave an elephant to Shajā'at Khān Dakhanī. As the governor of Jalalabad had written and represented the ruinous state of the fort of that place, I ordered

[315] Text wrongly has Māndhū.

what might be required for the repair of the said fort to be taken from the treasury of Lahore. Iftikhār Khān had done approved service in Bengal. On the request of the governor of that Subah I increased his original rank, which was 1,500, by 500. On the 28th a representation came from 'Abdu-llah Khān Fīrūz-jang, containing recommendations in favour of some of the zealous servants who had been sent with him to subdue the rebel Rana. As Ghaznīn Khān Jālwarī had shown the greatest zeal of all in this service, I increased by 500 personal and 400 horse his former rank, which was 1,500 personal and 300 horse. In the same manner each one of those persons was promoted according to his services.

Daulat Khān, who had been sent to Allahabad to bring the throne of black stone, came on Wednesday, the 4th of the month of Mihr (15th September, 1610), and had an audience and brought the stone safe and sound. In truth it was a wonderful slab, very black and shining. Many say it is of a species of touchstone; in length it was one-eighth less than four cubits, and in breadth 2 1/2 cubits and one *tasū,*[316] whilst its thickness may be three *tasū.* I ordered stone-cutters to carve suitable couplets on the sides of it. They had attached feet to it of the same kind of stone. I often sat on that throne.

As the brothers of Khān 'Ālam became security for him, I brought out of prison 'Abdu-s-Subḥān Khān, who was in confinement for certain offences, and promoted him to the rank of 1,000 personal and 400 horse, and appointed him to the faujdarship of the Subah of Allahabad, and gave him the jagir of

---

[316] A *tasū,* or *ṭasū,* is said in Wilson's Glossary to be the 24th part of a gaz or about a third of an inch. I.O. MS. makes the breadth $3\frac{1}{2}$ cubits 1 tasū. The slab is described in Keene's Guide and in the N.W.P. Gazetteer, Agra volume. One inscription has the date 1011, or 1602. Archæological Report, Iv, pp. 132-5, says it is 10 ft. $7\frac{1}{2}$ ins. long, 9 ft. 10 ins. broad, and 6 inches thick. It is supported on octagonal pedestals. See also Beale's Miftāḥu-t-tawārīkh, pp. 300, 301, where a representation of the stone and copies of the inscriptions are given.

Qāsim Khān, the brother of Islām Khān. I sent Tarbiyat Khān to the faujdarship of the Sarkar of Alwar. On the 12th of the same month a representation arrived from Khān Jahān that the Khankhanan, according to my order, had started for the Court in company with Mahābat Khān, and that Mīr Jamālu-d-dīn Ḥusain, who had been nominated by the Court to go to Bijapur, had also gone from Burhanpur, together with the wakils of 'Ādil Khān, to Bijapur. On the 21st of the same month I promoted Murtaẓā Khān to the subadarship of the Panjab, which is one of the largest charges in my dominions, and gave him a special shawl. Having appointed Tāj Khān, who was in the Subah of Multan to the governorship of Kabul, I added 500 horse to the rank of 3,000 personal and 1,500 horse already held by him. At the request of 'Abdu-llah Khān Fīrūz-jang, the son of Rānā Shankar was also promoted in rank. When Mahābat Khān, who had been sent to Burhanpur to ascertain the numbers of the forces of the Amirs appointed to the Deccan, and to bring the Khankhanan, arrived in the neighbourhood of Agra, he left the Khankhanan some stages off the city and came on in front himself, and was honoured with the good fortune of paying his respects and kissing the threshold. After a few days, on the 12th Ābān, the Khankhanan came and waited on me. As many of those who were loyal had represented the state of his affairs whether true or false, according to their ideas, and I was displeased with him, because the degree of favour and regard that I previously had observed in his case and that I had seen in my revered father had not produced its effect, I did justice in the matter, for previously to this a letter of appointment to the service of the Deccan for a certain time had been given to him, and he had proceeded there in attendance on Sulṭān Parwīz with other nobles for that important matter. After he arrived at Burhanpur he had not looked to the opportuneness of the time, and at an improper season for moving, and when forage and other necessaries had not been laid in, he had taken Sulṭān Parwīz and his forces above the Ghats, and by degrees, in consequence of want of concert among the Sardars and his treachery, and of conflicting opinions, things had come to such a pass that grain was obtained with difficulty, and not a *mān* was to be got for large sums of money. The affairs of the army became so confused that nothing went on properly, and horses, camels, and other four-footed beasts died. In consequence of the exigency of the time he had patched up a kind of peace with the enemy and withdrawn Sulṭān Parwīz and the army to Burhanpur. As this business did not turn out well, all the well-wishers of the State knew that this division (of counsels) and confusion had arisen from treachery and want of arrangement of the Khankhanan, and represented this to the Court. Although this appeared altogether incredible, at last this impression was left upon my mind, and a representation came from K͟hān Jahān to the effect that all this mischief and confusion had arisen through the treachery of the Khankhanan; either this service should be left entirely in his control, or, summoning him to Court, I should appoint to this duty this man whom I had myself cherished and brought up, and appoint 30,000 horse to support this slave (K͟hān Jahān himself), in order that in the space of two years, having freed the whole of the royal province, now in the possession of the enemy, and having brought the fort of Qandahar[317] and other forts on the border into the occupation of the servants of the Court, he should include in the royal dominions the province of Bijapur. If he did not complete this service in that time, he might be debarred from the good fortune of paying his respects (to me) and would not show his face to the servants of the Court. When the relations between the Sardars and the Khankhanan reached this point, I did not consider it advisable for him to be there any longer, and handed over the command to K͟hān Jahān and sent for him to Court. In reality the cause of my disinclination and want of favour to him was this.

[317] A fort in the Deccan "sixty miles north of Bidar" (Elliot, vi, 70).

The degree of inclination and disinclination towards him in future will be in accordance with whatever may become clear.

I favoured and promoted Sayyid 'Alī Bārha, who is one of our distinguished young men, with an increase of 500 personal and 200 horse beyond his previous rank, which was 1,000 personal and 500 horse, and gave Dārāb Khān, son of the Khankhanan, the rank of 1,000 personal and 500 horse, with the Sarkar of Ghazipur as his jagir. Previously to this I had had the daughter of Mīrzā Muẓaffar Ḥusain, son of Sulṭān Ḥusain Mīrzā Ṣafawī, ruler of Qandahar, betrothed to my son Sulṭān Khurram, and on this date, the 17th Ābān, as the marriage meeting had been arranged, I went to the house of Bābā Khurram and passed the night there. I presented most of the Amirs with robes of honour. Some of those confined in the fort of Gwalior I released, and especially Ḥājī Mirak. Islām Khān had collected 100,000 rupees from the *khāliṣa* (directly managed) parganahs. As he was at the head of the army and the service, I handed this over to him as a present. Giving a little gold and silver and some of every kind of jewellery and grain to trustworthy men, I determined that they should distribute them to the poor of Agra. On the same day a report came from Khān Jahān that Īraj, the son of the Khankhanan, had obtained leave from the prince, and according to orders he had despatched him to Court. With regard to what had been ordered in the case of Abū-l-fatḥ, of Bijapur, is the above-mentioned was an experienced man, and his being sent would cause despair to the other Sardars of the Deccan to whom promises had been made, he had (therefore) kept him under surveillance.[318] An order had been sent that as Kesho Dās, the son of Rāy Kalah (?), was in the service of Parwīz, if any impediment should occur in sending him, he (Khān Jahān) should despatch him whether he wished it or not.

---

318 So in MSS. Apparently Khān Jahān's meaning was that if this Deccani man were sent to Agra (as if to be punished) the other Deccani leaders would be discouraged.

Immediately on this becoming known to Parwīz, he gave him leave and said to Khān Jahān; "These few words from my mouth thou wilt represent, that as I would give my existence and life for the service of my visible God (Jahāngīr), what is there in the being or annihilation of Kesho Dās[319] that I should show any resistance in sending him? When they (i.e. the king) send for my confidential servants for any reason it produces a feeling of hopelessness and disquietude of mind in the rest, and becoming known in these regions gives an idea of disfavour on the part of our lord and Qibla (place looked towards in worship). As for the rest, it is His Majesty's order." From the date on which the fort of Ahmadnagar, by the efforts of my deceased brother Dāniyāl, came into the possession of the heads of the victorious State, up till now, the guardianship and preservation of that place had been entrusted to Khwāja Beg Mīrzā Ṣafawī, who was a relative of the asylum of pardon Shāh Ṭahmāsp. After the disturbance of the rebel Deccanis went to a great length, and they besieged the said fort, he had committed no fault in the duties of devotedness and holding of the fort. When the Khankhanan and the Amirs and other leaders who had assembled at Burhanpur in waiting on Parwīz devoted themselves to the driving back and defeat of the rebels, and from the differences of opinion and quarrels of the Amirs, and the absence of provision of forage and grain, those who looked after matters of importance brought this large army into improper roads and among hills and difficult passes, they in a short space of time rendered it wretched and impotent, and matters had come to such a pass and the difficulty with regard to grain was such that they were giving a life for a loaf. They then turned back helplessly with their objects unfulfilled. The garrison of the fort, who were expecting aid from this army, on hearing this news, lost heart and stability, and tumultuously wished to vacate the fort at once. When Khwāja Beg Mīrzā

[319] The text seems corrupt. Apparently I.O. MS. has Sargala, and this may have been Kesho Dās's title.

became aware of this he endeavoured to soothe and quiet the men, but though he did his best it had no good result. At last, under an agreement, he vacated the fort, and proceeded to Burhanpur, and on the day mentioned waited on the prince. Representations with regard to his coming reached me, and, as it was clear that he had not been wanting in bravery and loyalty, I ordered his rank of 5,000 personal and horse to be confirmed and a jagir to be given him. On the 9th a petition came from some of the Amirs in the Deccan that on the 22nd Sha'bān Mīr Jamālu-d-dīn Ḥusain had gone to Bijapur. 'Ādil Khān sent his wakil forward for 20 kos, and himself received him at a distance of 3 kos, and took the Mīr by the same road to his own residence.

As the desire to hunt overcame me, at a propitious hour determined by the astrologers, when a watch and six gharis had passed on the night of Friday, the 15th Ramaẓān, corresponding with the 10th Āzar in the 5th year (of my reign), I started to hunt, and made my first halt in the Dahrah Garden, which is near the city. At this stage I gave Mīr 'Alī Akbar leave to go into the city after bestowing on him 2,000 rupees and a special warm wrapper (*fargul*). In order that the grain and cultivation should not be trodden down by my men I ordered that all should remain in the city but the men who were actually wanted and my personal servants. Having entrusted the charge of the city to Khwāja Jahān I gave him his leave. On the 14th Sa'du-llah Khān, son of Sa'īd Khān, was given an elephant. On the 28th, corresponding with the 21st Ramaẓān, forty-four elephants, which Hāshim Khān, son of Qāsim Khān, had sent as an offering from Orissa, were produced before me. Of these one was very good and tame; this one I put in my private stud. On the 28th an eclipse (of the sun, *kusūf*) took place, in order to do away with the unluckiness of which I weighed myself against gold and silver ; it came to 1,800 tolas of gold and 4,900 rupees. This, along with several kinds of vegetables and sorts of animals such as elephants and horses and cattle, I ordered to be divided among deserving people who were unprovided for and helpless poor of the city of Agra and other cities in the neighbourhood.

As the affairs of the army which had been nominated for the subjugation of the Deccan under the command of Parwīz, and leadership of the Khankhanan and other high Amirs such as Rāja Mān Singh, Khān Jahān, Āṣaf Khān, the Amīru-l-umarā, and other mansabdars, and other leaders of every tribe and condition, had ended in this, that they had turned back from half-way and returned to Burhanpur, and all the confidential servants and news-writers who spoke the truth had sent in reports to the Court, that although there were many causes for the ruin of this army, yet the chief reason was the disagreement of the Amirs, especially the treachery of the Khankhanan, it came into my mind that I must send Khān A'z̤am with another fresh and powerful army to make amends for and set to rights some of the improper proceedings that had arisen from the disagreement of the Amirs that has been described. On the 11th of Day he (Khān A'z̤am) was honoured with the charge of this duty, and an order was given to the Diwans to make preparations and send him off quickly. I appointed Khān 'Ālam, Farīdūn Khān Barlās, Yūsuf Khān, son of Ḥusain Khān Tukriyah, 'Alī Khān Niyāzī, Bāz Bahādur Qalmāq, and other mansabdars, near to the number of 10,000 horse, to accompany him. It was settled that in addition to the ahadis who were appointed to this duty 2,000 others should accompany him, making altogether 12,000 horse. Having sent with him thirty lakhs of rupees and several elephants, I gave him his leave and presented him with a magnificent dress of honour, a jewelled sword-belt, a horse with a jewelled saddle, a private elephant, and 500,000 rupees for expenses. An order was given that the chiefs of the civil department should recover this from his jagir. The Amirs who were under his orders were honoured with robes of honour, horses, and presents. I increased by 500 more horse the rank held by Mahābat Khān, of 4,000 personal and 3,000 horse, and ordered him to conduct Khān A'ẓam and this army to Burhanpur, and having enquired into (the circumstances of) the destruction of the army, should give the order of the appointment of the Khān A'ẓam to the Amirs of those regions and make them of one purpose and counsel with him. He was to see the state of preparation of the army of those parts, and after arranging all matters should bring the Khankhanan with him to Court. On Sunday, the 4th Shawwal, when near the end of the day, I engaged in a cheetah hunt. I had determined that on this day and Thursdays no animals should be killed and I would eat no meat, on Sunday especially because of the respect my revered father had for that day in not being inclined to eat flesh on it, and in forbidding the killing of any animals for the reason that on the night of Sunday his own honoured birth had taken place. He used to say it was better on that day that all animals should be free from the calamity of those of a butcherly disposition. Thursday is the day of my accession. On that day also I ordered that animals should not be killed, so that whilst sporting I should not shoot an arrow or a gun at wild animals. In hunting with cheetahs Anūp Rāy, who is one of my close attendants, was heading the men who were with him in the hunt at a little distance[320] from me and came to a tree on which some kites were sitting. When his sight fell on those kites he took a bow and some pointless arrows (*tukkā*) and went towards them. By chance in the neighbourhood of that tree he saw a half-eaten bullock. Near it a huge, powerful tiger got up out of a clump that was near and went off. Though not more than two gharis of day remained, as he knew my liking for tiger-hunting, he and some of those who were with him surrounded the tiger and sent some one to me to give me the news. When it reached me I rode there at once in a state of excitement and at full speed, and Bābā Khurram, Rām Dās, I'timād Rāy, Ḥayāt Khān, and one or two

320 *Pāra dūrtar*, but it would seem from the Ma'āṣir, ii, 231, five lines from foot, that *pāra*, or *bāra*, is a word meaning a body of men. Perhaps it is *bārah*, ' twelve.

others went with me. On arriving I saw the tiger standing in the shade of a tree, and wished to fire at him from horseback, but found that my horse was unsteady, and dismounted and aimed and fired my gun. As I was standing on a height and the tiger below, I did not know whether it had struck him or not. In a moment of excitement I fired the gun again, and I think that this time I hit him. The tiger rose and charged, and wounding the chief huntsman, who had a falcon on his wrist and happened to be in front of him, sat down again in his own place. In this state of affairs, placing another gun on a tripod,[321] I took aim (*majrā*[322] *giriftam*). Anūp Rāy stood holding the rest, and had a sword in his belt and a baṭon (*kutaka*) in his hand. Bābā Khurram was a short distance off to my left, and Rām Dās and other servants behind him. Kamāl the huntsman (*qarāwul*) loaded the gun and placed it in my hand. When I was about to fire, the tiger came roaring towards us and charged. I immediately fired. The ball passed through the tiger's mouth and teeth. The noise of the gun made him very savage, and the servants who had crowded together could not stand his charge and fell over one another, so that I, through their pushing and shock, was moved a couple of paces from my place and fell down. In fact, I am sure that two or three of them placed their feet on my chest and passed over me. I'timād Rāy and the huntsman Kamāl assisting me, I stood up. At this moment the tiger made for those who were on the left-hand side. Anūp Rāy let the rest slip out of his hand and turned towards the tiger. The tiger, with the same activity with which he had charged, turned on him, and he manfully faced him, and struck him twice with both hands on the head with the stick he had in his hand. The tiger, opening his mouth, seized both of

---

[321] At p. 256 we have the phrase *majrā gīrand* applied to the directing of cannon against the buildings of Fort Ranthambhor. I confess that I do not know whether Jahāngīr fired the gun that was on the stand or the one that Kamāl loaded.

[322] *Majrā giriftam* seems rather to mean here 'adjusted the tripod,' for from what follows it appears that the gun was not then loaded. The Iqbāl-nāma, p. 47, has *māsha rā zīr kard*, 'applied the match ' (?).

Anūp Rāy's arms with it, and bit them so that his teeth passed through both, but the stick and the bracelets on his arms were helpful, and did not allow his arms to be destroyed. From the attack and pushing of the tiger Anūp Rāy fell down between the tiger's fore-feet, so that his head and face were opposite the tiger's chest. At this moment Bābā Khurram and Rām Dās came up to the assistance of Anūp Rāy. The prince struck the tiger on the loins with his sword, and Rām Dās also struck him twice with his sword, once on the shoulder-blade. On the whole it was very warm work, and Ḥayāt Khān struck the tiger several blows over the head with a stick he had in his hand. Anūp Rāy with force dragged his arms out of the tiger's mouth and struck him two or three times on the cheek with his fist, and rolling over on his side stood up by the force of his knees. At the time of withdrawing his arms from the tiger's mouth, as his teeth had passed through them, they were partly torn, and both his paws passed over his shoulders. When he stood up, the tiger also stood up and wounded him on the chest with his claws, so that those wounds troubled him for some days. As the ground was uneven, they rolled over each other, holding on like two wrestlers. In the place where I was standing the ground was quite level. Anūp Rāy says that God Almighty gave him so much intelligence that he bore the tiger over deliberately to[323] one side (in the original, that side), and that he knew no more. At this time the tiger left him and was making off. He in that state of bewilderment raised up his sword and followed him and struck him on the head. When the tiger turned his face round, he struck him another blow on the face, so that both his eyes were cut, and the skin of the eyebrows, which had been severed by the sword, fell over his eyes. In this state of affairs, a lamp-man of the name of Ṣāliḥ, as it was time to light the lamps, came in a

[323] Apparently the meaning is that he rolled the tiger over to the side furthest from Jahāngīr.

hurry and by a blind chance[324] came across the tiger. The tiger struck him one blow with his paw and knocked him down. To fall and give up his life were the same thing. Other people came in and finished the tiger's business. As Anūp Rāy had done this service to me and I had witnessed the way in which he offered his life, after he had recovered from the pain of his wounds and had the honour of waiting on me, I bestowed on him the title of Anīrā'ī Singh-dalan. Anīrā'ī[325] they call in the Hindi language the leader of an army, and the meaning of Singh-dalan is a tiger-slayer. Giving him a special sword of my own, I increased his mansab. I gave Khurram, son of Khān A'z̤am, who had been appointed to the governorship of the province of Junagadh, the title of Kāmil Khān. On Sunday, the 3rd Zī-l-qa'da, I employed myself in fishing, and 766 fish were caught; these were divided in my presence among the Amirs, *Ibachkiān* (?),[326] and most of the servants. I eat no fish but those that have scales, but not because the professors of the Shiah faith look on those without scales as unlawful, but the cause of my aversion is this, that I have heard from old men, and it has become known to me by experience as well, that fish without scales eat the flesh of dead animals and fish with scales do not eat it. From this cause, to eat them is contrary to my disposition. The Shiahs know[327] why they do not eat them and for what reason they consider them unlawful. One of my home-bred camels that was with me in the hunt carried five nilgaws that weighed 42 Hindustani maunds. I had before this sent for Naz̤īrī of Nīshāpūr, who excelled other men in the art of poetry, and passed his time in Gujarat as a merchant. At

---

324 *Kūragī*. The Iqbāl-nāma, p. 48, says the night was dark, and so the lamplighter blindly (*az kūragī*) fell upon the tiger and was killed. This tiger hunt and Jahāngīr's danger, etc., are described by William Finch (Purchas, i, 430).

325 Anīkini means an army in Sanskrit and Rai is a title meaning leadership.

326 Text, *Zangchiyān* (?). I.O. 181 has *Ibachkiyān*, i.e. people of the *Ibachkī-khāna* or closet. See Āyīn, Persian text, i, 42, and Blochmann, i, 46.

327 This is said ironically.

this time he came and waited on me, and imitating a poem of Anwarī,

> "Again, what youth and beauty this is for the world!"

laid before me a poem that he had composed on me. I presented him with 1,000 rupees, a horse, and a robe of honour as a gift for this poem. I had also sent for Ḥakīm Ḥamīd Gujarātī, whom Murtaẓā Khān greatly praised, and he came and waited on me. His good qualities and purity were better than his doctoring. He waited on me for some time. When it became known that there was no physician but himself in Gujarat, and I found he himself desired leave to go, I gave him and his sons 1,000 rupees and some shawls, and set aside a whole village for his maintenance; he went off to his native place quite happy. Yūsuf Khān, son of Ḥusain Khān Tukriyah, came from his jagir and waited on me. On Thursday, the 10th Zī-l-ḥijja, was the festival of the Qurbān (the sacrifice of Ishmael). As it is forbidden to take life on that day (Thursday), I ordered that on the Friday they should kill the sacrificial animals. Having sacrificed three sheep with my own hand, I mounted to go hunting, and returned when six gharis of night had passed. On this day was killed a nilgaw (commonly called blue bull) of the weight of 9 maunds and 35 seers. The story of this nilgaw is written because it is not devoid of strangeness. In the two past years, during which I had come to this same place to wander about and hunt I had shot at him each time with a gun. As the wounds were not in a fatal place, he had not fallen, but gone off. This time again I saw that nilgaw in the hunting-ground (*shikārgāh*), and the watchman recognized that in the two previous years he had gone away wounded. In short, I fired at him again three times on that day. It was in vain. I pursued him rapidly on foot for three kos, but however much I exerted myself I could not catch him. At last I made a vow that if this nilgaw fell I would have his flesh cooked, and for the soul of Khwāja Mu'īnu-d-dīn would give it to eat to poor people. I also vowed a muhr and one rupee to my revered father. Soon after this the nilgaw became worn out with moving, and I ran to his head and ordered them to make it lawful (cut its throat in the name of Allah) on the spot, and having brought it to the camp I fulfilled my vow as I had proposed. They cooked the nilgaw, and expending the muhr and rupee on sweets, I assembled poor and hungry people and divided them among them in my own presence. Two or three days afterwards I saw another nilgaw. However much I exerted myself and wished he would stand still in one place, so that I might fire at him, I could get no chance. With my gun on my shoulder I followed him till near evening until it was sunset, and despaired of killing him. Suddenly it came across my tongue, "Khwāja, this nilgaw also is vowed to you." My speaking and his sitting down were at one and the same moment. I fired at and hit him, and ordered him, like the first nilgaw, to be cooked and given to the poor to eat. On Saturday, the 19th Zī-l-ḥijja, I fished again. This time about 330 fish were caught. On the night of Wednesday, the 28th[328] of the same month, I encamped at Rūpbās. As this was one of my fixed hunting-places and there was an order that no one should hunt in the neighbourhood, a great number of antelope had come together in the desert there, so much so that they came into the inhabited parts and were not subject to any kind of molestation. I hunted for two or three days in those desert plains, and shot, and hunted with cheetahs many antelopes. As the hour for entering the city was near, making two halts on the way, I alighted on the night of Thursday, the 2nd Muḥarram, in the year 1020 (17th March, 1611), at the garden of 'Abdu-r-Razzāq Ma'mūrī, which is near, in fact close to, the city. On this night many of the servants of the Court, such as Khwāja Jahān, Daulat Khān, and a number who had remained in the city, came and waited on me. Īraj also, whom I had sent for from the Subah of the Deccan, had the honour of kissing the threshold. I stayed in that garden also on the Friday. On that day 'Abdu-r-Razzāq

---

[328] The text has 14th night, but I follow the I.O. MS. 181.

presented his own offerings. As this was the last day for hunting, an order was given that the duration of the hunt and the number of animals killed should be counted up to me. The time of the hunt was from the 9th of the month of Āẕar to the 29th Isfandārmuẕ of the 5th year, or three months and twenty days. In this time tigers 12, deer (*gāwzan*) 1, *chikārah* (gazelle) 44, *kūtāh-pācha* (hog-deer) 1 head, fawns 2 head, black buck 68 head, does 31 head, foxes 4, *kūrāra* deer 8, *pātal* (?) 1, bears 5, hyænas 3, hares 6, nilgaw 108, fish 1,096, eagle 1, bustard 1, peafowl 5, herons 5, partridges 5, brahminī ducks (*surḵẖāb*) 1, *sāras* 5, *dhīk* (?) 1; total, 1,414.

On Saturday, the 29th Isfandārmuẕ, corresponding to the 4th Muḥarram, I mounted an elephant and went to the city. From the garden of 'Abdu-r-Razzāq to the palace the distance is a kos and 20 *tanāb*. I scattered 1,500 rupees to the crowd. At the fixed hour I entered the palace. The bazars had been decorated with cloths after the manner of the New Year's feast. As at the hunting-time an order had been given to Ḵẖwāja Jahān to prepare in the *Maḥall* (Zenanah) a building fit for me to sit in, the said Ḵẖwāja had in the space of three months prepared and brought to perfection this kind of lofty building, and with folded hands (in humility) had done exceedingly active work. Coming off the dust of the road I entered that Paradise-like building and went to look round that abode, and it was very much to my taste. Ḵẖwāja Jahān was dignified with much praise and commendation. The offerings he had prepared were displayed to me in the same building. Some of these were approved and accepted and the remainder presented to him.

THE SIXTH NEW YEAR'S FEAST AFTER MY AUSPICIOUS ACCESSION.

Two gharis and forty seconds of day had passed on the Monday when the sun (lit. his honour the greatest star) entered his tower of honour, which is in the constellation of Aries. That day was the 1st Farwardīn, corresponding with the 6th Muḥarram[329] (21st March, 1611). The feast of the New Year having been prepared, I seated myself on the throne of good fortune. The Amirs and all the servants of the Court enjoyed the good fortune of waiting on me, and gave their congratulations. The offerings of the servants of the Court Mīrān Ṣadr Jahān, 'Abdu-llah Khān Fīrūz-jang, and Jahāngīr Qulī Khān, were laid before me. On Wednesday, the 8th Muḥarram, the offering of Rāja Kalyān, who had sent it from Bengal, was laid before me. On Thursday, the 9th of the same month, Shajā'at Khān and some of the mansabdars, who had come on summons from the Deccan, waited on me. I gave a jewelled waist-dagger to Razzāq-wirdī Ūzbeg. On the same day the New Year's offering of Murtaẓā Khān was laid before me. He had prepared all kinds of things. Having inspected all these, I took what I approved in the shape of valuable jewels, fine cloths, elephants, and horses, and gave back the rest. I presented a jewelled dagger to Abū-l-fatḥ Dakhanī, 3,000 rupees to Mīr 'Abdu-llah, and an Iraq horse to Muqīm Khān. I increased the rank of Shajā'at Khān, which was 1,500 personal and 100 horse, by 500 personal and horse. I had summoned him from the Deccan for the purpose of sending him to Bengal to Islām Khān, in reality to take his place permanently, and I entrusted him with the charge of that Subah. Khwāja Abū-l-ḥasan laid before me (as offerings) two rubies, one royal pearl, and ten rings. I gave Īraj, the son of Khānkhānān, a jewelled dagger. The rank of Khurram was 8,000 personal and 5,000 horse; I increased his personal allowance by 2,000, and increased that of Khwāja Jahān, which was 1,500 personal, 1,000 horse by

---

[329] Jahāngīr does not mention that it was in this year that he married Nūr-Jahān. He saw her on New Year's Day (Iqbāl nāma, p. 56), and it appears from a note of Jahāngīr on p. 132 of B.M. MS. Or. 3276 that he married her on 14th Khurdād (end of May, 1611). It was in the 11th year that she got the title of Nūr-Jahān. Before that she was known as Nūr-Maḥall. It would seem that Jahāngīr married Nūr-Jahān four years and a few days after her first husband's death.

500 personal, 200 horse. On 24th Muḥarram, 18th Farwardīn, the day of the ascendant, Yādgār 'Alī Sulṯān, ambassador of S͟hāh 'Abbās, ruler of Persia, who had come on a visit of condolence on the death of the late king and with congratulations on my accession, had the honour of waiting on me, and laid before me the gifts S͟hāh 'Abbās, my brother, had sent. He had brought good horses, cloth stuffs, and every kind of fitting present. After he had presented the gifts, on the same day I gave him a superb robe of honour and 30,000 rupees, which were equivalent to 1,000 Persian tumans. He handed me a letter in which were mingled congratulations and condolences for the death of my revered father. As in the letter of congratulation he expressed the greatest friendship, and omitted no point of regard and concord, it has pleased me to enter here an exact copy of it.

Copy of the letter of S͟hāh 'Abbās.

"May the sprinklings of the cloud of the grace of God and the dropping of the favour of the Almighty impart freshness to the gardens of wonderful men and inventors (of new things) ! May the flower-bed of sovereignty and rule and the mead of magnificence and exalted happiness of his Honour of heavenly dignity, of sun-like grandeur, the king whose fortune is young, of Saturn-like majesty, the renowned prince, possessing the authority of the spheres, the Khedive, the world-gripper (Jahāngīr) and country-conquering sovereign, the prince of the exaltedness of Sikandar, with the banner of Darius, he who sits on the throne of the pavilion of greatness and glory, the possessor of the (seven) climes, the increaser of the joys of good fortune and prosperity, adorner of the gardens of happiness, decorator of the rose-parterre, lord of the happy conjunction (of the planets), the opener of the countenance, the perfection of kinghood, expounder of the mysteries of the sky, the adornment of the face of learning and insight, index of the book of creation, compendium of human perfections, mirror of the glory of God, elevator of the lofty soul, increaser of good fortune and of the beneficent ascension, sun of the grandeur of the skies, the shadow of the benignity of the Creator, he who has the dignity of Jamshīd among the stars of the host of heaven, lord of conjunction, refuge of the world, river of the favours of Allah, and fountain of unending mercy, verdure of the plain of purity, may his land (lit. surface) be guarded from the calamity of the evil eye ; may his fountain of perfection be preserved in truth, his desire and love ; the tale of his good qualities and benevolence cannot be written.

"'The pen has not the tongue to express the secret of love.'

Although outwardly the distance (between us) prevents my attaining to the *ka'bah* of desire, yet he is the *qiblah* of my keen longing for spiritual intercourse. Thank God that by virtue of essential oneness this humble supplicant and that pure nursling of glory have in reality been united to one another. The distance of space and outward separation of the body not having prevented nearness of soul and spiritual union, my face is still towards friendship, and accordingly the dust of sorrow has not settled on the sunlike mirror of my mind, but it has received the reflection of the beauty of that exhibitor of perfection, and the olfactory of my soul has been ever scented with the sweet savour of friendship and love and the ambergris-perfumed breezes of affection and concord, and spiritual fellowship and perpetual union have rubbed off the rust from friendship.

"I sit beside thee in thought, and my heart is at ease,
For this is an union not followed by separation's pain.'

"Praise be given to the most mighty and pure God that the plant of the desire of true friends hath borne the fruit of fruition. Success (*maqṣūd*), that beauty who for years was hidden behind the veil, has by dint of humility and supplication at the throne of the Almighty, come forth and manifested herself from the hidden bridal chamber, and a ray of perfection has been thrown on the plain of the hopes of the expectants; she has ascended the auspicious throne and seated herself beside the king who adorns the assembly and enhances the glory of the tribune of the king of kings. The world-opening standard of the Caliphate and rule, and the sky-scraping umbrella of justice and world-sway of that creator of the diadem and throne, and that opener of the knots of knowledge and wisdom have cast the shade of equity and sovereignty and mercy over the heads of the inhabitants of the world. My hope is that the chief of desire-granters may make the auspicious ascension of that blessed rising of fortune brighten the crown and illuminate the throne, making it of good omen and prosperous to all, and may the things that appertain to kingship and rule of the world and the causes of dignity and prosperity be ever on the increase ! For long past the customs of amity and the ways of intimacy, which have been in existence between our ancestors, and now freshly have been re-established between this one who is bent on friendship and him who is intent on equity, demanded that when the good news of the accession of him who sits on the Gūrgānī throne and is the heir of the crown of Tīmūr reached this country, one of the confidants of the royal palace should be quickly nominated to convey congratulations, but inasmuch as the business of Āẕarbījān and the conquest of the province of Shirwān just then occurred, and until my loving mind was satisfied as to the affairs of that province, I could not return to my capital, some delay took place in the accomplishment of this important duty. Although outward ceremonial observances and politenesses have not much weight with people of knowledge and discernment, yet the observance of them is the observance of the dues of friendship. Of necessity, therefore, at this auspicious time when the attention of the servants of holy angels (?) has been withdrawn from the affairs of that province, which have been arranged in accordance with the desires of my well-wishers, and I am at ease in that quarter, I have returned and settled down in my capital of Isfahan, which is the permanent seat of rule. Therefore I have despatched Kamālu-d-dīn Yādgār 'Alī, who possesses the attributes of nobility, is perfect in sincerity and fully reliable, who is moreover of the number of devoted servants and Ṣūfīs of pure design of our family, to the most exalted Court, that after he has obtained the good fortune to salute you, to condole with you, and kissed the carpet of honour, and performed the dues of inquiry (after health, etc.) and congratulations, he may obtain leave to return, and may convey to the sincere mind of your well-wisher the good tidings of the safety of your angelic person and the health of your temperament that is of the brightness of the sun and increases joy. It is hoped that the tree of hereditary friendship and assiduousness, and the garden of intimacy and regard, both apparent and spiritual, which by the irrigation of the rivers of affection and the brooks of sincere regard acquire great splendour and greenness, not casting their leaves, may set in motion the cord of intimacy and drive away the misfortune of estrangement by the arrival of correspondence, which is the communication of the soul, and may connect by spiritual chains our visible friendship, and may favour the course and accomplishment of business.

" May God Almighty give the assistance of the secret powers to that living family of dignity and glory and that household of grandeur and good fortune."

Up to this is the copy of the letter of my brother Shāh 'Abbās.

My brothers Sulṭān Murād and Dāniyāl, who had died in the lifetime of my revered father, people had called by several names. I ordered that one of them should be called Shāhzāda maghfūr (the pardoned prince), and the other Shāhzāda marḥūm (the prince admitted to mercy). I promoted I'timādu-d-daulah and 'Abdu-r-Razzāq Ma'mūrī, who each held the rank of 1,500, to that of 1,800, and increased the horse-rank of Qāsim Khān, brother of Islām Kkankhanan, by 250. I dignified Īraj, eldest son of the Khankhanan, with the title of Shāh-nawāz Khān, and Sa'du-llah, son of Sa'īd Khān, with the appellation of Nawāzish Khān.

At the time of my accession I had increased weights and measures (lit. *gaz*), viz. to the extent of three ratis (small weight equal to eight barleycorns), in the weight of muhrs and rupees. At this time it was represented to me that in mercantile transactions it would be for the convenience of the people that muhrs and rupees should be of the same weight as previously. As in all affairs the contentment and ease of the people are to be looked to, I gave an order that from the present day, that is, the 11th Urdībihis͟ht in the 6th year of my reign, they should strike muhrs and rupees of the former weight in all the mints of my dominions. As before this, on Saturday, the 2nd of the month of Ṣafar, in the year 1020, the evil-dispositioned Aḥdād had heard that Kabul was deprived of an eminent leader, that K͟hān Daurān[330] was in the interior, and only Mu'izzu-l-mulk with a few servants of the aforesaid was in Kabul, thinking it a good opportunity he (Aḥdād) betook himself unexpectedly to Kabul with a large number of horsemen and foot-soldiers. Mu'izzu-l-mulk, according to the measure of his ability, displayed activity, and the Kabulis and other inhabitants, especially the Farmulī[331] tribe, barricaded up the streets and fortified their houses. The Afghans with some guns came in to the streets and bazars from different directions. The people from the shelter of their terraces and houses killed many of these wretches with arrows and guns, and Bargī,[332] one of the confidential leaders of Aḥdād, was killed. From the occurrence of this affair, for fear that the people from all sides and quarters should assemble and block the road for them to get out, giving up their hearts and feet (in a state of distraction), in fear and confusion they turned back. About 800 of those dogs went to jahannam (hell), and 200, having caught horses, hastily escaped with their lives from that deadly place. Nād 'Alī Maidānī, who was in Lahūgar, at last on the same day arrived there, and pursued them for a short distance. As the

---

330 K͟hān Daurān was away in the district of Ningnahar (Iqbāl-nāma, p. 53).

331 Text wrongly has Qizilbāshes.

332 Or Bārkī.

distance (between them) was too great and his band small, he turned back. For the energy he had shown in coming quickly, and for the activity displayed by Mu'izzu-l-mulk, they were both promoted in rank ; Nād 'Alī, who held that of 1,000 personal to that of 1,500, and Mu'izzu-l-mulk, who held the rank of 1,500, to 1,800. As it transpired that Khān Daurān and the Kabulis were in the habit of passing their days in carelessness, and the repelling of the evil disposition of Aḥdād had taken a long time, it occurred to me that as the Khankhanan was without employment I might appoint him and his sons to this duty. Soon after this idea occurred Qilīj Khān, to summon whom a firman had already been issued, came from the Panjab and obtained the honour of an audience. It became evident from the forehead of his circumstances (his manner) that he was annoyed at the duty of driving back the ill-dispositioned Aḥdād being assigned to Khānkhānān. As he faithfully promised to take up this duty, it was settled that the governorship of the Subah of the Panjab should belong to Murtaẓā Khān, and that the Khankhanan should remain at home, and that Qilīj Khān should be promoted to the rank of 6,000 personal and 5,000 horse, and be appointed to Kabul to drive back Aḥdād and the up-country robbers. I ordered the Khankhanan to have a jagir in the Subah of Agra in the Sarkars of Qanauj and Kalpi, that he might inflict condign punishment on the rebels of that region and exterminate them (pull them out by the roots). When I dismissed them I gave each of them special robes of honour and horses and elephants, and having received the robes of exaltation they started of. At the same time, on account of the sincerity of his friendship and his old services, I bestowed on I'timādu-d-daulah the rank of 2,000 personal and 500 horse, and presented him with a sum of 5,000 rupees by way of gift. Mahābat Khān, whom I had sent to make the necessary preparations for war for the victorious army of the Deccan and point out to the Amirs the desirability of concord and unanimity, paid his respects to me at the capital of Agra on the 12th of the month of Tīr, the 21st of Rabī'u-s̤-s̤ānī. It was brought to notice in a letter from Islām Khān that 'Ināyat Khān had performed approved service in the Subah of Bengal ; on this account I increased by 500 personal the rank he already held of 2,000. I also increased by 500 personal and 300 horse, so as to make it up altogether to 1,500 personal and 800 horse, the rank of Rāja Kalyān, who was one of the officials of that Subah. I appointed Hāshim Khān,[333] who was in Orissa, to the government of Kashmir, and sent his uncle, Khwāja Muḥammad Ḥusain, there to look after the affairs of that country until his arrival. In the time of my revered father his father, Muḥammad Qāsim, had conquered Kashmir. Chīn Qilīj, who was the eldest son of Qilīj Khān, came from the Subah of Kabul and waited on me. As in addition to his natural excellence he was a *khānazād* (houseborn one), he was honoured with the title of Khan, and according to the prayer of his father, and on condition of his undertaking service in Tīrah, I increased his rank by 500 personal and 300 horse. On the 14th Amardād, on account of the previous service and great sincerity and ability of I'timādu-d-daulah, I bestowed on him the high rank of the viziership of the kingdom, and on the same day presented a belt with a jewelled dagger to Yādgār 'Alī, ambassador of the ruler of Iran. As 'Abdu-llah Khān, who had been appointed to command the army against the rebel Rānā, promised to enter the province of the Deccan from the direction of Gujarat, I promoted him to be Subahdar of that province, and at his request appointed Rāja Bāso to the command of the army against the Rānā, increasing his rank by 500 horse. In place of Gujarat I conferred the Subah of Malwa on Khān A'ẓam and sent 400,000 rupees to provide for the army and warlike materials for the force that had been appointed to accompany 'Abdu-llah Khān by way of Nāsik, which is near the province of the Deccan. Ṣafdar Khān, with his

[333] The text has here the word *ghāyatan*, which does not seem to have much meaning. Erskine has 'without his knowledge,' so he probably had *ghā'ibāna* in his MS.

brothers, came from the Subah of Behar, and had the honour of kissing the threshold.

One of the royal slaves who was serving in the seal-cutting departments prepared and laid before me a design such as I had never seen or heard of before. As it is exceedingly strange, a detailed[334] description of it is given. In the shell of a filbert four compartments had been carved out of ivory. The first compartment was one of wrestlers, in which two men were engaged in wrestling, a third was standing with a spear in his hand, a fourth with a hard stone.[335] Another was sitting with his hands placed on the ground, while in front of him were laid a piece of wood, a bow and a pot. In the second a throne had been made above which a *shamiyāna* (a tent-fly or canopy) was depicted, and a man of wealth (a prince) was seated on the throne with one leg placed over the other and a pillow at his back. Five servants were standing around and before him, and tree-boughs threw a shade over the throne. In the third compartment is a company of rope-dancers, who have raised upright a pole with three ropes fastened to it. A rope-dancer upon it (qu. on the ropes ?[336]) has taken hold of his own right foot with his left hand behind his head, and standing on one foot has placed a goat on the top of the pole. Another person has thrown a drum on his neck and is beating it, whilst another man is standing with his hands lifted up and looking at the rope-dancer. Five other men are also standing, of whom one has a stick in his hand. In the fourth compartment there is a tree, below which the figure of the revered (*ḥaẓrat*) Jesus is shown. One person has placed his head at Jesus' feet, and an old man is

---

334 Compare Elliot, vi, 324.

335 *Sang-i-durshtī*. Elliot had the same reading and translates 'a heavy stone. 'But both MSS. have *sang u rasanī*, 'a stone and a cord,' query a sling, and this is certainly the right reading. See Iqbāl-nāma, p. 57.

336. Text *bar pāy*, but the I.O. MS. and Iqbāl-nāma, p. 58, have *bar bāzī* (' on the rope ' ? or perhaps ' is doing gymnastics').

conversing with Jesus and four others are standing by.[337] As he had made such a masterpiece, I honoured him with a present and with increased salary.

On the 30th Shahrīwar, Mīrzā Sulṭān, who had been sent for from the Deccan, came and waited on me. Ṣafdar Khān had an increase of rank conferred on him, and was appointed to go to the assistance of the army against the rebel Rānā. As 'Abdu-llah Khān Bahādur Fīrūz-jang had proposed to enter the neighbouring province of the Deccan by way of Nāsik, it occurred to me to appoint Rām Dās Kachhwāha, who was one of the sincere servants of my revered father, to accompany him in order that he might in every place look after him, and not allow him to be too rash and hasty. For this purpose I bestowed on him great favours, as well as the title of Raja, which he had not thought of for himself. I also gave him drums and the fort of Ranthanbūr, which is one of the noted castles in Hindustan, and honouring him with a superb robe of honour and an elephant and horse I dismissed him. I appointed Khwāja Abū-l-ḥasan, who had been transferred from the chief Diwanship, to the duty of the Subahdarship of the Deccan, as he had been for a long time in those regions in the service of my deceased brother (Dāniyāl). I honoured Abū-l-ḥasan, son of I'timādu-d-daulah, with the title of I'tiqād Khān, and having promoted the sons of Mu'aẓẓam Khān to fitting ranks sent them to Bengal to Islām Khān. At the request of Islām Khān, Rāja Kalyān was appointed to the government of the Sarkar of Orissa and had an increase in rank of 200 personal and horse. I presented Shajā'at Khān Dakhanī with 4,000 rupees. On the 7th Ābān Badī'u-z-zamān,

---

337 Note of Sayyid Ahmad (to the fourth compartment). "Evidently this masterpiece was not the work of a slave in the seal department, for no reason appears why the portrait of Jesus should be introduced into the fourth compartment. Probably this masterpiece was the work of Frank artists and had fallen into the hands of the slave, and he had ascribed it to his own workmanship. (Perhaps the scene depicted was the Transfiguration.)"

son of Mīrzā Shāhrukh, came from the Deccan and waited on me.

About this time, in consequence of the disturbances that had occurred in the country of Māwarā'a-n-nahr, many of the Amirs and Ūzbeg soldiers, such as Ḥusain Bī, Pahluwān Bābā, and Nauras Bī Darman, and Baram Bī and others came to Court and waited on me. They were all honoured with robes of honour, horses, cash, mansabs, and jagirs. On the 2nd Āzar Hāshim Khān came from Bengal and had the honour of kissing my threshold. I sent 500,000 rupees for the expenses of the victorious army of the Deccan, of which the leader was 'Abdu-llah Khān, to Ahmadabad in Gujarat by the hands of Rūp Khawāṣṣ and Shaikh Anbiyā. On the 1st day I went to the village of Samonagar, which is one of my fixed hunting-places, to hunt. Twenty-two antelope were killed, of which I myself killed sixteen and Khurram the other six. Remaining there two days and two nights, on the night of Sunday I returned to the city in health and safety, and one night this couplet threw its brilliance on my mind:—

> "As long as there's in heaven light for the sun,
> Be not the reflection far from the Shah's umbrella."

I ordered the lamplighters and the relators of stories that at the time of their salutations and telling stories they should commence with this couplet, and it is still in use. On Saturday, the 3rd day, a letter came from Khān A'ẓam that 'Ādil Khān Bījāpūrī had given up his evil ways and become penitent, and in the rank of servants was now more loyal than ever. On the 14th day, corresponding with the last day of Shawwāl, leave was given to Hāshim Khān to go to Kashmir. I gave a special wrapper[338] (*fargal*) to Yādgār 'Alī, ambassador of Persia. I presented I'tiqād Khān with one of my special swords called Sar-andāz (thrower of heads). Having honoured Shādmān, son of

---

[338] See Blochmann, p. 89, note. It came from Europe.

Khān A'ẓam, with the title of Shādmān Khān, I increased his rank to 1,700 personal and 500 horse. He was also honoured with a standard. Sardār Khān, brother of 'Abdu-llah Khān Fīrūz-jang, and Arslān Bī Ūzbeg, who had been appointed to the charge of Sīvistān,[339] were also presented with standards. I ordered that *jā'i-namāz* (prayer carpets) should be made of the skins of the antelopes I had myself killed, and be kept in the public audience hall for people to use in saying their prayers. By way of special respect to the Law I ordered that the Mīr-i-'Adl and Qāẓī, who are the pivot of affairs of the divine law, should not kiss the ground (before me), which is a kind of *sijda.* On Thursday, the 22nd day, I went again to Samonagar to hunt. As many antelope had collected together in that neighbourhood I had this time sent off Khwāja Jahān to prepare a qamargah and drive in the antelope into a broad place from all sides, to place canvas-walls (*sarā-parda*) and a *gulāl-bāṛ*[340] round it. They enclosed a kos and half of ground with sarapardas. When news came that the hunting-place had been prepared and a great deal of game had been confined, I went there and began to hunt on the Friday. Until the next Thursday I went every day to the qamargah with the ladies and hunted as much as I liked. Some of the deer were taken alive and some killed with arrows and guns. On the Sunday and Thursday, on which I do not fire guns at animals, they took them alive in nets. In these seven days 917 head, male and female, were caught, and of these 641 deer were caught alive. Four hundred and four head were sent to Fathpur to be let loose on the plain there, and with regard to 84 I ordered them to put silver rings in their noses and set them free in the same place. The 276 other antelope that had been killed with guns and arrows and by cheetahs were divided from day to day among the Begams and the slaves of the palace, and Amirs and servants of the palace. As I became very tired (*dilgīr*) of hunting, I gave

[339] In Scinde ; it is the same as Sahwan, and is on the Indus.

[340] Blochmann, p. 45.

orders to the Amirs to go to the *shikārgāh* (hunting-place) and hunt all that were left over, and myself returned in safety to the city. On the 1st Bahman, corresponding with the 17th Zī-l-qa'da, I ordered that in the large cities of my dominions, like Ahmadabad, Allahabad, Lahore, Delhi, Agra, etc., they should arrange bulghur-khanas (places for the distribution of cooked food) for the poor; thirty mahalls (districts) had been ordered. Six had already been established, and twenty-four other districts were now ordered. On the 4th Bahman I increased the rank of Rāja Bīr Singh Deo by 1,000 personal ; it was previously 4,000 personal and 2,000 horse : I gave him a jewelled sword. Another sword out of my special ones, that was called Shāh-bacha (king's child), was presented to Shāh-nawāz Khān. On the 16th Isfandārmuz, Badī'u-z-zamān, son of Mīrzā Shāhrukh, was appointed to the army against the rebel Rānā and a sword sent by his hand for Rāja Bāso. Having again heard that the Amirs on the borders interfere with authority in matters that do not concern them, and do not observe laws and regulations, I ordered[341] that the Bakhshis should circulate orders, to be obeyed amongst the Amirs of the borders, that hereafter they should not interfere in such things, which are the private affair of kings. The first thing is this, that they should not sit in the *jharokha* (private window), and should not trouble their officers and captains of the auxiliaries with keeping guard or saluting them, and should not have elephant fights, and should not inflict the punishment of blinding, and should not cut off ears and noses, and should not force Islam on anyone, and should not confer titles on their servants, and should not order the royal servants to do *kūrnish* or prostration, and should not force singers to remain on duty in the manner customary in (royal) darbars, and should not beat drums when they go out, and when they give a horse or elephant to anyone, whether to the king's attendants or to their own servants, they should not place reins

---

[341] Elliot, vi, 325.

or elephant's goads on their backs and make them perform obeisance. In going in procession they should not take with them on foot in their retinue the royal attendants. If they write anything to them they should not put a seal on it.[342] The regulations which have been styled the rules of Jahāngīr (Āyīn-i-Jahāngīrī) are now in force.[343]

THE SEVENTH NEW YEAR'S FESTIVAL AFTER THE AUSPICIOUS ACCESSION.

On Tuesday, the 1st Farwardīn of the seventh year from my accession on the 16th Muḥarram u-l-ḥarām (19th March, 1612) in the year 1021, the New Year's assembly that illuminates the world, and the festival that brings joy, were held in the capital of Agra. After four gharis of the night had passed on Thursday, the 3rd of the aforesaid month, the hour that the astrologers had chosen, I sat on the throne. I had ordered that, according to annual custom, the bazars should be decorated and the assembly should be kept up until the day of culmination (*rūz-i-sharaf*). Khusrau Bī Ūzbeg, who was known among the Uzbegs as Khusrau *Qimchī*,[344] came on these days and had the honour of waiting on me. As he was one of the influential men of Māwarā'a-n-nahr, I bestowed many favours on him, and gave him a fine robe of honour. I gave 15,000 rupees to Yādgār 'Alī, ambassador of the ruler of Iran, for his expenses. On the same day the offering of Afẓal Khān, which he had sent from the Subah of Behar, was laid before me. There were 30 elephants and 18 ponies (*gūnṭh*), and pieces of Bengal cloth, sandalwood, some

---

342 Both MSS. have *bar rū* instead of *bar ū*, ' in front ' or ' in the face ' of the letter, and this is no doubt the correct reading. See Iqbāl-nāma, p. 59. See Blochmann, p. 263, for the different places where seals are to be put. Jahāngīr's order apparently was that the provincial governors were not to impress their seals on the face of their letters or other documents.

343 The reference seems to be, not to these subsidiary regulations, but to the code of twelve rules promulgated by him at the commencement of his reign.

344 *Qūruqchī* in I.O. MS. and in Iqbāl-nāma, p. 60. Steingass gives it as meaning one who looks after the king's game, and as a sentinel.

pods of musk, aloes-wood (*Agallochum*), and all kinds of things. The offering of Khān Daurān was also produced before me. He had sent 45 head of horse and two strings of camels, porcelain from China, dressing-gowns (*pūstīnhā*[345]) of sable (*sammūr*), and other valuable presents procurable in Kabul and its neighbourhood. The officers of the palace had taken trouble about their offerings, and according to the yearly custom from day to day of the festival the offerings of the servants were laid before me. Having looked at them in detail, I took what I approved and gave them the remainder. On the 13th Farwardīn, corresponding with the 29th Muḥarram, a representation from Islām Khān arrived to the effect that through the blessing of Allah's favour and through the benign influence of the royal grace, Bengal had been freed from the disturbance of 'Uṡmān, the Afghan. Before the circumstances of this war are written down, some particulars with regard to Bengal will be recorded.[346] Bengal is a country of great extent, and in the second clime its length, from the port of Chittagong to Garī, is 450 kos; and its breadth, from the Northern hills to the boundary of Sarkar Madāran, 220 kos. Its revenue is about 60 krores of dams.[347] The former rulers of this place always had 20,000 horse, a lakh of foot-soldiers, 1,000 elephants, and 4,000 or 5,000 war-boats. From the time of Shīr Khān and his son Salīm Khān, this country was in the possession of the Afghans. When the throne of sovereignty of Hindustan in the hands of my revered father acquired beauty and splendour, he ordered the victorious forces (of the empire) into it, and for a long time made the conquest of it his object, until the aforesaid province, through the great efforts of the chiefs of the victorious State, passed from the possession of Dā'ūd Karānī, who was the last of its rulers. That wretch was killed in the fight with Khān Jahān, and his army

[345] Text has *pūsthā*, skins, but 1. 0. MS. has *pūstīnhā*.

[346] Copied from Āyīn. See Jarrett, ii, 115. See also Elliot, vi, 326.

[347] This is equal to one krore, fifty lakhs of rupees. The Sarkar of Orissa was included in Bengal, and its revenue is included in this. (Note of Sayyid Aḥmad.)

became scattered and in desperate condition. From that date until now the province is in the possession of the servants of the State. In the end a few of the remaining Afghans had remained in the corners and sides of the country, and kept a few distant places in their possession, until, by degrees, most of that body became despised and helpless, and were captured by the chiefs of the State in the places of which they had still possession. When the arrangement of the affairs of rule and empire, simply through the grace of God, became entrusted to this humble servant of the throne of Allah, in the first year after my accession I sent for Rāja Mān Singh, who had been appointed to the rule and government of that place, to Court, and sent Quṭbu-d-dīn Khān, who, out of all the officials, was distinguished as my foster-brother, in his place. As he entered the province he attained to martyrdom at the hand of one of those mischievous ones who had been appointed to that country, and that man, who had not thought of the consequences, also obtained the reward of his deeds, and was slain. I promoted Jahāngīr Qulī Khān, who was governor and a Jagirdar in the province of Behar, on account of his nearness to that neighbourhood, to the rank of 5,000 personal and horse, and ordered him to go to Bengal and take possession of the province. I sent an order to Islām Khān, who was at the capital of Agra, to go to Behar and consider that province his jagir. When a short time had passed under the rule of Jahāngīr Qulī Khān, he contracted a severe illness, in consequence of the bad water and air of that place, and by degrees the power of the disease and his weakness became so great as to end in his destruction. When the news of his death came to my hearing at Lahore, an order was issued in the name of Islām Khān to proceed as soon as possible to Bengal. When I appointed him to this important duty, most of the servants of the State made remarks on his youth and want of experience. As the excellence of his disposition and his natural capacity had been noticed by my judicious eye, I myself chose him for this duty. As it happened, the affairs of this province were carried on by him in such a manner as from the time when it first entered into the possession of the Chiefs of the everlasting State until this day has never been attained to by any of the servants of the Court. One of his noteworthy deeds was the driving away of the rebel 'Uṣmān, the Afghan. He frequently in the time of the late king encountered the royal forces, but his expulsion was not accomplished. When Islām Khān made Dhaka (Dacca) his place of abode and made the subjection of the Zamindars of that neighbourhood his chief object, it occurred to him that he should send an army against the rebel 'Uṣmān and his province. If he agreed to serve loyally, well and good, but if not, they should punish and annihilate him like other seditious people. At that time Shajā'at Khān[348] joined Islām Khan, and the lot of leading in this service[349] fell on his name. Several others of the State servants were also appointed to go with him, such as Kishwar Khān, Iftikhār Khān, Sayyid Ādam Bārha, Shaikh Achhay,[350] nephew of Muqarrab Khān, Mu'tamad Khān, the sons of Mu'aẓẓam Khān, Ihtimām Khān, and others. He took with him also some of his own men. At the hour when Mushtarī (Jupiter) was propitious, he started off this band, and appointed Mīr Qāsim, son of Mīrzā Murād, its chief paymaster and news-writer. He took also some of the Zamindars with him to show the road. The victorious armies started. When they reached the neighbourhood of 'Uṣmān's fort and land, they sent some eloquent men to admonish him and point out to him the way of loyalty, and bring him back from the road of rebellion to the right path. As much pride had seated itself in his brain-cup, and he had in his head a desire to seize the country, beside other fancies, he turned a deaf ear to their words and prepared himself

---

348 Also called Shaikh Kabīr Chishtī (Blochmann, p. 519 ; Ma'āṣiru-l-umarā, ii, 630).

349 Perhaps this is only rhetoric, but Abū-l-faẓl describes how lots were cast between him and Rāja Bīrbal as to who should go on the Yusufzai expedition.

350 *Ichī* means a hawk, but the meaning may be a Shaikh of Uch. *Acha* is given in Zenker as meaning a father in Turki. The Iqbāl-nāma has Ajha.

for conflict and fight. The battlefield happened to be on the bank of a nullah in a place which was a complete bog. On Sunday (12th March, 1612), the 9th Muḥarram, Shajā'at Khān, choosing the hour for the fight, arrayed the victorious forces, so that everyone should go to his place and be prepared for the battle. 'Uṣmān had not settled the battle for that day with himself. When he heard that the royal army had come prepared for battle, having no remedy he himself mounted and came to the bank of the nullah, and arrayed his own horse and foot opposite the victorious army. When the affair grew hot, and the two forces opposed each other, that foolish, obstinate man at the first onset threw his own fighting raging elephant against the advanced guard. After much fighting many of the leaders of the advanced guard, as Sayyid Ādam[351] Bārha and Shaikh Achhay, attained the dignity of martyrdom. Iftikhār Khān, the leader of the right wing, was in no way remiss in attacking, and sacrificed his own life. The band that was with him fought to such a degree that they were all cut to pieces. In the same way Kishwar[352] Khān and his band of the left wing bravely sacrificed themselves in the affair of their master, but many of the enemy (lit. those of dark fortune) were also wounded and killed. That evil one ('Uṣmān) took account of the combatants and ascertained that the leaders of the advanced guard and right and left wings were killed. The centre alone remained. He took no account of the killed and wounded on his own side, but attacked the centre (of the royal army) with the same energy. On this side the son and brothers and sons-in-law of Shajā'at Khān, as well as other officers, stopped the advance of those lost ones, and attacked them like tigers and leopards armed with claws and teeth. Some of them attained the dignity of martyrdom, and those that remained alive bore away fatal wounds. At this time ('Uṣmān) drove a

---

[351] Text wrongly has A'ẓam. See Blochmann, p. 521, note.

[352] Kishwar was the son of Jahāngīr's foster-brother Quṭbu-d-dīn, who was killed by Shīr-afgan.

raging elephant of the name of Gajpat,[353] which was his premier elephant, at Shajā'at Khān, who laid hold of his spear and struck the elephant. What does a raging elephant care for a javelin ! He then seized his sword and struck him two blows one after another. How did he regard these either! He then drew his dagger and struck him twice with it, but for this, too, he did not turn back, but overthrew Shajā'at Khān with his horse. Immediately he was separated from his horse ; calling out "Jahāngīr Shāh," he leapt up, and his equerry struck the elephant on both front legs a blow with a two-handed sword. As the elephant fell on his knees, the equerry pulled the elephant driver down off the elephant, and Shajā'at with the dagger he had in his hand, and while on foot, struck such blows on the trunk and forehead of the elephant that the elephant roared out at the pain and turned round. As he was severely wounded, he went to his own army and fell down. Shajā'at Khān's horse got up safely. As he was mounting his horse those vile ones drove another elephant at his standard-bearer, and overthrew his horse and standard. Shajā'at Khān gave a manly shout and roused the standard-bearer, saying: "Be bold : I'm alive and the standard is at my feet (?)."[354] At this critical moment all the servants of the State who were present seized their arrows and daggers and swords, and smote the elephant. Shajā'at himself came up and shouted to the standard-bearer to rise, and got another horse for the standard-bearer and mounted him on it. The standard-bearer unfurled the standard and maintained his ground. At the time of this struggle a (ball from a) gun struck that rebel on his forehead. However much they enquired for the man who fired it he could not be found. When this struck him, he recognized that he was a dead man. Yet for two watches, notwithstanding this fatal

---

[353] The Iqbāl-nāma and the B.M. MSS. call it Bakhla.

[354] These last words seem to be part of Shajā'at's speech, but see Iqbāl-nāma, p. 63. See also Elliot, vi, 329, and the translation of the Iqbāl-nāma account in Appendix L, Stewart's Cat. of Tippo Sultan's MSS., p. 275. The Iqbāl-nāma says that 'Us̤mān's corpulence compelled him to ride on an elephant.

wound, he urged on his men to the fight, and the battlefield was still deadly and the struggle warm. Afterwards the enemy turned their faces, and the victorious army pursued them, and continually striking them drove back those vile ones into the place where they had encamped. With arrows and guns those wretches would not allow the royal troops to enter the place where they were. When Walī, the brother of 'Uṣmān, and Mamrez, his ('Uṣmān's) son and other relations and followers became aware of 'Uṣmān's wound, they made up their minds that he would not recover from it, and that if they, defeated and put to flight, should go towards their fort none would reach it alive. They thought it best to remain for the night in the place where they had encamped, and towards the end of the night seek an opportunity and get to their fort. Two watches of night had passed when 'Uṣmān went to hell. In the third watch they raised his lifeless body, and leaving his tent and the things they had with them in the camp, proceeded to their fortress. The scouts of the victorious army, having obtained news of this, informed Shajā'at Khān. On the morning of Monday the loyalists assembled and decided to follow them, and not allow breathing-time to those of dark fortune. In the end, in consequence of the tired state of the soldiers, and in order to bury the martyrs and out of sympathy for the wounded, they were perplexed in their minds as to going or settling down (where they were). Just at this time 'Abdu-s-Salām, son of Mu'aẓẓam Khān, arrived with a body of servants of the State, altogether 300 horse and 400 musketeers (*tūpchī*). When this fresh body of men arrived it was determined to pursue, and they accordingly went on. When Walī, who after 'Uṣmān was the stock of the disturbance, learned that Shajā'at Khān with the victorious army had come together with another fresh force, he saw no resource for himself but to go to Shajā'at Khān on the straight line of faith and loyalty. In the end he sent a message that he who had been the cause of the disturbance had gone, and that the body of those who were left were servants and Musulmans. If he would give his word they would wait upon him and would agree to serve the State, giving their elephants as an offering. Shajā'at Khān and Mu'taqid Khān, who had arrived on the day of the battle and had done approved service, and all those who were loyal, in accordance with the necessity of the time and with what was best for the State, gave their word and encouraged them. On the next day, Walī and the sons, brothers, and sons-in-law of 'Uṣmān all came and waited upon Shajā'at Khān and the other servants of the State. They brought forty-nine elephants as an offering. After the completion of this work Shajā'at Khān, leaving some of the royal servants in Adhār[355] and the neighbourhood which was in the possession of that one of evil fortune, took with him Walī and the other Afghans, and on Monday, the 6th of the month of Ṣafar, came to Jahāngīrnagar (Dacca) and joined Islām Khān. When the joyful news reached in Agra this supplicant at the throne of Allah, he performed the

[355] The text has *dar adhār u ṭarf kih dar taṣarruf-i-ān tīra-rūzgār būd*. I do not know if *adhār* is the name of a place or what its meaning is. The I.O. MSS., Nos. 181 and 305, have *arhād*. Blochmann, p. 520, on the authority of the Makhzan-i-Afghānī, says the fight took place 100 kos from Dacca and in a place called Nek Ujya.l, and he points out in a note that there are several Ujyāls in Eastern Bengal. Possibly' Adhār is Udhār or Uzār, and a corruption of Ujyāl. The ' hills of Dacca,' referred to by Blochmann, might be Ran Bhawal or the Madhūpūr jungle. The Riyāzu-s-salāṭīn does not mention the site of the battle, and the translator, Maulawī 'Abdu-s-Salām, has in his note at p. 175 confounded two ' Īsā Khāns, and so drawn groundless inferences. Blochmann points out, p. 520, that the Ma'āṣiru-l-umarā says the prisoners were afterwards put to death. The passage is at vol. ii, p. 632. It says they were put to death by Jahāngīr's orders by 'Abdu-llah (who certainly was brute enough for anything). Jahāngīr, Tūzuk, p. 112, mentions the arrival of 'Uṣmān's sons and brothers at Court, so that Blochmann's statement at p. 520 about their being executed on the road is not correct. It appears, too, they came to Court after Shajā'at's death. Jahāngīr says (Tūzuk, p. 112) he made over the prisoners to responsible servants of government. 'Abdu-llah may have been one of these, and have got rid of his prisoners by killing them. It would appear that the battle with 'Uṣmān took place to the east or south-east of Dacca, and not near Orissa, as Stewart supposed.

prostrations of gratitude, and recognized that the driving away of this description of enemy was brought about simply through the unstinted mercy of the Almighty Giver. As a reward for this good service I promoted Islām Khān to the rank of 6,000 personal, and honoured Shajā'at Khān with the title of "Rustam of the age" (Rustam-zamān), as well as increased his rank by 1,000 personal and horse. I also increased the rank of other servants according to the measure of their services, and they were selected for other honours.

When this news first came of the killing of 'Uṣmān it appeared to be a joke, but by way of ascertaining the truth or falsehood of the words I took an omen from the divān of the tongue of the unseen world, Khwāja Ḥāfiẓ of Shiraz, and this ghazal[356] turned up:—

> "I make my eyes red and throw patience to the wilds,
> And in such a case throw my heart into the sea.
> I'm wounded by the shaft of heaven:
> Give wine, so that intoxicated I may cast a knot in the girdle of the Twins."

As this couplet was very appropriate to the occasion, I drew an omen from it. After some days news came again that the arrow of Fate, or rather of God, had struck 'Uṣmān, for however much they enquired for him, he who fired the shot was not

356 The lines occur in Hāfiẓ' divān, under the letter M, Brockhaus' ed., No. 396, but Jahāngīr has missed out two lines in his quotation. An Indian lithograph has *rakht* in the first line instead of *ṣabr*, but the latter reading occurs in Brockhaus. In the fourth line *nargis* is a mistake for *tīrkash*. *Tīr-i-falak*, 'the arrow of the spheres,' is also a name for the planet Mercury. *Tīrkash-i-Jauzā* means both a particular constellation in the sign Gemini, which is supposed to resemble a quiver in appearance, and also the strings of a musical instrument. The meaning of the lines seems to be, " I have been wounded by the shaft of heaven : give me wine that I may become intoxicated and be able to tie a knot in the quivergirdle of the Gemini. " The appositeness of the *fāl* is not very apparent, but the mention of an arrow was taken to be an allusion to the death of ' Uṣmān by a shot from an unknown hand.

made manifest. This has been recorded on account of its strange nature.

On the 16th Farwardīn, Muqarrab Khān, who is one of my chief retainers and the old confidants of the Jahangiri service, who had attained the rank of 3,000 personal and 2,000 horse, came from the fort of Cambay and had the honour of waiting on me. I had ordered him, on account of certain business, to go to the port of Goa[357] and buy for the private use of the government certain rareties procurable there. According to orders he went with diligence to Goa, and remaining there for some time, took at the price the Franks asked for them the rareties he met with at that port, without looking at the face of the money at all (i.e. regardless of cost). When he returned from the aforesaid port to the Court, he produced before me one by one the things and rareties he had brought. Among these were some animals that were very strange and wonderful, such as I had never seen, and up to this time no one had known their names. Although King Bābar has described in his Memoirs the appearance and shapes of several animals, he had never ordered the painters to make pictures of them. As these animals appeared to me to be very strange, I both described them and ordered that painters should draw them in the Jahāngīr-nāma, so that the amazement that arose from hearing of them might be increased. One of these animals in body is larger than a peahen and smaller than a peacock.[358] When it is in heat and displays itself, it spreads out its feathers like the peacock and dances about. Its beak and legs are like those of a cock. Its head and neck and the part under the throat are every minute of a different colour. When it is in heat it is quite red—one might say it had adorned itself with red coral—and after a while it becomes white in the same places, and looks like cotton. It sometimes looks of a turquoise colour. Like a

---

[357] Elliot, vi, 331.

[358] They call this in the English language a turkey, and the people of India call it *pīrū*; Persian-knowing Indians call it in Persian *jīlmurgh*.! They are now plentiful in India. (Note of Sayyid Ahmad.)

chameleon it constantly changes colour. Two pieces of flesh it has on its head look like the comb of a cock. A strange thing is this, that when it is in heat the aforesaid piece of flesh hangs down to the length of a span from the top of its head like an elephant's trunk, and again when he raises it up it appears on its head like the horn of a rhinoceros, to the extent of two finger-breadths. Round its eyes it is always of a turquoise colour, and does not change. Its feathers appear to be of various colours, differing from the colours of the peacock's feathers. He also brought a monkey of a strange and wonderful form. Its hands, feet, ears, and head are like those of a monkey, and its face like that of a fox. The colour of its eyes is like that of a hawk's eye, but the eyes are larger than those of a hawk. From its head to the end of its tail it is an ordinary cubit in length. It is lower than a monkey and taller than a fox. Its hair is like the wool of a sheep and its colour like that of ashes. From the lobe of its ear to its chin it is red and of the colour of wine. Its tail is two or three finger-breadths longer than half a cubit, quite different from that of other monkeys. The tail of this animal hangs down like the tail of a cat. Sometimes it makes a sound like a young antelope. On the whole it is a very strange beast. Of the wild birds which they call *tadrū* (pheasant) till now it has never been heard that they breed in captivity. In the time of my revered father they made great efforts to obtain eggs and young ones but it was not managed. I ordered them to keep some of them, male and female, in one place, and by degrees they bred. I ordered them to place the eggs under hens, and in a space of two years sixty or seventy young were produced and fifty or sixty grew up. Whoever heard of this matter was astonished. It was said that in the Wilāyat (Persia ?) the people there had made great efforts, but no eggs were produced and no young were obtained.

In these days I increased the mansab of Mahābat Khān by 1,000 personal and 500 horse, which thus became 4,000 personal and 3,500 horse. The mansab of I'timādu-d-daulah, original and increased, was fixed at 4,000 personal and 1,000 horse. To the mansab of Mahā Singh also an increase of 500 personal and horse was given : it was originally and with increase 3,000 personal and 2,000 horse. The mansab of I'tiqād Khān was increased by 500 personal and 200 horse, and made up to 1,000 personal and 300 horse. Khwāja Abū-l-ḥasan in these days came from the Deccan and waited on me. Daulat Khān, who had been appointed to the faujdarship of Allahabad and of the Sarkar of Jaunpur, came and paid his respects: an increase of 500 was made to his mansab, which was 1,000. On the day of culmination (*rūz-i-sharaf*), which was the 19th Farwardīn, I raised the mansab of Sulṭān Khurram, which was 10,000, to 12,000, and made that of I'tibār Khān, which was 3,000 personal and 1,000 horse, up to 4,000. I raised the mansab of Muqarrab Khān from 2,000 personal and 1,000 horse by 500 personal and horse ; and increased that of Khwāja Jahān, which was 2,000 personal and 1,200 horse, by 500. As these were the days of the New Year, many of the servants (of the State) obtained an increase of their mansabs. On the same day Dulīp came from the Deccan and waited on me. As his father Rāy Rāy Singh had died, I honoured him with the title of Rāy and clothed him in a dress of honour. Rāy Rāy Singh had another son, by name Sūraj Singh. Although Dulīp was his *ṭīkā* (marked with the *ṭīkā*) son, he wished Sūraj Singh to succeed him, in consequence of the love that he bore to his mother. When the circumstances of his death were reported to me, Sūraj Singh, in consequence of his want of intelligence and tender years, represented to me : "My father has made me his successor and given me the *ṭīkā*." This remark was not to my liking, and I said : "If thy father has given the *ṭīkā* to thee, we shall give it to Dulīp." Then marking the *ṭīkā* with my own hand, I presented the latter with his father's jagir and hereditary possessions. I bestowed on I'timādu-d-daulah an inkstand and jewelled pen. Rūdar, the father of Lakhmī Chand, Raja of Kumaon, who is one of the considerable Rajas of the hill country, had come in the time of the late King Akbar,[359] and when he came had petitioned[360] that the son of Rāja Ṭoḍar Mal might take him by the hand and bring him to wait on him. In consequence, the Raja's (Ṭoḍar Mal's) son had been appointed to bring him. Lakhmī Chand now similarly asked that the son of I'timādu-d-daulah might bring him to pay his respects. I sent Shāpūr[361] to bring him to wait on me. He laid before me rare things from his own hill country, such as *gūnṭh* ponies, and birds of prey, such as hawks, *jurra* (falcons), royal falcons, *qaṭās* (yaks), navels of musk, and skins of the musk antelope with the musk-bags on them, swords which in their language they call *khānḍā,* and daggers which they call *kaṭār,* and all kinds of things. Amongst the Rajas of this hill country this Raja is well known for the large quantities of gold he has. They say there is a gold-mine in his territory.[362]

In order to lay the foundation of a palace at Lahore, I sent there Khwāja Jahān Khwāja Dūst Muḥammad, who is well skilled in this kind of business.

As the affairs of the Deccan, in consequence of the disagreements among the Sardars and the carelessness of Khān A'ẓam, did not look well, and the defeat of 'Abdu-llah Khān had taken place, I had sent for Khwāja Abu-l-ḥasan to make enquiries into the real state of these quarrels. After much enquiry and investigation it became clear that the defeat of 'Abdu-llah Khān had been caused by his pride and his sharp temper, and not listening to words (of advice), and partly by the quarrels and want of agreement between the Amirs. Briefly, it had been determined that 'Abdu-llah Khān should start from the direction of Nāsik and Trimbak with the Gujarat army and the

359 Akbar-nāma, iii, 533. It was in the 33rd year.

360 He asked Ṭoḍar Mal's protection, but the son was sent (Akbar-nāma, iii, 533).

361 This name is not in all the MSS. It is another name for I'tiqād, son of I'timādu-d-daulah.

362 Blochmann, p. 508.

Amirs who had been appointed to accompany him. This army had been brought into proper order by trustworthy leaders and zealous Amirs, such as Rāja Rām Dās, Khān A'lam, Saif Khān, 'Alī Mardān Bahādur, Ẓafar Khān, and other servants of the State. The number of the army had passed 10,000 and come up to near 14,000. On the side of Berar it was settled that Rāja Mān Singh, Khān Jahān, the Amīru-l-umarā, and many other leaders should proceed. These two armies should be aware of each other's marches and halts, so that on an appointed day they might catch the enemy between the two. If this rule had been observed and their hearts had been in unison, and self-interest had not come between, it is most probable that Almighty God would have given them the victory of the day. When 'Abdu-llah Khān passed the Ghats and entered the enemy's country, he did not take care to send runners (*qāṣidān*) to bring intelligence from the other army, nor did he, in accordance with the arrangements, make his movements harmonise with theirs, so that on an appointed day they might take the enemy between two armies. Rather he relied on his own strength, and considered that if he could gain the victory alone it would be better. This idea fixed itself in his mind, and however much Rām Dās desired him to promise to go forward with due deliberation, it was of no use. The enemy, who were observing him closely, had sent a large number of leaders and Bargīs (Mahrattas) against him, and encounters took place with them every day. They did not fail to throw rockets and different fireworks at night. At last the enemy drew near, and yet he obtained no intelligence about the other army, though he had approached Daulatabad, which was the place of assembly of the Dakhanis. 'Ambar, the black-faced, had raised to sovereignty a child who, in his opinion, bore relationship to the family of Niẓāmu-l-mulk. In order that men might fully accept his (the child's) sovereignty, he raised him up and took him by the hand, and made himself the Peshwa and leader. He sent men again and again (against 'Abdu-llah), and the number of the enemy was continually increasing till at last they made an attack, and by throwing rockets and other fireworks made matters hot for him.[363] At length the loyalists thought it best, as no assistance had come to them from the other army and all the Dakhanis had turned against them, to retreat, at once and try some other arrangement. All agreed, and with one consent started off before dawn. The Dakhanis followed them to the boundaries of their own country, and the two armies, meeting every day, did not fail in fighting. In these days several of the ambitious and zealous young men were killed. 'Alī Mardān Khān Bahādur, behaving like a brave man, carried away terrible wounds and fell into the hands of the enemy, and showed his companions an example of fidelity to his salt and of life-sacrifice. Zū-l-faqār Beg also displayed manly actions, and a rocket struck him on the leg, and two days afterwards he died. When they entered the country of Rāja Bharjū,[364] who was one of those loyal to the throne, that body (the enemy) turned back, and 'Abdu-llah Khān proceeded towards Gujarat. The real truth is this, that if in going he had drawn his rein (gone slowly) and allowed the other army to have come up to him, the matter would have turned out according to the wish of the chief men of the victorious State.[365] As soon as the news of the retreat of 'Abdu-llah Khān reached the leaders of the army that was advancing from Berar, not seeing any advantage from further stay, they also retired, and joined the camp of Parwīz at 'Ādilābād in the neighbourhood of Burhanpur. When this intelligence reached me at Agra I was greatly agitated, and proposed to go there myself and destroy root and branch those servants who had become masters. The Amirs and other devoted ones would in no way consent to this. Khwāja Abū-l-ḥasan represented that as no one understood the business of that region as the Khankhanan did I ought to send him, and that he should again arrange matters that had fallen into disorder, and

---

363 Elliot, vi, 333.

364 Raja of Baglāna.

365 A periphrasis for Jahāngīr himself.

according to the exigencies of the time should compose differences so that affairs might return to their original condition. Other well-wishers being consulted, all their opinions were at one in this, that the Khankhanan must be sent and that Khwāja Abū-l-ḥasan should accompany him. Agreeing with this determination, those who had charge of the affairs of the Khankhanan and his companions obtained leave to go on Sunday, the 17th Urdībihisht, in the 7th year. Shāh-nawāz Khān, Khwāja Abū-l-ḥasan, Razzāq-birdī Ūzbeg, and several others of his associates paid their parting salutations on the same day. The Khankhanan was promoted to the rank of 6,000 personal, Shāh-nawāz Khān to that of 3,000 and horse, that of Dārāb Khān increased by 500 personal and 300 horse (altogether 2,000 personal and 1,500 horse), and to Raḥman-dād, his (the Khankhanan's) younger son, I also gave a fitting mansab. I presented the Khankhanan with a grand dress of honour, a jewelled dagger, a special elephant with *talāyir* (accoutrements), and an Iraq horse. In the same way I bestowed on his sons and companions dresses of honour and horses. In the same month Mu'izzu-l-mulk came from Kabul with his sons, and had the good fortune to kiss the threshold. Shyām Singh and Rāy Mangat Bhadauriya, who belonged to the army of Bangash, according to the request of Qilīj Khān, were promoted to higher mansabs. Shyām Singh had 1,500 personal and was increased by 500, and Rāy Mangat was also raised to a higher rank.

For a long time past news had come of the illness of Āṣaf Khān; sometimes the disease was got under and sometimes recurred, until he died at Burhanpur in the 63rd year of his age. His understanding and capacity were very good. He was very quick-witted. He also wrote poetry. He composed "Khusrau and Shīrīn," dedicating it to me, and called it the "Nūr-nāma" (the writing of light).[366] He had been ennobled in the time of my revered father and made Vizier. In the days when I was a prince

366 The history of Nūr, i.e. the history of Nūru-d-din Jahāngīr.

he had several times done foolish things, and most men, and indeed Khusrau himself, were of opinion that after my accession I would do unpleasant things (with regard to him). In a manner contrary to what had entered the minds of himself and others, I favoured him and promoted him to the rank of 5,000 personal and horse, and after he had for some time been Vizier with full authority, neglected no point in increasing favour towards him. After his death I gave mansabs to his sons and bestowed kindnesses on them. At last it was clear that his disposition and sincerity were not as they should be, and, considering his own evil deeds, he had always been suspicious with regard to me. They say he was aware of the conspiracy and disturbance that took place on the Kabul expedition, and had given support to the wretches. Indeed, I had no confidence that notwithstanding my favour and kindness to him he was not disloyal and of perverse fortune.

After a short space of time, on the 25th of the same month of Urdībihisht, the news of Mīrzā Ghāzī's death arrived. The said Mīrzā was of the ruling family of Thatta (Tatta), of the tribe of Tarkhānī. His father, Mīrzā Jānī, in the time of my revered father became loyal, and with the Khankhanan, who had been appointed to his province, he had the good fortune to have the honour of waiting on Akbar near Lahore. By the royal favour he was given his own province, and, choosing himself to serve at Court, he sent his men to the charge and administration of Thatta, and remained in the service while he lived. At last he died at Burhanpur. Mīrzā Ghāzī Khān, his son, who was at Thatta, in accordance with the firman of the late king obtained the government of that country. Sa'īd Khān, who was at Bhakar (Bukkur), received an order to console him and bring him to Court. The aforesaid Khan sent men to him to recommend loyalty to him. At last, having brought him to Agra, he procured him the honour of kissing the feet of my revered father. He was at Agra when my father died and I ascended the throne. After I arrived at Lahore for the pursuit of Khusrau news came that the

Amirs on the borders of Khurasan had assembled together and proceeded against Qandahar, and that Shāh Beg, the governor of that place, was shut up in the fort and looking out for assistance. Of necessity an army was appointed for the relief of Qandahar under the leadership of Mīrzā Ghāzī and other Amirs and generals. When this army reached the neighbourhood of Qandahar, the army of Khurasan, not seeing in themselves the power to await it, returned. Mīrzā Ghāzī, having entered Qandahar, handed over the country and the fort to Sardār Khān, who had been appointed to the government of the place, and Shāh Beg went to his own jagir. Mīrzā Ghāzī started for Lahore by way of Bhakar. Sardār Khān was only a short time at Qandahar before he died, and that province was again in need of a leader and master. This time I added Qandahar to Thatta and handed it over to Mīrzā Ghāzī. From that time till his death he remained there continuously in performance of the duties of its protection and government. His conduct towards the disaffected was excellent. As it was necessary to send a leader to Qandahar in the place of Mīrzā Ghāzī, I appointed Abū-l-bī Ūzbeg,[367] who was at Multan and in that neighbourhood, to that post. I promoted him in rank from 1,500 personal and 1,000 horse to 3,000 personal and horse, and honoured him with the title of Bahādur Khān and a standard. The governorship of Delhi and the protection and administration of that province was conferred on Muqarrab Khān. I dignified Rūp Khawāṣṣ, who was one of the personal servants of my revered father, with the title of Khawāṣṣ Khān, and, giving him the rank of 1,000 personal and 500 horse, bestowed on him the faujdarship of the Sarkar of Qanuj. As I had sought the daughter[368] of I'tiqād Khān, son of

---

[367] Should be Abū -n-nabī. See *infra*

[368] This was Arjumand Bānū or Mumtāz-mahall, the favourite wife of Shāh Jahān and the mother of fourteen of his children. She was the niece of Nūr-Jahān, her father being Nūr-Jahān's brother, the Āsaf Khān IV and Abū-l-ḥasan of Beale, who also had the names of I'tiqād Khān and Yamīnu-d-daulah. There is an account of the betrothal and wedding in the Pādshāh-nāma, i, 388. It seems that the betrothal took place five years and three months before the marriage, and

I'timādu-d-daulah, in marriage for Khurram, and the marriage festival had been arranged for, I went on Thursday, 18th Khūrdād, to his house, and stayed there one day and one night. He (Khurram) presented offerings (to me) and he gave jewels[369] to the Begams, and to his mothers (including stepmothers) and to the female servants of the harem, and dresses of honour to the Amirs.

I sent 'Abdu-r-Razzāq, the bakhshi of the palace (*darkhāna*), to settle the country of Thatta (Sind) until a Sardar should be appointed who could conciliate the soldiery and the cultivators, and so bring the province into order. I increased his rank and presented him with an elephant and a shawl (*parmnarm*), and sent him off. I made Mu'izzu-l-mulk bakhshi in his room. Khwāja Jahān, who had been sent to inspect the buildings in Lahore and to arrange about them, came in the end of this month and waited on me. Mīrzā 'Īsā Tarkhān, one of the relations of Mīrzā Ghāzī, had been appointed to the army of the Deccan. I sent for him to arrange about the business of Thatta, and on the same day he had the good fortune to pay his respects. As he was deserving of favour, he was given the rank of 1,000 personal and

---

when Shāh Jahān was 15 years old. At the time of the marriage Shāh Jahān was 20 years and 3 months old and Arjumand Bānū was 19 years and 1 month. 18th Khūrdād, 1021, would correspond to about the end of May, 1612, but the Padshāh-nāma gives the eve of Friday, 9th Rabī'u-lawwal of 1021, corresponding to 22nd Urdībihisht, as the day of the marriage. This would correspond to 30th April, 1612, so that apparently Jahāngīr's visit to the house (apparently I'timādu-d-daulah's, but possibly Shāh Jahān's) took place about a month after the marriage. Arjumand Bānī died in childbed at Burhanpur in 1040, or July, 1631, the chronogram being one word, viz. *gham,* ' grief.' She must have been born in 1591, and was in her 40th year when she died. She was not Shāh Jahān's first wife, for he was married to the daughter of Muẕaffar Ḥusain Ṣafawī, a descendant of Shāh Isma' īl of Persia, in September, 1610 (Rajab, 1019), but the betrothal to Arjumand was earlier than this. It was in Arjumand's honour that the Tāj was built.

[369] *Tūrhā*. The corresponding passage in the Iqbāl-nāma, p. 67, last line, shows that jewels are meant. The text omits the preposition *ba* before *Begamān*.

500 horse. The disease of *khūn-pāra*[370] had affected my health. By the advice of the physicians on Wednesday, the (date not given) of the said month, I drew about a sir (*āṣār*)[371] of blood from my left arm. As great lightness resulted, it occurred to me that if they were to call blood-letting 'lightening' it would be well. Nowadays this expression is made use of. To Muqarrab Khān, who had bled me, I gave a jewelled *khapwa* (dagger). Kishan Dās, accountant of the elephant department and stable, who from the time of the late king until now has been the clerk in charge of two departments, and for ages had been hopeful of the title of Raja and the rank of 1,000 personal, and before this had been gratified with a title, now had the rank of 1,000 conferred on him. Mīrzā Rustam, son of Sulṭān Ḥusain Mīrzā Ṣafawī, who had been appointed to the army of the Deccan, I sent for at his request. On Saturday, the 9th of the month of Tīr, he came with his sons and waited on me. He made an offering of a ruby and forty-six royal pearls. I increased the rank of Tāj Khān, the governor of Bhakar, who was one of the old Amirs of this State, by 500 personal and horse.

The tale of the death of Shajā'at Khān is a very strange affair. After he had performed such services and Islām Khān had given him leave to go to the Sarkar of Orissa, one night on the road he was riding on a female elephant *chaukandī-dār*[372] (? in a square howdah or four-pillared canopy), and had given a young eunuch a place behind him. When he left his camp they had fastened up an elephant that was in heat on the road. From the noise of the horses' hoofs and the movement of the horsemen he attempted to break his chain. On this account a great noise and confusion took place. When this noise reached the ear of the

---

[370] *Khān-pāra*, 'congestion of blood '; *pāra* or *bāra* is used to mean a collection or gathering. See Ma'āṣiru-l-umarā, ii, 221, where we have *bāra ya'nī jam'ī*. Erskine, in spite of his MS., reads *chūn pāra* and translates 'as quicksilver.'

[371] *Āṣār*, which, according to Forbes, is a sir weight.

[372] Perhaps it was only what is called a *chār-jāma* and not an enclosed howḍah.

eunuch, he in a state of bewilderment awoke Shajā'at Khān, who was asleep or in the insensibility of wine, and said : "An elephant in heat has got loose and is coming in this direction." As soon as he heard this he became confused and threw himself down from the front of the chaukandi. When he threw himself off his too struck against a stone and was torn open, and he died in two or three days of that same wound. In short, from hearing this affair I was completely bewildered. That a brave man on the mere hearing of a cry or a word coming from a child should become so confused and throw himself down without control from the top of an elephant is in truth a matter of amazement. The news of this event reached me on the 19th of the month of Tīr. I consoled his sons with kindnesses and the conferring of offices. If this accident had not happened to him, as he had done notable service, he would have obtained exaltation with greater favours and kindnesses.

"One cannot strive against destiny."

Islām Khān had sent 160 male and female elephants from Bengal ; they were brought before me and placed in my private elephant stables. Rāja Tekchand, the Raja of Kumaon, asked for leave to depart. As in the time of my father there had been given to his father 100 horses, I gave him the same number as well as an elephant, and while he was at Court bestowed on him dresses of honour and a jewelled dagger. Also to his brothers I gave dresses of honour and horses. I presented him with his territory according to previous arrangements, and he went back to his home happy and successful.

It happened incidentally that this verse of the Amīru-l-umarā was quoted:—

"Pass, O Messiah, o'er the heads of us slain by love;
Thy restoring one life is worth a hundred murders."[373]

---

373 The reference is to the Messiah as the restorer to life by His breath. For *baguzar*,' pass by,' Erskine had in his MS. *Maguzar* pass not. 'Apparently the verse

As I have a poetical disposition I sometimes intentionally and sometimes involuntarily compose couplets and quatrains. So the following couplet came into my head:—

> "Turn not thy cheek, without thee I cannot live a moment;
> For thee to break one heart is equal a hundred murders."

When I had recited this, everyone who had a poetical vein composed a couplet in the same mode. Mullā 'Alī Aḥmad,[374] the seal-engraver, of whom an account has been given previously, had not said badly—

> "O Censor, fear the weeping of the old vintner;
> Thy breaking one jar is equal to a hundred murders."

Abū-l-fatḥ Dakhanī,[375] who was one of the most considerable of 'Ādil Khān's Amirs, and had two years previously taken to being loyal and had entered himself among the leaders of the victorious army, on the 10th of Amurdād waited on me, and being accepted by my grace and favour had bestowed on him a special sword and a robe of honour, and after some days I also gave him a special horse. Khwājagī Muḥammad Ḥusain,[376] who had gone to Kashmir as the deputy for his brother's son, when he was satisfied in his mind with the state of affairs of that place,

---

means that it is more meritorious for the Messiah to restore one man to life than it is for another to slay a hundred infidels.

[374] 'Alī Aḥmad died suddenly two years before this, unless indeed the passage at p. 169 refers to the mimic and not to 'Alī Aḥmad. Probably the meaning is that 'Alī Aḥmad had made this couplet on some previous occasion, and that one of the courtiers now quoted it. His verse about the hundred murders may contain a play on the word *khūn*, ' blood, ' and refer to the spilling of the blood-like wine. It is difficult to understand how Jahāngīr came to introduce the verse into his Memoirs here. It does not seem to have any connection with the account of the Raja of Kumaon. Jahāngīr says it was quoted ' incidentally,' *bā taqarrubī*. Perhaps the word here means 'by way of parody,' or 'by way of paraphrase.' In the MS. used by Erskine the words of the first line seem to *be Maguzar Masī ḥ bar sar-i-mā*, and so Erskine translates "Pass not, O Messiah, over the heads of us victims of love." Perhaps maguzar means 'do not pass by.'

[375] This is the Dakhanī chief mentioned previously at p. 192.

[376] Blochmann, p. 485. He acted in Kashmir for his brother Hāshim.

came on the same day and waited on me. As a Sardar was needed to be sent for the governorship of Patna and the rule of that place, it occurred to me to send Mīrzā Rustam. Having raised his rank from 5,000 personal and 1,500 horse to 5,000 personal and horse, on the 26th Jumādā-s̤-s̤ānī, corresponding to the 2nd Shahrīwar, I gave him the government of Patna, and bestowing on him a special elephant, a horse with a jewelled saddle, a jewelled sword, and a superb dress of honour, I dismissed him. His sons and the sons of his brother Muzaffar Ḥusain Khān Mīrzā'ī were exalted with increased rank, elephants, horses, and dresses of honour, and sent off with him. I appointed Rāy Dulīp to support Mīrzā Rustam. As his residence was near that place, he collected a good body of men for that service. I increased his rank by 500 personal and horse, so that it became 2,000 with 1,000 horse, and also gave him an elephant. Abū-l-fatḥ Dakhanī had obtained a jagir in the Sarkar of Nagpur and that neighbourhood. He was dismissed in order that he might administer his jagir and look to the guarding and government of that country as well. Khusrau Bī Ūzbeg was appointed to the faujdarship of the Sarkar of Mewar. His rank of 800 personal and 300 horse was now increased to 1,000 personal and 500 horse, and I also presented him with a horse. As I had my eye on the old service of Muqarrab Khān, it occurred to me that I must not pass by the desire of his heart. I had increased his rank and he had obtained good jagirs, but he longed for a standard and drums, and he was now honoured with these as well. Ṣāliḥ, the adopted son of Khwāja Beg-Mīrzā Ṣafawī, was a youth of great bravery and zeal. I gave him the title of Khanjar Khān, and made him eager in the service.

On Thursday, the 22nd Shahrīwar, corresponding with 17th Rajab, 1021, the feast of my solar weighing took place in the house of Maryam-zamānī. It is an approved custom with me to weigh myself in this manner. The late king Akbar, who was the place of manifestation of kindness and grace, also approved of the custom, and twice in every year weighed himself against several sorts of metals, gold, silver, and many precious articles, once according to the solar and once according to the lunar year, and divided their total value, which was worth about a lakh of rupees, among faqirs and needy people. I also observe this annual custom and weigh myself in the same manner, and give those valuables to faqirs. Mu'taqid Khān, Diwan of Bengal, who had been relieved from that service, produced before me the sons and brothers and some of the servants of 'Usmān, whom Islām Khān had sent with him to the Court. The charge of each one of the Afghans was entrusted to a responsible servant. Then he (Mu'taqid) produced his own offering, which consisted of twenty-five elephants, two rubies, a jewelled *phūl kaṭāra*[377] (a kind of dagger), trustworthy eunuchs, Bengal stuffs, etc. Mīr Mīrān, son of Sulṭān Khwāja, who was in the Deccan army, obtained the honour of kissing the threshold and gave a ruby as an offering. As between Qilīj Khān, leader of the army of Bangash on the borders of Kabul, and the Amirs of that Subah, who had been sent as companions to him under his leadership, there were quarrels, especially with Khān Daurān, I sent Khwāja Jahān to make enquiry as to which side was in fault. On the 11th of the month of Mihr, Mu'taqid Khān was appointed to the high dignity of bakhshi, and his mansab was raised to 1,000 personal and 300 horse. Raising for the second time the mansabs of Muqarrab Khān a little, I made it 2,500 personal and 1,500 horse by an increase of 500. On the representation of the Khankhanan, Farīdūn Khān Barlās was raised to the mansab, original and increase, of 2,500 personal and 2,000 horse. Rāy Manohar received that of 1,000 personal and 800 horse, and Rāja Bīr Singh Deo that of 4,000 personal and 2,200 horse. Bhārat, grandson of Rāmchand Bandīlah, I, after the latter's death, honoured with the title of Raja. On the 28th Ābān, Zafar Khān, having come

---

[377] The *kaṭāra* was a long, narrow dagger. See Blochmann's Āyīn, pi. xli, fig. 9. But the word *phūl* (flower) is obscure. Perhaps it means the knot or crochet of jewels called by Chardin, iv, 164, ed. Rouen, " une enseigne ronde de pierreries," and which, he says, the Persians called ' rose de Poignard.'

according to summons from the Subah of Gujarat, waited on me. He brought as offerings a ruby and three pearls. On the 6th Āẕar, corresponding with the 3rd Shawwāl, news came from Burhanpur that the Amīru-l-umarā had died on Sunday, the 27th Ābān, in the parganah of Nihālpūr. After the illness he had at Lahore his intelligence appeared to be less, and a great loss of memory happened to him. He was very sincere. It is sad that he left no son capable of patronage and favour. Chīn Qilīj Khān came from his father, who was at Peshawar, on the 20th Āẕar, and offered (on his father's behalf) 100 muhrs and 100 rupees, and also presented the offerings he had of his own in the shape of a horse and cloth stuffs and other things. To the government of Behar I promoted Zafar Khān, who is one of the trustworthy house-born ones and foster-children, and increasing his mansab by 500 personal and horse, I made it up to 3,000 personal and 2,000 horse, and also honouring his brothers with robes of honour and horses, allowed them to go off to that province. He had always hoped that he might obtain some separate service in order that he might show his natural ability. I also desired to prove him and make this service the touchstone by which to try him. As it was the season for travelling and hunting, on Tuesday, the 2nd Ẕī-l-qa'da (25th December, 1612), corresponding with the 4th Day, I left Agra with the intention of hunting and encamped in the Dahrah garden, remaining there four days.[378] On the 10th of the same month the news came of the death of Salīma Sulṭān Begam, who had been ill in the city. Her mother was Gul-rukh Begam, daughter of King Bābar, and her father Mīrzā Nūru-d-dīn Muḥammad, of the Naqshbandī Khwājas. She was adorned with all good qualities. In women this degree of skill and capacity is seldom found. H.M. Humāyūn, by way of kindness (to Bairām), had betrothed her who was his sister's daughter to Bairām Khān. After his death, in

[378] He must have remained more than four days, for he got the news of Salīma's death while in the garden. See *infra*. Perhaps the date 10th refers to Day and not to Ẕī-l-qa'da. The Dahrah garden was in the environs of Agra.

the beginning of the reign of the late king Akbar, the marriage took place. After the said Khan had been killed, my revered father married her himself. She received mercy (died) in the 60th year of her age.[379] On the same day I marched from the Dahrah garden and sent I'timādu-d-daulah to bury her (lit. lift her up), and ordered him to place her in the building in the Mandākar garden which she herself had made. On the 17th of the month of Day, Mīrzā 'Alī Beg Akbarshāhī came from the army of the Deccan and waited on me. Khwāja Jahān, whom I had despatched to the Subah of Kabul, returned on the 21st of the same month and waited on me. The time for his going and coming had extended to three months and eleven days. He brought twelve muhrs and twelve rupees as an offering. On the same day Rāja Rām Dās also came from the victorious army of the Deccan and paid his respects, and made an offering of 101 muhrs. As robes of honour for the winter season had not been sent to the Amirs of the Deccan, they were forwarded by the hand of Ḥayāt Khān. As the port of Surat had been assigned in jagir to Qilīj Khān, he prayed that Chīn Qilīj (his son) might be despatched for it's guardianship and administration. On the 27th Day he had a dress of honour, and being honoured with a dress of honour and the title of Khān, and a standard, obtained leave to go. For the purpose of advising the Amirs of Kabul, and on account of the disagreements that had sprung up between them and Qilīj Khān, I sent Rāja Rām Dās, and bestowed on him a horse and robe of honour and 30,000 rupees for expenses. On the 6th Bahman, when my camp was in the parganah of Bārī, there

---

[379] This statement is wrong. Salīma was 76 when she died, she having been born on 4th Shawwāl, 945, or 23rd February, 1539. She died on or about 10th Zī-l-qa'da, 1021 (2nd January, 1613), so that she was 73 solar years old. See note in B.M. MS. Or. 171, Rieu, 257*a*, and an article in J.A.S.B. for 1906. The note is by the author of the Tārīkh-i-Muḥammadī and is at 72*a* of the B.M. MS. Or. 171, and the corresponding passage appears in MS. Or. 182, on p. 140. The chronogram of Salīma's birth was *Khūsh-ḥāl*, which yields 945. She was about $3\frac{1}{2}$ years older than Akbar.

came the news of the death of Khwājagī Muḥammad Ḥusain, who was of the ancient servants of this State. His elder brother, Muḥammad Qāsim Khān, in the time of my revered father, found great favour, and Khwāja Muḥammad Ḥusain as well was one of his confidential servants, and held employments such as that of superintendent of the kitchen (*bakāwul*) and such like. He left no son and was beardless, and not a single hair of moustache or whiskers appeared on him. At the time of speaking he spoke very shrilly, and was looked upon as an eunuch. Shāh-nawāz Khān, whom the Khankhanan had sent from Burhanpur to make certain representations, came on the 15th of the same month and waited on me. He presented 100 muhrs and 100 rupees. As the affairs of the Deccan, in consequence of the hasty proceedings of 'Abdu-llah Khān and the treachery of the Amirs, did not present a good prospect, the Dakhanis obtained an opportunity for speaking and began to talk of peace to the Amirs and well-wishers there. 'Ādil Khān embraced the robe of loyalty, and prayed that if the affairs of the Deccan were entrusted to him he would so arrange that some of the districts which had been taken out of the possession of the officers of the State should be restored. The loyal ones, looking to the necessities of the time, represented this, and a settlement of some kind was arrived at, and the Khankhanan undertook to settle matters. The Khān A'ẓam was also desirous of putting down the rebel Rānā, and begged for this service by way of obtaining merit (as a *ghāzī*). He was ordered to go to Malwa, which was his jagir, and after arranging matters there to take up this duty. The mansab of Abū-l-bī Ūzbeg[380] was increased by 1,000 personal and 500 horse to 4,000 personal and 3,500 horse. My hunting went on for 2 months and 20 days, and during that time I went out every day to hunt. As not more than 50 or 60 days remained before the world-illumining New Year, I returned, and on the 24th

[380] The real name appears to be Abū-n-nabī. He had the title of Bahādur Khān. See Ma'āṣiru-l-umarā, i, 400. In the Akbar-nāma, iii, 820 and 839, he is called Abū-1-baqā.

Isfandiyār encamped in the Dahrah garden. The courtiers and some of the mansabdars, who by order had remained in the city, came on that day and waited on me. Muqarrab Khān presented a decorated jar, Frank hats, and a jewelled sparrow (?). I remained three days in the garden, and on the 27th Isfandiyār entered the city. During this time[381] 223 head of deer, etc., 95 nilgaw, 2 boars, 36 cranes (or herons), etc., and 1,457 fish were killed.

THE EIGHTH NEW YEAR AFTER THE AUSPICIOUS ACCESSION.

The eighth year after my accession, corresponding with Muḥarram, 1022. On the night of Thursday, the 27th Muḥarram, corresponding with the 1st Farwardīn in the eighth year after my accession, after 3 1/2 gharis of day had elapsed, his honour the sun passed from the constellation of Pisces to that of Aries, which is his abode of rejoicing and victory. Early in the morning of the New Year's Day the feast was prepared and adorned after the custom of every year. At the end of that day I sat on the throne of State, and the Amirs and ministers of the State and the courtiers of the palace came to salute and congratulate me. On these days of happy augury I sat the whole day in the public audience hall. Those who had anything to ask or claim presented their petitions, and the offerings of the servants of the palace were laid before me. Abū-l-bī, governor of Qandahar, had sent for an offering Iraq horses and hunting dogs, and they were brought before me. On the 9th of the same month Afẓal Khān came from the Subah of Behar, and in waiting on me presented 100 muhrs and 100 rupees, as well as an elephant. On the 12th the offering of I'timādu-d-daulah was laid before me, consisting of jewels, cloths, and other things. That which pleased me attained to the dignity of acceptance. Of the elephants of Afẓal Khān's offering ten others were inspected on this day. On the 13th the offerings of Tarbiyat Khān were laid before me. Mu'taqid Khān bought a house at Agra, and passed some days

[381] This must refer to the 2 months and 20 days of hunting.

in that place. Misfortunes happened to him one after another. We have heard that prosperity and bad luck depend on four things : first, upon your wife ; second, upon your slave ; third, upon your house ; fourth, upon your horse. In order to know the prosperity or ill-luck of a house a rule has been established, indeed they say it is infallible. One must clear a small piece of the site from earth, and again strew the earth upon the same ground. If it cover it, one may call it middling good fortune for that house, neither prosperity nor misfortune ; if it become less (i.e. does not cover it exactly) it points to ill-luck, and if it does more (than cover it) it is fortunate and auspicious. On the 14th the mansab of I'tibār Khān was raised from 1,000 and 300 horse to 2,000 personal and 500 horse. I increased the mansab of Tarbiyat Khān by 500 personal and 50 horse, so that it became 2,000 personal and 850 horse. Hūshang, son of Islām Khān, who was in Bengal with his father, came at this time and paid his respects. He brought with him some Maghs, whose country is near Pegu and Arracan, and the country is still in their possession. I made some enquiries as to their customs and religion. Briefly they are animals in the form of men. They eat everything there is either on land or in the sea, and nothing is forbidden by their religion. They eat with anyone. They take into their possession (marry) their sisters by another mother. In face they are like the Qarā Qalmāqs, but their language is that of Tibet and quite unlike Turkī. There is a range of mountains, one end of which touches the province of Kāshghar and the other the country of Pegu. They have no proper religion or any customs that can be interpreted as religion. They are far from the Musulman faith and separated from that of the Hindus.

Two or three days before the Sharaf (the sun's highest point) my son Khurram desired me to go to his house that he might present his New Year's offerings from that place. I agreed to his request, and remained for one day and one night at his house. He presented his offerings. I took what I approved of and gave him back the rest. The next day Murtaẓā Khān presented his offerings. Every day until the day of culmination (*rūz-i-sharaf*) the offerings of one or of two or three of the Amirs were laid before me. On Monday, the 19th Farwardīn, the assembly of the Sharaf was held. On that auspicious day I sat on the throne of State, and an order was given that they should produce all sorts of intoxicating things, such as wine, etc., so that every one according to his desire might take what he liked. Many took wine. The offerings of Mahābat Khān were on this day brought to me. I gave one gold muhr of 1,000 tolas, which is called the star of destiny (*kaukab-i-ṭāli'*), to Yādgār 'Alī Khān, the ambassador of the ruler of Iran. The feast went off well. After the assembly broke up I ordered that they might carry off the furniture and decorations. The offering of the Muqarrab Khān had not been arranged on New Year's Day. All sorts of rareties and excellent presents were now produced which he had collected together. Amongst others, twelve Iraq and Arab horses that had been brought in a ship, and jewelled saddles of Frank workmanship[382] were produced before me. To the mansab of Nawāzish Khān 500 horse were added so as to make it one of 2,000 personal and horse. An elephant called Bansībadan, which Islām Khān had sent from Bengal, was brought to me and put among my special elephants. On the 3rd Urdībihisht, Khwāja Yādgār, brother of 'Abdu-llah Khān, came from Gujarat and waited on me ; he offered 100 Jahāngīrī muhrs. After he had been in attendance a few days he was honoured with the title of Sardār Khān. As a competent bakhshi had to be sent to the army of Bangash and those regions, I chose Mu'taqid Khān for this duty, and increased his mansab by 300 personal and 50 horse so that it became 1,500 with 350 horse, and dismissed him. It was settled that he must go quickly. I sent off Muḥammad Ḥusain Chelebī, who understood the purchase of jewels and collecting curiosities, with money to go by way of Iraq to Constantinople

---

382 *Zīn-i-muraṣṣa' kārī -i-Farangī*. The MSS. in the B.M. seem to have *zaram* instead of *zīn*.

and buy and bring for the Sarkar curiosities and rareties. For this purpose it was necessary that he should pay his respects to the ruler of Iran. I had given him a letter and a memorandum (of what he was to procure). Briefly, he saw my brother, S͟hāh 'Abbās, in Mashhad, and the king enquired from him what kind of things should be brought for his master's Sarkar. As he was urgent, Chelebī showed the list he had brought with him. In that list there were entered good turquoise and *mūmīyā* (bitumen) from the mine of Ispahan. He told him that these two articles were not to be bought, but he would send them for me. He authorized Uwaisī Tūpchī (gunner), who was one of his private servants, to hand over to him six bags (*ambāncha*) of turquoise earth holding about 30 seers, with 14 tolas of mumiya and four Iraq horses, one of which was a piebald, and he wrote a letter containing many, many expressions of friendship. With regard to the inferior quality of the turquoise dust (*k͟hāka*) and the small quantity of mumiya he made many apologies. The khaka appeared very inferior. Although the jewellers and makers of rings made every endeavour, no stone that was fit to be made into a finger ring could be produced. Probably in these days turquoise dust is not procurable from the mines such as it was in the time of the late king Ṭahmāsp. He mentioned all this in the letter. With regard to the effect of mumiya I had heard much from scientists, but when I tried it no result was apparent. I do not know whether physicians have exaggerated its effect, or whether its efficacy had been lessened by its being stale. At any rate, I gave it to a fowl with a broken leg to drink in larger quantity than they said and in the manner laid down by the physicians, and rubbed some on the place where it was broken, and kept it there for three days, though it was said to be sufficient to keep it from morning till evening. But after I had examined it, no effect was produced, and the broken place remained as it was.[383] In a separate letter the Shah had written a

[383] Jahāngīr's words seem to imply that he caused the fowl's leg to be broken in

recommendation of Salāmu-llah, the Arab. I immediately increased his mansab and his jagir.

I sent one of my private elephants with trappings to 'Abdu-llah Khān and gave another to Qilīj Khān. I ordered that assignments (*tankhwāh*) should be made to 12,000 horse on the establishment[384] of 'Abdu-llah Khān at the rate of three horses and two horses for each trooper. As previously with a view to service in Junagarh I had increased the mansab of his brother Sardār Khān by 500 personal and 300 horse, and had afterwards assigned the duty to Kāmil Khān, I ordered that he should retain his increase and that it should be counted (permanently) in his mansab. I increased the rank of Sarfarāz Khān, which was that of 1,500 personal and 500 horse, by 200 horse more. On the 27th Urdībihisht, corresponding with the 26th Rabī'u-l-awwal, in the eighth year of my reign, in the year 1022 of the Hijra era, on Thursday, the meeting for my lunar weighing took place in the house of Maryam-zamānī (his mother). Some of the money that was weighed I ordered to be given to the women and the deserving ones who had assembled in my mother's house. On the same day I increased by 1,000 the mansab of Murtaẓā Khān, so that it came to 6,000 personal and 5,000 horse. Khusrau Beg, a slave of Mīrzā Khān, came from Patna in the company of 'Abdu-r-Razzāq Ma'mūrī and waited on me, and Sardār Khān, brother of 'Abdu-llah Khān, obtained leave to go to Ahmadabad. An Afghan had brought from the Carnatic two goats that had

---

order to try the experiment. Manucci, i, 55, has a good deal to say about *mūmīyā*, though he admits that he had not himself witnessed its effects. I do not find that Hājī Bābā descants on its virtues, though at the end of the first chapter he says that his mother gave him an unguent which she said would cure all fractures. The Persian translator, no doubt rightly, has rendered the word 'unguent' by *mūmiyā*. With regard to the derivation of the word, may it not be connected with *mom*, 'wax'? Vullers has a long article on the word.

384 The text has *birādārī*, 'brotherhood,' but the true reading, as shown by the B.M. MSS., is bar *āwardī*, برآوردی, and this means either the establishment of 'Abdu-llah or a list submitted by him. Perhaps 'list' is a better translation, the word *āwardī* being connected with the *āwarda-nawīs* of Wilson's Glossary.

pāzahar (bezoar stones, an antidote against poison). I had always heard that an animal that has pazahar is very thin and miserable, but these goats were very fat and fresh. I ordered them to kill one of them, which was a female. Four pazahar stones became apparent, and this caused great astonishment.

It is an established fact that cheetahs in unaccustomed places do not pair off with a female, for my revered father once collected together 1,000 cheetahs. He was very desirous that they should pair, but this in no way came off. He had many times coupled male and female cheetahs together in gardens, but there, too, it did not come off. At this time a male cheetah, having slipped its collar, went to a female and paired with it, and after two and a half months three young ones were born and grew up. This has been recorded because it appeared strange. As cheetahs did not pair with cheetahs, (still less) had it ever been heard in former times (?) that tigers mated in captivity. As in the time of my reign wild beasts have abandoned their savagery, tigers have become so tame that troops of them without chains or restraint go about amongst the people, and they neither harm men nor have any wildness or alarm. It happened that a tigress became pregnant and after three months bore three cubs ; it had never happened that a wild tiger after its capture had paired. It had been heard from philosophers that the milk of a tigress was of great use for brightening eyes. Although we made every effort that the moisture of milk should appear in her breasts, we could not accomplish it. It occurs to me that as it is a raging creature, and milk appears in the breasts of mothers by reason of the affection they have for their young, as milk[385] comes into their breasts in connection with their young ones drinking and sucking at the time of their taking (the milk), their (the mothers') rage increases and the milk in their breasts is dried up.

---

[385] The sentence is very obscure. MS. No. 181 I.O. has *khūn*, 'blood', instead of chūn, 'as,' and perhaps the meaning is blood in the breasts turns to milk on account of love for their cubs, and then the sucking by the latter increases the mother's natural ferocity and the milk dries up.

At the end of Urdībihisht, Khwāja Qāsim, brother of Khwāja 'Abdu-l-'Azīz, who is of the Naqshbandī Khwājas, came from Māwarā'a-n-nahr and waited on me. After a few days 12,000 rupees were given to him as a present. As Khwāja Jahān had made a melon-bed in the neighbourhood of the city, when two watches of day had passed on Thursday, the 10th Khūrdād, I got into a boat and went to inspect the melon-bed, and took the ladies with me. We reached there when two or three gharis of day were left, and passed the evening in walking among the beds. A wonderfully sharp wind and whirlwind sprang up, so that the tents and screens fell down. I got into the boat and passed the night in it. I also passed part of the Friday in walking about the melon-bed, and returned to the city. Afẓal Khān, who for a long time had been afflicted with boils and other sores, died on the 10th Khūrdād. I transferred the jagir and hereditary land of Rāja Jagman, who had failed in his service in the Deccan, to Mahābat Khān. Shaikh Pīr, who is one of the emancipated ones who hold aloof from the attachments of the age, and who on account of the pure friendship that he bears towards me has chosen to be my companion and servant, had before this founded a mosque in the parganah of Mairtha, which is his native place. At this time he took occasion to mention the circumstance. As I found his mind bent on the completion of this building I gave him 4,000 rupees, so that he himself might go and expend it, and also gave him a valuable shawl and dismissed him. In the public audience hall there were two railings (*maḥjar*) of wood. Inside the first, Amirs, ambassadors, and people of honour sat, and no one entered this circle without an order. Within the second railing, which is broader than the first, the mansabdars of inferior rank,[386] ahadis, and those who had work to do are admitted. Outside this railing stand the servants of the Amirs and all the people who may enter the Diwankhana. As there was no difference between the first and

[386] In the B.M. MSS. the words are *man ṣabdārān-i-rīzā-mansab*. These last two words are wanting in the text.

second railings, it occurred to me that I should decorate the first with silver. I ordered this railing and the staircase that led from this railing to the balcony of the Jharokha, as well as the two elephants placed on the two sides of the seat of the Jharokha, which skilful people had made of wood, to be decorated with silver. After this was completed it was reported to me that 125 maunds of silver in Hindustani weight, equal to 880 maunds of Persia, had been used up ; indeed, it now assumed a worthy appearance.

On the 3rd of the month of Tīr, Muẓaffar Khān came from Thatta[387] and waited on me. He made an offering of twelve muhrs and a Koran with a jewelled cover, and two jewelled roses (?) (*dū gul*). On the 14th of the same month Ṣafdar Khān came from the Subah of Behar and waited on me, offering 101 muhrs. After Muẓaffar Khān had been some days in attendance, I increased his former mansab by 500 personal, and giving him a standard and a private shawl dismissed him to Thatta.[388]

I knew that every animal or living thing bitten by a mad dog died, but this had not been ascertained in the case of an elephant. In my time it so happened that one night a mad dog came into the place where was tied one of my private elephants, Gajpatī[389] by name, and bit the foot of a female elephant that was with mine. She at once cried out. The elephant-keepers at once ran in, and the dog fled away into a thorn-brake that is there. After a little while it came in again and bit my private elephant's fore-foot as well. The elephant killed it. When a month and five days had passed after this event, one day when it was cloudy the growling of thunder came to the ear of the female elephant, that was in the act of eating, and it of a sudden raised a cry and its limbs began to tremble. It threw itself on the ground, but rose again. For seven days water ran out of its mouth, then suddenly

[387] Text Patna, but B.M. MSS. have Thatta.

[388] Text has Patna.

[389] Text Kachhī, but it is Gajpatī in B.M. MSS.

it uttered a cry and showed distress. The remedies the drivers gave it had no effect, and on the eighth day it fell and died. A month after the death of the female elephant they took the large elephant to the edge of the river in the plain. It was cloudy and thundery in the same way. The said elephant in the height of excitement all at once began to tremble and sat down on the ground. With a thousand difficulties the drivers took it to its own place. After the same interval and in the same way that had happened to the female elephant this elephant also died. Great amazement was caused by this affair, and in truth it is a matter to be wondered at that an animal of such size and bulk should be so much affected by a little wound inflicted on it by such a weak creature.

As Khānkhānān had repeatedly begged for leave to be given to his son Shāh-nawāz Khān, on the 4th Amurdād I gave him a horse and a robe of honour and dismissed him to the Deccan. I promoted Ya'qūb Badakhshī, whose mansab was 150, to 1,500 personal and 1,000 horse, on account of the bravery he had displayed, and gave him the title of Khan as well as a standard.

The Hindus are in four divisions, and each of these acts according to its own rules and ways. In every year they keep a fixed day. The first is the caste of the Brahmans,[390] that is, those who know the Incomparable God. Their duties are of six kinds— (1) to acquire religious knowledge, (2) to give instructions to others, (3) to worship fire, (4) to lead men to the worship of fire, (5) giving something to the needy, (6) taking gifts. There is for this caste an appointed day, and that is the last day of the month of Sāwan, the second month of the rainy season.[391] They consider this an auspicious day, and the worshippers go on that day to the banks of rivers and tanks, and recite enchantments, breathe upon cords and coloured threads; on another day, which is the

---

[390] This seems taken from Abū-l-faẓl. See Jarrett, iii, 115. The third duty, which Jahāngīr calls " worshipping fire," is by Abū-l-faẓl termed Yāg, i.e. sacrifice.

[391] It is the day of the full moon in Sāwan that is holy.

first of the New Year, they fasten them on the hands of the Rajas and great men of the time, and look on them as (good) omens. They call this thread *rākhī,*[392] that is, preservation (*nigāh-dāsht*). This day occurs in the month of Tīr, when the world-heating sun is in the constellation of Cancer. The second caste is that of the Chhatrī, which is known as Khatrī. Their duty is to protect the oppressed from the evil of the oppressors. The customs of this caste are three things—(1) that they study religious science themselves but do not teach others ; (2) that they worship fire, but do not teach others to do so ; (3) that they give to the needy, but although they are needy take nothing themselves. The day of this caste is the *Bijay dasamīn,* 'the victorious tenth.'[393] On this day with them it is lucky to mount and go against one's enemy with an army. Rām Chand, whom they worship as their god, leading his army on that day against his enemy won a victory, and they consider this a great day, and, decorating their elephants and horses, perform worship. This day falls in the month of Shahrīwar,[394] when the Sun is in the mansion of Virgo, and on it they give presents to those who look after their horses and elephants. The third caste is that of Baish (Vaishya). Its custom is this, that they serve the other two castes of which mention has been made. They practise agriculture and buying and selling, and are employed in the business of profit and interest. This caste has also a fixed day which they call the Dewālī ; this day occurs in the month of Mihr when the sun is in the constellation of Libra, the 28th day of the lunar month. On the night of that day they light lamps, and friends and those who

---

392 Blochmann, p. 184, and Wilson's Glossary. Badayūnī (Lowe, p. 269) speaks of Akbar's wearing the *rākhī* on the 8th day of Virgo. I do not know why Jahāngīr calls the day after the last day of Sāwan the first day of the New Year. Perhaps *rūz-i-duyam* here means 'another day,' and not 'the next day'; but then, if so, why is it the rakhi day, for that is in Sāwan ? The Hindu New Year begins in Baisākh (April). It will be observed from Jarrett, ii, 17, that Sāwan is also the name of a month of a particular length. Perhaps Jahāngīr has confused the two things.

393 It is the 10th of Aswīn (September).

394 The text wrongly has *dar har māh* instead of only *dar māh*.

are dear assemble in each other's houses and pass their time busily in gambling. As the eyes of this caste are on profit and interest, they consider carrying over and opening new accounts on that day auspicious. The fourth caste is the Sudras, who are the lowest caste of the Hindus. They are the servants of all, and derive no profit from those things which are the specialities of every (other) caste. Thursday is the Holī, which in their belief is the last day of the year. This day occurs in the month of Isfandārmuz, when the sun is in the constellation of Pisces. On the night of this day they light fires at the head of the streets and ways, and when it becomes day they for one watch scatter the ashes on each other's heads and faces, and make a wonderful noise and disturbance, and after this wash themselves, put on their apparel, and walk about in the gardens and on the plains. As it is an established custom of the Hindus to burn the dead, to light fires on this night, which is the last night of the year that has passed, signifies that they burn the last year, which has gone to the abode of the dead. In the time of my revered father the Hindu Amirs and others in imitation of them performed the ceremony of rakhi in adorning him, making strings of rubies and royal pearls and flowers jewelled with gems of great value and binding them on his auspicious arms. This custom was carried on for some years. As they carried this extravagance to excess, and he disliked it, he forbade it. The brahmans by way of auguries used to tie these strings and (pieces of) silk according to their custom. I also in this year carried out this laudable religious practice, and ordered that the Hindu Amirs and the heads of the caste[395] should fasten rakhis on my arms. On the day of the rakhi, which was the 9th Amurdād, they performed the same rites, and other castes by way of imitation did not give up this bigotry ; this year I agreed to it, and ordered that the brahmans should bind strings (of cotton) and silk after the ancient manner. On this day by chance fell the anniversary of the death of the late

---

[395] The negative in text is wrong apparently. It does not occur in MS. No. 181 I.O. nor in the B.M. MSS., which have *ba* instead of *na*.

king.[396] The commemoration of such an anniversary is one of the standing rules and customs in Hindustan. Every year on the day of the death of their fathers and those who are dear to them, each according to his circumstances and ability prepares food and all kinds of perfumes, and the learned men, the respectable and other men assemble, and these assemblies sometimes last a week. On this day I sent Bābā Khurram to the venerated tomb to arrange the assemblage, and 10,000 rupees were given to ten trustworthy servants to divide among fakirs and those who were in want.

On the 15th of the month of Amurdād the offering of Islām Khān was laid before me. He had sent 28 elephants, 40 horses of that part of the country which are known as *ṭānghan,* 50 eunuchs, 500 *pargāla nafīs sitārkānī.*[397]

It had been made a rule that the events of the Subahs should be reported according to the boundaries of each, and news-writers from the Court had been appointed for this duty. This being the rule that my revered father had laid down, I also observe it, and much gain and great advantage are to be brought about by it, and information is acquired about the world and its inhabitants. If the advantages of this were to be written down it would become a long affair. At this time the news-writer of Lahore reported that at the end of the month of Tīr ten men had gone from the city to Amānābād, which lies at a distance of 12 kos. As the air was very hot, they took shelter under a tree. Soon afterwards wind and a dust-storm (*chakrī*) sprang up, and when it blew on that band of men they trembled, and nine of them died under the tree, and only one remained alive ; he was ill for

[396] That is, 9th Amurdād corresponded with the Ḥijra date of Akbar's death, viz. 13th Jumādā-ṣ-ṣānī, which this year, 1022, occurred in July. According to the solar calendar Akbar's death was in October.

[397] *Pargālas* seem to be clothes of some sort. Perhaps the word is another form of the *fargūl* of Blochmann, p. 89. The text has *sitārkānī. Sitār* means a veil, but probably we should read *Sonārgaonī,* 'of Sonargaon.' Both the MSS. give the number of elephants as 68 instead of 28 as in text.

a long time, and recovered with great difficulty. In that neighbourhood such bad air was created that numerous birds who had their nests in that tree all fell down and died, and that the wild beasts (beasts of the plain, perhaps cattle) came and threw themselves on to the cultivated fields, and, rolling about on the grass, gave up their lives. In short, many animals perished. On Thursday, the 13th Amurdād, having said my prayers (lit. counted my rosary), I embarked on board a boat for the purpose of hunting in the village of Samonagar, which is one of my fixed hunting - places. On the 3rd S͟hahrīwar, K͟hān 'Ālam, whom I had sent for from the Deccan in order to despatch him to Iraq in company with the ambassador of the ruler of Iran, came and waited on me at this place. He offered 100 muhrs. As Samonagar was in Mahābat K͟hān's jagir, he had prepared a delightful halting-place there on the bank of the river, and it pleased me greatly. He presented offerings of an elephant and an emerald ring. The former was put into my private stud. Up to the 6th S͟hahrīwar I was employed in hunting. In these few days 47 head of antelope, male and female, and other animals were killed. At this time Dilāwar K͟hān sent as an offering a ruby, which was accepted. I sent a special sword for Islām K͟hān. I increased the mansab of Ḥasan 'Alī Turkumān, which was 1,000 personal and 700 horse, by 500 personal and 100 horse. At the end of Thursday, the 20th of the same month, in the house of Maryam-zamānī, my solar weighing took place. I weighed myself according to the usual custom against metals and other things. I had this year attained to the age of 44 solar years. On the same day Yādgār 'Alī, ambassador of the ruler of Iran, and K͟hān 'Ālam, who had been nominated to accompany him from this side, received their leave to go. On Yādgār 'Alī there were bestowed a horse with a jewelled saddle, a jewelled sword, a vest without sleeves with gold embroidery, an aigrette with feathers and a *jīg͟ha* (turban ornament), and 30,000 rupees in cash, altogether 40,000 rupees, and on K͟hān 'Ālam a jewelled *khapwa* or *phūl kaṭāra* (a sort of dagger) with a pendant of royal pearls. On the 22nd of the same month I visited the venerated mausoleum of my revered father at Bihishtābād, riding on an elephant. On the way 5,000 rupees in small coin were scattered round, and I gave other 5,000 rupees to Khwāja Jahān to divide among the dervishes. Having said my evening prayers, I went back to the city in a boat. As the house of I'timādu-d-daulah was on the bank of the river Jumna, I alighted there until the end of the next day. Having accepted what pleased me of his offerings, I went towards the palace ; I'tiqād Khān's house was also on the bank of the river Jumna ; at his request I disembarked there with the ladies, and walked round the houses he had lately built there. This delightful place pleased me greatly. He had produced suitable offerings of cloth stuffs and jewels and other things ; these were all laid before me and most of them were approved. When it was near evening I entered the auspicious palace. As the astrologers had fixed an hour in this night for starting for Ajmir, when seven gharis of the night of Monday, the 2nd Sha'bān, corresponding with the 24th Shahrīwar, had passed, I started in happiness and prosperity with intent to go there from the capital of Agra. In this undertaking two things were agreeable to me, one a pilgrimage to the splendid mausoleum of Khwāja Mu'īnu-d-dīn Chishtī, from the blessing of whose illustrious soul great advantages had been derived by this dignified family, and whose venerable shrine I had not visited after my accession to the throne. The second was the defeat and beating back of the rebel Rānā Amar Singh, who is one of the most considerable of the Zamindars and Rajas of Hindustan, and whose headship and leadership and those of his ancestors all the Rajas and Rays of this province agree to. The administration has for long been in the hands of this family, and they have long borne rule towards the East, that is the Pūrab. They became in that time well known under the title of Rajas. After this they fell on the Deccan[398] and took possession of many of the countries of that region. In the

[398] See Jarrett, ii, 268, where it is said that an ancestor of Bāppa came to Berar.

place of Raja they have taken the title of Rāwal. After this they came into the hill country of Mewāt, and by degrees got into their possession the fort of Chitor. From that date until this day, which is in the eighth year after my accession, 1,471 years have passed.[399]

There are twenty-six others of this caste who have ruled for 1,010 years. They have the title of Rāwal, and from the Rāwal who was first known as Rāwal down to Rānā Amar Singh, the present Rānā, there are twenty-six individuals who have ruled for the space of 461 years. During this long time they have never bent their necks in obedience to any of the kings of the country of Hindustan, and have for most of the time been rebellious and troublesome, so much so that in the reign of the late king Bābar, Rānā Sāngā collected together all the Rajas, Rays, and Zamindars of this province, and fought a battle in the neighbourhood of Biyāna with 180,000 horse and several lakhs of footsoldiers. By the aid of Almighty God and the assistance of fortune the victorious army of Islām prevailed against the infidel forces, and a great defeat happened to them. The details of this battle have been given in the Memoirs of King Bābar. My revered father (may his bright tomb be the abode of unending Grace) exerted himself greatly to put down these rebels, and several times sent armies against them. In the twelfth year after his accession he set himself to capture the fort of Chitor, which is one of the strongest forts of the inhabited world, and to overthrow the kingdom of the Rānā, and after four months and ten days of siege took it by force from the men of Amar Singh's father, after much fighting, and returned after destroying the fort. Every time the victorious forces pressed him hard in order to capture him or make him a fugitive, but it so happened that this was not

[399] According to Tod, Bāppa, the ancestor of the Rānā, acquired Chitor in A.D. 728. Jahāngīr makes twenty-six princes rule for 1,010 years and twenty-six others only reign for 461 years ! Tod says the legendary ancestor Kenek Sen, the sixty-third from Loh, the son of Rām, emigrated from the Panjab to Gujarat in 145 A.D. Perhaps the Mewāt of the Tūzuk is a mistake for Mewār.

effected. In the end of his reign, on the same day and hour that he proceeded to the conquest of the Deccan, he sent me with a large army and reliable Sardars against the Rānā. By chance these two affairs, for reasons which it would take too long to recount, did not succeed. At last I came to the throne, and as this matter was only half done, the first army I sent to the borders was this one. Making my son Parwīz its leader, the leading nobles who were at the capital were appointed to this duty. I sent abundant treasure and artillery with him. As every matter depends on its own season, at this juncture the unhappy affair of Khusrau occurred, and I had to pursue him to the Panjab. The province and the capital of Agra remained void. I had necessarily to write that Parwīz should return with some of the Amirs and take charge of Agra and the neighbourhood. In short, this time again the matter of the Rānā did not go off as it should. When by the favour of Allah my mind was at rest from Khusrau's disturbance, and Agra became again the alighting place of the royal standards, a victorious army was appointed under the leadership of Mahābat Khān, 'Abdu-llah Khān, and other leaders, and from that date up to the time when the royal standards started for Ajmir his country was trodden under foot by the victorious forces. As finally the affair did not assume an approved form, it occurred to me that, as I had nothing to do at Agra, and I was convinced that until I myself went there the affair would not be set to rights , I left the fort of Agra and alighted at the Dahrah garden. On the next day the festival of the Dasahrā took place. According to the usual custom they decorated the elephants and horses, and I had them before me. As the mothers and sisters of Khusrau repeatedly represented to me that he was very repentant of his deeds, the feelings (lit. sweat) of fatherly affection having come into movement, I sent for him and determined that he should come every day to pay his respects to me. I remained for eight days in that garden. On the 28th news arrived that Rāja Rām Dās, who was doing service in Bangash and the neighbourhood of Kabul with Qilīj Khān, had died. On the 1st of the month of Mihr I marched from the garden, and dismissed Khwāja Jahān to look after the capital of Agra and guard the treasure and the palace, and gave him an elephant and a special robe (*fargul*). On the 2nd Mihr news arrived that Rāja Bāso had died in the thanah of Shahabad,[400] which is on the border of the territory of Amar. On the 10th of the same month I halted at Rūp Bās, which has now been named Amānābād. Formerly this district had been given as jagir to Rūp Khawāṣṣ. Afterwards, bestowing it on Amānu-llah, son of Mahābat Khān, I ordered it to be called by his name. Eleven days were passed at this halting-place. As it is a fixed hunting-place, I every day mounted to go hunting, and in these few days 158 antelopes, male and female, and other animals were killed. On the 25th of the month I marched from Amānābād. On the 31st, corresponding with the 8th Ramaẓān, Khwāja Abū-l-ḥasan, whom I had sent for from Burhanpur, came and waited on me, and presented as offerings 50 muhrs, 15 jewelled vessels, and an elephant, which I placed in my private stud. On the 2nd Ābān, corresponding with the 10th Ramaẓān, news came of the death of Qilīj Khān. He was one of the ancient servants of the State, and obtained the mercy of God in the 80th year of his age. He was employed at Peshawar in the duty of keeping in order the Afghans full of darkness.[401] His rank was 6,000 personal and 5,000 horse. Murtaẓā Khān Dakhanī was unrivalled in the art of *pūlta-bāzī,* which in the language of the Dakhanis they call *yagānagī,* and the Moguls *shamshīr-bāzī,* 'sword-play' (fencing). For some time I studied it with him. At this time I exalted him with the title of Warzish Khān (Exercise - Khān). I had established a custom that deserving people and dervishes should be brought before me every night, so that I might bestow on them, after personal enquiry into their condition, land, or gold, or clothes. Amongst these was a man who represented to me

[400] Probably the town of that name in the Rajputana State of Jhalāwar. See "Rajputana Gazetteer," ii, 211.

[401] The Raushanīs, called by their enemies the Tārīkīs.

that the name Jahāngīr, according to the science of *abjad* (numerals reckoned by letters), corresponded to the great name "Allah Akbar."[402] Considering this a good omen, I gave him who discovered (this coincidence) land, a horse, cash, and clothing. On Monday, the 5th Shawwāl, corresponding to the 26th Ābān, the hour for entering Ajmir was fixed. On the morning of the said day I went towards it. When the fort and the buildings of the shrine of the revered Khwāja appeared in sight, I traversed on foot the remainder of the road, about a kos. I placed trustworthy men on both sides of the road, who went along giving money to fakirs and the necessitous. When four gharis of day had passed, I entered the city and its inhabited portion, and in the fifth ghari had the honour of visiting the venerated mausoleum. After visiting it I proceeded to the auspicious palace, and the next day ordered all those present in this honoured resting-place, both small and great, belonging to the city, and travellers, to be brought before me, that they might be made happy with numerous gifts according to their real circumstances. On the 7th Āzar I went to see and shoot on the tank of Pushkar, which is one of the established praying-places of the Hindus, with regard to the perfection of which they give (excellent) accounts that are incredible to any intelligence, and which is situated at a distance of three kos from Ajmir. For two or three days I shot waterfowl on that tank, and returned to Ajmir. Old and new temples which, in the language of the infidels, they call Deohara[403] are to be seen around this tank. Among them Rānā Shankar, who is the uncle of the rebel Amar, and in my kingdom is among the high nobles, had built a Deohara of great magnificence, on which 100,000 rupees had been spent. I went to see that temple. I found a form cut out of black stone, which from the neck above was in the shape of a pig's head, and the rest of the body was like that of a man. The worthless religion of the Hindus is this, that once on a time for

[402] Both Jahāngīr and Allah Akbar yield 288.

[403] Sanskrit Devaharā, 'an idol temple.'

some particular object the Supreme Ruler thought it necessary to show himself in this shape ; on this account they hold it dear and worship it.[404] I ordered them to break that hideous form and throw it into the tank. After looking at this building there appeared a white dome on the top of a hill, to which men were coming from all quarters. When I asked about this they said that a Jogī lived there, and when the simpletons come to see him he places in their hands a handful[405] of flour, which they put into their mouths and imitate the cry of an animal which these fools have at some time injured, in order that by this act their sins may be blotted out. I ordered them to break down that place and turn the Jogī out of it, as well as to destroy the form of an idol there was in the dome. Another belief they have is that there is no bottom to this tank. After enquiry it appeared that it is nowhere deeper than 12 cubits. I also measured it round and it was about 1 1/2 kos.

On the 16th Āzar news came that the watchmen had marked down a tigress. I immediately went there and killed it with a gun and returned. After a few days a nilgaw (blue bull) was killed, of which I ordered them to take off the skin in my presence and cook it as food for the poor. Over 200 people assembled and ate it, and I gave money with my own hand to each of them. In the same month news came that the Franks of Goa had, contrary to treaty, plundered four cargo vessels[406] that frequented the port of Surat in the neighbourhood of that port; and, making prisoners a large number of Musulmans, had taken possession of the goods and chattels that were in those ships. This being very disagreeable to my mind, I despatched Muqarrab Khān, who is

---

404 "Rajputana Gazetteer," ii, 69.

405 Instead of *kaff ārdi*, 'a handful of flour,' the R.A.S. 'MS. Has *kaf az way*, 'his spittle,' and this seems more likely.

406 Text *ajnabī*, 'foreign' or 'strange,' and Dowson had the same reading, for at vi, 337, we have the translation 'ships engaged in the foreign trade of Surat.' But I adopt the reading of I.O. MS. 181, which is *ajnāsī*, as it does not seem likely that Jahāngīr would interest himself about 'foreign' ships.

in charge of the port, on the 18th Āẕar, giving him a horse and elephant and a dress of honour, to obtain compensation for this affair. On account of the great activity and good services of Yūsuf Khān and Bahāduru-l-mulk in the Subah of the Deccan, I sent standards for them.

It has been written that my chief object, after my visit to the Khwāja, was to put a stop to the affair of the rebel Rānā. On this account I determined to remain myself at Ajmir and send on Bābā Khurram, my fortunate son. This idea was a very good one, and on this account, on the 6th of Day, at the hour fixed upon, I despatched him in happiness and triumph. I presented him with a *qabā* (outer coat) of gold brocade with jewelled flowers and pearls round the flowers, a brocaded turban with strings of pearls, a gold woven sash with chains of pearls, one of my private elephants called Fatḥ Gaj, with trappings, a special horse, a jewelled sword, and a jewelled *khapwa,* with a *phūl kaṭāra.* In addition to the men first appointed to this duty under the leadership of Khān A'ẓam, I sent 12,000 more horse with my son, and honoured their leaders, each according to his condition, with special horses and elephants and robes of honour, and dismissed them. Fidā'ī Khān was nominated to the paymastership of this army. At the same time Ṣafdar Khān was despatched to the government of Kashmir in place of Hāshim Khān. He received a horse and robe of honour. On Wednesday, the 11th, Khwāja Abū-l-ḥasan was made general paymaster (*bakhshī-kul*), and received a dress of honour. I had ordered them to make a large caldron[407] at Agra for the revered mausoleum of the Khwāja. On this day it was brought, and I ordered them to cook food for the poor in that pot, and collect together the poor of Ajmir to feed them whilst I was there. Five thousand people assembled, and all ate of this food to their fill. After the food I gave money to each of the dervishes with my own hand. At this

[407] "Rajputana Gazetteer," ii, 63. There are now two large caldrons (*dīg*) inside the dargāh enclosure.

time Islām Khān, governor of Bengal, was promoted to the mansab of 6,000 personal and horse, and a flag was given to Mukarram Khān, son of Mu'āẓẓam Khān.

On the 1st of Isfandārmuz, corresponding with the 10th Muḥarram, 1023 (20th February, 1614), I left Ajmir to hunt nilgaw, and returned on the 9th. I halted at the fountain of Ḥāfiẓ Jamāl,[408] two kos from the city, and passed the night of Friday[409] there. At the end of the day I entered the city. In these twenty days ten nilgaw had been killed. As the good service of Khwāja Jahān and the smallness of his force for the defence and government of Agra and that neighbourhood were brought to my notice, I increased his mansab by 500 personal and 100 horse. On the same day Abū-l-fatḥ Dakhanī came from his jagir and waited on me. On the 3rd of the same month news came of the death of Islām Khān ; he had died on Thursday, the 5th Rajab, in the year 1022 (21st August, 1613). In one day, without any previous illness, this inevitable event occurred. He was one of those born and brought up in the house (house-born). The naturally good disposition and knowledge of affairs that showed themselves in him were seen in no one else. He ruled Bengal with entire authority, and brought within the civil jurisdiction of the province countries that had never previously come under the sway of any of the jagirdars or into the possession of any of the Chiefs of the State. If death had not overtaken him he would have done perfect service.

The Khān A'ẓam had himself prayed that the illustrious prince should be appointed to the campaign against the Rānā, yet, notwithstanding all kinds of encouragement and gratification on the part of my son (Shāh Jahān), he would not

---

[408] Ḥāfiẓ Jamāl was the name of the saint Mu' īnu-d-dīn's daughter ("Rajputana Gazetteer," ii, 62). It lies at the back of the Taragarh hill, and is now commonly called Nūr-chashma. The fountains, etc., are in a ruined state. Sir Thomas Roe visited this place (id., p. 123).

[409] *Shab-i-jum'a,* which is Friday eve according to Blochmann.

apply himself to the task, but proceeded to act in his own unworthy manner. When this was heard by me, I sent Ibrāhīm Ḥusain, who was one of my most trusty attendants, to him, and sent affectionate messages to him to say that when he was at Burhanpur he had daily begged this duty of me, as he considered it equivalent to the happiness of both worlds, and had said in meetings and assemblies that if he should be killed in this enterprise he would be a martyr, and if he prevailed, a ghāzī. I had given him whatever support and assistance of artillery he had asked for. After this he had written that without the movement of the royal standards to those regions the completion of the affair was not free of difficulty. By his counsel I had come to Ajmir, and this neighbourhood had been thus honoured and dignified. Now that he had himself prayed for the prince, and everything had been carried out according to his counsel, why did he withdraw his foot from the field of battle and enter the place of disagreement ? To Bābā Khurram, from whom up till now I had never parted, and whom I sent in pure reliance on his (Khān A'ẓam's) knowledge of affairs, he should show loyalty and approved good-will, and never be neglectful day or night of his duty to my son. If, contrariwise, he should draw back his foot from what he had agreed to, he must know that there would be mischief. Ibrāhīm Ḥusain went, and impressed these words on his mind in the same detailed way. It was of no avail, as he would not go back from his folly and determination. When Bābā Khurram saw that his being in the affair was a cause of disturbance, he kept him under observation and represented that his being there was in no way fitting, and he was acting thus and spoiling matters simply on account of the connection he had with Khusrau.[410] I then ordered Mahābat Khān to go and bring him from Udaipur, and told Muḥammad Taqī, the diwan of buildings, to go to Mandesūr and bring his children and dependants to Ajmir.

410 Khusrau was married to his daughter.

On the 11th of the month news came that Dulīp, son of Rāy Singh, who was of a seditious and rebellious disposition, had been heavily defeated by his younger brother, Rāo Sūraj Singh, who had been sent against him, and that he was making disturbance in one of the districts of the Sarkar of Ḥiṣṣar. About this time Hāshim of Khost, the faujdar, and the jagirdars of that neighbourhood seized him, and sent him as a prisoner to Court. As he had misbehaved repeatedly, he was capitally punished, and this was a warning to many of the seditious. In reward for this service an increase of 500 personal and 200 horse was made to the mansab of Rāo Sūraj Singh. On the 14tḥ of the month a representation came from my son Bābā Khurram that the elephant 'Ālam-gumān, of which the Rānā was very fond, together with seventeen other elephants, had fallen into the hands of the warriors of the victorious army, and that his master would also soon be captured.

THE NINTH NEW YEAR'S FEAST AFTER MY AUSPICIOUS ACCESSION.

The commencement of the ninth year after my auspicious accession, corresponding with the Hijra year 1023 (1614).

Two watches and one ghari had passed on the night of Friday, the 9th Ṣafar (21st March, 1614), when the world-warming sun shed his rays on the constellation of Aries, which is his house of dignity and honour ; it was the first morning of the month of Farwardīn. The assembly for the New Year's festival took place in the pleasant regions of Ajmir, and at the time of entry (of the sun into Aries), which was the propitious hour, I seated myself on the throne of good fortune. They had in the usual manner decorated the palace with rare cloth-stuffs and jewels and gem-decked things. At this auspicious moment the elephant 'Ālam-gumān,[411] which was fit to be entered in the private stud, with the seventeen other male and female

[411] The "Arrogant of tḥe Earth" (Tod).

elephants which my son Bābā Khurram had sent of the Rānā's elephants, were presented before me, and the hearts of the loyal rejoiced. On the 2nd day of the New Year, knowing it to be propitious for a ride, I mounted it and scattered about much money. On the 3rd I conferred on I'tiqād Khān a mansab of 3,000 personal and 1,000 horse, increasing thus that which he had already, which was of 2,000 personal and 500 horse, and I distinguished him with the title of Āṣaf Khān, with which title two of his family had been previously honoured. I also increased the mansab of Dayānat Khān by 500 personal and 200 horse. At the same time I promoted I'timādu-d-daulah to the mansab of 5,000 personal and 2,000 horse. At the request of Bābā Khurram I increased the mansab of Saif Khān Bārha by 500 personal and 200 horse, that of Dilāwar Khān by the same number, that of Kishan Singh by 500 horse, and that of Sarfarāz Khān by 500 personal and 300 horse. On Sunday, the 10th, the offering of Āṣaf Khān was produced before me, and on the 14th I'timādu-d-daulah produced his own offering. From these two offerings I took what pleased me and gave back the rest. Chīn Qilīj Khān, with his brothers, relations, and the army and retinue of his father, came from Kabul[412] and waited on me. Ibrāhīm Khān, who had a mansab of 700 personal and 300 horse, having been promoted to that of 1,500 personal and 600 horse, was appointed jointly with Khwāja Abū-l-ḥasan to the exalted dignity of paymaster of the household. On the 15th of this month Mahābat Khān, who had been appointed to bring Khān A' ẕ am and his son 'Abdu-llah, came and waited on me. On the 19th the assembly of honour was held. On that day the offering of Mahābat Khān was laid before me, and I sent a private elephant called Rūp Sundar for my son Parwīz. When that day had passed I ordered them to deliver Khān A' ẕ am into the charge of Āṣaf Khān, that he might keep him in the fort of Gwalior. As my object in sending him to the fort was in case some disagreement

[412] Perhaps this means Peshawar, for apparently Qilīj was there when he died.

and disturbance should occur in the matter of the Rānā in consequence of the attachment that he had to Khusrau, I ordered him not to be kept in the fort like a prisoner, but that they should provide everything necessary for his comfort and convenience in the way of eating and clothing. On the same day I promoted Chīn Qilīj Khān to a mansab of 2,500 personal and 700 horse. To the rank of Tāj Khān, who had been appointed to the charge of the province of Bhakar, I added 500 personal and horse. On the 18th Urdībihisht I forbade Khusrau to pay his respects. The reason was this, that through the affection and fatherly love (I bore him) and the prayers of his mother and sisters, I had ordered again that he should come every day to pay his respects (*kūrnish*). As his appearance showed no signs of openness and happiness, and he was always mournful and dejected in mind, I accordingly ordered that he should not come to pay his respects. In the time of my revered father, Muẓaffar Ḥusain Mīrzā and Rustam Mīrzā, sons of Sulṭān Ḥusain Mīrzā, nephews of Shāh Ṭahmāsp Ṣafawī, who had in their possession Qandahar and Zamīndāwar and that neighbourhood, sent petitions to the effect that in consequence of the nearness to Khurasan and the coming of 'Abdu-llah Khān Ūzbeg to that country, they could not leave the charge of looking after the country and come (to pay their respects), but that if he (Akbar) would send one of the servants of the palace they would hand over the country to him, and themselves come to pay their respects. As they repeatedly made this request, he sent Shāh Beg Khān, who is now honoured with the title of Khān Daurān, to the governorship of Qandahar and Zamīndāwar and that neighbourhood, and wrote firmans full of favour to the Mīrzās summoning them to the Court. After their arrival favours appropriate to the case of each were bestowed on them, and he gave them a territory equal to two or three times the collections of Qandahar. In the end, the management expected from them was not achieved, and by degrees the territory deteriorated. Muẓaffar Ḥusain Mīrzā died during the lifetime of my revered father, and he sent Mīrzā Rustam with the

Khankhanan to the Subah of the Deccan, where he had a small jagir. When the throne was honoured by my succession, I sent for him from the Deccan with the intention of showing him favour and sending him to one of the border territories. About the time he came Mīrzā Ghāzī Tarkhān, who held the governorship of Thatta and Qandahar and that neighbourhood, died. It occurred to me to send him to Thatta, so that he might show there his natural good qualities and administer that country in an approved manner. I promoted him to a mansab of 5,000 personal and horse, 200,000 rupees were given to him for expenses, and I despatched him to the Subah of Thatta. My belief was that he would do good service[413] on those borders. In opposition to my expectation he did no service, and committed so much oppression that many people complained of his wickedness. Such news of him was heard that it was considered necessary to recall him. One of the servants of the Court was appointed to summon him, and I sent for him to Court. On the 26th Urdībihisht they brought him. As he had committed great oppression on the people of God, and inquiry into this was due according to the requirements of justice, I handed him over to Anīrā'ī Singh-dalan that he might enquire into the facts, and that if guilty he might receive prompt punishment and be a warning to others. In those days the news also came of the defeat of Aḥdād, the Afghan. The facts are that Mu'taqid Khān came to Pūlam[414] Guzar (ferry?), in the district of Peshawar, with an

[413] According to the Ma'āṣir, iii, 486, in the biography of 'Īsā Khān, Rustam was sent to put down the Tarkhāns, and succeeded in doing so. See also ibid., p. 438, in the biography of Rustam, where it is said that Jahāngīr told him to send away the Arghuns. Perhaps the passage in Ma'āṣir, p. 438, which according to Blochmann, p. 314, means that Rustam ill-treated the Arghuns, rather means that he intrigued with them but oppressed the peasantry.

[414] Though the text has Pūlam, the real word seems to be Ilam or Ailam. Ailam Guzar appears to be a pass in a range of hills. It may, however, be a ferry on the Kabul River. That river seems to be also known as the Shāh 'Ālam, and there is a ferry on it of that name. The text speaks of Kot Tīrāh as 8 kos from Jalalabad, but Tīrāh is much further away. The B.M. MSS. have *Kotal-i-Tīrāh*, 'the Tīrāh defile.'

army, and Khān Daurān with another force in Afghanistan and blocked the path of that rascal (lit. black-faced one). Meanwhile a letter came to Mu'taqid Khān from Pish Bulagh that Aḥdād had gone to Koṭ Tīrāh, which is 8 kos from Jalalabad, with a large number of horse and foot, and had killed a few of those who had chosen to be loyal and obey, and made prisoners of others, and was about to send them to Tīrāh, and intended to make a raid on Jalalabad and Pish Bulagh. Immediately on hearing this news Mu'taqid Khān started in great haste with the troops he had with him. When he arrived at Pish Bulagh he sent out spies to ascertain about the enemy. On the morning of Wednesday, the 6th, news reached him that Aḥdād was in the same place. Placing his trust on the favour of God, which is on the side of this suppliant at the throne of Allah, he divided the royal army into two, and went towards the enemy, who, with 4,000 or 5,000 experienced men, had seated themselves haughtily in complete carelessness, and did not suspect that besides Khān Daurān's there was an army in the neighbourhood that could oppose itself to them. When news came that the royal forces were coming against that ill-fortuned man, and the signs of an army were becoming manifest, in a state of bewilderment he distributed his men into four bodies, and seating himself on an eminence a gunshot away, to get to which was a difficult matter, he sent his men to fight. The musketeers of the victorious army assailed the rebel with bullets, and sent a large number to hell. Mu'taqid Khān took the centre of his army to his advanced guard, and, not giving the enemy more than time to shoot off their arrows two or three times, swept them clean away, and pursuing them for 3 or 4 kos, killed nearly 1,500 of them, horse and foot. Those left of the sword took to flight, most of them wounded and with their arms thrown away. The victorious army remained for the night in the same place on the battlefield, and in the morning proceeded with 600 decapitated heads[415] towards Peshawar and

[415] Compare Price's Jahāngīr, p. 94. It appears from that account that Mu'taqid *alias* Lashkar Khān was originally called Abū-l- ḥusain. According to the account

made pillars of the heads there. Five hundred horses and innumerable cattle and property and many weapons fell into their hands. The prisoners of Tīrāh were released, and on this side no well-known men were killed. On the night of Thursday, the 1st of Khūrdād, I proceeded towards Pushkar to shoot tigers, and on Friday killed two of them with a gun. On the same day it was represented to me that Naqīb Khān had died. The aforesaid Khān was one of the Saifī Sayyids, and was originally from Qazwin. The tomb of his father, Mīr 'Abdu-l-Laṭīf, is at Ajmir. Two months before his death his wife,[416] between whom and her husband there was a great affection, and who for twelve days was ill with fever, drank the unpleasant draught of death. I ordered them to bury him by the side of his wife, whom they had placed in the Khwāja's venerated mausoleum. As Mu'taqid Khān had done approved service in the fight with Aḥdād, in reward he was exalted with the title of Lashkar Khān. Dayānat Khān, who had been sent to Udaipur in the service of Bābā Khurram and to convey certain orders, came on the 7th Khūrdād and gave good account of the rules and regulations made by Bābā Khurram. Fidā'ī Khān, who in the days of my princehood was my servant, and whom after my accession I had made bakhshi in this army, and who had obtained favour, gave up the deposit of his life on the 12th of the same month. Mīrzā Rustam, as he showed signs of repentance and regret for his misdeeds, and generosity demanded that his faults should be pardoned, was, in the end of the month, summoned to my presence, and I satisfied his mind, and having given him a dress of honour, ordered him to pay his respects to me. On the night of Sunday, the 11th of the month of Tīr, a female elephant in the private elephant stud gave birth to a young one in my presence. I had repeatedly ordered them to ascertain the period of their gestation; at last it became evident that for a female young one it

there, the prisoners were brought to Jahāngīr with the decapitated heads of 17,000 (!) suspended from their necks !

416 She was a daughter of Mīr Maḥmūd, Akbar's secretary (Blocmniann, p. 449).

was 18 months and for a male 19 months. In opposition to the birth of a human being, which is in most cases by a head delivery, young elephants are born with their feet first. When the young one was born, the mother scattered dust upon it with her foot, and began to be kind and to pet it. The young one for an instant remained fallen, and then rising, made towards its mother's breasts. On the 14th the assembly of Gulāb - pāshī (sprinkling of rose-water) took place ; from former times this has been known as *āb-pāshī* (water-sprinkling), and has become established from amongst customs of former days. On the 5th Amurdād (middle July, 1614) came news of the death of Rāja Mān Singh.[417] The aforesaid Raja was one of the chief officers of my revered father. As I had sent many servants of the State to serve in the Deccan, I also appointed him. After his death in that service, I sent for Mīrzā Bhāo Singh, who was his legitimate heir. As from the time when I was prince he had done much service with me, although the chiefship and headship of their family, according to the Hindu custom, should go to Mahā Singh, son[418] of Jagat Singh, the Raja's eldest son, who had died in the latter's lifetime, I did not accept him, but I dignified Bhāo Singh with the title of Mīrzā Rāja, and raised him to the mansab of 4,000 personal and 3,000 horse. I also gave him Amber, the native place of his ancestors, and, soothing and consoling the mind of Mahā Singh, increased his former mansab by 500, and gave him as an *in'ām* the territory of Garha.[419] I also sent him a jewelled dagger belt, a horse, and dress of honour. On the 8th of this month of Amurdād I found a change in my health, and by degrees was seized with fever and headache. For fear that some injury might occur to the country and the servants of God, I kept this secret from most of those familiar with and near to me , and did not inform the physicians and hakims. A few days passed in

---

[417] Mān Singh died in the Deccan in 1614, and apparently in the month of June.

[418] Text *pidar* by mistake for *pisar*.

[419] Garha, described as Bāndhū in Ma'āṣir, ii, 175. It is Garha-Katanga, i.e. Jabalpur.

this manner, and I only imparted this to Nūr-Jahān Begam, than whom I did not think anyone was fonder of me; I abstained from eating heavy foods, and, contenting myself with a little light food, went every day, according to my rule, to the public Dīwān-khāna (hall of audience), and entered the Jharokha and *ghusal-khāna* (parlour) in my usual manner, until signs of weakness showed themselves in my skin.[420] Some of the nobles[421] became aware of this, and informed one or two of my physicians who were trustworthy, such as Ḥakīm Masīḥu-z-zamān, Ḥakīm Abū-l-qāsim, and Ḥakīm 'Abdu-sh-Shakūr. As the fever did not change, and for three nights I took my usual wine, it brought on greater weakness. In the time of disquietude, and when weakness prevailed over me, I went to the mausoleum of the revered Khwāja, and in that blessed abode prayed to God Almighty for recovery, and agreed to give alms and charity. God Almighty, in His pure grace and mercy, bestowed on me the robe of honour of health, and by degrees I recovered. The headache, which had been very severe, subsided under the remedies of Ḥakīm 'Abdu-sh-Shakūr, and in the space of twenty-two days my state returned to what it was before. The servants of the palace, and indeed the whole of the people, made offerings for this great bounty. I accepted the alms of no one, and ordered that everyone in his own house should distribute what he wished among the poor. On the 10th Shahrīwar news came that Tāj Khān, the Afghan, governor of Thatta,[422] had died ; he was one of the old nobles of the State.

During my illness it had occurred to me that when I completely recovered, inasmuch as I was inwardly an ear-bored slave of the Khwāja (Mu'īnu-d-dīn) and was indebted to him for my existence, I should openly make holes in my ears and be enrolled among his ear-marked slaves. On Thursday, 12th

---

420 Perhaps the meaning is that there was an eruption.

421 *Buzurgān*, which perhaps here means elder ladies of the harem.

422 This is Tāsh Beg (Blochmann, p. 457). The text wrongly has Patna.

Shahrīwar,[423] corresponding to the month of Rajab, I made holes in my ears and drew into each a shining pearl. When the servants of the palace and my loyal friends saw this, both those who were in the presence and some who were in the distant borders diligently and eagerly made holes in their ears, and adorned the beauty of sincerity with pearls and rubies which were in the private treasury, and were bestowed on them, until by degrees the infection caught the Ahadis and others. At the end of the day of Thursday, the 22nd of the said month, corresponding with the 10th Sha'bān, the meeting for my solar weighing was arranged in my private audience hall, and the usual observances were carried out. On the same day Mīrzā Rāja Bhāo Singh, gratified and prosperous, returned to his native country with the promise that he would not delay (there) more than two or three months. On the 27th of the month of Mihr news came that Farīdūn Khān Barlās had died at Udaipur. In the clan of Barlās no leader remained but he. As his tribe had many claims on this State and endless connection with it, I patronised his son Mihr 'Alī, and raised him to the mansab of 1,000 personal and horse. On account of the approved services of Khān Daurān, I increased by 1,000 his mansab, which became 6,000 personal and 5,000 horse, original and increase. On the 6th Ābān the *qarāwuls* (*shikārīs*) reported that three tigers had been met at a distance of 6 kos. Starting after midday, I killed all three of them with a gun. On the 8th of the month the festival of the Dewālī came on. I ordered the attendants of the palace to have games with each other for two or three nights in my presence ; winnings and losings took place. On the 8th of this month they brought to Ajmir the body of Sikandar Mu'īn Qarāwul (Shikārī), who was one of my old attendants and had done much service for me when I was prince, from Udaipur, which was the place where my son Sulṭān Khurram was staying. I ordered the qarawuls and his fellow-tribesmen to take his body and bury it

[423] Jahāngīr was born in this month, which then corresponded to Rajab.

on the bank of Rānā Shankar's tank. He was a good servant to me. On the 12th Āzar two daughters whom Islām Khān in his lifetime had taken from the Zamindar of Kūch (Behar), whose country is on the boundary of the eastern provinces, together with his son and 94 elephants, were brought before me. Some of the elephants were placed in my private stud. On the same day, Hūshang, Islām Khān's son, came from Bengal, and had the good fortune to kiss the threshold, and presented as offerings two elephants, 100 muhrs, and 100 rupees. On one particular night in Day I dreamt that the late king (Akbar) said to me: "Bābā, forgive for my sake the fault of 'Azīz Khān, who is the Khān A'ẓam." After this dream, I decided to summon him from the fort (of Gwalior).

There is a ravine in the neighbourhood of Ajmir that is very beautiful. At the end of this ravine a spring appears which is collected in a long and broad tank, and is the best water in Ajmir. This valley and spring are well known as Ḥāfiẓ Jamāl. When I crossed over to this place I ordered a suitable building to be made there, as the place was good and fit for developing. In the course of a year a house and grounds were made there, the like of which those[424] who travel round the world cannot point out. They made a basin 40 gaz by 40, and made the water of the spring rise up in the basin by a fountain. The fountain leaps up 10 or 12 gaz. Buildings are laid on the edge of this basin, and in the same way above, where the tank and fountain are, they have made agreeable places and enchanting halls and resting-rooms pleasant to the senses. These have been constructed and finished off in a masterly style by skilled painters and clever artists. As I desired that it should be called by a name connected with my august name, I gave it the name of Chashma-i-Nūr, or the

[424] Is this an allusion to some complimentary remark of Sir Thomas Roe? Sir Thomas did not come to Ajmir till December, 1615, but Jahāngīr is here apparently writing of what happened a year after his visit to *Ḥāfiẓ* Jamāl. The chronogram was 1024 (1615).

fountain of light.' In short, the one fault it has is this, that it ought to have been in a large city, or at a place by which men frequently pass. From the day on which it was completed I have often passed Thursdays and Fridays there. I ordered that they should think out a chronogram for its completion. Sa'īdā Gīlānī, the head of the goldsmiths, discovered it in this clever hemistich:—

" The palace[425] of Shāh Nūru-d-dīn Jahāngīr " (1024).

I ordered them to put a stone with this carved upon it on the top of the portico of the building.

In the beginning of the month of Day, merchants came from Persia and brought pomegranates of Yazd and melons from Kārīz, which are the best of Khurasan melons, so many that all the servants of the Court and the Amirs of the frontiers obtained a portion of them and were very grateful to the True Giver (God) for them. I had never had such melons and pomegranates. It seemed as if I had never had a pomegranate or a melon before. Every year I had had melons from Badakhshan and pomegranates from Kabul, but they bore no comparison with the Yazd pomegranates and the Kārīz melons. As my revered father (may God's light be his witness !) had a great liking for fruit, I was very grieved that such fruits had not come to Hindustan from Persia in his victorious time, that he might have enjoyed and profited by them. I have the same regret for the *Jahāngīrī 'iṭr* (so-called otto of roses), that his nostrils were not gratified with such essences. This 'itr is a discovery which was made during my reign through the efforts of the mother of Nūr-Jahān Begam. When she was making rose-water a scum formed on the surface of the dishes into which the hot rose-water was poured from the jugs. She collected this scum little by little; when much rosewater was obtained a sensible portion of the scum was collected. It is of

[425] Maḥall-i-Shāh Nūru-d-dīn Jahāngīr, 1024 (1615). See Proceedings A.S.B. for August, 1873, pp. 159-60.

such strength in perfume that if one drop be rubbed on the palm of the hand it scents a whole assembly, and it appears as if many red rosebuds had bloomed at once. There is no other scent of equal excellence to it. It restores hearts that have gone and brings back withered souls. In reward for that invention I presented a string of pearls to the inventress. Salīma[426] Sulṯān Begam (may the lights of God be on her tomb) was present, and she gave this oil the name of 'itr-i-Jahangiri.'

Great difference appeared in the climates of India. In this month of Day, in Lahore, which is between Persia and Hindustan, the mulberry-tree bore fruit of as much sweetness and fine flavour as in its ordinary season. For some days people were delighted by eating it. The news-writers of that place wrote this. In the same days Ba<u>kh</u>tar <u>Kh</u>ān Kalāwant, who was closely connected with 'Adil <u>Kh</u>ān, inasmuch as he ('Ādil) married his own brother's daughter to him, and made him his preceptor in singing and *durpat*[427] *guftan,* appeared in the habit of a dervish. Summoning him and enquiring into his circumstances, I endeavoured to honour him. In the first assembly I gave him 10,000 rupees in cash and 50 pieces of cloth of all sorts and a string of pearls, and having made him a guest of Āṣaf <u>Kh</u>ān, ordered him to enquire into his circumstances. It did not appear whether he had come without 'Ādil <u>Kh</u>ān's permission, or the latter had sent him in this guise in order that he might find out the designs of this Court and bring him news about them. Considering his relationship to 'Ādil <u>Kh</u>ān, it is most probable that he has not come without 'Ādil <u>Kh</u>ān's knowledge. A report by Mīr Jamālu-d-dīn Ḥusain, who at this time was (our) ambassador at Bijapur, corroborates this idea, for he writes that 'Ādil <u>Kh</u>ān has, on account of the kindness which has been

---

[426] Salīma died in the 7th year, so that the discovery must have occurred some time before this mention of it.

[427] Hindustani, *dhurpad,* "petit poëme ordinairement composè de cinq hémistiches sur une même rime." "It was invented by Rāja Mān of Gwalior" (Garcin de Tassy, Hist. Litt. Hindouie, i, 12).

shown by H.M. (Jahāngīr) to Bakhtar Khān, been very gracious to him (Jamālu-d-dīn). Every day he has shown him more and more favour, keeps him beside him at nights, and recites to him durpats, which he ('Ādil Khān) has composed, and which he calls *nauras*[428] (Juvenilia). "The remainder of the facts will be written on the day when I get my dismissal."

In these days they brought a bird from the country of Zīrbād (Sumatra, etc., Blochmann, p. 616) which was coloured like a parrot, but had a smaller body. One of its peculiarities is that it lays hold with its feet of the branch or perch on which they may have placed it and then makes a somersault, and remains in this position all night and whispers to itself. When day comes it seats itself on the top of the branch. Though they say that animals also have worship, yet it is most likely that this practice is instinctive. It never drinks water, and water acts like poison upon it, though other birds subsist on water.

In the month[429] of Bahman there came pieces of good news one after the other. The first was that the Rānā Amar Singh had elected for obedience and service to the Court. The circumstances of this affair are these. My son of lofty fortune, Sulṭān Khurram, by dint of placing a great many posts, especially in some places where most people said it was impossible to place them on account of the badness of the air and water and the wild nature of the localities, and by dint of moving the royal forces one after another in pursuit, without regard to the heat or excessive rain, and making prisoners of the families of the inhabitants of that region, brought matters with

---

[428] See Rieu, 741*b*, who calls the *nauras* a treatise on music composed by Ibrāhīm 'Ādil Shāh II. This 'Ādil Shāh was Firishta's patron, and reigned till 1626. Jamālu-d-dīn is the dictionary-maker and friend of Sir T. Roe. The sentence about reporting the remainder of the facts seems to be an extract from his report. Muḥammad Wāriṣ, in his continuation of the Pādshāh-nāma, B.M. MS. Add. 6556, p. 438, mentions, with reprobation, that 'Ādil Shāh had given his niece in marriage to a singer.

[429] Translated Elliot, vi, 339.

the Rānā to such a pass that it became clear to him that if this should happen to him again he must either fly the country or be made prisoner. Being without remedy, he chose obedience and loyalty, and sent to my fortunate son his maternal uncle, Subh Karan, with Haridās Jhālā, who was one of the men in his confidence, and petitioned that if that fortunate son would ask forgiveness for his offences and tranquillise his mind, and obtain for him the auspicious sign-manual,[430] he would himself come and wait on my son, and would send his son and successor Karan to Court, or he, after the manner of other Rajas, would be enrolled amongst the servants of the Court and do service. He also begged that he himself might be excused from coming to Court on account of his old age. Accordingly my son sent them in company with his own Diwan Mullā Shukru-llah, whom after the conclusion of this business I dignified with the title of Afẓal Khān, and Sundar Dās, his major-domo, who, after this matter was settled, was honoured with the title of Rāy Rāyān, to the exalted Court, and represented the circumstances. My lofty mind was always desirous, as far as possible, not to destroy the old families. The real point was that as Rānā Amar Singh and his fathers, proud in the strength of their hilly country and their abodes, had never seen or obeyed any of the kings of Hindustan, this should be brought about in my reign. At the request of my son I forgave the Rānā's offences, and gave a gracious farman that should satisfy him, and impressed on it the mark of my auspicious palm.[431] I also wrote a farman of kindness to my son that if he could arrange to settle the matter I should be much pleased. My son also sent them[432] with Mullā Shukru-llah and Sundar Dās to the Rānā to console him and make him hopeful of

---

430 Lit. procure for him the sign of the blessed *panja* (five fingers). The sign-manual was that of Jahāngīr. See below. See also Tod's Rajasthan, reprint, i, 411, for a representation of the *panja*; also p. 383, note id.

431 *Panja mubārak* (Tod's Rajasthan, i, 383 and 411).

432 Perhaps the uncle and Haridas, or the *īnhā*, 'them,' may mean the farman. See Elliot, vi, 340, which has 'my letters.' Tod has translated this part of the Tuzuk, i, 382.

the royal favour. They gave him the gracious farman with the sign-manual of the auspicious hand, and it was settled that on Sunday, the 26th of the month of Bahman, he and his sons should come and pay their respects to my son. The second piece of good news was the death of Bahādur, who was descended from the rulers of Gujarat, and was the leaven of disturbance and mischief (there). Almighty God had annihilated him in His mercy : he died of a natural illness. The third piece of news was the defeat of the Warzā (Portuguese Viceroy), who had done his best to take the castle and port of Surat. In the roadstead[433] of the port of Surat a fight took place between the English, who had taken shelter there, and the Viceroy. Most of his ships were burnt by the English fire. Being helpless he had not the power to fight any more, and took to flight. He sent some one to Muqarrab Khān, who was the governor of the ports of Gujarat, and knocked at the door of peace, and said that he had come to make peace and not to make war. It was the English who had stirred up the war. Another piece of news was that some of the Rajputs, who had determined to attack and kill 'Ambar (misprinted Ghīr), had made an ambush, and finding a good opportunity had gained access to him, when a slight wound had been inflicted on him by one of them. The men who were round 'Ambar (again misprinted Ghīr) had killed the Rajputs and taken 'Ambar to his quarters. A very little[434] more would have made an end of him. In the end of this month, when I was employed in hunting in the environs of Ajmir, Muḥammad Beg, an attendant on my fortunate son Sulṭān Khurram, came and brought a report from that son, and stated that the Rānā had come with his

---

[433] The text has *khaurmiyān*, and I.O. 181 has *khaur-i-bandar*. *Khaur* means a bay or gulf in Arabic. The battle is that between Captain Downton and the Portuguese, which took place in January, 1615, and is described in Orme's Hist., Fragments, p. 351, etc. See also Danvers' "Portuguese in India," ii, 170. The engagement was in the Swally channel.

[434] Elliot, vi, 340. As Mr. Rogers remarks, the sentence is not easily intelligible. Probably the translation should be, "No one remained (all the Rajputs having been killed) who could finish off Malik 'Ambar."

sons and paid his respects to the prince ; " the details would be made known by the report." I immediately turned the face of supplication to the Divine Court, and prostrated myself in thanksgiving. I presented a horse, an elephant, and a jewelled dagger to the aforesaid Muḥammad Beg, and honoured him with the title of Z̲ū-l-faqār K̲h̲ān.[435] From the report it appeared that on Sunday, the 26th Bahman, the Rānā paid his respects to my fortunate son with the politeness and ritual that servants pay their respects, and produced as offerings a famous large ruby that was in his house, with some decorated articles and seven elephants, some of them fit for the private stud, and which had not fallen into our hands and were the only ones left him, and nine horses.

My son also behaved to him with perfect kindness. When the Rānā clasped his feet and asked forgiveness for his faults, he took his head and placed it on his breast, and consoled him in such a manner as to comfort him. He presented him with a superb dress of honour, a jewelled sword, a horse with a jewelled saddle, and a private elephant with silver housings, and, as there were not more than 100 men with him who were worthy of complete robes of honour (*sar u pā*), he gave 100 sarupa and 50 horses and 12 jewelled *khapwa* (daggers). As it is the custom of the Zamindars that the son who is the heir-apparent should not go with his father to pay his respects to a king or prince, the Rānā observed this custom, and did not bring with him Karan, the son who had received the *ṭīkā*. As the hour (fixed by astrology) of the departure of that son of lofty fortune from that place was the end of that same day, he gave him leave, so that, having himself gone, he might send Karan to pay his respects. After he had gone, Karan also came and did so. To him also he gave a superb dress of honour, a jewelled sword and dagger, a horse with a gold saddle, and a special elephant, and

[435] Probably the father or grandfather of the Muḥammad Beg Z̲ū-l-faqār who was a servant of Aurangzīb (Ma'ā s̤iru-l-umarā, ii, 89).

on the same day, taking Karan in attendance, he proceeded towards the illustrious Court. On the 3rd Isfandārmuz my return to Ajmir from hụnting took place. From the 17th Bahman up to that date, during which I was hunting, one tigress with three cubs and thirteen nilgaw had been killed. The fortunate prince encamped on Saturday, the 10th of the same month, at the village of Devrānī, which is near the city of Ajmir, and an order was given that all the Amirs should go to meet him, and that each should present an offering according to his standing and condition, and on the next day, Sunday, the 11th, he should have the good fortune to wait upon me. The next day the prince, with great magnificence, with all the victorious forces that had been appointed to accompany him on that service, entered the public palace. The hour for him to wait on me was when two watches and two gharis of the day had passed, and he had the good fortune to pay his respects, and performed his prostrations and salutations. He presented 1,000 ashrafis and 1,000 rupees by way of offering, 1,000 muhrs and 1,000 rupees by way of charity. I called that son forward and embraced him, and having kissed his head and face, favoured him with special kindnesses and greetings. When he had finished the dues of service and had presented his offerings and charities, he petitioned that Karan might be exalted with the good fortune of prostrating himself and paying his respects. I ordered them to bring him, and the Bakhshis with the usual ceremonies of respect produced him. After prostration and salutation were completed, at the request of my son Khurram, I ordered them to place him in front on the right hand of the circle. After this I ordered Khurram to go and wait on his mothers, and gave him a special dress of honour, consisting of a jewelled *chārqab* (sleeveless vest), a coat of gold brocade, and a rosary of pearls. After he had made his salutation, there were presented to him a special dress of honour, a special horse with a jewelled saddle, and a special elephant. I also honoured Karan with a superb robe of honour and a jewelled sword, and the Amirs and mansabdars had the honour of prostrating themselves and paying their respects, and presented their offerings. Each of these, according to his service and rank, was honoured with favours. As it was necessary to win the heart of Karan, who was of a wild nature and had never seen assemblies and had lived among the hills, I every day showed him some fresh favour, so that on the second day of his attendance a jewelled dagger, and on the next day a special Iraqi horse with jewelled saddle, were given to him. On the day when he went to the darbar in the female apartments, there were given to him on the part of Nūr-Jahān Begam a rich dress of honour, a jewelled sword, a horse and saddle, and an elephant. After this I presented him with a rosary of pearls of great value. On the next day a special elephant with trappings (*talāyir*) were given. As it was in my mind to give him something of every kind, I presented him with three hawks and three falcons, a special sword, a coat of mail, a special cuirass, and two rings, one with a ruby and one with an emerald. At the end of the month I ordered that all sorts of cloth stuffs, with carpets and cushions (named *takiya*) and all kinds of perfumes, with vessels of gold, two Gujrati carts, and cloths, should be placed in a hundred trays. The Ahadis carried them in their arms and on their shoulders to the public audience hall, where they were bestowed on him.

Ṣ̤ābit Khān[436] at the paradise - resembling assemblies was always addressing unbecoming speeches and making palpable allusions to I'timādu-d-daulah and his son Āṣaf Khān. Once or twice, showing my dislike of this, I had forbidden him to do so, but this was not enough for him. As I held very dear I'timādu-d-daulah's goodwill towards me, and was very closely connected with his family, this matter became very irksome to me. As one night without reason and without motive he began to speak unpleasant words to him, and said them to such an extent that signs of vexation and

436 R.A.S. MS. has Dayānat Khān, and so has I.O. MS. 181.

annoyance became evident in I'timādu-d-daulah's face, I sent him next morning, in the custody of a servant of the Court, to Āṣaf Khān to say that as on the previous evening he had spoken unpleasant words to his father, I handed him over to him, and he might shut him up either there or in the fort of Gwalior, as he pleased ; until he made amends to his father I would never forgive his fault. According to the order Āṣaf Khān sent him to Gwalior fort. In the same month Jahāngīr Qulī Khān was promoted to an increased mansab, and was given that of 2,500 personal and 2,000 horse. Aḥmad Beg Khān, who is one of the old retainers of the State, committed some faults on the journey to the Subah of Kabul, and Qilīj Khān, who was the commander of the army, had repeatedly complained of his making himself disagreeable. Necessarily I summoned him to Court, and in order to punish him handed him over to Mahābat Khān to confine him in the fort of Ranṭambhor. Qāsim Khān, governor of Bengal, had sent two rubies as an offering, and they were laid before me. As I had made a rule that they should bring before me after two watches of the night had passed the dervishes and necessitous people who had collected in the illustrious palace, this year also after the same manner I bestowed on the dervishes with my own hand and in my own presence 55,000 rupees and 190,000 bighas of land, with fourteen entire villages, and twenty-six ploughs,[437] and 11,000 *kharwār*[438] (ass-loads) of rice; I presented as well 732 pearls, of the value of 36,000 rupees, to the servants who by way of loyalty had bored their ears.

At the end of the aforesaid month news came that when four and a half gharis of night had passed on Sunday, the 11th of the month, in the city of Burhanpur, God Almighty had

---

437 *Qulba.* It does not appear that this is a land-measure.

438 *Kharwār.* It is a weight. See Jarrett, ii, 394, where a kharwar is said to be equal to ten Hindustani maunds.

bestowed on Sultān Parwīz a son by the daughter of Prince Murād. I gave him the name of Sultān Dūr-andīsh[439] (long-thoughted).

THE TENTH NEW YEAR'S FESTIVAL AFTER MY AUSPICIOUS ACCESSION.

When 55 seconds had passed on Saturday, 1st Farwardīn, in my 10th year, corresponding with the 8th[440] of the month of Ṣafar (March, 1615), 1024 Hijra, the sun from the constellation of Pisces entered the house of honour of Aries. When three gharis had passed on the night of Sunday I seated myself on the throne of State. The New Year's feast and ceremonials were prepared in the usual manner. The illustrious princes, the great Khans, the chief officers and Ministers of State made their salutations of congratulation. On the 1st of the month the mansab of I'timādu-d-daulah was increased from 5,000 personal and 2,000 horse by 1,000 personal and horse. Special horses were given to the Kunwar Karan, Jahāngīr Qulī Khān, and Rāja Bīr Singh Deo. On the 2nd the offering of Āṣaf Khān was laid before me ; it was an approved offering of jewels and jewelled ornaments and things of gold, of cloth stuffs of all kinds and descriptions, and was looked over in detail. That which I approved was worth 85,000 rupees. On this day a jewelled sword with a belt and band (?) (*band u bār*) was given to Karan, and an elephant to Jahāngīr Qulī Khān. As I had made up my mind to proceed to the Deccan, I gave an order to 'Abdu-l-Karīm Ma'mūrī, to go to Mandu and prepare a new building for my private residence and repair the buildings of the old kings. On the 3rd day the offerings of Rāja Bīr Singh Deo were laid before me and one ruby, some pearls, and one elephant had the honour of being accepted. On the 4th day the mansab of Muṣṭafā Khān was increased by 500 personal

[439] Probably this was the son who died in the 14th year (Tūzuk, p. 282).

[440] Should be 18th. See Elliot, vi, 341. I.O. 181 has 20th, and this is probably correct, *bīstam* and *hashtam* being often mistaken for one another by the copyists. B.M. MS. Add. 26215 has *dūshamba*, Monday, instead of *shamba*, Saturday.

and 200 horse to 2,000 personal and 250 horse. On the 5th I gave a standard and drums to I'timādu-d-daulah, and an order was given him to beat his drums. The mansab of Āṣaf Khān was increased by 1,000 personal and horse to 4,000 personal and 2,000 horse, and having increased the mansab of Rāja Bīr Singh Deo by 700 horse, I dismissed him to his own country, directing that he should present himself at Court at stated periods. On the same day the offering of Ibrāhīm Khān was laid before me. Some of all the kinds of things pleased me. Kishan Chand, of the sons of the Rajas of Nagarkot, was honoured with the title of Raja. On Thursday, the 6th, the offerings of I'timādu-d-daulah were laid before me at Chashma-i-Nūr; a large meeting had been arranged, and by way of favour the whole of his offerings were inspected. Of the jewels and jewelled things and choice cloth stuffs the value of 100,000 rupees was accepted, and the remainder given back. On the 7th day I increased by 1,000 personal the mansab of Kishan Singh, which had been 2,000 personal and 1,500 horse. On this day a tiger was killed in the neighbourhood of Chashma-i-Nūr. On the 8th I gave Karan the mansab of 5,000 personal and horse, and gave him a small rosary of pearls and emeralds with a ruby in the centre, which in the language of the Hindus is called *smaran* (Sanskrit for 'remembrance'). I increased the mansab of Ibrāhīm Khān by 1,000 personal and 400 horse, so as to make it 2,000 personal and 1,000 horse, original and increase. The mansab of Ḥājī Bī Ūzbeg was increased by 300 horse, and that of Rāja Shyām Singh by 500 personal so as to make it 2,500 personal and 1,400 horse. On Sunday, the 9th, there was an eclipse of the sun, when twelve gharis of the day had passed. It began from the west, and four out of five parts of the sun were eclipsed in the knot of the dragon. From the commencement of the seizure until it became light eight gharis elapsed. Alms of all kinds, and things in the shape of metals, animals, and vegetables, were given to fakirs and the poor and people in need. On this day the offering of Rāja Sūraj Singh was laid before me ; what was taken was of the value of 43,000 rupees. The offering of Bahādur Khān, the governor of Qandahar, was also laid before me on this day ; its total value came to 14,000 rupees. Two watches of the night had passed on the night of Monday, the 29th Ṣafar (30th March, 1615), in the ascension of Sagittarius, when a boy was born to Bābā Khurram by the daughter of Āṣaf Khān ; I gave him the name of Dārā Shukūh. I hope that his coming will be propitious to this State conjoined with eternity, and to his fortunate father. The mansab of Sayyid 'Alī Bārha was increased by 500 personal and 300 horse, so as to bring it to 1,500 personal and 1,000 horse. On the 10th the offering of I'tibār Khān was laid before me, and what was of the value of 40,000 rupees was accepted. On this day the mansab of Khusrau Bī Ūzbeg was raised by 300 horse, and that of Manglī Khān by 500 personal and 200 horse. On the 11th the offering of Murtaẓā Khān was laid before me. Of it seven rubies, one rosary of pearls, and 270 other pearls were accepted, and their value was 145,000 rupees. On the 12th the offerings of Mīrzā Rāja Bhāo Singh and Rāwat Shankar were laid before me. On the 13th, out of the offering of Khwāja Abū-l-ḥasan, one *qutbī* (Egyptian ?) ruby, one diamond, one string of pearls, five rings, four pearls, and some cloths, altogether the value of 32,000 rupees, were accepted. On the 14th the mansab of Khwāja Abū-l-ḥasan, which was 3,000 personal and 700 horse, was increased by 1,000 personal and 500 horse, and that of Wafādār Khān, of 750 personal and 200 horse, by 2,000 personal and 1,200 horse. On the same day Muṣṭafā Beg, the ambassador of the ruler of Iran, had the good fortune to wait upon me. After completing the matter of Gurjistan (Georgia), my exalted brother sent him with a letter consisting of expressions of friendship and assurances of sincerity, with several horses, camels, and some stuffs from Aleppo, which had come for that fortunate brother from the direction of Rūm. Nine large European hunting dogs, for which a request had gone, were also sent by him.

Murtaẓā Khān, on this day, obtained leave to go for the capture of the fort of Kāngra, the equal of which for strength they cannot point to in the hill country of the Panjab or even all the habitable world. From the time when the sound of Islam reached the country of Hindustan up to this auspicious time when the throne of rule has been adorned by this suppliant at the throne of Allah, none of the rulers or kings has obtained possession of it. Once in the time of my revered father, the army of the Panjab was sent against this fort, and besieged it for a long time. At length they came to the conclusion that the fort was not to be taken, and the army was sent off to some more necessary business. When he was dismissed, I gave Murtaẓā Khān a private elephant with trappings. Rāja Sūraj Mal, son of Rāja Bāso, as his country was near that fort, was also appointed, and his previous mansab was increased by 500 personal and horse. Rāja Sūraj Singh also came from his place and jagir and waited on me, and presented an offering of 100 ashrafis. On the 17th the offering of Mīrzā Rustam was laid before me. Two jewelled daggers, one rosary of pearls, some pieces of cloth, an elephant, and four Iraq horses were accepted, and the rest returned ; their value was 15,000 rupees. On the same date the offering of I'tiqād Khān, of the value of 18,000 rupees, was laid before me. On the 18th the offering of Jahāngīr Qulī Khān was inspected. Of jewels and cloth stuffs the value of 15,000 rupees was accepted. The mansab of I'tiqād Khān, which was 700 personal and 200 horse, I increased by 800 personal and 300 horse, so that with original and increase it came to 1,500 personal and 500 horse. Khusrau Bī Ūzbeg, who was one of the distinguished soldiers, died of the disease of dysentery. On the 8th day, which was Thursday, after two watches and four and a half gharis had passed, the *sharaf* (highest point of the sun's ascension) began. On this auspicious day I ascended the throne in happiness and prosperity, and the people saluted and congratulated me. When one watch of the day remained I went to the Chashma-i-Nūr. According to agreement the offering of Mahābat Khān was laid before me at that place. He had arranged beautiful jewels and jewellery, with cloth stuff and articles of all kinds that were pleasing to me.

Among these, a jewelled khapwa (dagger), which at his request the royal artificers had made, and the like of which in value there did not exist in my private treasury, was worth 100,000 rupees. In addition to this, jewels and other things of the value of 138,000 rupees were taken. Indeed, it was a splendid offering. To Muṣṭafā Beg, the ambassador of the ruler of Iran, I gave 20,000 *darab,* or 10,000 rupees. On the 21st I sent robes of honour by the hand of 'Abdu-l-Ghafūr to fifteen of the Amirs of the Deccan. Rāja Bikramājīt obtained leave to go to his jagir, and a special shawl (*parm naṙm*[441]) was given to him. On the same day I gave a jewelled waist-dagger to Muṣṭafā Beg, the ambassador. I increased the mansab of Hūshang, the son of Islām Khān, which was 1,000 personal and 500 horse, by 500 personal and 200 horse. On the 23rd, Ibrāhīm Khān was promoted to the Subah of Behar. Zafar Khān was ordered to present himself at Court. To the mansab of Ibrāhīm Khan, which was 2,000 personal and 1,000 horse, I added 500 personal and 1,000 horse. Saif Khān on the same day was dismissed to his jagir, as well as Ḥājī Bī Ūzbeg, who was honoured with the title of Ūzbeg Khān. Bahāduru-l-mulk, who belonged to the army of the Deccan, and held the mansab of 2,500 personal and 2,100 horse, received an increase of 500 personal and 200 horse. An increase of 200 was made in the mansab of Khwāja Taqī, which was 800 personal and 180 horse. On the 25th an increase of 200 horse was made in the rank of Salāmu-llah, the Arab, so that it became 1,500 personal and 1,000 horse. I presented Mahābat Khān with the black piebald horse out of my special horses which the ruler of Iran had sent the. At the end of the day of Thursday I went to the house of Bābā Khurram and remained there till a watch of the night had passed. His second offering was laid before me on that day. On the first day he paid his respects he laid before me a celebrated ruby of the Rānā, which, on the day of his paying his respects, he

441 Akbar used the word *parm narm,* 'very soft,' as a substitute for 'shawl' (Blochmann, p. 90).

had made an offering of to my son, and which the jewellers valued at 60,000 rupees. It was not worthy of the praise they had given it. The weight of this ruby was eight *tānk,*[442] and it was formerly in the possession of Rāy Maldeo, who was the chief of the tribe of the Rāṭhors and one of the chief rulers (or Rays) of Hindustan. From him it was transferred to his son Chandar Sen, who, in the days of his wretchedness and hopelessness, sold it to Rānā Uday Singh. From him it went to Rānā Partāp, and afterwards to this Rānā Amar Singh. As they had no more valuable gift in their family, he presented it on the day that he paid his respects to my fortunate son Bābā Khurram, together with the whole of his stud of elephants, which, according to the Indian idiom, they call *gheta chār.*[443] I ordered them to engrave on the ruby that at the time of paying his respects Rānā Amar Singh had presented it as an offering to Sulṭān Khurram. On that day certain other things from among the offerings of Bābā Khurram were accepted. Among them was a little crystal box of Frank work, made with great taste, with some emeralds, three rings, four Iraq horses, and various other things, the value of which was 80,000 rupees. On the day on which I went to his house he had prepared a great offering, in fact there were laid before me things and rarities worth about four or five lakhs of rupees. Of these the equivalent of 100,000 rupees was taken away and the balance given to him.

On the 28th the mansab of Khwāja Jahān, which was 3,000 personal and 1,800 horse, was increased by 500 personal and 400 horse. In the end of the month I presented Ibrāhīm Khān with a

---

442 According to Gladwin, 96 tanks = one sir. Four mashas make a tank, and a masha is about 18 grains troy.

443. Text *kheta chār*. But the two B.M. MSS. which I have consulted have no *yā*, and have *khatta* or *ghatta chār*. I think that the word must be घटा, *ghaṭā*, which in Sanskrit means a troop of elephants assembled for war. I am not sure what the word *chār* means, but perhaps it is only an affix. According to Abū -l-faẓl a herd of (wild) elephants is called *sahn* (Blochmann, p. 122).

horse, a robe of honour, a jewelled dagger, a standard and drums, and dismissed him to the province of Behar. The office of *'arẓ-mukarrir* (reviser of petitions), that belonged to K͟hwājagī Ḥājī Muḥammad, as he had died, I gave to Muk͟hliṣ K͟hān, who was in my confidence. Three hundred horse were increased in the mansab of Dilāwar K͟hān, who now had 1,000 personal and horse. As the hour of the leave-taking of Kunwar Karan was at hand, I was desirous of showing him my skill in shooting with a gun. Just at this time the *qarāwulān* (shikaris) brought in news of a tigress. Though it is an established custom of mine only to hunt male tigers, yet, in consideration that no other tiger might be obtained before his departure, I went for the tigress. I took with me Karan, and said to him that I would hit it wherever he wished me to do so. After this arrangement I went to the place where they had marked down the tiger. By chance there was a wind and disturbance in the air, and the female elephant on which I was mounted was terrified of the tigress and would not stand still. Notwithstanding these two great obstacles to shooting, I shot straight towards her eye. God Almighty did not allow me to be ashamed before that prince, and, as I had agreed, I shot her in the eye. On the same day Karan petitioned me for a special gun, and I gave him a special Turkish one.

As on the day for his departure I had not given Ibrāhīm K͟hān an elephant, I now gave him a special elephant, and I also sent an elephant to Bahāduru-l-mulk and one to Wafādār K͟hān. On the 8th Urdībihis͟ht the assemblage for my lunar weighing was held, and I weighed myself against silver and other things, distributing them amongst the deserving and needy. Nawāzis͟h K͟hān took leave to go to his jagir, which was in Malwa. On the same day I gave an elephant to K͟hwāja Abū-l-ḥasan. On the 9th they brought K͟hān A'ẓam, who had come to Agra from the fort of Gwalior, and who had been sent for. Though he had been guilty of many offences, and in all that I had done to him I was right, yet when they brought him into my presence and my eye fell on him, I perceived more shame in myself than in him.

Having pardoned all his offences, I gave him the shawl I had round my waist. I gave Kunwar Karan 100,000 *darab*. On the same day Rāja Sūraj Singh brought a large elephant of the name of Ran-rāwat, which was a celebrated elephant of his, as an offering. In fact, it was such a rare elephant that I put it into my private stud. On the 10th the offering of Khwāja Jahān, which he sent me from Agra by the hand of his son, was laid before me. It was of all kinds of things, of the value of 40,000 rupees. On the 12th the offering of Khān Daurān, which consisted of forty-five[444] horse two strings of camels, Arabian dogs (greyhounds), and hunting animals (hawks ?), was brought before me. On the same day seven other elephants from Rāja Sūraj Singh were also brought to me as an offering, and were placed in my private stud. Taḥayyur Khān, after he had been in attendance on me for four months, to-day got leave to go. A message was sent to 'Ādil Khān. I impressed on him the profit and loss of friendship and enmity, and made an agreement (with Taḥayyur Khān) that all these words should be repeated to 'Ādil Khān, and he should bring him back to the path of loyalty and obedience. At the time of his taking leave I also bestowed on him certain things. On the whole, in this short time, what with the gifts bestowed on him by me privately, by the princes, and those given him by the Amirs according to order, the account mounted up to about 100,000 rupees that he had received. On the 14th the rank and reward of my son Khurram were fixed. His mansab had been one of 12,000 personal and 6,000 horse, and that of his brother (Parwīz) 15,000 personal and 8,000 horse. I ordered his mansab to be made equal with that of Parwīz, besides other rewards. I gave him a private elephant of the name of Panchī Gaj,[445] with accoutrements of the value of 12,000 rupees. On the 16th an elephant was given to Mahābat Khān. On the 17th the mansab of Rāja Sūraj Singh, which was 4,000 personal and 3,000 horse, was

[444] *Panj tuqūz*, i.e. 9 by 5. The text has . تاقور, *tāqūr*.

[445] The B.M. MSS. seem to have *panch kunjar*, 'five elephants,' i.e. equal to five elephants (?).

increased by 1,000, and it was raised to 5,000. At the request of 'Abdu-llah Khān the mansab of Khwāja 'Abdu-l-Laṭīf, which was 500 personal and 200 horse, was raised by 200, and it was ordered to be 1,000 personal and 400 horse. 'Abdu-llah, the son of Khān A'ẓam, who was imprisoned in the fort of Ranṭambhor, was sent for at the request of his father. He came to the Court, and I took the chains off his legs and sent him to his father's house. On the 24th, Rāja Sūraj Singh presented me with another elephant, called Fauj-sangār ('ornament of the army '), by way of offering. Although this is also a good elephant, and has been placed in my private stud, it is not to be compared with the first elephant (he sent), which is one of the wonders of the age, and is worth 20,000 rupees. On the 26th, 200 personal were added to the mansab of Badī'u-z-zamān, son of Mīrzā Shāhrukh ; it was 700 personal and 500 horse. On the same day Khwāja Zainu-d-dīn, who is of the Naqshbandī Khwājas, came from Māwarā'a-n-nahr and waited on me, bringing as an offering eighteen horses. Qizilbāsh Khān, who was one of the auxiliaries of the province of Gujarat, had come to Court without the leave of the governor. I ordered that an ahadi should put him into confinement, and that he be sent back to the governor of Gujarat, so that others might not desire to do the same. The mansab of Mubārak Khān Sazāwal I raised 500 personal, so that it should be 1,500 personal and 700 horse. On the 29th I gave Khān A'ẓam 100,000 rupees, and ordered that the parganahs of Ḍāsna and Kāsna,[446] which are equivalent to 5,000 personal, should be made his jagir. At the end of the same month I gave leave to Jahāngīr Qulī Khān, with his brothers and other relatives, to go to Allahabad, which had been appropriated to them as jagir. At this meeting twenty horse, a *qabā* (*parm narm*) of Cashmere cloth, twelve deer, and ten Arabian dogs were given to Karan. The next day, which was the 1st Khūrdād, forty horse, the next day forty-one horse, and the third day twenty, amounting in the space of three days to 101

[446] In Sarkār Delhi (Jarrett, ii, 287).

head, were given as a present to Kunwar Karan. In return for the elephant Fauj-sangār, an elephant worth 10,000 rupees out of my private stud was presented to Rāja Sūraj Singh. On the 5th of the month ten turbans (*chīra*), ten coats (*qaba*), and ten waist-bands were given to Karan. On the 20th I gave him another elephant.

In these days the news-writer of Kashmir had written that a Mullā of the name of Gadā'ī, a disciplined dervish, who for forty years had lived in one of the monasteries of the city, had prayed the inheritors of that monastery two years[447] before he was to deliver over the pledge of his life that he might select a corner in that monastery as a place for his burial. They said, " Let it be so." In short, he selected a place. When the time for his delivery came he informed his friends and relations and those who were dear to him that an order had reached him that, delivering over the pledge (of life) he had, he should turn towards the last world. Those who were present wondered at his words, and said that the prophets had no such information, and how could they believe such words ? He said, " Such an order has been given to me." He then turned to one of his confidants, who was of the sons of the Qāẓīs of the country, and said : " You will expend the price[448] of my Koran, which is worth 700 tankas, in carrying me (to the grave). When you hear the call to Friday's prayer you will enquire for me." This conversation took place on the Thursday, and he divided all the goods in his room among his acquaintance and disciples, and went, and at end of the day bathed at the baths. The Qāẓī-zāda aforesaid came before the call for prayer, and enquired as to the health of the Mullā. When he came to the door of the cell he found the door closed and a servant sitting there. He asked the slave what had happened,

---

[447] The text does not expressly say that the dervish foretold two years before his death the period of his death, but apparently Jahāngīr means this, for he goes on to speak of the time mentioned for his delivery. See also Iqbāl-nāma, p. 81, where the dervish is called Ḥāfiẓ, and where it is added that the whole population of Srinagar followed the bier.

[448] Lit. give it, for the Koran cannot be directly sold.

and the servant said, " The Mullā has enjoined me that until the door of the cell open of its own accord I must not go in." Shortly after these words were said the door of the cell opened. The Qāẓī-zāda entered the cell with that servant and saw that the Mullā was on his knees with his face turned toward the qibla, and had given up his soul to God. Happy the state of the freed who can fly away from this place of the snares of dependence with such ease !

By the increase of 200 personal and 50 horse in the mansab of Karam Sen Rāṭhor, I raised it to 1,000 personal and 300 horse. On the 11th of this month the offering of Lashkar Khān, which consisted of three strings of Persian camels and twenty cups and plates from Khiṭā (China) and twenty Arabian dogs, was brought before me. On the 12th a jewelled dagger was bestowed on I'tibār Khān, and to Karan I gave a plume (*kalgī*) worth 2,000 rupees. On the 14th I gave a dress of honour to Sar-buland[449] Rāy, and gave him leave to go to the Deccan.

On the night of Friday, the 15th, a strange affair occurred. By chance on that night I was at Pushkar. To be brief, Kishan, own brother to Rāja Sūraj Singh, was in great perturbation through Gobind Dās, the Vakil of the said Raja having some time ago killed his nephew, a youth of the name of Gopāl Dās. The cause of the quarrel it would take too long to tell. Kishan Singh expected that, as Gopāl Dās was also the nephew of the Raja (Sūraj Singh), the latter would kill Gobind Dās. But the Raja, on account of the experience and ability of Gobind Dās, relinquished the idea of seeking revenge for his nephew's death. When Kishan saw this neglect on the part of the Raja, he resolved himself to take revenge for his nephew, and not allow his blood to pass away unnoticed. For a long time he kept this matter in his mind, until on that night he assembled his brothers, friends, and servants, and told them that he would go that night

[449] Text *pisar*, 'son of Buland Rāy,' but from the B. M. MSS. it appears that *pisar* is a mistake for Sar.

to take Gobind Dās's life, whatever might happen, and that he did not care what injury might happen to the Raja. The Raja was in ignorance of what was happening, and when it was near dawn Kishan came with Karan, his brother's son, and other companions. When he arrived at the gate of the Raja's dwelling he sent some of the experienced men on foot to the house of Gobind Dās, which was near the Raja's. He himself (Kishan) was on horseback, and stationed himself near the gate. The men on foot entered Gobind Dās's house, and killed some of those who were there on guard. Whilst this fight was going on Gobind Dās awoke, and seizing his sword in a state of bewilderment was coming out from one side of the house to join the outside watchmen. When the men on foot had finished killing some of the people, they came out of the tent to endeavour to find out Gobind Dās, and, meeting him, they finished his affair (killed him). Before the news of the killing of Gobind Dās reached Kishan, he, unable to bear it any more, dismounted and came inside the dwelling. Although his men protested in a disturbed state that it was not right to be on foot, he would in no way listen to them. If he had remained a little longer and the news of his enemy having been killed had reached him, it is possible that he would have escaped safe and sound, mounted as he was. As the pen of destiny had gone forth after another fashion, as soon as he alighted and went in, the Raja, who was in his *maḥall* (female apartment), awoke at the uproar among the people, and stood at the gate of his house with his sword drawn. People from all sides were aroused and came in against the men who were on foot. They saw what the number of men on foot was, and came out in great numbers and faced Kishan Singh's men, who were about ten in number. In short, Kishan Singh and his nephew Karan, when they reached the Raja's house, were attacked by these men and both of them killed. Kishan Singh had seven and Karan nine wounds. Altogether in this fight 66 men on the two sides were killed, on the Raja's side 30 and on Kishan Singh's 36. When the sun rose and illumined the world with its light, this business was revealed, and the Raja saw that his brother, his nephew, and some of his servants, whom he considered dearer than himself, were killed, and the whole of the rest had dispersed to their own places. The news reached me in Pushkar, and I ordered them to burn those who were killed, according to their rites, and inform me of the true circumstances of the affair. In the end it became clear that the affair had happened in the manner in which it has been written here, and that no further enquiry was necessary.

On the 8th Mīrān Ṣadr Jahān came from his native place and waited on me with an offering of 100 muhrs. Rāy Sūraj Singh was dismissed to his duty in the Deccan. I presented him with a couple of pearls for his ears and a special Kashmir shawl (*parm narm*). A pair of pearls were also sent to Khān Jahān. On the 25th I increased the mansab of I'tibār Khān by 600 horse, so as to bring it to 5,000 personal and 2,000 horse. On the same day Karan obtained leave to go to his jagir. He received a present of a horse, a special elephant, a dress of honour, a string of pearls of the value of 50,000 rupees, and a jewelled dagger which had been completed for 2,000 rupees. From the time of his waiting on me till he obtained leave, what he had had in the shape of cash, jewellery, jewels, and jewelled things was of the value of 200,000 rupees, with 110 horses, five elephants, in addition to what my son Khurram bestowed on him at various times. I gave Mubārak Khān Sazāwal a horse and an elephant, and appointed him to accompany him. I sent several verbal messages to the Rānā. Rāja Sūraj Singh also obtained leave to go to his native country, with a promise to return in two months. On the 27th, Pāyanda Khān Moghul,[450] who was one of the old Amirs of the State, gave up the deposit of his life.

At the end of this month news came that the ruler of Iran had executed his eldest son Ṣafī Mīrzā. This was a cause of great

[450] Blochmann, p. 387. Possibly he was the part author of a translation of Bābār's Commentaries.

bewilderment. When I enquired into it they said that at Darash,[451] which is one of the noted cities of Gīlān, he ordered a slave of the name of Bihbūd to kill Ṣafī Mīrzā. The slave found an opportunity, early in the morning on the 5th of Muḥarram, in the year 1024 (25th January, 1615), when the Mīrzā was returning from the baths towards his house, and finished his affair for him with two wounds from a sword (*sīkhakī*).[452] After a great part of the day had passed, while his body lay between the water and the mud, Shaikh Bahā'u-d-dīn Muḥammad, who was the best known man in the country for learning and holiness, and on whom the Shah had full reliance, reported the affair, and, obtaining leave to lift him up, took his corpse and sent it to Ardabīl, where was the burial-ground of his ancestors. Although much enquiry was made of travellers from Iran, no one would say a word of this affair that satisfied my mind with regard to it. The killing of a son must have some powerful motive in order to do away with the disgrace of it.

On the 1st of the month of Tīr I gave an elephant of the name of Ranjīt with its trappings to Mīrzā Rustam and another to Sayyid Alī Bārha. Mīrak Ḥusain, a relation of Khwāja Shamsu-d-dīn, was appointed bakhshi and news-writer of the Subah of Behar, and took leave to go. I gave Khwāja 'Abdu-l-Laṭīf Qūsh-begī (the falconer) an elephant and a dress of honour, and dismissed him to his jagir. On the 9th of the same month I gave a jewelled sword to Khān Daurān, and a jewelled dagger was sent for Allahdād, the son of Jalālā the Afghan, who had become loyal. On the 13th took place the meeting for the festival of the

[451] The name is wrong. The Iqbāl-nāma, p. 84, has Rasht (Rashd), which is a well-known town on the Caspian.

[452] According to the Iqbāl-nāma the true reading is *sanjakī* (see p. 84). But Olearius, who gives a full account of the murder (p, 352 of English translation, ed. 1662), says Bihbūd gave him two stabs with a *chentze,* which is a kind of poniard.

Āb-pāshān[453] (rose-water scattering), and the servants of the Court amused themselves with sprinkling rose-water over each other. On the 17th, Amānat Khān was appointed to the port of Cambay. As Muqarrab Khān proposed to come to Court, the (charge of the) aforesaid port was changed. On the same day I sent a jewelled waist-dagger to my son Parwīz. On the 18th the offering of Khānkhānān was laid before me. He had prepared all kinds of jewellery and other things, jewels with jewelled things, such as three rubies and 103 pearls, 100 rubies (*yāqūt*), two jewelled daggers and an aigrette adorned with rubies and pearls, a jewelled water-jar, a jewelled sword, a quiver bound with velvet, and a diamond ring, altogether of the value of about 100,000 rupees, in addition to jewels and jewelled things, cloth from the Deccan and Carnatic, and all kinds of gilt and plain things, with fifteen elephants and a horse whose mane reached the ground. The offering of Shāh-nawāz Khān (his son) also, consisting of five elephants, 300 pieces of all kinds of cloth, was brought before me. On the 8th I honoured Hūshang with the title of Ikrām Khān. Rūz-afzūn, who was one of the princes of the Subah of Behar and who had been from his youth one of the permanent servants of the Court, having been honoured by admission into Islam, was made Raja of the province of his father, Rāja Sangrām.[454] Though the latter had been killed in opposing the leaders of the State, I gave him an elephant and leave to go to his native place. An elephant was presented to Jahāngīr Qulī Khān. On the 24th, Jagat Singh, son of Kunwar Karan, who was in his 12th year, came and waited on me, and presented petitions from his grandfather, the Rānā Amar Singh, and from his father. The signs of nobility and high birth were evident on his face. I pleased him with a dress of honour and kindness. To the mansab of Mīrzā 'Īsā Tarkhān an addition of

---

[453] A Persian festival in memory of a rain which fell on the 13th Tīr and put an end to a famine (Bahār-i-'ajam).

[454] Sangrām was Raja of Kharkpur in Behar, and was killed in battle with Jahāngīr Qulī Khān (Blochmann, p. 446, note).

200 personal was made, so that it attained to 1,200 personal and 300 horse. In the end of the month, having honoured Shaikh Ḥusain Rohīla with the title of Mubāriz Khān, I dismissed him to his jagir. Ten thousand darabs (5,000 rupees) were given to the relations of Mīrzā Sharafu-d-dīn Ḥusain Kāshgharī, who at this time had come and had the honour of kissing the threshold. On the 5th Amurdād, to the mansab of Rāja Nathmal, which was 1,500 personal and 1,100 horse, an addition of 500 personal and 100 horse was made. On the 7th, Kesho (Dās) Mārū, who had a jagir in the Sarkar of Orissa, and who had been sent for to Court on account of a complaint[455] against the governor of the Subah of that place, came and paid his respects. He produced as an offering four elephants. As I had a great desire to see my *farzand* (son) Khān Jahān (Lodī), and for the purpose of enquiring into important matters connected with the Deccan, it was necessary for him to come at once, I sent for him. On Tuesday, the 8th of the same month, he waited on me, and presented as an offering 1,000 muhrs, 1,000 rupees, 4 rubies, 20 pearls, 1 emerald, and a jewelled *phūl kaṭāra,* the total value being 50,000 rupees. On the night of Sunday, as it was the anniversary of the great Khwāja (Mu'īnu-d-dīn), I went to his revered mausoleum, and remained there till midnight. The attendants and Sufis exhibited ecstatic states, and I gave the fakirs and attendants money with my own hand; altogether there were expended 6,000 rupees in cash, 100 *ṣ̈aub-kurta* (a robe down to the ankles), 70 rosaries of pearls,[456] coral and amber, etc. Mahā Singh, grandson of Rāja Mān Singh, was honoured with the title of Raja, and a standard and drums given him. On the 16th an Iraq horse out of my private stable and another horse were presented to Mahābat Khān. On the 19th an elephant was given to Khān A'ẓ̈am. On the 20th, 200 horse were added to the mansab of Kesho (Dās) Mārū, which was

[455] *Shakwā'i-ṣāḥib-i-Sūba.* I presume it means a complaint against the governor, and perhaps one made by Kesho.

[456] The pearls are omitted in the MSS.

2,000 personal and 1,000 horse, and he was dignified with a dress of honour. An increase of 200 personal and horse was made to the mansab of Khwāja 'Āqil, which was 1,200 personal and 600 horse. On the 22nd, Mīrzā Rāja Bhāo Singh took leave to go to Amber, which was his ancient native place, and had given him a special Kashmir *phūp* (?) robe.[457] On the 25th, Aḥmad Beg Khān, who was imprisoned at Ranṭambhor, paid his respects to me, and his offences were pardoned on account of his former services. On the 28th, Muqarrab Khān came from the Subah of Gujarat and waited on me, and offered an aigrette and a jewelled throne.[458] An increase of 500 personal and horse was made to the mansab of Salāmu-llah, the Arab, and it was brought to 2,000 personal and 1,100 horse. On the 1st of the month of Shahrīwar the following increases were made in the rank of a number of men who were going on service to the Deccan :—To Mubāriz Khān 300 horse, making 1,000 personal and horse. Nāhir Khān was also raised to 1,000 personal and horse. Dilāwar Khān was raised by 300 horse to 2,500 personal and horse. Manglī Khān's rank was increased by 200 horse to 1,500 personal and 1,000 horse. Girdhar, the son of Ray Sāl, had the rank of 800 personal and horse bestowed on him, and Ilf Khān Qiyām Khān the same mansab, original and increase. Yādgār Ḥusain was raised to 700 personal and 500 horse, and Kamālu-d-dīn, son of Shīr Khān, to the same mansab. One hundred and fifty horse were added to the rank of Sayyid 'Abdu-llah Bārha, which then came to 700 personal and 300 horse, original and increase. On the 8th of the said month I bestowed one Nūrjahānī muhr, which is equal to 6,400 rupees, on Muṣṭafā Beg, the ambassador of the ruler of Iran, and presented five cheetahs to Qāsim Khān, governor of Bengal. Mīrzā Murād, eldest son of Mīrzā Rustam, on the 12th of the same month was honoured with the title of Iltifāt Khān. On the night of the 16th, corresponding with the *Shab-i-barāt*

---

457 It is *phūl* in MS. No. 181.

458 *Takhtī*, qu. a signet ? No. 181 has a *lāl takhtī*.

(consecrated to the memory of forefathers), I ordered them to light lamps on the hills round the Ānā Sāgar tank and on its banks, and went myself to look at them. The reflection of the lamps fell on the water and had a wonderful appearance. I passed the most of that night with the ladies of the mahall on the bank of that tank.

On the 17th, Mīrzā Jamālu-d-dīn Ḥusain,[459] who had gone as an ambassador to Bijapur, came and waited on me, and presented three rings, the stone of one of which was a cornelian from Yemen, of great beauty and pureness of water, the like of which is seldom seen among the cornelians of Yemen. 'Ādil Khān sent a person of the name of Sayyid Kabīr Khān on his own part with the said Mir, and forwarded as offerings elephants with gold and silver fittings, Arab horses, jewels and jewelled things, and all kinds of cloth made in that country. On the 24th of this month they were brought before me with a letter he had brought. On the same day the assembly for my solar weighing was held. On the 26th, Muṣṭafā Beg, the ambassador, took his leave. In addition to what had been bestowed on him during the time of his attendance, I gave him 20,000 rupees more in cash and a dress of honour, and in answer to the letter he had brought sent a friendly letter written in the perfection of friendship. On the 4th of the month of Mihr the mansab of Mīr Jamālu-d-dīn Ḥusain, which was 2,000 personal and 500 horse, was fixed at 4,000 personal and 2,000 horse. On the 5th, Mahābat Khān, in company with Khān Jahān, who had been appointed to serve in the Deccan, at the hour that had been appointed for him, took his leave ; he was honoured with a dress of honour, a jewelled dagger, a *phūl kaṭāra,* a special sword, and an elephant. On the 8th, Khān Jahān took his leave, and I presented him with a dress of honour, and a special *nādirī* (a dress), and an ambling horse with a saddle, a special elephant, and a special sword. On the same date 1,700 horse of those under the command of

[459] Sir Thomas Roe's friend.

Mahābat Khān were ordered to have assignments (*tankhwāh*) for two or three horses given them. The whole of the men who were at this time appointed for service in the Deccan were 330 mansabdars, 3,000 ahadis, 700 horse from the Ūymaqs, and 3,000 Dalazāk Afghans. Altogether there were 30,000[460] cavalry, and 3,000,000 rupees of treasure, and an efficient artillery, and war elephants. They proceeded on this duty. The mansab of Sarbuland Rāy was increased by 500 personal and 260 horse, and came to 2,000 personal and 1,500 horse. Bāljū, nephew of Qilīj Khān, was promoted to the mansab of 1,000 personal and 700 horse, original and increase. I also increased Rāja Kishan Dās's mansab by 500. At the request of Khān Jahān, the mansab of Shāhbāz Khān Lodī, who belonged to the Deccan force, was fixed, original and increase, at 2,000 personal and 1,000 horse ; and 200 horse were added to the mansab of Wazīr Khān. The mansab of Suhrāb Khān, son of Mīrzā Rustam, was fixed at 1,000 personal and 400 horse, original and increase. On the 14th of the same month 1,000 was added to the mansab of Mīr Jamālu-d-dīn Ḥusain, and by increasing it also by 500 horse he was raised to the exalted rank of 5,000 personal and 2,500 horse. On the 19th, Rāja Sūraj Singh, with his son Gaj Singh, who had gone home, came and paid their respects, and presented as offerings 100 muhrs and 1,000 rupees. I gave Sayyid Kabīr, who had been sent by 'Ādil Khān, one Nūrjahānī muhr, which weighed 500 *tūlcha.* On the 23rd, ninety elephants of those which Qāsim Khān had acquired from the conquest of the country of Kūch (Behar), and the conquest of the Maghs and the zamindars of Orissa, were brought before me and placed in the special elephant houses. On the 26th, Irādat Khān was raised to the rank of Mīr-sāmānī (head butler), Mu'tamad Khān to that of Bakhshi of the Ahadis, Muḥammad Riẓā Jābirī to that of Bakhshi of the Subah of the Panjab and news-writer of that place. Sayyid Kabīr, who had come on the part of 'Ādil Khān to beg pardon for the offences of

[460] Text wrongly has 3 instead of 30.

the rulers (*dunyā-dārān*) of the Deccan, and to promise the restoration of the fort of Ahmadnagar and the royal territory which had been taken out of the possession of the chiefs of the victorious State through the rebellion of certain rebels, came and waited on me, and obtained leave to go on this date; and, having received a dress of honour, an elephant, and a horse, started off. As Rāja Rāj Singh Kachhwāha had died in the Deccan, I promoted his son Rām Dās to the mansab of 1,000 personal and 400 horse. On the 4th of Ābān, drums were given to Saif Khān Bārha and his mansab increased by 300 horse, so as to bring it up to 3,000 personal and 2,000 horse. On the same date I released Rāja Mān, who was in confinement in the fort of Gwalior, on the security of Murtaẓā Khān, and, confirming his mansab, sent him to the said Khān for duty at the fort of Kāngra. At the request of Khān Daurān, an increase of 300 horse was ordered to the mansab of Ṣādiq Khān, raising it to 1,000 personal and horse. Mīrzā ʻĪsā Tarkhān came from the province of Sambhal, which was his jagir, and waited on me, and offered 100 muhrs. On the 16th, Rāja Sūraj Singh obtained leave to go to his duty in the Deccan, and I increased his mansab by 300 horse, so as to make it 5,000 personal and 3,300 horse ; he received a dress of honour and a horse, and started. On the 18th I confirmed the mansab of Mīrzā ʻĪsā, original and increase, at 1,500 personal and 800 horse, and gave him an elephant and a dress of honour, and he took leave to go to the Deccan.

On the same day the news of the death of the wretch Chīn Qilīj was received by a letter from Jahāngīr Qulī Khān. After the death of Qilīj Khān, who was one of the old servants of this State, I had made this inauspicious man an Amir, and shown him great favour, and given him in jagir such a place as Jaunpur. I also sent his other brothers and relations with him and made them his deputies. He had one brother of the name of Lahorī,[461] of a very wicked disposition. It was reported to me that the

[461] Apparently because born in Lahore (see Blochmann, p. 500).

servants of God (people) were greatly oppressed by his conduct. I sent an ahadi to bring him (Lahorī) from Jaunpur. At the coming of the ahadi, suspicion without any cause prevailed over Chīn Qilīj, and it came into his mind to run away, taking his misguided brother with him. Leaving his mansab, his government, place, and jagir, money, property, children, and people, he took a little money and gold and a few jewels and went with a small body among the zamindars. This news arrived a few days ago and caused great astonishment. In short, to whatever zamindar he went he took money[462] from him (?) and then let him go (?), until news came that he had entered the country of Johaṭ.[463] When this news reached Jahāngīr Qulī Khān, he sent some of his men to take and bring that thoughtless one. They took him as soon as they arrived, and were intending to take him to Jahāngīr Qulī Khān, when he at that very moment went to hell. Some of those who had accompanied him said that for some days previously he had contracted an illness and it had killed him. But this was heard of him as well, that he committed suicide, in order that they might not take him to Jahāngīr Qulī Khān in this state. In any case, they brought his body with his children and servants who were with him to Allahabad. They made away with most of the money that he had, and the zamindars took it from him. Alas, that salt (i.e. loyalty) should not have brought such black-faced wretches to condign punishment!

[462] According to I.O. MS. 181 every zamindar took some money from Chīn Qilīj and sent him out of his estate, and this seems to be the probable meaning, for we are told later on that the zamindars plundered Chīn Qilīj.

[463] Tirhut. R.A.S. MS. has "It chanced that the zamindar of this place was with Jahāngīr Qulī, and the latter sent him with some people to seize Chīn Qilīj." I.O. MS. has the same, and this seems correct. The text has "It chanced that the zamindar of that place was spending some days in that neighbourhood (?)." Perhaps a negative has been omitted before 'spending.' I.O. MS. seems to have Johirhat as the name of the zamindar's estate.

"Behind the duty that lies on all people is
the duty to the sovereign and benefactor " (?).[464]

On the 22nd, at the request of Khān Daurān, 200 horse were added to the mansab of Nād 'Alī Maidānī, one of the officers appointed to Bangash, which brought it to 1,500 personal and 1,000 horse ; 100 horse were also added to the mansab of Lashkar Khān, which was 2,000 personal and 900 horse. On the 24th I confirmed the mansab of Muqarrab Khān, which was 3,000 personal and 2,000 horse, and increased it to 5,000 personal and 2,500 horse. On the same day I bestowed the title of Khan on Qiyām, son of Shāh Muḥammad Qandahārī, who was an Amīr-zāda, and was in service as a huntsman. On the 5th of the month of Āzar a jewelled dagger was given to Dārāb Khān, and by the hand of Rāja Sārang Deo dresses of honour were bestowed on the Amirs of the Deccan. As some (evil) things had been heard about Ṣafdar Khān, governor of Kashmir, I dismissed him from the government, and favouring Aḥmad Beg Khān on account of his previous services, I promoted him to be Subadar of Kashmir, and confirmed his mansab of 2,500 personal and 1,500 horse, honoured him with a jewelled waist-dagger and a dress of honour, and gave him leave. By the hand of Ihtimām Khān I sent winter dresses of honour to Qāsim Khān, governor of Bengal, and the Amirs that were attached to that province. On the 15th of the month there was laid before me the offering of Maka'ī, son of Iftikhār Khān, consisting of an elephant, *goṭ*[465] horses, and pieces of cloth. He was honoured with the title of Muruwwat Khān. At the request of I'timādu-d-daula, I had sent for Dayānat Khān, who was in the fort of Gwalior, and he had the good fortune to pay his respects ; his property, which had been confiscated, was restored to him.

[464] Apparently the verse is quoted with reference to Jahāngīr Qulī's failure to exact retribution from the zamindars. There is an account of Chīn Qilīj in the Ma'aṣir, iii, 351.

[465] *Gūnṭh,* a breed of small horses or ponies.

At this time Khwāja Hāshim, of Dahbīd, who at this day vigorously maintains in Transoxiana the profession of a dervish, and in whom the people of that country have great belief, sent a letter by the hand of one of his disciples pointing out his old devotion (to the royal family) and connection and friendship of his ancestors with this illustrious family, together with a *farjī*[466] and a bow and a couplet which the late king Bābar had made for a saint of the name of Khwājagī, who also belonged to that sect of dervishes. The last hemistich is as follows :—

"We are bound to the Khwājagī and are servants to the Khwājagī."

I also with my own pen wrote some lines in the style of that writing, and sent impromptu quatrains with 1,000 Jahāngīrī muhrs to the said Khwāja—

" O thou whose kindness to me is ever more and more,
The State has remembrance of thee, O Dervish,
As from good tidings our heart is rejoiced,
We are glad that thy kindness passes all bounds. "

As I ordered that whoever had the poetic temperament should recite (compose ?) this quatrain,[467] Ḥakīm Masīḥu-z-zamān said, and said very well—

"Although we have the business of kingship before us,
Every moment more and more we think on the dervishes.
If the heart of our Dervish be gladdened by us
We count that to be the profit of our kingship."

I gave the Ḥakīm 1,000 muhrs for the composition of this quatrain. On the 7th of the month of Day, when I was coming back from Pushkar and returning to Ajmir, on the way forty-two wild pigs were taken.

On the 20th, Mīr Mīrān came and waited on me. A summary of his circumstances and of his family is now written. On the

---

466 A *farjī* is a coat (see Blochmann, p. 89).

467 Text *īn rubī'ī,* 'this quatrain,' which does not seem to make sense. Perhaps *īn* here should be *āyīn-i-rub ā 'ī,* ' the rules or the custom of a quatrain. 'Similarly, *īn kitābat* five lines down may be *āyīn-i-kitābat*,' the rules of writing.'

side of his father[468] he is the grandson of Mīr Ghiyās̤u-d-dīn Muḥammad Mīr Mīrān, son of Shāh Ni'matu-llah Walī. During the reigns of the Ṣafawī kings the family had attained to great respect, so that Shāh T̤ahmāsp gave his own sister Jānish[469] Khānim to Shāh Ni'matu-llah, and so on account of his being a great Shaikh and of his being an instructor he was made a relative and a son-in-law (of kings). On the side of his mother he was the daughter's son of Shāh Isma'īl Khūnī (Isma'īl II, the Bloody). After the death of Shāh Ni'matu-llah, his son Ghiyās̤u-d-dīn Muḥammad Mīr Mīrān received great consideration, and the late Shāh (T̤ahmāsp) gave to his eldest son in marriage a daughter from the royal family. He gave the daughter of the above-mentioned Shāh Isma'īl to another son of his, Khalīlu-llah, to whom Mīr Mīrān was born. The aforesaid Mīr Khalīlu-llah, seven or eight years before this, had come from Persia and waited on me at Lahore. As he belonged to a high and saintly family, I was much interested in his affairs, and gave him a mansab and a jagir, and honoured and cherished him. After the seat of government was at Agra, in a short time he was attacked by bilious[470] diarrhœa from eating too many mangoes, and in ten or twelve days gave up his soul to the Creator. I was grieved at his going, and ordered what he had left in cash and jewels to be sent to his children in Persia. Meanwhile Mīr Mīrān, who was 22 years old, became a qalandar and dervish, and came to me at Ajmir in a way that nobody on the road could recognize him. I soothed all the troubles of his mind and the miseries of his inward and outward condition, and gave him a mansab of 1,000 personal and 400 horse, and presented him with 30,000 darabs in cash. He is now in waiting and attendance on me.

---

[468] His father was Khalīlu-llah, previously mentioned in the Tūzuk, and who had lately died (Iqbāl-nāma, p. 84, and Tūzuk, pp. 62 and 69). T̤ahmāsp gave Ni'matu-llah's daughter in marriage to his own son Isma'īl.

[469] Khānish Khānim in Ma'āsir, iii, 339.

[470] *Ishāl-i-kabd.*

On the 12th, Ẓafar Khān, who had been removed from the Subah of Behar, came and waited on me, and made an offering of 100 muhrs, as well as three elephants. On the 15th of Day I increased the mansab of Qāsim Khān, the Subahdar of Bengal, by 1,000 personal and horse, so as to make it 4,000 personal and horse. As the diwan and bakhshi of Bengal, Ḥusain Beg and Ṭāhir, had not done approved service, Mukhliṣ Khān, who was one of the confidential servants of the Court, was nominated to these duties. I conferred on him a mansab of 2,000 personal and 700 horse, and also gave him a standard. The duty of *'arẓ-mukarrir* (reviser of petitions) I ordered to be given to Dayānat Khān. On the 25th, Friday, the weighing of my son Khurram took place. Up to the present year, when he is 24 years old, and is married and has children, he has never defiled himself with drinking wine. On this day, when the assembly for his weighing was held, I said to him : " Bābā, thou hast become the father of children, and kings and kings' sons have drunk wine. To-day, which is the day of thy being weighed, I will give thee wine to drink, and give thee leave to drink it on feast days and at the time of the New Year, and at all great festivals. But thou must observe the path of moderation, for wise men do not consider it right to drink to such an extent as to destroy the understanding, and it is necessary that from drinking only profit should be derived." Bū 'Alī (Avicenna), who is one of the most learned of hakims and physicians, has written this quatrain—

> "Wine is a raging enemy, a prudent friend;
> A little is an antidote, but much a snake's poison.
> In much there is no little injury,
> In a little there is much profit."

With much trouble wine was given to him. I had not drunk it till I was 15[471] years old, except when in the time of my infancy

---

[471] Two I.O. MSS. and the R.A.S. MS. have 18 instead of 15. Elliot has "up to my fourteenth" year. Jahāngīr was born in Rabī', 977, or 31st August, 1569, and the beginning of wine-drinking to which he refers must have taken place at earliest in January, 1586. He tells us that it was after the death of Muḥammad Ḥakīm, and

two or three times my mother and wet-nurses gave it by way of infantile remedy. They asked for a little spirit from my revered father, and gave it me to the extent of a tola mixed with water and rosewater to take away a cough, designating it as medicine. At the time when the camp of my revered father had been pitched in order to put down the disturbance of Yūsufza'e Afghans at the fort of Attock, which is on the bank of the Nīlāb (Indus) River, one day I had mounted to go out to hunt. When I had moved about a good deal and the signs of weariness had set in, a gunner of the name of Ustād Shāh-qulī, a wonderful gunner out of those under my revered uncle Mīrzā Muḥammad Ḥakīm, said to me that if I would take a cup of wine it would drive away the feeling of being tired and heavy. It was in the time of my youth, and as I felt disposed towards it I ordered Maḥmūd, the Āb-dār (person in charge of drinking water, etc.), to go to the house of Ḥakīm 'Alī and bring me an intoxicating draught. He sent me[472] the amount of one and a half cups of yellow wine of a sweet taste in a little bottle. I drank it, and found its quality agreeable. After that I took to drinking wine, and increased it from day to day until wine made from grapes ceased to intoxicate me, and I took to drinking arrack (*'araq*, spirits), and by degrees during nine years my potions rose to twenty cups of doubly distilled spirits, fourteen during the daytime and the remainder at night. The weight of this was six Hindustani sirs or one and a half maunds of Iran. The extent of my eating in those

---

at the time when his father was at Attock. Now Akbar arrived there on 15th Muḥarram, 994, according to Niẕāmu-d-dīn, and on 12th Day, 994, according to Abū-l-faẓl, iii, 976, i.e. about the end of December, 1585, and at that time Jahāngīr was 17 years and 4 months of age, or in his 18th year. He continued to drink heavily for nine years, i.e. till he was 26 (17 + 9), then he moderated for seven years, i.e. till he was 33, and he kept to that for fifteen years more, i.e. till he was 48 These years were lunar years, and he tells that at the time of writing he was 47 years and 9 months old, according to the lunar calendar. It seems to follow that the MSS. are right, and that we should read 18.

[472] Elliot, vi, 341.

days was a fowl[473] with bread and vegetables (lit. radish).[474] In that state of matters no one had the power to forbid me, and matters went to such a length that in the crapulous state from the excessive trembling of my hand I could not drink from my own cup, but others had to give it me to drink, until I sent for Ḥakīm Humām, brother of Ḥakīm Abū-l-fatḥ, who was of the most intimate with my revered father, and informed him of my state. He, with excessive sincerity and unfeigned burning of heart, said to me without hesitation, " Lord of the world, by the way in which you drink spirits, God forbid it, but in six months matters will come to such a pass that there will be no remedy for it." As his words were said out of pure good-will, and sweet life was dear to me, they made an impression on me, and from that day I began to lessen my allowance and set myself to take *filūnīyā*.[475] In

---

[473] The two good I. O. MSS. have, not *murgh* or *murghī*, but *tughdarī* or *tūghdarī*, a 'bustard, 'unless indeed the word be *taghaddī*, 'breakfast.' But probably the word is *tughdarī*, a bustard, and the reference is to the particular memorable day when he first drank wine. His food that day, he says, was a bustard with bread and a radish (*turb*).

[474] Blochmann. *Calcutta Review*, 1869, has 'turnips.'

[475] *Filūnīyā*. The word is not given in ordinary dictionaries, but it is explained in Dozy's Supplement. It is stated there that it is a sedative electuary, and that the word is derived from the Greek, being φιλωυια, which is the name of an antidote or drug invented by Philon of Tarsus. There is an account of Philon and a reference to his drug in Smith's Classical Dictionary. Philon lived in or before the first century after Christ, and is referred to by Galen and others. The word as given there is φιλωυειον. We are not told what it was made of. In Price's Jahāngīr, filuniya, misread there as Kelourica, is described by Jahāngīr as brother's son to *tiryāq*, i.e. theriaca (see Price, p. 6). *Tiryāk* or *tiryāq* is supposed to be a Greek word (see Lane), and means an antidote against poison, etc. It is so used in the verse from Avicenna quoted by Jahāngīr to his son Shāh Jahān. See D'Herbelot, s.v. *Teriak*. But it is also often used apparently as a synonym for opium. The mixing of wine with spirits was intended to dilute the potation, for hitherto Jahāngīr had been taking raw spirit. A *miṣqāl* is said to be $63\frac{1}{2}$ grains troy, and so 18 misqals would be about 3 ounces, and the six cups would be about $1\frac{1}{2}$ lb. troy. In Elliot, Jahāngīr is made to say that he does not drink on Thursdays and Fridays. But the *Shab-i-jum'a*, as Blochmann has pointed out

proportion as I diminished my liquor, I increased the amount of filuniya.

I also ordered that the arrack should be diluted with wine of the grape so that there should be two parts wine and one part arrack. Every day I diminished the quantity I took, and in the course of seven years I brought it down to six cups. The weight of each cupful was 18 1/4 misqals. It is now fifteen years that I have drunk at this rate, neither more nor less. And my drinking time is the night except on the day of Thursdays, as it is the day of the blessed accession. Also on the eve[476] of Friday, which is the most blessed eve of the week, and is the prelude to a blessed day (I do not drink). I drink at the end of each day with these two[477] exceptions, for it does not appear right that this eve (Thursday night) should be spent in neglect, and that there should be an omission (on Friday) of returning thanks to the True Benefactor. On the day of Thursday and on the day of Sunday I do not eat meat. Not on Thursday, because it is the day of my auspicious accession, and not on Sunday, because it is the birthday of my revered father, and he greatly honoured and held dear the day. After some time I substituted opium for filuniya. Now that my age has arrived at 46 solar years and 4 months, I eat eight surkhs (a red berry used as a weight) of opium when five gharis of day have passed, and six surkhs after one watch of night.

---

elsewhere, Āyīn translation, p. 171, n. 3, means Thursday night or Friday eve, and this is clearly the case here, for Jahāngīr speaks of the eve's being followed by a blessed day. It should be noted that there is no connection in Jahāngīr's mind between abstaining from wine and abstaining from meat. He did not eat meat on Thursdays or Sundays because he did not approve of taking life on these days, but he drank on both of them.

476 Cf. Blochmann's translation and *Calcutta Review* for 1869.

477 I understand the two exceptions (*dū chīz*) to be that on Thursdays he drank in the daytime, contrary to the general rule of only drinking at night, and that on Thursday evenings he did not drink.

I gave a jewelled dagger to 'Abdu-llah Khān by the hand of Maqṣūd 'Alī. Shaikh Mūsā, a relation of Qāsim Khān, was dignified with the title of Khān, and promoted to the mansab of 800 personal and 400 horse, and was allowed to go to Bengal. The mansab of z̤afar Khān was increased to 500 personal and horse, and he was appointed to duty in Bangash. On the same day Muḥammad Ḥusain, brother of Khwāja Jahān, was given the faujdarship of the Sarkar of Ḥiṣṣār and dismissed, his mansab being increased by 200 horse to raise it to 500 personal and 400 horse, with the gift of an elephant. On the 5th Bahman an elephant was conferred on Mīr Mīrān. When the merchant 'Abdu-l-Karīm left Iran for Hindustan, my exalted brother Shāh 'Abbās sent me by his hand a rosary of cornelian from Yemen and a cup of Venetian workmanship, which was very fine and rare. On the 9th of the same month they were laid before me. On the 18th some offerings of many kinds of jewelled ornaments, etc., which Sulṭān Parwīz had sent to me, were laid before me. On the 7th Isfan-dārmuz, Ṣādiq, nephew of I'timādu-d-daulah, who was permanently employed as Bakhshi, was honoured with the title of Khān. I had also conferred this title on Khwāja 'Abdu-l-'Azīz. According to what was right, I called him by the title of 'Abdu-l-'Azīz Khān and Ṣādiq by that of Ṣādiq Khān. On the 10th, Jagat Singh, son of Kunwar Karan, who had obtained leave to go to his native country, when he took leave was presented with 20,000 rupees, a horse, an elephant, a dress of honour, and a special shawl. Five thousand rupees, a horse, and a dress of honour were also given to Haridās Jhālā, who was one of the confidants of the Rānā and tutor to Karan's son. By his hand I also sent a mace of gold (*shashparī*) for the Rānā.

On the 20th of the same month, Rāja Sūraj Singh, son of Rāja Bāso, who on account of the nearness of his dwelling-place to it had been sent with Murtaẓā Khān to capture the fort of Kāngra, came on my summons and waited on me. The aforesaid Khān had entertained certain suspicions with regard to him, and on this account, considering him an undesirable companion, had repeatedly sent petitions to the Court, and wrote things about him until an order was received to summon him.

On the 26th, Niẓāmu-d-dīn Khān came from Multan and waited on me. In the end of this year news of victory and prosperity came in from all sides of my dominions. In the first place, this was with regard to the disturbance of Aḥdād, the Afghan, who for a long time past had been in rebellion in the hill country of Kabul, and round whom many of the Afghans of that neighbourhood had assembled, and against whom from the time of my revered father until now, which is the 10th year after my accession, armies have always been employed. He by degrees was defeated, and, falling into a wretched state, a part of his band was dispersed and a part killed. He took refuge for some time in Charkh, which was a place on which he relied, but Khān Daurān surrounded it and closed the road for entry and exit. When there remained no grass for his beasts or means of living for men in the fortress, he at night brought down his animals from the hills and grazed them on the skirts, and accompanied them himself, in order that he might set an example to his men. At last this intelligence reached Khān Daurān. He then appointed a body of his leaders and experienced men to go into ambush on an appointed night in the neighbourhood of Charkh. That band went and hid itself at night in places of refuge, and Khān Daurān rode on the same day in that direction. When those ill-fated ones brought out their cattle and let them loose to graze, and the ill-conditioned Aḥdād himself passed by the places of ambush with his own band, suddenly a dust rose in front of him. When they enquired it became known that it was Khān Daurān. In a state of bewilderment he endeavoured to turn back, and the scouts announced to the aforesaid Khān that it was Aḥdād. The Khān gave his horse the reins and went at Aḥdād ; the men who were in ambush also blocked the road and attacked him. The fight lasted till midday in consequence of the broken nature of the ground and the thickness of the jungle ; at last defeat fell on the Afghans and they betook themselves to the hill:

about 300 fighting men went to hell and 100 were taken prisoners. Aḥdād could not regain the stronghold and hold on there. Necessarily he turned his face towards Qandahar. The victorious troops entering Char<u>kh</u>, burnt all the places and houses of those ill-fortuned ones, and destroyed and rooted them up from their foundations.

Another[478] piece of news was the defeat of the ill-starred 'Ambar and the destruction of his unfortunate army. Briefly, a band of the influential leaders and a body of Bargīs (Mahrattas), who are a hardy lot and who are the centre of resistance in that country, becoming angry with 'Ambar, showed an intention to be loyal, and begging for quarter from <u>Sh</u>āh-nawāz <u>Kh</u>ān, who was in Bālāpūr with an army of royal troops, agreed to interview the said <u>Kh</u>ān, and being satisfied, Ādam <u>Kh</u>ān, Yāqūt <u>Kh</u>ān, and other leaders, and the Bargīs Jādo[479] Rāy and Bāpū Kāṭiyā, came and interviewed him. <u>Sh</u>āh-nawāz <u>Kh</u>ān gave each of them a horse, an elephant, money, and dress of honour, according to their quality and condition, made them hot in duty and loyalty, and marching from Balapur started against the rebel 'Ambar in their company. On the road they fell in with an army of the Dakhanis, whose leaders were Maḥalldār,[480] Dāni<u>sh</u> (Āta<u>sh</u> ?), Dilāwar, Bijlī, Fīrūz, and others, and routed it.

> "With broken arms and loosened loins,
> No strength in their feet, no sense in their heads."[481]

They reached the camp of that ill-starred one, and he from excessive pride determined to fight with the victorious troops. Having collected those rebels who were with him and 'Ādil

---

[478] Elliot, vi, 343.

[479] The MSS. have Jādūn Rāy and Bāba Chokanth (Jīū Kantli ?). The Ma'ā s̤ īru-l-umarā, ii, 646, has Mālūjī Kāntiya. The text has Bābū Kāntiya.

[480] The text is corrupt. The Ma'ā s̤ ir, id., has Āta<u>sh</u> instead of Dāni<u>sh</u>.

[481] The text is corrupt. In the second line of the verse the text has *guft,* which seems meaningless, and two I.O. MSS. and B. M.MS. Add. 26,215 have *jang,* battle.' The R.A.S. MS. has *pāy,* 'feet,' which seems to me the best reading. Possibly *guft* should be read *kift,*' shoulder.'

Khān's army and that of Quṭbu-l-mulk together, and preparing their artillery, he started to meet the royal troops until a space of not more than 5 or 6 kos remained between. On Sunday, the 25th Bahman, the armies of light and darkness approached each other and the scouts became visible. Three watches of day had passed when cannon and rocket firing began. In the end Dārāb Khān, who was in command of the vanguard, with other leaders and zealous men such as Rāja Bīr Singh Deo, Rāy Chand, 'Alī Khān the Tatar, Jahāngīr Qulī Beg Turkmān, and other lions of the forest of bravery, drew their swords and charged the vanguard of the enemy. Performing the dues of manliness and bravery, they scattered this army like the Banātu-n-na'sh (' Daughters of the Bier,' i.e. the Great Bear); and not stopping there they attacked the enemy's centre. Turning on the army opposed to them, such a hand-to-hand struggle took place that the onlookers remained bewildered. For nearly two gharis this combat went on. Heaps of the dead lay there, and the ill-starred 'Ambar, unable to offer further opposition, turned his face to flight. If darkness[482] and gloom had not come on at the cry of those black-fortuned ones, not one of them would have found the road to the valley of safety. The crocodiles of the river of conflict followed the fugitives for 2 or 3 kos. When horses and men could move no more and the defeated were scattered, they drew rein and returned to their places. The whole of the enemy's artillery, with 300 laden camels that carried rockets, war elephants, Arab and Persian horses, weapons and armour beyond reckoning, fell into the hands of the servants of the State, and there was no counting the slain and the fallen. A great many of the leaders fell alive into their hands. The next day the victorious troops, marching from the place of victory, proceeded to Karkī, which was the nest of those owlish ones, and seeing no

---

[482] The text is corrupt. In the second line of the verse the text has *guft*, which seems meaningless, and two I.O. MSS. and B. M.MS. Add. 26,215 have *jang*, battle.' The R.A.S. MS. has *pāy*, 'feet,' which seems to me the best reading. Possibly *guft* should be read *kift*,' shoulder.'

trace of them they encamped there, and obtained news that they during that night and day had fallen miserably in different places. For some days the victorious army, delayed at Karkī, levelled with the dark earth the buildings and houses of the enemy, and burnt that populous place. In consequence of the occurrence of certain events, to describe which in detail would take too long here, they returned from that place and descended by the Rohan Khanḍa Pass. In reward for this service I ordered increases to be made in the mansabs of a number who had shown zeal and bravery.

The third piece of news was the conquest of the province of Khokharā[483] and the acquisition of the diamond mines, which were taken by the excellent exertions of Ibrāhīm Khān. This province is one of the dependencies of the Subah of Behar and Patna. There is a river there from which they procure diamonds. At the season when there is little water, there are pools and water-holes, and it has become known by experience to those who are employed in this work that above every water-hole in which there are diamonds, there are crowds of flying animals of the nature of gnats, and which in the language of India they call *jhīngā* (?).[484] Keeping the bed of the stream in sight as far as it is accessible, they make a collection of stones (*sangchīn*) round the water-holes. After this they empty the water-holes with spades and shovels to the extent of a yard or 1 1/2 yards and dig up the area. They find among the stones and sand large and small

---

[483] It will be remembered that Jahāngīr has called 'Ambar's army the army of darkness, alluding perhaps to 'Ambar's being an Abyssinian.

[484] Elliot, vi, and Blochmann, p. 479, n. 3.

[483] Perhaps it should be *phangā* or *feringha,* a grasshopper, or it may be *jhīngur,* a cockroach. Presumably the country was covered with thick jungle, and the cloud of insects indicated where water was. Erskine's MS. has *chika.* B.M. Or. 3276 has *chika* or *jika*. Possibly the word is *jhīngur,* a cockroach (see Blochmann in J.A.S.B. for 1871, vol. xl). He quotes a Hindustani Dict., which says that the *jhīngā* is what in Arabic is called the *jarādu-l-baḥr* or water-locust. The river referred to by Jahāngīr is the Sankh of I.G. , xii, 222. V. Ball, Proc. A. S.B. for 1881, p. 42, suggests that the *jhīngā* may be thunder-stones!

diamonds[485] and bring them out. It occasionally happens that they find a piece of diamond worth 100,000 rupees. Briefly, this province and this river were in possession of a Hindu Zamindar of the name of Durjan Sāl, and although the governors of the Subah frequently sent armies against him and went there themselves, in consequence of the difficult roads and thickness of the jungles they contented themselves with taking two or three diamonds and left him in his former condition. When the aforesaid Subah was transferred from Ẓafar Khān, and Ibrāhīm Khān was appointed in his place, at the time of his taking leave I ordered him to go and take the province out of the possession of that unknown and insignificant individual. As soon as he arrived in the province of Behar he assembled a force and went against that Zamindar. According to former custom he sent some of his men with a promise to give some diamonds and some elephants, but the Khān did not agree to this and entered impetuously into the province. Before the fellow could collect his men he found guides and invaded it. Just when the zamindar received this news, the hills and vales that are his abode were beleaguered. Ibrāhīm sent men about to find him and they got hold of him in a cave with several women, one of whom was his mother, while others were also his father's wives. They arrested him, and also one of his brothers. They searched and took from them the diamonds they had with them. Twenty-three male and female elephants also fell into Ibrāhīm s hands. In reward for this service the mansab of Ibrāhīm Khān, original and increase, was made up to 4,000 personal and horse, and he was exalted with the title of Fatḥ-jang. Orders were also given for an increase in the mansabs of those who accompanied him on this service and had shown bravery. That province is now in possession of the imperial servants of the State. They carry on work in the bed of the stream, and bring to Court whatever diamonds are found.

---

485 Compare Tavernier's account of the searching for diamonds in Sambhalpur (vol. ii, p. 311, of ed. of 1676).

A large diamond, the value of which has been estimated at 50,000 rupees, has lately been brought from there. If a little pains are taken, it is probable that good diamonds will be found and be placed in the jewel-room.

THE ELEVENTH NEW YEAR'S FEAST AFTER THE AUSPICIOUS ACCESSION.

Fifteen gharis of day had passed on Sunday, the last day of Isfandārmuz̲, corresponding with the 1st Rabī'u-l-awwal (19th March, 1616), when from the mansion of Pisces the sun cast the ray of prosperity on the palace of Aries. At this auspicious hour, having performed the dues of service and supplication at the throne of Almighty God, I ascended the throne of State in the public audience hall, the area of which was laid out with tents and canopies (*s̲h̲āmiyānahā*), and its sides adorned with European sereens, painted gold brocades, and rare cloths. The princes, Amirs, the chief courtiers, the ministers of State, and all the servants of the Court performed their congratulatory salutations. As Ḥāfiẓ Nād 'Alī, *gūyanda* (singer), was one of the ancient servants, I ordered that whatever offerings were made on the Monday by anyone in the shape of cash or goods should be given to him by way of reward. On the 2nd day (of Farwardīn) the offerings of some of the employés were laid before me. On the 4th day the offering of K̲h̲wāja Jahān, who had sent them from Agra, and which consisted of several diamonds and pearls, of jewelled things, cloth stuffs of all kinds, and an elephant, worth altogether 50,000 rupees, was brought before me. On the 5th day, Kunwar Karan, who had been given leave to go to his home, returned and waited on me. He presented as offering 100 muhrs, 1,000 rupees, an elephant with fittings, and four horses. To the mansab of Āṣaf K̲h̲ān, which was 4,000 personal and 2,000 horse, I on the 7th made an addition of 1,000 personal and 2,000 horse, and honoured him with drums and a standard. On this day the offering of Mīr Jamālu-d-dīn Ḥusain was laid before me ; what he offered was approved and accepted. Among the things was a jewelled dagger which had been made under his superintendence.[486] On its hilt was a yellow ruby[487] (*yāqūt-i-zard*), exceeding clear and bright, in size equal to half a hen's egg. I had never before seen so large and beautiful a yellow ruby. Along with it were other rubies of approved colour and old emeralds. Brokers (*muqīmān*) valued it (the dagger) at 50,000 rupees. I increased the mansab of the said Mīr by 1,000 horse, which brought it to 5,000 personal and 3,500 horse. On the 8th I increased the mansab of Ṣādiq Ḥāziq by 300 personal and horse, and that of Irādat Khān by 300 personal and 200 horse, so as to raise each to 1,000 personal and 500 horse. On the 9th the offering of Khwāja Abū-l-ḥasan was laid before me ; of jewelled ornaments and cloth stuffs, what was of the value of 40,000 rupees was accepted, and the remainder I made a present to him. The offering of Tātār Khān Bakāwul-begī, consisting of one ruby (*la'l*), one *yāqūt*, a jewelled *takhtī* (signet ?), two rings, and some cloths, was accepted. On the 10th three elephants which Rāja Mahā Singh sent from the Deccan, and 100 and odd pieces of gold brocade, etc., which Murtaẓā Khān sent from Lahore, were laid before me. On this date Dayānat Khān presented his offering of two pearl rosaries, two rubies, six large pearls, and one gold tray, to the value of 28,000 rupees. At the end of Thursday, the 11th, I went to the house of I'timādu-d-daulah in order to add to his dignity. He then presented me with his offering, and I examined it in detail. Much of it was exceedingly rare. Of jewels there were two pearls worth 30,000 rupees, one *quṭbī* ruby which had been purchased for 22,000 rupees, with other pearls and rubies. Altogether the value was 110,000 rupees. These had the honour of acceptance, and of cloth, etc., the value

---

[486] Text, *khūd-huniarkārī*, 'his own workmanship,' but the MSS. have *khūd-sarkārī*. See also Iqbāl-nāma, p. 87, which says that Jamālu-d-d-īn had had it made in Bījāpūr.

[487] Really a topaz. Tavernier points out that the natives call various precious stones rubies, distinguishing them by their colour.

of 15,000 rupees was taken. When I had finished inspecting the offering I passed nearly one watch of the night in conviviality and enjoyment. I ordered that cups (of wine) should be given to the Amirs and servants. The ladies of the *maḥall* (harem) were also with me, and a pleasant assembly was held. After the festive assembly was over I begged I'timādu-d-daulah to excuse me, and went to the hall of audience. On the same day I ordered Nūr-maḥall Begam to be called Nūr-Jahān Begam. On the 12th the offering of I'tibār Khān was laid before me. They had made a vessel (*z̤arf*) in the form of a fish, jewelled with beautiful gems, exceedingly well shaped and calculated to hold my allowance.[488] This, with other jewels and jewelled things and cloth stuffs, the value of which was worth 56,000 rupees, I accepted and gave back the rest. Bahādur Khān, governor of Qandahar, had sent seven Iraq horses and nine *tuqūz* (81 ?) of cloth stuffs. The offerings of Irādat Khān and Rāja Sūraj Mal, son of Rāja Bāso, were laid before me on the 13th. 'Abdu-s-Subḥān, who held a mansab of 1,200 personal and 600 horse, was promoted to 1,500 personal and 700 horse. On the 15th the Subahdarship of the province of Thatha was transferred from Shamshīr Khān Ūzbeg to Muz̤affar Khān. On the 16th the offering of I'tiqād Khān, son of I'timādu-d-daulah, was laid before me. Of this the equivalent of 32,000 rupees was taken, and I gave back the rest to him. On the 17th the offering of Tarbiyat Khān was inspected. Of jewels and cloth what was valued at 17,000 rupees was approved. On the 18th I went to the house of Āṣaf Khān, and his offering was presented to me there. From the palace to his house was a distance of about a kos. For half the distance he had laid down under foot velvet woven with gold and gold brocade and plain velvet, such that its value was represented to me as 10,000 rupees. I passed that day until midnight at his house with the ladies. The offerings he had prepared were laid before me in

488 Text, *ba-andāza-i-mu'tād-i-man*, 'of capacity corresponding to my custom.' Presumably it was a drinking-cup, and held Jahāngīr's customary potation.

detail. Jewels, jewelled ornaments, and things of gold and beautiful cloth stuffs, things of the value of 114,000 rupees, four horses, and one camel were approved of. On the 19th (Farwardīn), which was the day of honour (*rūz-i-sharaf*) of the sun, a grand assembly was held in the palace. In order to observe the auspicious hour, when $2\frac{1}{2}$ gharis of day were left of the aforesaid day, I seated myself on the throne. My son Bābā Khurram at this blessed hour laid before me a ruby of the purest water and brilliancy, which they pronounced to be of the value of 80,000 rupees. I fixed his mansab, which was 15,000 personal and 8,000 horse, at 20,000 personal and 10,000 horse. On the same day my lunar weighing took place. I increased the mansab of I'timādu-d-daulah, which was 6,000 personal and 3,000 horse, to 7,000 personal and 5,000 horse, and bestowed on him a *tūmān tūgh* (horse-tail standard), and ordered his drums to be beaten after those of my son Khurram. I increased the mansab of Tarbiyat Khān by 500 personal and horse, so as to bring it to 3,500 personal and 1,500 horse. The mansab of I'tiqād Khān was increased by 1,000 personal and 400 horse. Niẓāmu-d-dīn Khān was promoted to 700 personal and 300 horse, and appointed to the Subah of Behar. Salāmu-llah, the Arab, was honoured with the title of Shajā'at Khān, and, being dignified with a necklace of pearls, became one of the royal[489] servants. I promoted Mīr Jamālu-d-dīn Injū to the title of 'Aẓudu-d-daulah (Arm of the State). On the 21st Almighty God gave Khusrau a son by the daughter of Muqīm, son of Mihtar Fāẓil Rikāb-dār (stirrup-holder). To Allah-dād, the Afghan, who, accepting my service, had separated himself from the evil-minded Aḥdād and come to Court, I gave 20,000 darabs (10,000 rupees). On the 25th came the news of the death of Rāy Manohar, who had been attached to the army of the Deccan. Giving his son a mansab of 500 personal

---

[489] *Ḥadqa-ba-gūshān*. Apparently referring to his being one of those who bored their ears in imitation of Jahāngīr.

and 300 horse, I bestowed upon him his father's place and property. On the 26th the offering of Nād 'Alī Maidānī, consisting of nine horses, several bits (? *dahāna kīsh*[490]), and four Persian camels (*wilāyatī*), was brought before me. On the 28th I presented Bahādur Khān, governor of Qandahar, Mīr Mīrān, son of Khalīlu-llah, and Sayyid Bāyazīd, governor of Bhakar, each with an elephant. On the 1st Urdībihisht, at the request of 'Abdu-llah Khān, I presented drums to his brother Sardār Khān. On the 3rd I gave Allah-dād Khān, the Afghan, a jewelled *khapwa* (dagger). On the same day news came that Qadam,[491] one of the Afrīdī Afghans who had been loyal and obedient, and to whom the *rāh-dārī* (transit dues) of the Khaibar Pass belonged, from some slight suspicion had withdrawn his feet from the circle of obedience and raised his head in sedition. He had sent a force against each of the posts (*thāna*), and wherever he and his men went, through the carelessness of those men (in the posts), had plundered and killed many of the people. Briefly, in consequence of the shameful action of this senseless Afghan, a new disturbance broke out in the hill country of Kabul. When this news arrived I ordered Hārūn, brother of Qadam, and Jalāl, his son, who were at Court, to be apprehended and handed over to Āṣaf Khān to be imprisoned in the fort of Gwalior. By the manifestation of the Divine mercy and kindness and the signs of God's favour, an affair took place at this time which is not devoid of strangeness. After the victory over the Rānā my son presented me in Ajmir with an exceedingly beautiful and clear ruby, valued at 60,000 rupees. It occurred to me that I ought to bind this ruby on my own arm. I much wanted two rare pearls of good water of one form to be a fit match for this kind of ruby. Muqarrab Khān had procured one grand pearl of the value of 20,000 rupees, and given it to me as a New Year's offering. It occurred to me that if I could procure a pair to it they would

[490] The text is corrupt. The true reading seems to be *ṣad dāna-i-kīsh*,' one hundred pieces of muslin ' (?). I.O. 181 seems to have *kabsh*, 'rams.'

[491] Here follow two unintelligible words, *Pagāna Bankāna*.

make a perfect bracelet. Khurram, who from his childhood had had the honour of waiting on my revered father, and remained in attendance on him day and night, represented to me that he had seen a pearl in an old turban (*sar-band*) of a weight and shape equal to this pearl. They produced an old *sar-pīch* (worn on the turban), containing a royal pearl of the same quality, weight, and shape, not differing in weight even by a trifle, so much so that the jewellers were astonished at the matter. It agreed in value, shape, lustre, and brilliance; one might say they had been shed from the same mould. Placing the two pearls alongside of the ruby, I bound them on my arm, and placing my head on the ground of supplication and humility, I returned thanks to the Lord that cherished His slave, and made my tongue utter His praise—

"Who succeeds with hand and tongue?
He who performs the dues of thanks."

On the 5th (Urdībihisht) 30 Iraq and Turki horses that Murtaẓā Khān had sent from Lahore were brought before me, as also 63 horses, 15 camels, male and female, a bundle of crane's (*kulang*) plumes, 9 *'āqirī* (?),[492] 9 veined[493] fish-teeth, 9 pieces of china from Tartary, 3 guns, etc., from Khān Daurān, which he had sent from Kabul, were accepted. Muqarrab Khān presented an offering of a small elephant from Abyssinia which they had brought by sea in a ship. In comparison with the elephants of Hindustan it presents some peculiarities. Its ears are larger than the ears of the elephants of this place, and its trunk and tail are longer. In the time of my revered father I'timād Khān of Gujarat sent a young elephant[494] as an offering ; by degrees it grew up and was very fiery and bad-tempered. On the 7th a jewelled dagger was given to Muẓaffar Khān, governor of Thatha. On the

[492] Perhaps this should be *faghfūrī*, porcelain.'

[493] *Jauhar-dār*, defined by Vullers as bone or wood bearing veins, i.e. striated.

[494] See Akbar-nāma, ii, 315. It was sent before Jahāngīr was born. It, too, was an African elephant.

same day news came that a band of Afghans[495] had attacked 'Abdu-s-Subḥān, brother of Khān 'Ālam, who was stationed at one of the posts, and had laid siege to his post. 'Abdu-s-Subḥān, with certain other mansabdars and servants who had been appointed to go with him, had behaved valiantly. But at last, in accordance with the saying—

"When gnats get wings they smite the elephant,"

those dogs overcame them, and elevated 'Abdu-s-Subḥān with several of the men of the post to the dignity of martyrdom.[496] As a condolence for this affair a gracious farman and a special dress of honour were sent to Khān 'Ālam, who had been appointed ambassador to Iran (and was still in that country). On the 14th the offering of Mukarram Khān, son of Mu'azzam Khān, came from Bengal. It consisted of jewels and articles procurable in that province, and was brought before me. I increased the mansab of some of the jagirdars of Gujarat. Of these, Sardār Khān, whose mansab was that of 1,000 personal and 500 horse, was raised to 1,500 personal and 300[497] horse, and had a standard given to him as well. Sayyid Qāsim, son of Sayyid Dilāwar Bārha, was raised to an original and increased mansab of 800 personal and 450 horse, and Yār Beg, nephew of Aḥmad Qāsim Koka, to one of 600 personal with 250 horse. On the 17th there came the news of the death of Razzāq of Merv, the Ūzbeg who belonged to the army of the Deccan. He was well skilled in war, and one of the distinguished Amirs of Māwarā'a-n-nahr. On the 21st, Allah-dād, the Afghan, was honoured with the title of Khān, and his mansab, which was 1,000 personal and 600 horse, was raised to 2,000 personal and 1,000 horse. Three hundred thousand rupees out of the treasury of Lahore were ordered as a reward and for expenses to Khān Daurān, who had greatly exerted himself in the Afghan disturbance. On the 28th,

---

495 Here the two words referred to at note 2 on p. 321 are repeated.

496 Ma'āṣiru-l-umarā, i, 736. Khān 'Ālam's name was Mirzā Barkhūrdār.

497 This seems wrong ; the number of horse would probably not be reduced.

Kunwar Karan obtained leave to go home for his marriage. I conferred on him a dress of honour, a special Iraq horse with a saddle, an elephant, and a jewelled waist-dagger. On the 3rd of this month (Khūrdād) the news of the death of Murtaẓā Khān came. He was one of the ancients of this State. My revered father had brought him up and raised him to a position of consequence and trust. In my reign also he obtained the grace of noteworthy service, namely, the overthrow of Khusrau. His mansab had been raised to 6,000 personal and 5,000 horse. As he was at this time Subahdar of the Panjab, he had undertaken the capture of Kāngra, to which in strength no other fort in the hill country of that province or even in the whole inhabited world can be compared. He had obtained leave to go on this duty. I was much grieved in mind at this news ; in truth, grief at the death of such a loyal follower is only reasonable. As he had died after spending his days in loyalty, I prayed to God for pardon for him. On the 4th Khūrdād the mansab of Sayyid Niẕām was fixed, original and increase, at 900 personal and 650 horse. I gave Nūru-d-dīn Qulī the post of entertainer to the ambassadors from all parts. On the 7th news came of the death of Saif Khān Bārha ; he was a brave and ambitious young man. He had exerted himself in an exemplary way in the battle with Khusrau. He bade farewell to this perishable world in the Deccan through cholera (*haiẓa*). I conferred favours on his sons. 'Alī Muḥammad, who was the eldest and most upright of his children, was given the mansab of 300[498] personal and 400 horse, and his ('Alī Muḥammad's) brother, by name Bahādur, that of 400 personal and 200 horse. Sayyid 'Alī, who was his nephew, received an increase in rank of 500 personal and horse. On the same day Khūb-Allah, son of Shāh-bāz Khān Kambū, received the title of Ran-bāz Khān. On the 8th[499] the mansab of Hāshim Khān, original and increase, was fixed at 2,500 personal and 1,800

---

[498] So in text, but No. 181 has 600, and this is more likely, for the number of horse is never, I think, larger than the *zāt* rank.

[499] I.O. MSS. have 18th.

horse. On this date I bestowed 20,000 *darabs* (10,000 rupees) on Allah-dād Khān, the Afghan. Bikramājīt, Raja of the province of Bāndhū, whose ancestors were considerable zamindars in Hindustan, through the patronage of my fortunate son Bābā Khurram, obtained the blessing of paying his respects to me, and his offences were pardoned. On the 9th,[500] Kalyān of Jesalmīr, to summon whom Rāja Kishan Dās had gone, came and waited on me. He presented 100 muhrs and 1,000 rupees. His elder brother Rāwal Bhīm was a person of distinction. When he died he left a son 2 months old, and he too did not live long. In the time when I was prince I had taken his daughter in marriage, and called her by the title of Malika-Jahān[501] (queen of the world). As the ancestors of this tribe had come of ancient loyal people, this alliance took place. Having summoned the aforesaid Kalyān, who was the brother of Rāwal Bhīm, I exalted[502] him with the *ṭīka* of Rāja and the title of Rāwal. News came that after the death of Murtaẓā Khān loyalty was shown by Rāja Mān, and that, after giving encouragement to the men of the fort of Kāngra an arrangement had been made that he should bring to Court the son of the Raja of that country, who was 29 years old. In consequence of his great zeal in this service, I fixed his mansab, which was 1,000 personal and 800 horse, at 1,500 personal and 1,000 horse. Khwāja Jahān was promoted from his original and increased mansab to that of 4,000 personal and 2,500 horse. On this date[503] an event occurred such that, although I was greatly desirous of writing it down, my hand and heart have failed me. Whenever I took my pen my state became bewildered, and I helplessly ordered I'timādu-d-daulah to write it.

---

500 I.O. MSS. have 20th.

501 The two I.O. MSS. have the following sentence here : "On this day it happened that however much I tried to write, my heart and hand would not act. Whenever I seized the pen my condition altered. At last I had to tell I'timādu-d-daulah to write."

502 This sentence is not in the I.O. MSS.

503 Here comes the passage which the two I.O. MSS. enter higher up.

"An ancient sincere slave, I'timādu-d-daulah, by order writes in this auspicious volume[504] that on the 11th[505] Khūrdād the traces of fever were seen in the pure daughter[506] of Shāh Khurram of lofty fortune, for whom His Majesty showed much affection as the early fruit of the garden of auspiciousness. After three days pustules (*ābila*) appeared, and on the 26th of the same month, corresponding with Wednesday, the 29th Jumādā-l-awwal (15th June, 1616), in the year 1025, the bird of her soul flew from her elemental cage and passed into the gardens of Paradise. From this date an order was given that Chār-shamba (Wednesday) should be called Kam-shamba (or *Gum-shamba*). What shall I write as to what happened to the pure personality of the shadow of God in consequence of this heartburning event and grief-increasing calamity ? Inasmuch as it happened after this manner to that soul of the world, what must be the condition of those other[507] servants whose life was bound up with that pure personality ? For two days the servants were not received in audience, and an order was given that a wall should be built in front of the house which had been the abode of that bird of paradise, so that it might not be seen. In addition to this he did not adorn the gate of the hall of audience (did not come there). On the third day he went in an agitated state to the house of the illustrious prince, and the servants had the good fortune to pay their salutations and found fresh life. On the road, however much the Ḥaẓrat (the Emperor) desired to control himself, the tears flowed from the auspicious eyes, and for a long time it was so that at the mere hearing of a word from which came a whiff of pain, the state of the Ḥaẓrat became bewildered. He remained for

---

[504] I.O. MS. 181 has "writes that on the 11th," etc.

[505] The I.O. MSS. add here "of the 11th year."

[506] Probably this is the Chimnī Begam, a daughter of Shāh Jahān, whose grave is near that of the saint Khwāja Mu' īnu-dx-dīn Chishtī ("Rajputana Gazetteer," ii, 62). Probably Chimnī should be Chamanī, which means 'verdant' and comes from *chaman*, a garden. Perhaps she died of smallpox. It was in the summer.

[507] Apparently the reference is to the parents of the child and to the grandfather, that is, the writer of this notice.

some days in the house of the prince of the inhabitants of the world, and on Monday[508] of Tīr, Divine month, he went to the house of Āṣaf Khān, and turned back thence to the Chashma-i-Nūr, and for two or three days employed himself there. But as long as he was in Ajmir he could not control himself. Whenever the word 'friendship' reached his ear, the tears would drop from his eyes unrestrained, and the hearts of his faithful followers were torn in pieces. When the departure of the cortège of fortune to the Subah of the Deccan took place, he gained a little composure."

On this date Prithī Chand, son of Rāy Manohar, obtained the title of Ray and the mansab of 500 personal and 400 horse, and a jagir in his native place. On Saturday, the 11th, I went from the Chashma-i-Nūr to the palace at Ajmir. On the eve of Sunday, the 12th, after 37 seconds had passed, at the time of the ascension of Sagittarius to the 27th degree, by the calculations of the Hindu astronomers, and the 15th degree of Capricorn, by the calculations of the Greeks, there came from the womb of the daughter of Āṣaf Khān (wife of Khurram) a precious pearl into the world of being. With joy and gladness at this great boon the drums beat loudly, and the door of pleasure and enjoyment was opened in the face of the people. Without delay or reflection the name of Shāh Shajā'at came to my tongue. I hope that his coming will be auspicious and blessed to me and to his father. On the 12th a jewelled dagger[509] and an elephant were bestowed on Rāwal Kalyān of Jesalmīr. On the same day arrived the news of the death of Khawāṣṣ Khān, whose jagir was in the Sarkar of Qanauj. I gave an elephant to Rāy Kunwar, Diwan of Gujarat. On the 22nd of the same month (Tīr) I added 500 personal and horse to the mansab of Rāja Mahā Singh, so as to make it one of 4,000 personal and 3,000 horse. The mansab of 'Alī Khān Tatārī,

---

508 I.O. MSS. have Monday, the 6th Tir, and say that Jahāngīr went to Chashma-i-Nūr on the 9th, which they say was a Thursday. And we see later that Jahāngīr speaks of Saturday as the 11th.

509 The word 'dagger' is omitted in the text.

who before this had been exalted with the title of Nuṣrat Khān, was fixed at 2,000 personal and 500 horse, and a standard was also conferred on him. With a view to the accomplishment of certain purposes, I had made a vow that they should place a gold railing with latticework at[510] the enlightened tomb of the revered Khwāja. On the 27th of this month it was completed, and I ordered them to take and affix it. It had been made at a cost of 110,000 rupees. As the command and leading of the victorious army of the Deccan had not been carried out to my satisfaction by my son Sulṭān Parwīz, it occurred to me to recall him, and send Bābā Khurram as the advanced guard of the victorious army, inasmuch as the signs of rectitude and knowledge of affairs were evident in him, and that I myself would follow him, so that this important matter would be carried through in one and the same campaign. With this object a farman had already been sent in the name of Parwīz ordering him to start for the Subah of Allahabad, which is in the centre of my dominions. Whilst I was engaged in the campaign, he would be entrusted with the guarding and administration of that region. On the 29th of the same month a letter came from Bihārī Dās, the news-writer of Burhānpūr, that the prince on the 20th had left the city safely and well and gone towards the aforesaid Subah. On the 1st Amurdād I bestowed a jewelled turban on Mīrzā Rāja Bhāo Singh. An elephant was conferred on the shrine of Kushtīgīr. On the 18th, Lashkar Khān had sent four ambling (*rāhwār*) horses, and they were brought before me. Mīr Mughal was appointed to the faujdarship of the Sarkar of Sambal in the place of Sayyid 'Abdu-l-Wāriṡ, who had obtained the governorship of the Subah of Qanauj in the place of Khawāṣṣ Khān. His mansab, in view of that duty, was fixed at 500 personal and horse. On the 21st the offering of Rāwal Kalyān of Jesalmīr was laid before me ; it was 3,000 muhrs, 9 horses, 25 camels, and 1 elephant. The mansab of Qizil-bāsh Khān was

510 I.O. MSS. have *bar·daur*, 'round.'

fixed, original and increase, at 1,200 personal and 1,000 horse. On the 23rd, Shajā'at Khān obtained leave to go to his jagir that he might arrange the affairs of his servants and his territory, and present himself at the time agreed upon. In this year,[511] or rather in the 10th year after my accession, a great pestilence appeared in some places in Hindustan. The commencement of this calamity was in the parganahs of the Panjab, and by degrees the contagion spread to the city of Labore. Many of the people, Musulmans and Hindus, died through this. After this it spread to Sirhind and the Dū'āb, until it reached Delhi and the surrounding parganahs and villages, and desolated them. At this day it had greatly diminished. It became known from men of great age and from old histories that this disease had never shown itself in this country[512] (before). Physicians and learned men were questioned as to its cause. Some said that it came because there had been drought for two years in succession and little rain fell ; others said it was on account of the corruption of the air which occurred through the drought and scarcity. Some attributed it to other causes. Wisdom is of Allah, and we must submit to Allah's decrees!

" What does a slave who bows not his neck to the order ?"

On 5th Shahrīwar 5,000 rupees towards her expenses were sent to the mother of Mīr Mīrān, the daughter of Shāh Isma'īl II, by merchants who were proceeding to the province of Iraq. On the 6th a letter came from 'Ābid Khān,[513] bakhshi and news-writer of Ahmadabad, to the purport that 'Abdu-llah Khān Bahādur Fīrūz-jang had quarrelled with him because he had recorded among (current) events certain affairs that had been unpleasing to him, and had sent a body of men against him, and

511 Elliot, vi, 346. There is a better account of the plague in the Iqbāl-nāma, pp. 88, 89.

512 The words are *dar wilāyat,* and may mean 'any country' or 'any foreign country.'

513 The son of the historian Niẓāmu-d-dīn. Sir T. Roe refers to this affair.

had insulted him by carrying him away to his house, and had done this and that to him. This matter appeared serious to me, and I was desirous at once to cast him out of favour and ruin him. At last it occurred to me to send Dayānat Khān to Ahmadabad to enquire into this matter on the spot from disinterested people to see if it had actually occurred, and, if so, to bring 'Abdu-llah Khān with him to the Court, leaving the charge and administration of Ahmadabad to Sardār Khān, his brother. Before Dayānat Khān started, the news reached Fīrūz-jang, and he in a state of great perturbation confessed himself an offender and started for the Court on foot. Dayānat Khān met him on the road, and seeing him in a strange condition, as he had wounded his feet with walking, he put him on horseback, and taking him with him came to wait on me. Muqarrab Khān, who is one of the old servants of the Court, from the time when I was a prince had continually wanted the Subah of Gujarat. It thus occurred to me that, as this kind of action on the part of 'Abdu-llah Khān had come about, I might fulfil the hope of an ancient servant and send him to Ahmadabad in the place of the aforesaid Khān. A fortunate hour was chosen in these days, and I appointed him to be ruler of the Subah. On the 10th the mansab of Bahādur Khān, governor of Qandahar, which was 4,000 personal and 3,000 horse, was increased by 500 personal.

Shauqī, the mandolin player, is the wonder of the age. He also sings Hindi and Persian songs in a manner that clears the rust from all hearts. I delighted him with the title of Ānand Khān: Ānand in the Hindi language means pleasure and ease.

Mangoes[514] used not to be in season in the country of Hindustan after the month of Tīr (June–July), (but) Muqarrab

[514] Text *Anand*, but this makes no sense. The I.O. MSS. have *amba*, mangoes, and though the remark seems abrupt this is no doubt the correct reading. Jahāngīr was particularly fond of mangoes, and perhaps he is here playing on the similarity between the words *amba* and *anand*.

Khān had established gardens in the parganah of Kairāna,[515] which is the native place of his ancestors, and looked after the mangoes there in such a manner as to prolong the season for more than two months, and sent them every day fresh into the special fruit storehouse. As this was altogether an unusual thing to be accomplished, it has been recorded here. On the 8th a beautiful Iraq horse of the name of La'l Bī-bahā (priceless ruby) was sent for Parwīz by the hand of Sharīf, one of his attendants.

I had ordered quick-handed stone-cutters to carve full-sized figures of the Rānā and his son Karan out of marble. On this day they were completed and submitted to me. I ordered them to be taken to Agra and placed in the garden[516] below the *jharoka* (exhibition-window). On the 26th the meeting for my solar weighing was held in the usual manner. The first weight came to 6, 514 *tūlcha* of gold. I was weighed twelve times against different things ; the second weighing was against quicksilver, the third against silk, the fourth against various perfumes, such as ambergris and musk, down to sandalwood, *'ūd, bān,* and so on, until twelve weighings were completed. Of animals, according to the number of years that I had passed, a sheep, a goat,[517] and a fowl (for each year) were given to fakirs and

---

515 In Sarkār Sahāranpur (Jarrett, ii, 292). It is now in the Muẓaffarnagar district (I.G., vii, 308).

516. " It is a pity that no trace of these is left at Agra. Had there been, they would have been the wonder of the age "(note of Sayyid Aḥmad). Perhaps they are the two figures which have generally been supposed to have been put up by Akbar and to represent Chitor heroes. The word *tarkīb* in the text may mean that they were mounted statues. But then the description of them as marble statues would be wrong.

517 Text has *gūsfand-i-nar*, 'a ram,' but the MSS. have *gūsfand u bar,* or *buz,* and it is evident that the true reading is 'a sheep, a goat.' See Blochmann, p. 266, where goats are mentioned among the animals distributed by Akbar. The number of animals distributed corresponded with the years of Jahāngīr's age (48) multiplied by 3, and so would be 48 x 3 = 144 (see Blochmann, I.c.). The weight of Jahāngīr was 6, 514 tulchas, and Blochmann (p. 267, n.) takes this to be the same as tolas, and estimates Jahāngīr's weight at 210 $\frac{1}{2}$ lb. troy or 15 stone. Probably this is

dervishes. This rule has been observed from the time of my revered father up to the present day in this enduring State. They divide after the weighing all these things among the fakirs and those in need to the value of about 100,000 rupees.

This day a ruby which Mahābat Khān had purchased at Burhanpur for 65,000 rupees from 'Abdu-llah Khān Fīrūz-jang was laid before me, and was approved of. It is a ruby of beautiful form. The special mansab of Khān Ā'ẓam was fixed at 7,000 personal, and an order was passed that the diwani establishment should pay an equivalent to that in a *tankhwāh jāgīr.* At the request of I'timādu-d-daulah, what had been deducted from the mansab of Dayānat on account of former proceedings was allowed to remain as before. 'Aẓudu-d-daulah, who had obtained the Subah of Malwa in jagir, took his leave, and was dignified with the gift of a horse and a dress of honour. The mansab of Rāwal Kalyān of Jesalmir was fixed at 2,000 personal and 1,000 horse, and it was ordered that that province (Jesalmir) should be given him as tankhwah. As the (auspicious) hour of his departure was on that same day, he took leave to depart for his province well pleased and exalted with the gift of a horse, an elephant, a jewelled sword, a jewelled *khapwa* (dagger), a robe of honour, and a special Kashmir shawl. On the 31st Muqarrab Khān took leave to go to Ahmadabad, and his mansab, which was 5,000 personal and 2,500 horse, was fixed at 5,000 personal and horse, and he was honoured with a dress of

---

excessive, and his weight might be 82 sir or about 2 maunds, i.e. 164 lb. or 11 $\frac{1}{2}$ stone. The perfumes against which he was weighed were ambergris, not amber (which has no scent), ' ūd, i.e. lignum aloes, and *bān* (not *pān* as in text), which apparently is the same as *lubān*, 'frankincense ' (see the chapter on perfumes in Blochmann, p. 77). I am not sure of the meaning of the phrase *ba-dast nīhāda*. The MSS. have not the preposition *ba*. Perhaps the meaning is 'put them into the hands of the fakirs.' Jahāngīr was born on the 18th Shahrīwar, 977 = 31st August, 1569. The weighings described in the text took place on the 26th Shahrīwar. Perhaps this was because his birthday was on the 24th Shahrīwar according to the Jalālī year.

honour, a *nādirī* (a kind of dress), a *takma*[518] of pearls, whilst two horses from my private stable, a special elephant, and a jewelled sword were also bestowed on him. He went off to the aforesaid Subah with delight and in a state of happiness. On the 11th of Mihr, Jagat Singh, son of Kunwar Karan, came from his native place and waited on me. On the 16th, Mīrzā 'Alī Beg Akbarshāhī came from the province of Oudh, which had been given him in jagir, and waited on me. He presented as offerings 1,000 rupees, and he produced before me an elephant which one of the zamindars of that province possessed, and which he had been ordered to take from him. On the 21st the offering of Qutbu-l-mulk, the ruler of Golcondah, consisting of some jewelled ornaments, was inspected by me. The mansab of Sayyid Qāsim Bārha was fixed, original and increase, at 1,000 personal and 600 horse. On the eve of Friday, the 22nd, Mīrzā 'Alī Beg, whose age had passed 75 years, gave up the deposit of his life. Great[519] services had been performed by him for this State. His mansab rose by degrees to 4,000. He was one of the distinguished heroes of this family (*jawānān-i īn ulūs*)[520] and of a noble disposition. He left neither son nor other descendants. He had the poetic temperament. As his inevitable destiny had been fulfilled[521] on the day on which he went to pay his devotions at the venerated mausoleum of Khwāja Mu'īnu-d-dīn, I ordered them to bury him in the same blessed place.

At the time when I gave leave to the ambassadors of 'Ādil Khān of Bijapur, I had requested that if in that province there

---

[518] Generally written *taghma*, 'a badge of honour,' 'a medal,' etc.

[519] See Tūzuk, p. 11, Blochmann, p. 482, and Ma'āṣiru-l-umarā, iii, 355. The statement at Tūzuk, p. 11, about Delhi seems a mistake, and is not in the MSS. Mīrzā 'Alī came from Badakhshan. He is frequently mentioned in vol. iii of the Akbar-nāma.

[520] This is the same phrase as, according to the MSS., occurs at p. 11. Apparently the ulūs referred to is the Timuride family to which Jahāngīr belonged. It is connected with Mīrzā 'Alī's title of Akbarshāhi.

[521] See in Blochmann, l.c., the affecting story of his death.

were a wrestler, or a celebrated swordsman, they should tell 'Ādil Khān to send him to me. After some time, when the ambassadors returned, they brought a Mughal, by name Shīr 'Alī, who was born at Bijapur, and was a wrestler by profession and had great experience in the art, together with certain sword-players. The performances of the latter were indifferent, but I put Shīr 'Alī to wrestle with the wrestlers and athletes who were in attendance on me, and they could none of them compete with him. One thousand rupees, a dress of honour, and an elephant were conferred on him ; he was exceedingly well made, well shaped, and powerful. I retained him in my own service, and entitled him "the athlete of the capital." A jagir and mansab were given him and great favours bestowed on him. On the 24th, Dayānat Khān, who had been appointed to bring 'Abdu-llah Khān Bahādur Fīrūz-jang, brought him and waited on me, and presented as an offering 100 muhrs. On the same date Rām Dās, the son of Rāja Rāj Singh, one of the Rajput Amirs who had died on duty in the Deccan, was promoted to a mansab of 1,000 personal and 500 horse. As 'Abdu-llah Khān had been guilty of faults, he made Bābā Khurram his intercessor, and on the 26th, in order to please him, I ordered the former to pay his respects to me. He waited upon me with a face of complete shame, and presented as offerings 100 muhrs and 1,000 rupees. Before the coming of 'Ādil Khān's ambassadors I had made up my mind that, having sent Bābā Khurram with the vanguard, I should myself proceed to the Deccan and carry out this important affair, which for some reasons had been put off. For this reason I had given an order that except the prince no one should represent to me the affairs of the rulers of the Deccan. On this day the prince brought the ambassadors and laid their representation before me. After the death of Murtaẓā Khān, Rāja Mān and many of the auxiliary Sardars had come to Court. On this day, at the request of I'timādu-d-daulah, I appointed Rāja Mān as the leader in the attack on the fort of Kāngra. I appointed all the men to accompany him, and according to the condition and rank of each made him happy with a present—a horse, an elephant, a robe of honour, or money—and gave them leave. After some days I conferred on 'Abdu-llah Khān, at the request of Bābā Khurram, a jewelled dagger, as he was exceedingly broken-hearted and grieved in mind, and an order was passed that his mansab should continue as it was before, and that he should remain in attendance on my son among those appointed for duty in the Deccan. On the 3rd Ābān I ordered the mansab of Wazīr Khān, who was in attendance on Bābā Parwīz, to be, original and increase, 2,000 personal and 1,000 horse. On the 4th, Khusrau, who was in the charge, for safe keeping, of Anīrā'ī Singh-dalan, for certain considerations was handed over to Āṣaf Khān. I presented him with a special shawl. On the 7th (Ābān), corresponding with the 17th Shawwāl (28th October, 1616), a person of the name of Muḥammad Riẓā Beg, whom the ruler of Persia had sent as his representative, paid his respects. After performing the dues of prostration and salutation (*kūrnish, sijda, taslīm*), he laid before me the letter he had brought. It was decided that he should produce before me the horses and other presents he had brought with him. The written and verbal messages sent were full of friendship, brotherhood, and sincerity. I gave the ambassador on that same day a jewelled tiara (*tāj*) and a dress of honour. As in the letter much friendliness and affection were displayed, an exact copy is recorded in the Jahāngīr-nāma.[522]

On Sunday, the 18th Shawwāl, corresponding to the 8th Ābān,[523] the camp equipage of my son Bābā Khurram left Ajmir

522 This letter being of the usual Persian style, and having nothing to do with Jahāngīr's history, is omitted. It relates to the sending of Muḥammad Ḥusain Chelebī with presents to the emperor, and to the offering his services for the purchase of jewels, etc.

523 Text 20th Ābīn, but the MSS. have 8th, and this is clearly right. By the latter part of the sentence Jahāngīr means that Shāh Jahān was to start first, and that he himself was to leave afterwards. The "auspicious palace" referred to in the next sentence is apparently Shāh Jahān's establishment. Jahāngīr did not leave for about a fortnight. Though Shāh Jahān and the establishment (*daulat-khāna-i-*

for the purpose of the conquest of the provinces of the Deccan, and it was decided that my son aforesaid should start by way of advanced guard, followed by the glorious standards (of Jahāngīr). On Monday, the 19th, corresponding with the 9th Ābān, when three gharis of day had passed, the auspicious palace moved in the same direction in the like manner. On the 10th the mansab of Rāja Sūraj Mal, who had been appointed to accompany the prince, was made up, original and increase, to 2,000 personal and horse. On the night of the 19th Ābān, after my usual custom, I was in the *ghusul-khāna.* Some of the Amirs and attendants, and by chance Muḥammad Riẓā Beg, the ambassador of the ruler of Persia, were present. When six gharis had passed, an owl came and sat on top of a high terrace roof belonging to the palace, and was hardly visible, so that many men failed to distinguish it. I sent for a gun and took aim and fired in the direction that they pointed out to me. The gun, like the decree of heaven, fell on that ill-omened bird and blew it to pieces. A shout arose from those who were present, and involuntarily they opened their lips in applause and praise. On the same night I talked with the ambassador of my brother Shāh 'Abbās, and at last the conversation turned on the slaying of Ṣafī Mīrzā, his (the Shah's) eldest son. I asked him because this was a difficulty in my mind. He represented that if his slaughter had not been carried out at that time he would certainly have attempted the Shah's life. As this intention became manifest from his behaviour, the Shah was beforehand with him and ordered him to be killed. On the same day the mansab of Mīrzā Ḥasan, son of Mīrzā Rustam, was fixed, original and increase, at 1,000 personal and 300 horse. The mansab of Mu'tamad Khān,[524] who had been appointed to the post of paymaster of the army with Bābā Khurram, was settled at 1,000 personal and 250 horse. The time for the leave-taking of Bābā Khurram had been fixed as

---

humāyūn) made a start on the 8th or 9th Ābān, he did not finally leave till the 20th Ābān. See *infra*.

[524] Author of Iqbāl-nāma.

Friday, the 20th (Ābān). At the end of this day he paraded before me the pick of his men armed and ready in the public hall of audience. Of the distinguished favours bestowed on the aforesaid son one was the title of <u>Sh</u>āh, which was made a part of his name. I ordered that thereafter he should be styled <u>Sh</u>āh Sulṭān <u>Kh</u>urram. I presented him with a robe of honour, a jewelled *chārqab,* the fringe and collar of which were decorated with pearls, an Iraq horse with a jewelled saddle, a Turki horse, a special elephant called Bansī-badan,[525] a carriage, according to the English fashion,[526] for him to sit and travel about in, a jewelled sword with a special *pardala* (sword-belt) that had been taken at the conquest of the fort of Ahmadnagar, and was very celebrated, and a jewelled dagger. He started with great keenness. My trust in Almighty God is that in this service he may gain renown (lit. become red-faced). On each of the Amirs and mansabdars, according to his quality and degree, a horse and an elephant were conferred. Loosening a private sword from my own waist, I gave it to 'Abdu-llah <u>Kh</u>ān Fīrūz-jang. As Dayānat <u>Kh</u>ān had been appointed to accompany the prince, I gave the duty of *'arẓ-mukarrir* (reviser of petitions) to <u>Kh</u>wāja Qāsim Qilīj <u>Kh</u>ān. Previously[527] to this a band of thieves had carried off a certain sum of money from the royal treasury in the *kotwālī chabūtara* (Police Office). After some days seven men of that band, with their leader, of the name of Nawal, were caught, and a portion of that money was recovered. It occurred to me that as they had been guilty of such boldness I ought to punish them severely. Each was punished in exemplary fashion, and I ordered Nawal, the leader of them all, to be thrown under the feet of an elephant. He petitioned that if I would give the order he would fight the elephant. I ordered it to be so. They produced a very furious elephant. I bade them put a dagger into his hand

[525] 'Of body like Krishna, or like a flute'?

[526] According to Roe, it was not the English carriage, but a copy. Perhaps Jahāngīr had the original carriage and <u>Sh</u>āh Jahān the copy.

[527] Elliot, vi, 346.

and bring him in front of the elephant. The elephant several times threw him down, and each time that violent and fearless man, although he witnessed the punishments of his comrades, got up again and bravely and with a stout heart struck the elephant's trunk with the dagger, so that the animal refrained from attacking him. When I had witnessed this pluck and manliness, I ordered them to inquire into his history. After a short time, according to his evil nature and low disposition, he ran away in his longing for his own place and abode. This annoyed me greatly, and I ordered the jagirdars of that neighbourhood to hunt him up and apprehend him. By chance he was caught a second time, and this time I ordered that ungrateful and unappreciative one to be hanged. The saying of Shaikh Muṣliḥu-d-dīn Sa'dī accords with his case—

> "In the end a wolf's cub becomes a wolf,
> Although he be brought up with man."

On Tuesday,[528] the 1st Zī-l-qa'da (10th November, 1616), corresponding with the 21st Ābān, after two watches and five gharis of the day had passed, in good condition and with a right purpose I mounted the Frank carriage, which had four horses attached to it, and left the city of Ajmir. I ordered many of the Amirs to accompany me in carriages, and at about sunset alighted at a halting-place about 1 3/4 kos distant, in the village of Deo Rāy (Dorāī ?).[529] It is the custom of the people of India that if the movement of kings or great men for the conquest of a country is towards the east they should ride a tusked elephant, and if the movement is towards the west on a horse of one colour ; if towards the north in a palanquin or a litter (*singhāsan*), and if towards the south, that is, in the direction of the Deccan (as on this occasion), on a *rath,* which is a kind of cart (*arāba*) or *bahal* (two-wheeled car). I had stayed at Ajmir for five days less

[528] The day was Saturday, not Tuesday, and it is Saturday in the MSS.

[529] Elliot has Deo Rānī, and it is Deo Rānī in I.O. MS. 305.

than three years.[530] They consider the city of Ajmir, which is the place of the blessed tomb of the revered Khwāja Mu'īnu-d-dīn, to be in the second clime. Its air is nearly equable. The capital of Agra is to the east of it ; on the north are the townships (district) of Delhi, and on the south the Subah of Gujarat. On the west lie Multan and Deālpūr. The soil of this province is all sandy ; water is found with difficulty in the land, and the reliance for cultivation is on moist[531] soil and on the rainfall. The cold season is very equable, and the hot season is milder than in Agra. From this subah in time of war 86,000[532] horse and 304,000 Rajput foot are provided. There are two large lakes in this city; they call one of these the Bīsal[533] and the other the Ānāsāgar. The Bīsal tank is in ruins and its embankment is broken. At this time I ordered it to be repaired. The Ānāsāgar at the time that the royal standards were there was always full of water and waves. This *tāl* is 1 1/2 kos and 5 *tanāb* (lit. tent-ropes) (in circumference?). Whilst at Ajmir I visited nine times the mausoleum of the revered Khwāja, and fifteen times went to look at the Pushkar lake; to the Chashma-i-Nūr I went thirty-eight times. I went out to hunt tigers, etc., fifty times. I killed 15 tigers, 1 cheetah, 1 black-ear (lynx), 53 nilgaw, 33 gazelle (*gawazn*), 90 antelope, 80 boars, and 340 water-fowl. I encamped seven times at Deo Rāy (Deo Rānī) (Dorāī?). At this halt 5 nilgaw and 12 water-fowl were killed. Marching on the 29th from Deo Rāy, my camp was pitched at the village of Dāsāwalī, 2 kos and 1 1/2 quarters distant from

---

530 Jahāngīr arrived in Ajmir on the 26th Ābān, 1022, and left it on the 21st Ābān, 1025. The Muhammadan dates are 5th Shawwāl, 1022, and 1st Zī-l-qa'da, 1025 = 18th November, 1613, and 10th November, 1616.

531 Text *tar* but MSS. have *abtar*, i.f. inferior and perhaps low land The text seems corrupt.

532 MSS. have 86,500 horse and : 347,000 foot, and this agrees with the Āyīn (Jarrett, ii, 272).

533. Text wrongly has Nīl. The lank in question is the Bīsalya tank of the Rajputana Gazetteer, ii, 4, which was made by Bīsal Deo Chohān about 1050 A.D. It is described in Tod's "Personal Narrative," i, 824. of Calcutta reprint. It is, or was, about 8 miles in circumference and is about a mile west of the Ānāsāgar. which was made by Bīsal Deo's grandson.

Deo Rāy. On this day I gave an elephant to Mu'tamad Khān. I stayed the next day at this village. On this day a nilgaw was killed, and I sent two of my falcons to my son Khurram. I marched from this village on the 3rd Āzar, and pitched at the village of Bādhal (Māwal?), 2 1/4 kos distant. On the road six water-fowl, etc., were killed. On the 4th, having gone 1 1/2 kos, Rāmsar,[534] which belongs to Nūr-Jahān Begam, became the place for the alighting of honour and glory. A halt was made at this place for eight days. In the place of Khidmat-gār Khān I here appointed Hidāyatu-llah *mīr-tūzak* (master of ceremonies). On the 5th day 7 antelope, 1 kulang (crane), and 15 fish were killed. The next day Jagat Singh, son of Kunwar Karan, received a horse and a robe of honour and took leave for his native place. A horse was also given to Kesho Dās Lālā and an elephant to Allah-dād Khān Afghān. On the same day I killed a gazelle, 3 antelope, 7 fish, and 2 water-fowl. On that day was heard the news of the death of Rāja Syām Singh, who belonged to the army of Bangash. On the 7th day 3 antelope, 5 water - fowl, and a *qashqaldāgh*[535] (coot) were killed. On Thursday and the eve of Friday, as Rāmsar belongs to the jagir of Nūr-Jahān, a feast and entertainment were prepared. Jewels, jewelled ornaments, fine cloths, sewn tapestry, and every kind of jewellery were presented as offerings. At night on all sides and in the middle of the lake, which is very broad, lamps were displayed. An excellent entertainment was arranged. In the end of the said Thursday, having also sent for the Amirs, I ordered cups for most[536] of the servants. On my journeys by land some boats are always taken along with the victorious camp ; the boatmen convey them on carts. On the day after this entertainment I went to fish in these boats, and in a short time 208 large fish came into

---

[534] About 20 miles south-east of Ajmir.

[535] This is the name of a water-bird in Turkī. It is also called *māgh* and water-crow *(zāgh-i-āb)*, and in Hindī *jalkawā* (note of Sayyid Ahmad).

[536] Probably the meaning is that he allowed those who wished to drink to do so. Many, or at least some, would be abstainers.

one net. Half of these were of the species of *rahū*. At night I divided them among the servants in my own presence. On the 13th Āẕar I marched from Rāmsar, and hunting for 4 kos along the road, the camp was pitched at the village of Balodā.[537] Here I stayed for two days. On the 16th, moving 3 1/4 kos, I alighted at the village of Nihāl.[538] On the 18th the march was one of 2 1/4 kos. On this day I gave an elephant to Muḥammad Riẓā Beg, ambassador of the ruler of Persia. The village of Jonsā became the halting-place of the tents of greatness and prosperity. On the 20th I marched to the halting-place of Deogāon ; I hunted along the road for a distance of 3 kos. I stayed at this place for two days, and at the end of the day went out to hunt. At this stage a strange affair was witnessed. Before the royal standards arrived at this halting-place, an eunuch went to the bank of a large tank there is in the village, and caught two young *sāras*, which are a kind of crane ; at night, when we stopped at this halting-place, two large saras appeared making loud cries near the ghusul-khana (parlour), which they had placed on the edge of the tank, as if somebody were exercising oppression on them. They fearlessly began their cries and came forward. It occurred to me that certainly some kind of wrong had been done to them, and probably their young had been taken. After enquiry was made the eunuch who had taken the young saras brought them before me. When the saras heard the cries of these young ones, they without control threw themselves upon them, and suspecting that they had had no food, each of the two saras placed food in the mouths of the young ones, and made much lamentation. Taking the two young ones between them, and stretching out their wings and fondling them, they went off to their nest. Marching on the 23rd 3 3/4 kos, I alighted at the village of Bahāsū (Bhālū ?). Here there was a halt of two days, and each day I rode to hunt. On the 26th the royal standards moved and the halt was outside of the village of Kākal. A halt was made

[537] Namūda in MSS.

[538] Sahāl in MSS.

after traversing 2 kos. On the 27th the mansab of Badī'u-z-zamān, son of Mīrzā Shāhrukh, original and increased, was fixed at 1,500 personal and 750 horse. Marching on the 29th 2 3/4 kos, a halt was made at the village of Lāsā, near parganah Boda.[539] This day corresponded with the festival of Qurbān (19th December, 1616). I ordered them to observe the ordinances of that day. From the date on which I left Ajmir up to the end of the aforesaid month, viz. the 30th Āzar, 67 nilgaw, antelope, etc., and 37 waterfowl, etc., had been killed. A march was made from Lāsā on the 2nd Day, and I marched and hunted for 3 kos 10 *jarīb,* and halted in the neighbourhood of the village of Kānṛā. On the 4th a march of 3 1/4 kos was made to the village of Sūraṭh. Marching 4 1/2 kos on the 6th, a halt was made near the village of Barora (Bardaṛā?). On the 7th, when there was a halt, 50 water-fowl and 14 qashqaldagh (coot) were killed. The next day was a halt as well. On this day 27 water-fowl became a prey. On the 9th a march of 4 1/8 kos was made. Hunting and overthrowing prey, I alighted at the halting-place of Khūsh Tāl. At this stage a report came from Mu'tamad Khān that when the territory of the Rānā became the halting-place of Shāh Khurram, though there had been no agreement to this effect (i.e. to the Rānā's meeting him), the fame and dignity of the victorious army had introduced a commotion into the pillars of his patience and firmness, and he had come and paid his respects to him when he halted at Dūdpūr,[540] which was on the border of his jagir, and observing all the dues and ceremonies of service he had neglected not the smallest portion of them. Shāh Khurram had paid him every attention, and pleased him with the gift of a dress of honour, a *chārqab,* a jewelled sword, a jewelled khapwa, Persian and Turki horses, and an elephant, and dismissed him with every honour. He had also favoured his sons and relations

---

[539] In Sarkār Marosor (Jarrett, ii, 208). It was in Malwa. But the I.O. MSS. have Nauda.

[540] Text Ūdaipūr, but this was not on the border of the Ṛānā's territory, and the MSS. have Dūdpūr.

with dresses of honour, and out of his offering, which consisted of five elephants, twenty-seven horses, and a tray full of jewels and jewelled ornaments, had taken three horses and given back the remainder. It was settled that his son Karan should attend on the stirrup of Bābā Khurram in this expedition with 1,500 horse. On the 10th the sons of Rāja Mahā Singh came from their jagir and native place (Amber) and waited on me in the neighbourhood of Ranṭambhor, making an offering of three elephants and nine horses. Each one of them, according to his condition, received an increase of mansab. As the neighbourhood of the said fort became a halting-place for the royal standards, I released some of the prisoners who were confined in that fort. At this place I halted for two days and each day went to hunt. Thirty-eight water-fowl and qashqaldagh (coot) were taken. On the 12th I marched, and after going 4 kos halted at the village of Koyalā. On the road I killed fourteen water-fowl and an antelope. On the 14th, having traversed 3 3/4 kos, I halted in the neighbourhood of the village of Ekṭorā,[541] killing on the road a blue bull, twelve herons (*karwānak*), etc. On the same day Āghā Fāzil, who had been appointed deputy for I'timādu-d-daulah at Lahore, was dignified with the title of Fāẓil Khān. At this stage they had erected the royal lodging (*daulat-khāna*) on the bank of a tank, which was exceedingly bright and pleasant. On account of the pleasantness of the place I halted two days there, and at the end of each went to hunt water-fowl. To this place the younger son of Mahābat Khān, by name Bahrawar, came from the fort of Ranṭambhor, which is his father's jagir, to pay his respects to me. He had brought two elephants, both of which were included in my private stud. I promoted Ṣafī, son of Amānat Khān, to the title of Khān, and, increasing his mansab, made him bakhshi and news-writer of the Subah of Gujarat. Having travelled 4 $\frac{1}{2}$ kos on the 17th, I halted at the

[541] Perhaps the Toda of Sir T. Roe.

village of Lasāyā.[542] During the halt I killed one water-fowl and twenty-three saṇd-grouse (*durrāj*). As I had sent for Lashkar Khān to Court on account of the disagreement that had occurred between him and Khān Daurān, I at this place appointed 'Ābid Khān,[543] bakhshi and news-writer, in his stead. On the 19th, having made a march of $2\frac{1}{4}$ kos, an encampment was made in the neighbourhood of the village of Kūrāka (Korān ?),[544] which is situated on the bank of the Chambal. On account of the excellence of the place and the pleasantness of its air and water, a halt took place here for three days. Every day I sat in a boat and went to hunt water-fowl and to wander over the river. On the 22nd[545] there was a march, and having traversed $4\frac{1}{2}$ kos, shooting on the road, the victorious camp was pitched at the villages of Sulṭānpūr and Chīla Mala (Chīlāmīlā ?). On this day of halt I bestowed on Mīrān Ṣadr Jahān 5,000 rupees, and gave him leave to proceed to the place assigned to him as his jagir. Another 1,000 rupees were given to Shaikh Pīr. On the 25th I marched and hunted for $3\frac{1}{2}$ kos and encamped at the village of Bāsūr.[546] According to fixed rules one halt and one march took place, and on the 27th I marched and hunted $4\frac{1}{8}$ kos and encamped at the village of Chārdūha (Varadhā ?). Two days halt took place here. In this month of Day 416 animals were killed, namely, 97 sand-grouse (durraj), 192 qashqaldagh, 1 saras, 7 herons, 118 water-fowl, and 1 hare. On the 1st Bahman,

542 Lyāsā in MSS.

543 Son of Niẓāmu-d-d-īn the historian.

544 Gorāna in MSS. and the distance $2\frac{1}{4}$ kos and 1 *jarīb*.

545 23rd in MSS.

546 Mānpūr in text.

corresponding with the 12th Muḥarram, 1026 (20th January, 1617), seating myself in boats with the ladies, I went forward one stage. When one ghari of day remained I arrived at the village of Rūpāheṛā, the halting-place, the distance being 4 kos and 15 jarib. I shot five sand-grouse. On the same day I sent by the hands of Kaikana winter dresses of honour to twenty-one Amirs on duty in the Deccan, and ordered him to take 10,000[547] rupees from those Amirs as a thanksgiving for the dresses of honour. This halting-place had much verdure and pleasantness. On the 3rd a march took place. As on the previous day, I embarked in a boat, and after traversing 2 1/8 kos the village of Kākhā-dās (Kākhāvās ?)[548] became the encamping place of the victorious camp. As I came hunting on the way, a sand-grouse fell flying into a thicket. After much search it was marked, and I ordered one of the beaters to surround the thicket and catch it, and went towards it myself. Meanwhile another sand-grouse rose, and this I made a falcon seize. Soon afterwards the beater came and laid the sand-grouse before me. I ordered them to satisfy the falcon with this sand-grouse, and to keep the one we had caught, as it was a young bird. (But) before the order reached him the head huntsman fed the falcon with the sand-grouse (the second one, viz. that which the falcon had caught). After a while the beater represented to me that if he did not kill the sand-grouse it would die (and then could not be eaten as not properly killed). I ordered him to kill it if that was the case. As he laid his sword on its throat, it with a slight movement freed itself from the sword and flew away. After I had left the boat and mounted my horse, suddenly a sparrow (*kunjishk*) by the force of the wind struck the head of an arrow that one of the beaters who was in my retinue had in his hand, and immediately fell down and died. I was amazed and bewildered at the tricks of destiny; on one side it preserved the sand-grouse, whose time had not arrived, in a short time from three such dangers, and on the other hand made

---

547 MSS. 2,000 rupees.

548 Perhaps Kānha Dās.

captive in the hand of destruction on the arrow of fate the sparrow whose hour of death had come—

"The world-sword may move from its place, But it will cut no vein till God wills."

Dresses of honour for the winter had also been sent by the hand of Qarā, the *yasāwul* (usher), to the Amirs at Kabul. I halted at this place on account of the pleasantness of the spot and the excellence of the air. On this day there came the news of the death of Nād 'Alī Khān Maidānī at Kabul. I honoured his sons with mansabs, and at the request of Ibrāhīm Khān Fīrūz-jang[549] increased the mansab of Rāwat Shankar by 500 personal and 1,000 horse. On the 6th there was a march, and going for 4 1/8 kos by the pass known as Ghāṭe Chāndā, the royal camp was pitched at the village of Amḥār (Amjār?). This valley is very green and pleasant and good trees are seen in it. Up to this stage, which is the limit of the country of the Subah of Ajmir, 84 kos had been traversed. It was also a pleasant stage. Nūr-Jahān Begam here shot with a gun a *qarīsha* (?), the like of which for size and beauty of colour had never been seen. I ordered them to weigh it, and it came to 19 tolas and 5 mashas. The aforesaid village is the commencement of the Subah of Malwa, which is in the second clime. The length[550] of this Subah from the extremity of the province of Gaṛha to the province of Bānswāla (Bānswaṛā?) is 245 kos, and its breadth from the parganah of Chanderī to the parganah of Nandarbār is 230 kos. On the east is the province of Bāndho, and on the north the fort of Narwar, on the south the province of Baglānā, and on the west the Subahs of Gujarat and Ajmir. Malwa is a large province abounding in water and of a pleasant climate. There are five rivers in it in addition to streams, canals, and springs, namely, the

---

549 Should be Fath-jang as in MSS.

550 Jarrett, ii, 195.

Godavarī,[551] Bhīmā, Kālīsindh, Nīrā, and Narbada. Its climate is nearly equable. The land of this province is low, but part of it is high. In the district of Dhār, which is one of the noted places of Malwa, the vine gives grapes twice in the year, in the beginning of Pisces and the beginning of Leo, but the grapes of Pisces are the sweeter. Its husbandmen and artificers are not without arms. The revenue of the province is 24,700,000 dams. When needful there are obtained from it about 9,300[552] horse and four lakhs, 70,300 foot-soldiers, with 100 elephants. On the 8th, moving on 3 1/2 kos, an encampment was made near Khairābād. On the road 14 sand-grouse and 3 herons were killed, and having traversed and shot over 3 kos the camp was pitched at the village of Sidhārā. On the 11th, while there was a halt, I mounted at the end of the day to hunt, and killed a blue bull. On the 12th, after traversing 4 1/4 kos, a halt was made at the village of Bachhayārī. On that day Rānā Amar Singh had sent some baskets of figs. In truth it is a fine fruit, and I had never seen such delicious figs in India. But one must eat only a few of them; it does harm to eat many. On the 14th there was a march; having traversed 4 1/8 kos, I encamped at the village of Balbalī. Rāja Jānbā, who is an influential zamindar in these regions, had sent two elephants as an offering, and they were brought before me. At the same stage they brought many melons grown in Kārīz near Herat. Khān 'Ālam had also sent 50 camels. In former years they had never brought melons in such abundance. On one tray they brought many kinds of fruit—Kārīz melons, melons from Badakhshan and Kabul, grapes from Samarkand[553] and Badakhshan, apples from Samarkand, Kashmir, Kabul, and from Jalalabad, which is a dependency of Kabul, and pineapples, a

551 The name seems to be wrong. Jahāngīr is evidently copying from the Āyīn, and the rivers mentioned there (Jarrett, ii, 195) are the Narbada, Sipra, Kālīsindh, Betwa, and the Kodī (or Godī).

552 29,668 (Jarrett, ii, 198).

553 The MSS. also have sweet pomegranates from Yezd, and sub-acid (*may-khwush*) ones from Farāh, and pears from Badakhshau (see Elliot, vi, 348).

fruit that comes from the European ports, plants of which have been set in Agra. Every year some thousands are gathered in the gardens there which appertain to the private domains (*khāliṣa-i-sharīfa*)[554] ; *kaula,*[555] which are similar in form to an orange, but smaller and better in flavour. They grow very well in the Subah of Bengal. In what language can one give thanks for such favours? My revered father had a great liking for fruit, especially for melons, pomegranates, and grapes. During his time the Kārīz melons, which are the finest kind, and pomegranates from Yezd, which are celebrated throughout the world, and Samarkand grapes had not been brought to Hindustan. Whenever I see these fruits they cause me great regret. Would that such fruit had come in those days, so that he might have enjoyed them !

On the 15th, which was a halting day, news came of the death of Mīr 'Alī, son of Farīdūn Khān Barlās, who was one of the trusted *amīr-zādas* (descended from amirs) of this family (the Timurides). On the 16th a march took place. Having traversed 41/8 kos, the camp of heavenly dignity was pitched near the village of Girī. On the road the scouts brought news that there was a lion in this neighbourhood. I went to hunt him and finished him with one shot. As the braveness of the lion (*shīr babar*) has been established, I wished to look at his intestines. After they were extracted, it appeared that in a manner contrary to other animals, whose gall-bladder is outside their livers, the gall-bladder of the lion is within his liver (?). It occurred to me that the courage of the lion may be from this cause. On the 18th, after traversing 2 3/4 kos, the village of Amriyā was our halting - place. On the 19th, which was a halt, I went out to hunt. After going 2 kos, a village came to view exceedingly sweet and pleasant. Nearly 100 mango-trees were seen in one garden; I had seldom seen mango-trees so large and green and pleasant. In the same garden I saw a *bar*-tree (a banyan), exceedingly large. I

---

554 The MSS. have *khā ṣ ṣa-i-sharīfa*.

555 Qu. *komla* ? Instead of *qābiltar* the MSS. have *mā'iltar*.

ordered them to measure its length, breadth, and height in yards (*gaz*). Its height from the surface to the highest branch (*sar-shākh*) was 74 cubits (*z̤ira'*). The circumference of its trunk was $44\frac{1}{2}$ cubits and its breadth[556] $175\frac{1}{2}$ measured by the gaz. This has been recorded as it is very unusual. On the 20th was a march, and on the road a blue bull was shot with a gun. On the 21st, which was a halt, I went out to hunt at the end of the day. After returning, I came to the house of I'timādu-d-daulah for the festival of Khwāja Khiẓr, whom they call Khiẓrī; I remained there till a watch of the night had passed, and then feeling inclined for food I went back to the royal quarters. On this day I honoured I'timādu-d-daulah as an intimate friend by directing the ladies of the harem not to veil their faces from him. By this favour I bestowed everlasting honour on him. On the 22nd an order was given to march, and after $3\frac{1}{8}$ kos were traversed the camp was pitched at the village of Būlgharī (Nawalkheṛī ?). On the road two blue bulls were killed. On the 23rd day of Tīr, which was a halt, I killed a blue bull with a gun. On the 24th, traversing 5 kos, the village of Qāsim-kheṛā was the halting-place. On the road a white animal[557] was killed, which resembled the *kūtāh pāya* (hog-

---

556 *Pahnā'ī*. Its area or shade. Perhaps the $175\frac{1}{2}$ are yards, not cubits.

557 Evidently the four-horned antelope, the *Tetracerus quadricornis* of Blanford, p. 520, and which has the Hindustani name of *doda*. Blanford describes its colour as dull pale brown. "The posterior horns are much larger than the anterior ones, which are situated between the orbits and are often mere knobs. It is the only Indian representative of the *duikarbok* of Africa. Another Indian name is *chausingha*. In jungle this species and the hog-deer may easily be mistaken the one for the other. It is not gregarious, and moves with a peculiar jerky action." The resemblance between the four-horned antelope and the hog-deer–the *kūtāh pāycha* or short-legged deer of Bābar and Jahāngīr–may account for Blanford's giving *doda* as a native name for the hog-deer (*Cervus porcinus*). For Babar's

deer); it had four horns, two of which were opposite the extremities of its eyes, and two finger-breadths in height, and the two other horns four finger-breadths towards the nape of the neck. These were four finger-breadths in height. The people of India call this animal *dūdhādhārīt* (*dudhāriyā* ?). The male has four horns and the female none. It was said that this kind of antelope has no gall-bladder, but when they looked at its intestines the gall-bladder was apparent, and it became clear that this report has no foundation. On the 25th, which was a halt, at the end of the day I rode out to hunt and killed a female nilgaw with my gun. Bāljū, nephew of Qilīj Khān, who held the mansab of 1,000 personal and 850 horse, and had a jagir in Oudh, I promoted to 2,000 personal and 1,200 horse, dignified him with the title of Qilīj Khān, and appointed him to the Subah of Bengal. On the 26th a march took place, and after traversing 4 3/4 kos a halt was made at the village of Dih Qāẓiyān, which is in the neighbourhood of Ujjain. A number of mango-trees in this place had blossomed. They had pitched the tents on the bank of a lake, and had prepared an enchanting place. Pahāṛ, son of Ghaznīn[558] Khān, was capitally punished at this stage. Cherishing this unlucky one after the death of his father, I had given him the fort and province of Jālaur, which was the place of his ancestors. As he was of tender years, his mother used to forbid him certain evil practices. That eternally black-faced one with some of his companions one night came into the house and killed his own full mother with his own hand. This news reached me and I ordered them to bring him. After his crime was proved against him, I or dered them to put him to death (*kih ba biyāsā rasānīdand*). At this halting-place a tamarind[559] tree came to view,

---

description of the *kūtāh pāya* or *pāycha* see Erskine, p. 317. Gladwin in his history of Jahāngīr writes the native name as *Dirdhayan*.

558 Blochmann, p. 493.

559 Text, *khurmā*, a date, but evidently the *khurmā-i-Hind* or the tamarind, i.e. ' the palm of India,' is meant (see Bābar's Mem., Erskine, p. 324). I do not understand the measurements. The word *yak*, ' one,' before the word shākh is not in the MSS.

the form and habit of which were somewhat strange. The original tree had one trunk; when it had grown to 6 gaz, it turned into two branches, one of which was 10 and the other 9 1/2 gaz. The distance between the two branches was 4 1/2 gaz. From the ground to the place where the branches and leaves came to an end (?), there were on the side of the large branch 16 gaz, and on the other branch 15 1/2 gaz. From the place whence the branches and green leaves began (?) to the top (trunk?) of the tree was 2 1/2 gaz, and the circumference was 2 3/4 gaz. I ordered them to make a *chabūtara* (platform) round it of the height of 3 gaz. As the trunk was very straight and well-shaped, I told my artists to depict it in the illustrations to the Jahāngīr-nāma. A march was made on the 27th. After traversing 2 1/8 kos, a halt was made at the village of Hinduwāl[560] ; on the road a blue bull was killed. On the 28th, after traversing 2 kos, the village of Kāliyādaha became the halting-place. Kāliyādaha is a building which was made by Nāṣiru-d-dīn, son of Ghiyā ṣ u-d-dīn, son of Sul ṭ ān Maḥmūd Khaljī, who was ruler of Malwa. In the time of his rule he had made it in the neighbourhood of Ujjain, which is one of the most celebrated cities in the Subah of Malwa. They say that the heat overcame him so much that he passed his time in the water. He made this building in the middle of the river, and divided its waters into canals, and brought the water on all sides, as well as inside and outside, of the house, and made large and small reservoirs suited to the place. It is a very pleasant and enjoyable place, and one of the noted habitations of Hindustan. Before it. was decided to halt at this place I sent architects and ordered them to clean up the place again. On account of its

---

and is, I think, wrong. I think the 16 gaz and $15\frac{1}{2}$ gaz are the lengths of the two branches, and that the measurements $2\frac{1}{2}$ and $2\frac{3}{4}$ gaz refer to the length and circumference of the two branches at the place when they started from the trunk and before they put out leaves.

560 Hindwas or Hindāwas in MSS.

pleasantness I remained in this place for three days. At the same place Shajā'at Khān came from his jagir and waited on me. Ujjain is one of the old cities, and is one of the seven established places of worship of the Hindus. Rāja Bikramājīt, who introduced the observation of the heavens and stars into Hindustan, lived in this city and province. From the time of his observations until now, which is the 1026th Hijra year (1617 A.D.) and the 11th year from my accession, 1,675[561] years have passed. The deductions of the astronomers of India are all based on his observations. This city is on the bank of the River Sipra. The belief[562] of the Hindus is that once in some year at an uncertain time the water of this river turns into milk. In the reign of my revered father, at the time when he had sent Abū-l-faẓl to set in order the affairs of my brother Shāh Murād, he sent a report from that city that a large body of Hindus and Musulmans had borne testimony that some days previously at night this river had become milk, so that people who took water from it that night found in the morning their pots full of milk.[563] As this obtained currency it has been recorded, but my intelligence will in no way agree to it. The real truth of this affair is known to Allah. On the 2nd Isfandārmuz I embarked in a boat from Kāliyādaha, and went to the next stage. I had frequently heard that an austere Sanyāsī[564] of the name of Jadrūp many years ago retired from the city of Ujjain to a corner of the desert and employed himself in the worship of the true God. I had a great desire for his acquaintance, and when I was at the capital of Agra I was desirous of sending for and seeing him. In the end, thinking of the trouble it would give him, I did not

---

561 This is in accordance with and probably derived from Bābar's Commentaries, Erskine, p. 51, where he says that 1,584 years have elapsed from the time when Bikramājīt made his observatory. Erskine takes this to show that Bābar was writing in 934, and if we add 92 years, or the difference between 934 and 1026, we get 1,676 years (or 1,675 if we take the year to be 1025).

562 See Jarrett, ii, 196. Abū-1-faẓl says there that the flow occurred a week before his arrival at Ujjain.

563 Cf. Jarrett, ii, 196.

564 *Sanyāsī -i-mnrtāz.*

send for him. When I arrived in the neighbourhood of the city I alighted from the boat and went 1/8 kos on foot to see him. The place he had chosen to live in was a hole on the side of a hill which had been dug out and a door made. At the entrance there is an opening in the shape of a *miḥrāb*,[565] which is in length (? height) 1 gaz and in breadth 10 *gira* (knots, each 1/16 of a gaz), and the distance from this door to a hole which is his real abode is 2 gaz and 5 knots in length and in breadth 11 1/4 knots. The height from the ground to the roof is 1 gaz and 3 knots. The hole whence is the entrance to the abode is in length 5 1/2 knots and its breadth 3 1/2 knots. A person of weak body (thin ?) can only enter it with a hundred difficulties. The length and breadth of the hole are such. It has no mat and no straw. In this narrow and dark hole he passes his time in solitude. In the cold days of winter, though he is quite naked, with the exception of a piece of rag that he has in front and behind, he never lights a fire. The Mulla of Rūm (Jalālu-d-dīn) has put into rhyme the language of a dervish—

"By day our clothes are the sun, By night our mattress and blanket the moon's rays."

He bathes twice a day in a piece of water near his abode, and once a day goes into the city of Ujjain, and nowhere but to the houses of three brahmins whom he has selected out of seven, who have wives and children and whom he believes to have religious feelings and contentment. He takes by way of alms five

---

565 Text, *miḥrābī-shakl uftāda*, 'a place like a prayer-niche.' Possibly the true reading is *majrā bī-shakl uftāda*,' a passage without form.' However, the MSS. have *miḥrāb*. The account in the text may be compared with the Ma'āṣiru-l-umarā, i, 574, and with the Iqbāl-nāma, p. 94. The measurements of the mouth of the hole in the Ma'āṣir are taken from the Iqbāl-nāma, and differ from the account in the Tūzuk. The Ma'āṣir, following the Iqbāl-nāma, calls the ascetic Achhad or Ajhad. It also gives his subsequent history. He went to Mathura and was there cruelly beaten by Ḥakim Beg. Jahāngīr's visit to Jadrūp is referred to by Sir Thomas Roe, who mentions a report that the saint was said to be 300 years old. Jahāngīr does not say any such nonsense.

mouthfuls of food out of what they have prepared for their own eating, which he swallows without chewing, in order that he may not enjoy their flavour; always provided that no misfortune has happened to their three houses, that there has been no birth, and there be no menstruous woman in the house. This is his method of living, just as it is now written. He does not desire to associate with men, but as he has obtained great notoriety people go to see him. He is not devoid of knowledge, for he has thoroughly mastered the science of the Vedānta, which is the science of Sufism. I conversed with him for six gharis; he spoke well, so much so as to make a great impression on me. My society also suited him. At the time when my revered father conquered the fort of Āsīr, in the province of Khandesh, and was returning to Agra, he saw him in the very same place, and always remembered him well.

The learned of India have established four modes of life for the caste of brahmins, which is the most honoured of the castes of Hindus, and have divided their lives into four periods. These four periods they call the four *āsram.*[566] The boy who is born in a brahmin's house they do not call brahmin till he is 7 years old, and take no trouble on the subject. After he has arrived at the age of 8 years, they have a meeting and collect the brahmins together. They make a cord of *mūnj* grass, which they call *mūnjī,* in length 2 1/4 gaz, and having caused prayers and incantations to be repeated over it, and having had it made into three strands, which they call *sih tan,* by one in whom they have confidence, they fasten it on his waist. Having woven a *zunnār* (girdle or thread) out of the loose threads, they hang it over his right[567] shoulder. Having given into his hand a stick of the length of a little over 1 gaz to defend himself with from hurtful things and a copper vessel for drinking-water, they hand him over to a learned brahmin that he may remain in his house for twelve

566 See Jarrett, iii, 271, etc. The Sanskrit word is Āsrama, or Āshrama.

567 Left shoulder in Āyīn.

years, and employ himself in reading the Vedas, which they believe in as God's book. From this day forward they call him a brahmin. During this time it is necessary that he should altogether abstain from bodily pleasures. When midday is passed he goes as a beggar to the houses of other brahmins, and bringing what is given him to his preceptor, eats it with his permission. For clothing, with the exception of a loin cloth (*lungī*) of cotton to cover his private parts, and 2 or 3 more gaz of cotton which he throws over his back, he has nothing else. This state is called *brahmacharya,* that is, being busied with the Divine books. After this period has passed, with the leave of his preceptor and his father, he marries, and is allowed to enjoy all the pleasures of his five senses until the time when he has a son who shall have attained the age of 16 years. If he does not have a son, he passes his days till he is 48 in the social life. During this time they call him a *grihast,* that is, householder. After that time, separating himself from relatives, connections, strangers, and friends, and giving up all things of enjoyment and pleasure, he retires to a place of solitude from the place of attachment to sociality (*ta'alluq-i-ābād-i-kas̤rat*), and passes his days in the jungle. They call this condition *bānprasta,*[568] that is, abode in the jungle. As it is a maxim of the Hindus that no good deed can be thoroughly performed by men in the social state without the partnership of the presence of a wife, whom they have styled the half of a man, and as a portion of the ceremonies and worshippings is yet before him (has to be accomplished), he takes his wife with him into the jungle. If she should be pregnant, he puts off his going until she bear a child and it arrive at the age of 5 years. Then he entrusts the child to his eldest son or other relation, and carries out his intention. In the same way, if his wife be menstruous, he puts off going until she is purified. After this he has no connection with her, and does not defile himself with communication with her, and at night he sleeps

[568] Sanskrit, Vānaprastha.

apart.[569] He passes twelve years in this place, and lives on vegetables which may have sprung up of themselves in the desert and jungle. He keeps his zunnar by him and worships fire. He does not waste his time in looking after his nails or the hair of his head, or in trimming his beard and moustaches. When he completes this period in the manner related, he returns to his own house, and having commended his wife to his children and brothers and sons-in-law, goes to pay his respects to his spiritual guide, and burns by throwing into the fire in his presence whatever he has in the way of a zunnar, the hair of his head, etc., and says to him: "Whatever attachment (*ta'alluq*) I may have had, even to abstinence and worshipping and will, I have rooted up out of my heart." Then he closes the road to his heart and to his desires and is always employed in contemplation of God, and knows no one except the True Cause of Being (God). If he speak of science it is the science of Vedānta, the purport of which Bābā Fighānī has versified in this couplet—

"There's one lamp in this house, by whose rays
Wherever I look there is an assembly."

They call this state *sarvabiyās,*[570] that is, giving up all. They call him who possesses it *sarvabiyāsī.*

After interviewing Jadrūp I mounted an elephant and passed through the town of Ujjain, and as I went scattered to the right and left small coins to the value of 3,500 rupees, and proceeding 1 3/4 kos alighted at Dā'ūd-kheṛā, the place where the royal camp was pitched. On the 3rd day, which was a halting day, I went, from desire for association with him, after midday, to see Jadrūp, and for six gharis enjoyed myself in his company. On this day also he uttered good words, and it was near evening

---

569 Text *qa ṭ 'ī dar miyān ālat nihāda,* but apparently this should be *ālat qat' ba miyān nihāda* ; that is, "membrum virile in involucris reponens."

570 Text, *sarb biyāsm,* which may mean 'distributing everything.' The Iqbal-nama, p. 96, has *sarb nāsī* 'destroying everything.'

when I entered my palace. On the 4th day I journeyed 3 $\frac{1}{4}$ kos and halted at the village of Jarāo[571] in the Pārāniyā garden. This is also a very pleasant halting - place, full of trees. On the 6th there was a march; after proceeding for 4 3/4 kos I halted on the bank of the lake of Debālpūr Bheriyā. On account of the pleasantness of the place and the delights of the lake, I halted at this stage for four days, and at the end of each day, embarking in a boat, employed myself in shooting ducks (*murghābī*) and other aquatic animals. At this halting-place they brought *fakhrī* grapes from Ahmadnagar. Although they are not as large as the Kabul fakhri grapes, they do not yield to them in sweetness.

At the request of my son Bābā Khurram the mansab of Badī'u-z-zamān, son of Mīrzā Shāhrukh, was fixed at 1,500 personal and 1,000 horse. On the 11th I marched, and after proceeding for $3\frac{1}{4}$ kos halted in the parganah Daulatabad. On the 12th, which was a halt, I rode out to hunt. In the village of Shaikhūpūr, which belonged to the said parganah, I saw a very large and bulky banyan-tree, measuring round its trunk $18\frac{1}{2}$ gaz, and in height from the root to the top of the branches $128\frac{1}{4}$ cubits. The branches spread a shade for $203\frac{1}{2}$ cubits. The length of a branch, on which they have represented the tusks of an elephant, was 40 gaz. At the time when my revered father passed by this, he had made an impression of his hand by way of a mark at the height of $3\frac{3}{4}$ gaz from the ground. I ordered them also to make the mark of my hand 8 gaz above another root. In order that these two hand-marks might not be effaced in

---

[571] I.O. MS. No. 306 says nothing about a garden, but speaks of a village Khirwār and of halting under a mango-tree. Nor does No. 305 mention a garden.

the course of time, they were carved on a piece of marble and fastened on to the trunk of the tree. I ordered them to place a *chabūtara* and platform round the tree.

As at the time when I was prince I had promised Mīr Ẓiyā'u-dīn Qazwīnī, who was one of the Saifī Sayyids, and whom during my reign I have honoured with the title of Muṣṭafā Khān, to give the parganah of Maldah, which is a famous parganah in Bengal, to him and his descendants[572] in *āl tamghā* (perpetual royal grant), this great gift was bestowed in his honour at this halting-place. On the 13th a march took place. Going separately from this camp to look round the country and hunt with some of the ladies and intimates and servants, I proceeded to the village of Ḥāṣilpūr, and whilst the camp was pitched in the neighbourhood of Nālcha (Bālchha ?) I halted at the village of Sāngor. What shall be written of the beauty and sweetness of this village? There were many mango-trees, and its lands were altogether green and delightful. On account of its greenness and pleasantness I halted here for three days. I gave this village to Kamāl Khān, the huntsman, in place of Kesho Dās Mārū. An order was passed that they should hereafter call it Kamālpūr. At this same halting-place occurred the night of Shīvrāt (Shivrātri). Many Jogis collected. The ceremonies of this night were duly observed, and I met the learned of this body in social intercourse. In these days I shot three blue bulls. The news of the killing of Rāja Mān reached me at this place. I had appointed him to head the army that had been sent against the fort of Kāngṛā. When he arrived at Lahore he heard that Sangrām, one of the zamindars of the hill-country of the Panjab, had attacked his place and taken possession of part of his province. Considering it of the first importance to drive him out, he went against him. As Sangrām had not the power to oppose him, he left the country of which he had taken possession and took refuge in difficult hills and places. Rāja Mān pursued him

[572] Cf. Elliot, vi, 348. The MSS. say nothing about two sons.

there, and in his great pride, not looking to the means by which he himself could advance and retreat, came up to him with a small force. When Sangrām saw that he had no way to flee by, in accordance with this couplet—

"In time of need when no (way of) flight is left,
The hand seizes the edge of the sharp sword."[573]

A fight took place, and according to what was decreed, a bullet struck Rāja Mān and he delivered his soul to the Creator thereof. His men were defeated and a great number of them killed. The remainder, wounded, abandoned their horses and arms, and with a hundred alarms escaped half-dead.

On the 17th I marched from Sāngor, and after proceeding 3 kos came again to the village of Ḥāṣilpūr. On the road a blue bull was killed. This village is one of the noted places in the Subah of Malwa. It has many vines and mango-trees without number. It has streams flowing on all sides of it. At the time I arrived there were grapes contrary to the season in which they are in the Wilayat (Persia or Afghanistan). They were so cheap and plentiful that the lowest and meanest could get as much as they desired. The poppy had flowered and showed varied colours. In brief, there are few villages so pleasant. For three days more I halted in this village. Three blue bulls were killed with my gun. From Ḥāṣilpūr on the 21st in two marches I rejoined the big camp. On the road a blue bull was killed. On Sunday, the 22nd, marching from the neighbourhood of Nālcha (Bālchha ?), I pitched at a lake that is at the foot of the fort of Māndū. On that day the huntsmen brought news that they had marked down a tiger within 3 kos. Although it was Sunday, and on these two days, viz. Sunday and Thursday, I do not shoot, it occurred to me that as it is a noxious animal it ought to be done away with. I proceeded towards him, and when I arrived at the place it was sitting under the shade of a tree. Seeing its mouth, which was

573 From the "Gulistān."

half open, from the back of the elephant, I fired my gun. By chance it entered its mouth and found a place in its throat and brain, and its affair was finished with that one shot. After this the people who were with me, although they looked for the place where the tiger was wounded, could not find it, for on none of its limbs was there any sign of a gunshot wound. At last I ordered them to look in its mouth. From this it was evident that the bullet had entered its mouth and that it had been killed thereby. Mīrzā Rustam had killed a male wolf and brought it. I wished to see whether its gall-bladder was in its liver like that of the tiger, or like other animals outside its liver. After examination it was clear that the gall-bladder was also inside the liver. On Monday, the 23rd, when one watch had passed in a fortunate ascension and a benign hour, I mounted an elephant and approached the fort of Māndū. When a watch and three gharis of day had passed, I entered the houses which they had prepared for the royal accommodation. I scattered 1,500 rupees on the way. From Ajmir to Māndū, 159 kos, in the space of four months and two days, in forty-six marches and seventy-eight halts, had been traversed. In these forty-six marches our halts were made on the banks of tanks or streams or large rivers in pleasant places which were full of trees and poppy-fields in flower, and no day passed that I did not hunt while halting or travelling. Riding on horseback or on an elephant I came along the whole way looking about and hunting, and none of the difficulties of travelling were experienced; one might say that there was a change from one garden to another. In these huntings there were always present with me Āṣaf Khān, Mīrzā Rustam, Mīr Mīrān, Anīrā'ī, Hidāyatu-llah, Rāja Sārang Deo, Sayyid Kāsū, and Khawāṣṣ Khān. As before the arrival of the royal standards in these regions I had sent 'Abdu-l-Karīm, the architect, to look to the repair of the buildings of the old rulers in Māndū, he during the time the camp halted at Ajmir had repaired some of the old buildings that were capable of repair, and had altogether rebuilt some places. In short, he had made ready a house the like of which for pleasantness and sweetness has probably not been made anywhere else. Nearly 300,000 rupees, or 2,000 Persian tumans, were expended on this. There should be such grand buildings in all great cities as might be fit for royal accommodation. This fort is on the top of a hill 10 kos in circumference; in the rainy season there is no place with the fine air and pleasantness of this fort. At nights, in the season of the *qalbu-l-asad* (Cor leonis or Regulus, the star *a* of Leo), it is so cold that one cannot do without a coverlet, and by day there is no need for a fan (*bād-zan*). They say[574] that before the time of Rāja Bikramājīt there was a Raja of the name of Jai Singh Deo. In his time a man had gone into the fields to bring grass. While he was cutting it, the sickle he had in his hand appeared to be of the colour of gold. When he saw that his sickle had been transmuted, he took it to a blacksmith of the name of Mādan[575] to be repaired. The blacksmith knew the sickle had been turned into gold. It had before this been heard that there was in this country the alchemist's stone (*sang-i-pāras*), by contact with which iron and copper became gold. He immediately took the grasscutter with him to that place and procured the stone. After this he brought to the Raja of the time this priceless jewel. The Raja by means of this stone made gold, and spent part of it on the buildings of this fort and completed them in the space of twelve years. At the desire of that blacksmith he caused them to cut into the shape of an anvil most of the stones that were to be built into the wall of the fort. At the end of his life, when his heart had given up the world, he held an assembly on the bank of the Narbada, which is an object of worship among the Hindus, and, assembling brahmins, made presents to each of cash and jewels. When the turn of a brahmin came who had long been associated

---

574 Cf. Jarrett, ii, 197. The story is also told with many more details in Price's Jahāngīr, p. 108, etc.

575 Text, Mādan. But the name is Māndan, as MS. No. 181 and the Āyīn-i-Akbari (Jarrett, ii, 197) show. The legend is intended to show how Māndū got its name (see also Tiefenthaler, i, 353).

with him, he gave this stone into his hand. He from ignorance became angry and threw the priceless jewel into the river. After he came to know the true state of the affair he was a captive to perpetual sorrow. However much he searched, no trace of it was found. These things are not written in a book; they have been heard, but my intelligence in no way accepts this story. It appears to me to be all delusion. Māndū[576] is one of the famous Sarkars of the Subah of Malwa. Its revenue is 1,390,000 dams. It was for a long time the capital of the kings of this country. There are many buildings and traces of former kings in it, and up till now it has not fallen into ruin.

On the 24th I rode to go round and see the buildings of the old kings, and went first to the Jāmi' mosque, which is one built by Sulṭān Hūshang Ghūrī. A very lofty building came to view, all of cut stone, and although 180 years have passed since the time of its building, it is as if the builder had just withdrawn his hand from it. After this I went to the building containing the tombs of the Khaljī rulers. The grave of Naṣīru-d-dīn, son of Sulṭān Ghiyāṣu-d-dīn, whose face is blackened for ever, was also there. It is well known that that wretch advanced himself by the murder of his own father, Ghiyāṣu-d-dīn, who was in his 80th year. Twice he gave him poison, and he twice expelled it by means of a *zahr-muhra* (poison antidote, bezoar) he had on his arm. The third time he mixed poison in a cup of sherbet and gave it to his father with his own hand, saying he must drink it. As his father understood what efforts he was making in this matter, he loosened the zahr-muhra from his arm and threw it before him, and then turning his face in humility and supplication towards the throne of the Creator, who requires no supplication, said: "O Lord, my age has arrived at 80 years, and I have passed this time in prosperity and happiness such as has been attained to by no king. Now as this is my last time, I hope that Thou wilt not seize Naṣīr for my murder, and that

---

[576] Elliot, vi. 348.

reckoning my death as a thing decreed Thou wilt not avenge it." After he had spoken these words, he drank off that poisoned cup of sherbet at a gulp and delivered his soul to the Creator. The meaning of his preamble was that he had passed the time of his reign in enjoyment such as has not been attained to by any of the kings. When in his 48th year he came to the throne, he said to his intimates and those near him, "In the service of my revered father I have passed thirty years in warfare and have committed no fault in my activity as a soldier; now that my turn to reign has arrived, I have no intention to conquer countries, but desire to pass the remainder of my life in ease and enjoyment." They say that he had collected 15,000 women in his harem. He had a whole city of them, and had made it up of all castes, kinds, and descriptions— artificers, magistrates, qazis, kotwals, and whatever else is necessary for the administration of a town. Wherever he heard of a virgin possessed of beauty, he would not desist (lit. did not sit down from his feet) until he possessed her. He taught the girls all kinds of arts and crafts, and was much inclined to hunt. He had made a deer park and collected all kinds of animals in it. He often used to hunt in it with his women. In brief, in the period of thirty-two years of his reign, as he had determined, he went against no enemy, and passed this time in ease and enjoyment. In the same way no one invaded his country. It is reported that when Shīr Khān, the Afghan, in the time of his rule, came to the tomb of Naṣīru-d-dīn, he, in spite of his brutish nature, on account of Naṣīru-d-dīn's shameful conduct, ordered the head of the tomb to be beaten with sticks. Also when I went to his tomb I gave it several kicks, and ordered the servants in attendance on me to kick the tomb. Not satisfied with this, I ordered the tomb to be broken open and his impure remains to be thrown into the fire. Then it occurred to me that since fire is Light, it was a pity for the Light of Allah to be polluted with burning his filthy body; also, lest there should be any diminution of torture for him in another state from being thus burnt, I ordered them to throw his crumbled bones, together with his decayed limbs; into the Narbada. During his lifetime he always passed his days in the water in consequence of the heat that had acquired a mastery over his temperament. It is well known that in a state of drunkenness he once threw himself into one of the basins at Kāliyādaha, which was very deep. Some of the attendants in the harem exerted themselves and caught his hair in their hands and drew him out of the water. After he had come to his senses they told him that this thing had happened. When he had heard that they had pulled him out by the hair of his head, he became exceedingly angry, and ordered the hands of the attendants to be cut off. Another time, when an affair of this kind took place, no one had the boldness to pull him out and he was drowned. By chance, after 110 years had passed since his death, it came to pass that his decayed limbs also became mingled with the water.

On the 28th, as a reward for the buildings of Māndū having been completed through his excellent exertions, I promoted 'Abdu-l-Karīm to the rank of 800 personal and 400 horse, and dignified him with the title of Ma'mūr Khān (the architect-Khān). On the same day that the royal standards entered the fort of Māndū, my son of lofty fortune, Sulṭān Khurram, with the victorious army, entered the city of Burhanpur, which is the seat of the governor of the province of Khandesh.

After some days, representations came from Afẓal Khān and the Rāy Rāyān, to whom at the time of leaving Ajmir my son had given leave to accompany the ambassador to 'Ādil Khān, reporting that when the news of our coming reached 'Ādil Khān he came out for 7 kos to meet the order and the litter of the prince, and performed the duties of salutation and respect which are customary at Court. He did not omit a hair's point of such ceremonies. At the same interview he professed the greatest loyalty, and promised that he would restore all those provinces that 'Ambar of dark fate had taken from the victorious State, and agreed to send to the Court with all reverence a fitting offering with his ambassadors. After saying this he brought the ambassadors in all dignity to the place that had been prepared for them. On the same day he sent some one to 'Ambar with a message of the matters it was necessary to acquaint him with. I heard this news from the reports of Afẓal Khān and the Rāy Rāyān.

From Ajmir up to Monday, the 23rd of the aforesaid[577] month, during four months, 2 tigers, 27 blue bulls, 6 *chītal* (spotted deer), 60 deer, 23 hares and foxes, and 1,200 water-fowl and other animals had been killed. On these nights I told the story of my former hunting expeditions and the liking I had for this occupation to those standing at the foot of the throne of the Caliphate. It occurred to me that I might make up the account of my game from the commencement of my years of discretion up to the present time. I accordingly gave orders to the news-writers, the hunt-accountants and huntsmen, and others employed in this service to make enquiries and tell me of all the animals that had been killed in hunting. It was shown that from the commencement of my 12th year, which was in 988 (1580), up to the end of this year, which is the 11th year after my accession and my 50th lunar year, 28,532 head of game had been taken in my presence. Of these, 17,167 animals I killed myself with my gun or otherwise, viz.: Quadrupeds, 3,203; viz., tigers, 86; bears, cheetahs, foxes, otters (*ūdbilāo*), and hyænas, 9; blue bulls, 889; *mhāka,* a species of antelope, in size equal to a blue bull, 35 head; of antelope, male and female, *chikāra, chītal,* mountain goats, etc., 1,670[578] ; rams (*qūj*) and red deer, 215; wolves, 64; wild buffaloes, 36; pigs, 90; *rang,* 26; mountain sheep, 22; *arghalī,* 32; wild asses, 6; hares, 23. Birds, 13,964; viz., pigeons, 10,348; *lagaṛ-jhagaṛ* (a species of hawk), 3; eagles, 2; *qalīwāj* (*ghalīwāj,* kite), 23; owls (*chughd*), 39; *qautān* (goldfinch?), 12; kites (*mūsh-khwur,* mice-

---

[577] Monday, the 23rd Isfandārmuz, the day on which he reached Māndū. It was about the 6th March, 1617.

[578] The MSS. have 1,672.

eaters), 5; sparrows, 41; doves, 25; owls (*būm*), 30; ducks, geese, cranes, etc., 150; crows, 3,276. Aquatic animals, 10 *magar machha,* that is, crocodiles[579] (*nahang*).

THE TWELFTH NEW YEAR'S FEAST AFTER MY AUSPICIOUS ACCESSION.

One ghari of day remained of Monday, the 30th of the aforesaid (Isfandiyār) month, corresponding to the 12th Rabī'u-l-awwal, 1026 (20th March, 1617), when the sun changed from the constellation of Pisces into the pleasure-house of Aries, which is his abode of honour and good fortune. At the very time of transit, which was a fortunate hour, I sat upon the throne. I had ordered that according to the usual custom they should decorate the public audience hall with fine cloths, etc. Notwithstanding that many of the Amirs and chief men of the State were in attendance on my son Khurram, a meeting was arranged which was not inferior to those of previous years. I presented the offerings of Tuesday[580] to Ānand Khān. On the same day, which was the 1st Farwardīn of the 12th year (21st or 22nd March, 1617), a representation arrived from Shāh Khurram to the effect that the New Year's festival had been arranged for in the same manner as in previous years, but as the days of travelling and service had occurred the annual offerings of the servants would be remitted. This proceeding of my son was much approved. Remembering my dear son in my prayers, I besought for him

---

[579] See Elliot, vi, 351 and 362, note. Jahāngīr only gives details of the 17,167 animals killed by himself. The *mhāka* is possibly a clerical error for *mār-khwur*. The text says it is allied to the *gawazn*, but the MSS. have *gūr*, a wild ass. The details of the quadrupeds come to 3,203, the total stated by Jahāngīr. The details of the birds come to 13,954, but the 10 crocodiles bring up the figures to 13,964, and the total 3,203 + 13,964 comes to the 17,167 mentioned. It has been suggested to me that the *mhāka* of the text is the *mahā* or swamp-deer of the Terai, *Rucervs Duvaucelli*.

[580] The MSS. have Saturday instead of Tuesday, and this seems reasonable, for there were no offerings on Tuesday (see *infra*).

from the throne of Allah his welfare in both worlds, and ordered that on this New Year's Day no one should present offerings.

In consequence of the disturbance that tobacco brings about in most temperaments and constitutions, I had ordered that no one should smoke it (lit. draw). My brother Shāh 'Abbās had also become aware of the mischief arising from it, and had ordered that in Iran no one should venture to smoke. As Khān 'Ālam (ambassador to Persia) was without control in continual smoking of tobacco, he frequently practised it. Yādgār 'Alī Sulṭān, ambassador of the ruler of Iran, represented to Shāh 'Abbās that Khān 'Ālam could never be a moment without tobacco, and he (Shāh 'Abbās) wrote this couplet in answer—

"The friend's envoy wishes to exhibit tobacco;
With fidelity's lamp I light up the tobacco-market."

Khān 'Ālam in answer wrote and sent this verse—

"I, poor wretch, was miserable at the tobacco notice;
By the just Shah's favour the tobacco-market became brisk."

On the 3rd of the same month, Ḥusain Beg, the diwan of Bengal, had the good fortune to kiss the threshold, and made an offering of twelve elephants, male and female. Ṭāhir, bakhshi of Bengal, who had been accused of several offences, obtained the favour of paying his respects to me, and presented before me an offering of twenty-one elephants. Twelve of these were approved and the remainder I conferred on him. On this day a wine-feast was arranged, and I gave wine to most of the servants who were engaged in waiting on me, and made them all heated with the wine of loyalty. On the 4th the huntsmen sent news that they had marked down a lion in the neighbourhood of the Shakkar[581] tank, which is inside the fort and one of the famous constructions of the rulers of Malwa. I at once mounted and went towards that game. When the lion appeared he charged the

[581] Text, Sakar. Now locally called the Sāgan, 'sea,' tank.

ahadis and the retinue and wounded ten[582] or twelve of them. At last I finished his business with three shots[583] (lit. arrows) from my gun, and removed his evil from the servants of God. On the 8th the mansab of Mīr Mīrān, which was 1,000 personal and 400 horse, was fixed at 1,500 personal and 500 horse. On the 9th, at the request of my son Khurram, I increased the mansab of Khān Jahān by 1,000 personal and horse, making it thus 6,000 personal and horse; that of Ya'qūb Khān, which was 1,500 personal with 1,000 horse, was made 2,000 personal and 1,500 horse; that of Bahlūl Khān Miyāna[584] was increased by 500 personal and 300 horse to 1,500 personal and 1,000 horse; and that of Mīrzā Sharafu-d-dīn Kāshgharī, by whom and his son great bravery had been shown in the Deccan, was increased to 1,500 personal and 1,000 horse. On the 10th Farwardīn, corresponding with the 22nd Rabī'u-l-awwal, 1026, my lunar weighing took place. On this day two 'Iraq horses from my private stable and a dress of honour were conferred on my son Khurram and sent to him by Bahrām Beg. I increased the mansab of I'tibār Khān to 5,000 personal and 3,000 horse. On the 11th, Ḥusain Beg, of Tabriz, whom the ruler of Iran had sent to the ruler of Golconda by way of embassy, as, in consequence of the quarrel of the Franks with the Persians, the road of the Mīr had been closed,[585] waited upon me with the ambassador of the ruler of Golconda. Offerings came from him of two horses and some *tuqūz*[586] (nine-pieces?) of cloth from the Deccan and Gujarat. On the same day an 'Iraq horse from my private stable was bestowed on Khān Jahān. On the 15th, 1,000 personal were added to the mansab of Mīrzā Rāja Bhāo Singh, raising it to 5,000 personal and 3,000 horse. On the 17th, 500 horse were added to the mansab of Mīrzā Rustam, and

582 The MSS. only speak of twelve.

583 The MSS. seem to have merely *ba tīr-i-bandūq*, 'with bullets.'

584 Biyāna in text.

585 That is, apparently, the journey back by sea from the Deccan. The MSS. have Hasan instead of Ḥusain, and say the route by Ormuz was closed. Perhaps the *ba Mīr* of text is a mistake for *bar baḥr*,' by sea.

586 *Tuqūz* means nine in Turkī.

I made it up to 5,000 personal and 1,000 horse; that of Ṣādiq Khān was fixed at 1,500 personal and 700 horse, original and increase; Irādat Khān in the same manner was raised to the mansab of 1,500 and 600 horse. To the mansab of Anīrā'ī 500 personal and 100 horse were added, and it was made one of 1,500 personal and 500 horse. Three gharis of Saturday, the 19th, remained when the beginning of the *sharaf* (day of sun's culmination) occurred, and at the same time I again took my seat on the throne. Of the thirty-two prisoners from the army of the rebel 'Ambar who had been captured by the servants of the victorious State in the battle won by Shāh-nawāz Khān and the defeat of that disastrous man ('Ambar), I had handed one man over to I'tiqād Khān. The guards who had been appointed to keep him showed carelessness and let him escape. I was much annoyed at this, and I forbade I'tiqād Khān to come to wait on me for three months. As the said prisoner's name and condition were unknown, he was not caught again, although they showed activity in the matter. At last I ordered the captain of the guards who had been careless in keeping him to be capitally punished. I'tiqād Khān on this day, at the request of I'timādu-d-daulah, had the good fortune to pay his respects to me.

As for a long time no good had been heard of the affairs of Bengal and of the conduct of Qāsim Khān, it entered my mind to send to the Subah of Bengal Ibrāhīm Khān Fatḥ-jang, who had carried on successfully the affairs of the Subah of Behar and had brought a diamond mine into the possession of the State, and to despatch Jahāngīr Qulī Khān, who had a jagir in the Subah of Allahabad, in his place to Behar. I sent for Qāsim Khān to Court. At the same hour on the auspicious day (the day of culmination) an order was given that they should write royal farmans to the effect that *sazāwalān* (revenue collectors) should be appointed to take Jahāngīr Qulī Khān to Behar and to send Ibrāhīm Khān

Fatḥ-jang to Bengal. Patronizing Sikandar,[587] the jeweller, I promoted him to the mansab of 1,000 personal and 300 horse.

On the 21st I gave leave to Muḥammad Riẓā, ambassador of the ruler of Iran, and bestowed on him 60,000 darbs, equal to 30,000 rupees, with a dress of honour. As an equivalent to the souvenir (*yād-būdī*) that my brother Shāh 'Abbās had sent to me, I forwarded with the aforesaid ambassador certain presents of jewelled things which the rulers of the Deccan had sent, with cloths and rare things of every kind fit for presentation, of the value of 100,000 rupees. Among these was a crystal cup that Chelebī[588] had sent from 'Iraq. The Shah had seen this cup and said to the ambassador that if his brother (Jahāngīr) would drink wine out of it and send it to him it would be a great mark of affection. When the ambassador represented this, having drunk wine several times out of the cup in his presence, I ordered them to make a lid and a saucer for it and sent it along with the presents. The lid was of enamel (*mīnā-kārī*). I ordered the Munshis of mercurial writing (*'Uṭārid-raqm*) to write in due form an answer to the letter he had brought.

On the 22nd the scouts brought in news of a tiger. Mounting immediately, I went against the tiger and with three shots I delivered the people from his wickedness, and himself from the wickedness of his vile nature. Masīḥu-z-zamān produced before me a cat, and represented that it was a hermaphrodite, and that in his house it had young ones, and that when it had connection with another cat, young were born to the latter.

On the 25th the contingent of I'timādu-d-daulah passed before me in review on the plain under the jharoka. There were 2,000 cavalry well horsed, most of whom were Moghuls, 500 foot armed with bows and guns, and fourteen elephants. The

---

[587] The I. O. MSS. seem to have Sakakdar or Sakakandar.

[588] It appears from Shāh 'Abbās's letter to Jahāngīr (Tūzuk, p. 165) that Muḥammad Ḥusain Chelebī had been employed by Jahāngīr to collect curios in Persia.

bakhshis reckoned them up and reported that this force was fully equipped and according to rule. On the 26th a tigress was killed. On Thursday, the 1st Urdībihisht, a diamond that Muqarrab Khān had sent by runners was laid before me; it weighed 23 *surkh,* and the jewellers valued it at 30,000 rupees. It was a diamond of the first water, and was much approved. I ordered them to make a ring of it. On the 3rd the mansab of Yūsuf Khān was, at the request of Bābā Khurram, fixed at 1,000 with 1,500 horse, and in the same way the mansabs of several of the Amirs and mansabdars were increased at his suggestion. On the 7th, as the huntsmen had marked down four tigers, when two watches and three gharis had passed I went out to hunt them with my ladies. When the tigers came in sight Nūr-Jahān Begam submitted that if I would order her she herself would kill the tigers with her gun. I said, "Let it be so." She shot two tigers with one shot each and knocked over the two others with four shots. In the twinkling of an eye she deprived of life the bodies of these four tigers. Until now such shooting was never seen, that from the top of an elephant and inside of a howdah (*'amārī*) six shots should be made and not one miss, so that the four beasts found no opportunity to spring or move.[589] As a reward for this good shooting I gave her a pair of bracelets[590] (*pahunchī*) of diamonds worth 100,000 rupees and scattered 1,000 ashrafis (over her). On the same day Ma'mūr Khān (the architect-Khan) obtained leave to go to Lahore to complete the buildings of the palace there. On the 10th the death of Sayyid Wāriṡ, who was faujdar of the Subah of Oudh, was reported. On the 12th, as Mīr Maḥmūd asked for a faujdarship, I dignified him with the title of

---

[589] Note by Sayyid Aḥmad. They say that a poet recited this impromptu couplet—

"Though Nūr-Jahān be in form a woman,
In the ranks of men she's a tiger-slayer."

The point of this couplet is that before Nūr-Jahān entered Jahāngīr's harem she was the wife of Shīr-afgan, the tiger-slayer. The line may also read "In battle she is a man-smiter and a tiger-slayer."

[590] The two I.O. MSS. have "a pair of pearls and a diamond."

Tahawwur Khān, and, increasing his mansab, appointed him to the faujdarship of some of the parganahs of the Subah of Multan. On the 22nd, Ṭāhir, the bakhshi of Bengal, who had been forbidden to pay his respects, waited upon me and presented his offerings. Eight elephants were also presented as the offering of Qāsim Khān, governor of Bengal, and two as that of Shaikh Modhū. On the 28th, at the request of Khān Daurān, an order was given for the increase of the mansab of 'Abdu-l-'Azīz Khān by 500. On the 5th Khurdād the duty of the Diwanship of Gujarat was given to Mīrzā Ḥusain in supercession of Kesho. I dignified him with the title of Kifāyat Khān. On the 8th, Lashkar Khān, who had been appointed bakhshi of Bangash, came and waited on me; he offered 100 muhrs and 500 rupees. Some days before this Ūstād Muḥammad Nāyī (flute-player), who was unequalled in his craft, was sent by my son Khurram at my summons. I had heard some of his musical pieces[591] (*majlis-sāz*), and he played a tune which he had composed for an ode (*ghazal*) in my name. On the 12th I ordered him to be weighed against rupees; this came to 6,300 rupees. I also gave him an elephant with a howdah,[592] and I ordered him to ride on it and, having packed[593] his rupees about him, to proceed to his lodging. Mullā Asad, the story-teller, one of the servants of Mīrzā Ghāzī, came on the same day from Tattah and waited on me. As he was a reciter and story-teller full of sweetness and smartness. I liked his society, and I made him happy with the title of Maḥẕūẕ Khān, and gave him 1,000 rupees, a dress of honour, a horse, an elephant, and a palanquin. After some days I ordered him to be weighed against rupees, and his weight came up to 4,400. He

[591] There is a fuller account of this flute-player in Price's Jahāngīr, p. 114. The melody which he composed in Jahāngīr's name is there called by Price sent Jahāngirī. (The text does not give the name Jahāngīr.) It is there stated that Shāh Jahān brought the flute-player with him from Burhanpur and introduced him.

[592] *Hauza-dāri*, 'with a basin-shaped litter on it.'

[593] The word *pāshīda*, 'scattered,' does not occur in the I. O. MSS. But perhaps the word has two opposite meanings.

was raised to the mansab of 200 personal and 20 horse. I ordered him always to be present at the meetings for talk (*gap*). On the same day Lashkar Khān brought his men to the *darshan jharoka* before me. There were 500 horse, 14 elephants, and 100 musketeers. On the 24th news came that Mahā Singh, grandson of Rāja Mān Singh, who was entered among the great officers, had died from excessive wine-drinking at Bālāpūr in the province of Berar. His father also had died at the age of 32[594] from the drinking of wine beyond measure. On the same day they had brought to my private fruit-house many mangoes from all parts of the province of the Deccan, Burhanpur, Gujarat, and the parganahs of Malwa. Although this province is well known and celebrated for the sweetness, freedom from stringiness, and size of its mangoes, and there are few mangoes that equal its mangoes—so much so that I often ordered them to be weighed in my presence, when they were shown to come to a seer or 1 1/4 seer or even more—yet in sweetness of water and delicious flavour and digestibility the mangoes of Chaprāmau,[595] in the province of Agra, are superior to all the mangoes of this province and of all other places in India.

On the 28th I sent for my son Bābā Khurram a special gold-embroidered *nādirī* of a fineness such as had never been produced before in my establishment; I ordered the bearer to tell him that as this rarity had the speciality that I had worn it on the day I quitted Ajmir for the conquest of the Deccan, I had sent it to him. On the same day I placed the turban from my own head, just as it was, on the head of I'timādu-d-daulah, and honoured him with this favour. Three emeralds, a piece of jewelled *ūrbasī*,[596] and a ruby signet ring that Mahābat Khān had sent by

---

594 Father and son both died apparently at the same age.

595 It was in Sarkar Qanauj (Jarrett, ii, 185). It is Chibrāmau of I.G., iii, 97, and is in Farrukhabad district.

596 *Ūrvasī* is the name of an Apsara or celestial nymph. Probably it is here the name of a dress. (In Forbes's Hindustani Dictionary *ūrbasī* is said to denote a particular kind of ornament worn on the breast.)

way of offering were laid before me. They came to 7,000 rupees in value. On this day, by the mercy and favour of Allah, continued rain fell. Water in Māndū had become very scarce and the people were agitated about the matter, so that most of the servants had been ordered to go to the bank of the Narbada. There was no expectation of rain at that season. In consequence of the agitation of the people I turned by way of supplication to the throne of God, and He in His mercy and grace gave such rain that in the course of a day and a night tanks, ponds (*birkahā*), and rivers became full, and the agitation of the people was changed to complete ease. With what tongue can I render thanks for this favour? On the 1st of Tīr a standard was presented to Wazīr Khān. The offering of the Rānā, consisting of two horses, a piece of Gujarati cloth, and some jars of pickles and preserves, was laid before me. On the 3rd, Mu'azzā[597] (?) brought news of the capture of 'Abdu-l-Laṭīf, a descendant of the rulers of Gujarat, who had always been the originator of mischief and disturbance in that Subah. As his capture was a reason for the contentment of the people, praise was given to God, and I ordered Muqarrab Khān to send him to Court by one of his mansabdars. Many of the zamindars in the neighbourhood of Māndū came and waited on me, and laid offerings before me. On the 8th, Rām Dās, son of Rāja Rāj Singh Kachhwāha, was given the *ṭīka* of a Raja, and I honoured him with that title. Yādgār Beg, who was known in Māwarā'a-n-nahr (Transoxiana) as Yādgār Qūrchī, and had not been without connection and influence with the ruler of that country, came and waited on me. Of all his offerings a white china cup on a stand was the most approved. The offering of Bahādur Khān, governor of Qandahar, consisting of nine horses, nine *tuqūz* of fine cloth (81 pieces ?), two black foxes' skins, and other things, was brought before me. Also on this day the Rāja of

[597] The MSS. have *maghra*, which may be connected with the Arabic *maghr*, 'travelling quickly.' It may be the name of a courier, or merely mean 'quickly.'

Gadeha, Pem[598] Narāyan, had the good fortune to wait on me, and made an offering of seven elephants, male and female. On the 10th a horse and dress of honour were given to Yādgār Qūrchī. On the 13th was the feast of rose-water scattering (*gulāb-pāshān*). The rites due to that day were performed. Shaikh Maudūd Chishtī, one of the officers of Bengal, was honoured with the title of Chishtī Khān, and I presented him with a horse. On the 14th, Rāwal Samarsī (Samarsi ṃ ha), son of Rāwal Ūday Singh, zamindar of Bānswāla, waited on me; he gave as offering 30,000 rupees, three elephants, a jewelled *pān-dān* (box for betel), and a jewelled belt. On the 15th nine diamonds which Ibrāhīm Khān Fatḥ-jang, the governor of Behar, had sent along with Muḥammad Beg from the mine, and from the collections of the zamindars of that place, were laid before me. Of these, one weighed 14 1/2 tanks, and was of the value of 100,000 rupees. On the same day Yādgār Qūrchī was presented with 14,000 darbs, and I promoted him to the mansab of 500 personal and 300 horse. I fixed the mansab of Tātār Khān, *bakāwul-begī* (chief steward), original and increase, at 2,000 personal and 300 horse, and each of his sons was separately promoted to an increased mansab. At the request of Prince Sulṭ̤ān Parwīz, I increased the personal mansab of Wazīr Khān by 500.

On the 29th, which was the auspicious day of Thursday, Sayyid 'Abdu-llah Bārha, the envoy of my son of good fortune, Bābā Khurram, waited on me, and presented a letter from that son containing news of a victory over the provinces of the Deccan. All the chiefs, laying the head of duty in the noose of obedience, had consented to service and humility, and laid before him the keys of forts and strongholds, especially the fort of Ahmadnagar. In gratitude for this great favour and beneficence, placing the head of supplication on the throne of

---

598 Apparently it should bo Bhim; see *infra*. Gadeha is probably Gadhī in Khandesh; see Lethbridge's "Golden Book of India," p. 138. It is the Garvī of I.G., v, 33, and is one of the Bhīl States in the Dāng Tract.

that God who requires no return, I opened my lips in thankfulness, and, humbling myself, ordered them to beat the drums of rejoicing. Thanks be to Allah that a territory that had passed out of hand has come back into the possession of the servants of the victorious State, and that the seditious, who had been breathing the breath of rebellion and boasting, have turned towards supplication and weakness, and become deliverers of properties and payers of tribute. As this news reached me through Nūr-Jahān Begam, I gave her the parganah of Boda (Ṭoḍā ?),[599] the revenue of which is 200,000 rupees. Please God, when the victorious forces enter the province of the Deccan and its forts, and the mind of my excellent son Khurram is satisfied with regard to their possession, he will bring with the ambassadors such an offering from the Deccan as no other king of this age has received. It was ordered that he should bring with him the Amirs who were to receive jagirs in this Subah, in order that they might have the honour of waiting on me. They will thereafter get leave to depart, and the glorious royal standards will return with victory and rejoicing to the capital of Agra. Some days before the news of this victory reached me, I took one night an augury from the diwan of Khwāja Ḥāfiẓ as to what would be the end of this affair, and this ode turned up—

"The day of absence and night of parting from the friend are o'er.
I took this augury; the star passed and fulfilment came."[600]

When the secret tongue (*lisānu-l-ghaib*) of Ḥāfiẓ showed such an ending it gave me a strong hope, and accordingly, after

---

599. There was a Bodah in Sarkār Marosor in Malwa, but its revenue was only 2 $\frac{1}{2}$ lakhs of dams (Jarrett, ii, 208). The two I.O. MSS. and Debi Prasad's Hindi version have Ṭoḍā. Ṭoḍā was in Ajmir, Rantambhor Sarkar, and its revenue in Akbar's time was 1 $\frac{1}{2}$ lakhs of rupees (Jarrett, ii, 275).

600. Ode 192 of Brockhaus' edition, p. 112, first couplet.

twenty-five days, the news of victory arrived. In many of my desires I have resorted to the Khwāja's diwan, and (generally) the result has coincided with what I found there. It is seldom that the opposite has happened.

On the same day I added 1,000 horse to the mansab of Āṣaf Khān, and raised it to that of 5,000 personal and horse. At the end of the day I went with the ladies to look round the building of the Haft Manẓar[601] (seven storeys), and at the beginning of the evening returned to the palace. This building was founded by a former ruler of Malwa, Sulṭān Maḥmūd Khaljī. It has seven storeys, and in each storey there are four chambers (*ṣuffa*) containing four windows. The height of this tower (*mīnār*) is 54 1/2 cubits, and its circumference 50 yards (*gaz*). There are 171 steps from the ground to the seventh storey. In going and returning I scattered 1,400 rupees.[602]

On the 31st I honoured Sayyid 'Abdu-llah with the title of Saif Khān, and having exalted him with a dress of honour, a horse, an elephant, and a jewelled dagger, gave him leave and sent him to do duty with my son of lofty fortune. I also sent by him a ruby of the value of more than 30,000 rupees for my son. I did not regard its value, but as for a long time I used to bind it on my own head, I sent it him by way of good augury, considering it lucky for him. I appointed Sulṭān Maḥmūd, a son-in-law of Khwāja Abū-l-ḥasan bakhshi, to be bakhshi and news-writer of the Subah of Behar, and when he took leave I gave him an elephant. At the end of the day of Thursday, 5th Amurdād, I went with the ladies to see the Nīl-kunḍ, which is one of the

601 This is the building described by William Finch. See the Journal of John Jourdain, ed. by Foster for the Hakluyt Society, App. D. Finch speaks of a high turret 170 steps high. The tower was the Tower of Victory erected by Sulṭan Maḥmūd I in 1443 to commemorate a victory over the Raja of Chitor. "The stump of it has been found." Jourdain speaks of six storeys. It was built of green stone like marble.

602 Two hundred rupees per storey (?).

most[603] pleasant places in the fort of Mandu (Māṇḍogaṛh). Shāh-budāgh Khān, who was one of my revered father's most considerable Amirs, at the time when he held this province in jagir, built in this place an exceedingly pleasing and enjoyable building. Delaying there till two or three gharis of night had passed I returned to the auspicious palace.

As several indiscretions on the part of Mukhliṣ Khān, diwan and bakhshi of the Subah of Bengal, had come to my ears, I reduced his mansab by 1,000 personal and 200 horse. On the 7th a war (*mastī*) elephant from among those sent as offerings by 'Ādil Khān, by name Gaj-rāj, was sent to Rānā Amr Singh. On the 11th, I went out to hunt, and came one stage from the fort. There was excessive rain, and the mud was such that there was hardly any moving. For the convenience of the people and the comfort of the animals I gave up this undertaking, and passing the day of Thursday outside, returned on Friday eve. On the same day Hidāyatu-llah, who is very well suited to carry out the rules and movements (in travelling) of the headquarters (lit. presence), was honoured with the title of Fidā'ī Khān. In this rainy season rain fell in such quantities that old men said that they did not remember such rain in any age. For nearly forty days there was nothing but cloud and rain, so that the sun only appeared occasionally. There was so much wind that many buildings, both old and new, fell down. On the first night there was[604] such rain and thunder and lightning as has seldom been heard of. Nearly twenty women and men were killed, and the foundations even of some of the stone buildings were broken up. No noise is more terrifying than this. Till the middle of the month was passed, wind and rain increased. After this they gradually became less. What can be written of the verdure and self-grown fragrant plants? They covered valley and plain and

---

603 Blochmann, p. 371, and Ma'āṣiru-l-umarā, ii, 537. Now locally called the Nil-kanth, ' blue neck.

604 The text misses out a conjunction before *ṣadā*.

hill and desert. It is not known if in the inhabited world there exists another such place as Mandu for sweetness of air and for the pleasantness of the locality and the neighbourhood, especially in the rainy season. In this season, which lasts for months and extends up to the hot weather, one cannot sleep inside houses without coverlets, and in the day the temperature is such that there is no need for a fan or for change of place. All that could be written would still fall short of the many beauties of the place. I saw two things that I had not seen in any other place in Hindustan. One was the tree of the wild plantain that grows in most of the uncultivated places in the fort, and the other the nest of the wagtail (*mamūla*), which they call in Persian the *dum-sīcha* (tail-wagger). Up till now none of the hunters had pointed out its nest. By chance in the building I occupied there was its nest, and it brought out two young ones.

Three watches of day had passed on Thursday, the 19th, when I mounted with the ladies in order to go round and see the courts and buildings on the Shakkar tank, founded by former rulers of Malwa. As an elephant had not been conferred on I'timādu-d-daulah on account of his government of the Panjab, I gave him on the road one of my private elephants of the name of Jagjot. I remained in this enchanting place until the evening, and was much delighted with the pleasantness and greenness of the surrounding open spaces. After performing my evening prayer and counting my rosary, we returned to our fixed residence. On Friday an elephant named Ran-bādal (cloud of war ?), which Jahāngīr Qulī Khān had sent as an offering, was brought before me. Having adopted for myself certain special cloths and cloth-stuffs, I gave an order that no one should wear the same but he on whom I might bestow them. One was a *nādirī* coat that they wear over the *qabā* (a kind of outer vest). Its length is from the waist down to below the thighs, and it has no sleeves. It is fastened in front with buttons, and the people of Persia call it *kurdī* (from the country of the Kurds). I gave it the name of nadiri. Another garment is a ṭ̤ūs shawl, which my revered father had adopted as a dress. The next was a coat (qaba) with a folded collar (*batū girībān*). The ends of the sleeves were embroidered. He had also appropriated this to himself. Another was a qaba with a border, from which the fringes of cloth were cut off and sewn round the skirt and collar and the ends of the sleeve. Another was a qaba of Gujarati satin, and another a *chīra* and waistbelt woven with silk, in which were interwoven gold and silver threads.

As the monthly pay of some of Mahābat Khān's horsemen, according to the regulation of three and two horsed men, for the performance of duty in the Deccan, had become increased and the service[605] had not been performed, I gave an order that the civil officers (*dīwāniyān*) should levy the difference from his jagir. In the end of Thursday, the 26th, corresponding with the 14th Sha'bān, which is the Shab-i-barāt, I held a meeting in one of the houses of the palace of Nūr-Jahān Begam, which was situated in the midst of large tanks, and summoning the Amirs and courtiers to the feast which had been prepared by the Begam, I ordered them to give the people cups and all kinds of intoxicating drinks according to the desire of each. Many asked for cups, and I ordered that whoever drank a cup should sit according to his mansab and condition. All sorts of roast meats, and fruits by way of relish, were ordered to be placed before everyone. It was a wonderful assembly. In the beginning of the evening they lighted lanterns and lamps all round the tanks and buildings, and a lighting up was carried out the like of which has perhaps never been arranged in any place. The lanterns and lamps cast their reflection on the water, and it appeared as if the whole surface of the tank was a plain of fire. A grand entertainment took place, and the drinkers of cups took more cups than they could carry.

---

[605] Apparently the meaning is that the standard of two and three horses had not been kept up.

"A feast was arranged that lighted up the heart,
It was of such beauty as the heart desired.
They flung over this verdant mead
A carpet broad as the field of genius.
From abundance of perfume the feast spread far,
The heavens were a musk-bag by reason of incense,
The delicate ones of the garden (the flowers) became glorious,
The face of each was lighted up like a lamp."[606]

After three of four gharis of night had passed, I dismissed the men and summoned the ladies, and till a watch of night (remained?) passed the time in this delightful place, and enjoyed myself. On this day of Thursday several special things had happened. One was that it was the day of my ascension of the throne; secondly, it was the Shab-i-barāt; thirdly, it was the day of the *rākhī,* which has already been described, and with the Hindus is a special day. On account of these three pieces of good fortune I called the day Mubārak-shamba.

On the 27th, Sayyid Kāsū was dignified with the title of Parwarish Khān. Wednesday, in the same way that Mubārak-shamba had been a fortunate one for me, had fallen out exactly the opposite. On this account I gave this evil day the name of Kam-shamba, in order that this day might always fail from the world (lessen). On the next day a jewelled dagger was conferred on Yādgār Qūrchī, and I ordered that after this he should be styled Yādgār Beg. I had sent for Jay Singh, son of Rāja Mahā Singh. On this day he waited on me and presented an elephant as an offering. A watch and three gharis of Mubārak-shamba, the 2nd of Shahriyār, had passed, when I rode to look round the Nīl-kund and its neighbourhood; thence I passed on to the plain of the 'Īd-gāh on the top of a mound that was very green and pleasant. Champa flowers and other sweet wild herbs of that plain had bloomed to such a degree that on all sides on which

606 Some lines of this agree with the verses in the Akbar-nāma, ii, 190. The last two lines are quoted again in the account of the 15th year (p. 299 of Persian text).

the eye fell the world looked like a world of greenery and flowers. I entered the palace when a watch of night had passed.

As it had been several times mentioned to me that a kind of sweetmeat was obtained from the wild plantain such that dervishes and other poor people made it their food. I wished to enquire into the .matter. What I found was that the fruit of the wild plantain was an exceedingly hard and tasteless thing. The real fact is that in the lower part (of the trunk) there is a thing shaped like a fir - cone from which the real fruit of the plantain comes out. On this a kind of sweetmeat forms which has exactly the juiciness and taste of *pālūda*. It appears that men eat this and enjoy it.[607]

With regard to carrier pigeons (*kabūtar-i-nāma-bar*), it had been stated to me in the course of conversation that in the time of the Abbaside Caliphs they taught[608] the Baghdad pigeons who were styled 'letter-carriers' (*nāma-bar*), and were one-half larger[609] than the wild pigeon. I bade the pigeon-fanciers to teach their pigeons, and they taught some of them in such a manner that we let them fly from Mandu in the early morning, and if there was much rain they reached Burhanpur by 2 $\frac{1}{2}$ pahars (watches) of the day, or even in 1 $\frac{1}{2}$ pahars. If the air was very

---

607 The account is obscure. Elliot's translation is "In the root of the tree is found a lump of sweet substance which is exactly like that of Faluda. It is eaten by the poor." The text and some MSS. have *yak pārcha-i-shīrīnī,* but B.M. Or. 3276 has *yak pāra*. Roxburgh says nothing about any such growth on the wild plantain. *Fālūda* or *pālūda* is the name of a sweetmeat.

608 It is curious that the word *amūkhta*, 'taught,' in the text, and which appears to be almost necessary for the sense, does not occur either in the two I.O. MSS. or in the R.A.S. one. Burhanpur is about 100 miles as the crow flies south-south-east of Mandu.

609 The text has *par*,'feathers,' instead of the sign of the comparative *tar*, but the MSS. have *kalāntar.*

clear most of them arrived by one pahar of the day and some by four gharis (hours) of the day.

On the 3rd a letter came from Bābā Khurram, announcing the coming of Afẓal Khān and Rāy Rāyān and the arrival of the ambassadors of, Ādil Khān, and their bringing suitable offerings of jewels, jewelled things, elephants, and horses, offerings such as had never come in any reign or time, and expressing much gratitude for the services and loyalty of the aforesaid Khān, and his faithfulness to his word and duty. He asked for a gracious royal firman bestowing on him the title of *farzand* (son) and for other favours, which had never yet been vouchsafed in his honour. Since it was very gratifying to me to please my son, and his request was reasonable, I ordered that the Munshis of the mercurial pen should write a farman in the name of 'Ādil Khān, conveying every kind of affection and favour, and exceeding in his praise ten or twelve times what had been previously written. They were ordered in these farmans to address him as farzand. In the body of the farman I wrote this couplet with my own hand—

"Thou'st become, at Shāh Khurram's request,
Renowned in the world as my son" (*farzandī*).

On the 4th day this farman was sent off with its copy, so that my son Shāh Khurram might see the copy and send off the original. On Mubārak-shamba, the 9th, I went with the ladies to the house of Āṣaf Khān. His house was situated in the valley, and was exceedingly pleasant and bright. It had several valleys round it; in some places there were flowing waterfalls, and mango and other trees exceedingly green and pleasant and shady. Nearly 200 or 300 *keora* shrubs (*gul-i-keoṛā, Pandanus odoratissimus*) grew in one valley. In fine that day passed in great enjoyment. A wine party was held and cups were presented to the Amirs and intimates, and an offering from Āṣaf Khān was laid before me. There were many rare things. I took whatever I approved, and the remainder was given to him. On the same day Khwāja Mīr, son of Sulṯān Khwāja, who had come on a summons from Bangash, waited on me, and presented as an offering a ruby, two pearls, and an elephant. Rāja Bhīm Narāyan, a zamindar of the province of Gadeha, was promoted to the mansab of 1,000 personal and 500 horse. An order was given that a jagir should be provided him out of his native country. On the 12th a letter came from my son Khurram that Rāja Sūraj Mal, son of Rāja Bāso, whose territory is near the fort of Kangra, had promised that in the course of a year he would bring that fort into the possession of the servants of the victorious State. He also sent his letter which covenanted for this. I ordered that after comprehending his desires and wishes, and satisfying himself with regard to them, he should send off the Raja to wait on me, so that he might set about the said duty. On the same day, which was Monday, the 11th, corresponding with the 1st Ramaẕān (2nd September, 1617), after four gharis and seven pals had passed, a daughter was born to my son by the mother of his other children, who was the daughter of Āṣaf Khān. This child was named Rūshan-ārā Begam. As the Zamindar of Jaitpūr, which is in the jurisdiction[610] of Mandu, in consequence of wickedness had not had the felicity of kissing the threshold, I ordered Fidā'ī Khān to proceed against him with some mansabdars and 400 or 500 musketeers and plunder his country. On the 13th one elephant was given to Fidā'ī Khān and one to Mīr Qāsim, son of Sayyid Murād. On the 16th Jay Singh, son of Rāja Mahā Singh, who was 12 years old, was promoted to the mansab of 1,000 personal and horse. To Mīr Mīrān, son of Mīr Khalīlu-llah, I gave an elephant which I had myself approved, and another to Mullā

---

[610] The word is *ḥawālī,* which is sometimes translated 'neighbourhood,' and has been so translated here by Mr. Rogers. But either Jahāngīr has made a mistake or the word *ḥawālī* is capable of a wide interpretation, for Jaitpūr appears to be Jaitpūr in Kathiawar. See Jarrett, ii, 258, and I.G., vii, 192. Possibly Mandu is a mistake for Bāndhū. But there is a Jetgarh in Malwa (Jarrett, ii, 200).

'Abdu-s-Sattār.[611] Bhoj, son of Rāja Bikramājīt Bhadauriyā, after his father's death, came from the Deccan and waited on me, and presented 100 muhrs as an offering. On the 17th it was represented that Rāja Kalyān had come from the province of Orissa, and proposed to kiss my threshold. As some unpleasant stories had been told with regard to him, an order was given that they should hand him over with his son to Āṣaf Khān to enquire into the truth of what had been said about him. On the 19th an elephant was given to Jay Singh. On the 20th 200 horses were added to the mansab of Kesho Dās Mārū, so that it came, original and increase, to 2,000 personal and 1,200 horse. On the 23rd, having distinguished Allah-dād, the Afghan, with the title of Rashīd Khān, I gave him a *parm-narm* (shawl). The offering of Rāja Kalyān Singh, consisting of eighteen elephants, was brought before me; sixteen elephants were included in my private elephant stud, and I presented him with two. As the news had arrived from Iraq of the death of the mother of Mīr Mīrān, daughter of Shāh Isma'īl II, of the race of the Ṣafawī kings, I sent him a dress of honour and brought him out of the robes of mourning. On the 25th Fidā'ī Khān received a dress of honour, and, in company with his brother Rūḥu-llah and other mansabdars, obtained leave to go to punish the Zamindar of Jaitpur. On the 28th, having come down from the fort with the intention of seeing the Narbada and to hunt in its neighbourhood, I took the ladies with me, and halted two stages down on the bank of the river. As there were many mosquitoes and fleas, I did not stay more than one night. Having come the next day to Tārāpūr, I returned on Friday, the 31st. On the 1st of the month of Mihr, Muḥsin Khwāja, who at this time had come from Transoxiana, received a dress of honour and 5,000 rupees. On the 2nd, after enquiry into the matters of Rāja Kalyān, with regard to which a report had been received, and which Āsaf Khan had been appointed to investigate, as he appeared

[611] Probably this was the author who collaborated with Jerome Xavier. See Rieu's Catalogue, iii, 1077.

innocent, he enjoyed the good fortune to kiss the threshold, and presented as an offering 100 muhrs and 1,000 rupees. His offering of a string of pearls, consisting of eighty pearls and two rubies, with a bracelet with a ruby and two pearls, and the golden figure of a horse studded with jewels, was laid before me. A petition from Fidā'ī Khān arrived stating that when the victorious army entered the province of Jaitpur the zamindar had elected to run away. He could not oppose Fidā'ī, and his country was ravaged. He now repented of what he had done, and intended to come to the Court, which was the asylum of the world, and proffer service and obedience. A force with Rūḥu-llah was sent in pursuit of him to capture and bring him to Court, or to lay waste and ruin his domain and imprison his women and dependants, who had gone into the country of the neighbouring zamindars. On the 8th Khwāja Niẓām came and laid before me fourteen pomegranates from the port of Mukhā (Mocha), which they had brought to Surat in the space of fourteen days, and in eight days more to Mandu. The size of these was the same as that of the Thatta pomegranates. Though the pomegranates of Thatta are seedless and these have seeds,[612] yet they are delicate, and in freshness excel those of Thatta. On the 9th news came that while Rūḥu-llah was passing through the villages, he came to know that the women and dependants of the Jaitpūrī zamindar were in a certain village. He remained outside, and sent men into the village to make enquiries and to bring out the persons who were there. Whilst he was making enquiries, one of the devoted servants of the zamindar came along with the villagers. Whilst his men were scattered here and there, and Rūḥu-llah with some servants had brought out his furniture and was sitting on a carpet, that devoted servant came behind him and struck him with a spear; the blow was fatal and the spearhead came out at his breast. The pulling out of the spear

[612] I.O. MS. 305 has *dāna-ī-nāzikī*, 'soft (or small) seeds.'

and the reverting[613] to his original (dying) of Rūḥu-llah took place together. Those who were present sent that wretch to hell. All the men who had been scattered about put on their armour and attacked the village. Those doomed men (*k͟hūn-giriftahā*) had the disgrace of harbouring[614] rebels and sedition-mongers, and were killed in the course of an astronomical hour. They brought into captivity their wives and daughters, and, setting fire to the village, made it so that nothing was seen but heaps of ashes. They then lifted up the body of Rūḥu-llah and went and joined Fidā'ī K͟hān. With regard to the bravery and zeal of Rūḥu-llah, there was no dispute; at the most, his carelessness brought about this turn of fortune. No traces of habitation remained in that region; the zamindar of that place went into the hills and jungles and concealed and obliterated himself. He then sent someone to Fidā'ī K͟hān and begged for pardon for his offences. An order was given that he should be allowed quarter and brought to Court.

The mansab of Muruwwat K͟hān was fixed, original and increase, at 2,000 personal and 1,500 horse, on condition that he should destroy Harbhān,[615] Zamindar of Chandra-koṭa, from whom travellers endured great annoyance. On the 13th Rāja Sūraj Mal, together with Taqī, the bakhshi who was in attendance on Bābā K͟hurram, came and waited on me. He represented all his requirements. His engagement to perform the work was approved, and at the request of my son he was honoured with a standard and drums. To Taqī, who had been appointed with him, a jewelled *khapwa* (dagger) was given, and

---

613 Note 181 has *wāṣil gas͟htan*, 'becoming united '(to the Deity).

614 *Jā dādan*, 'to give way,' the meaning apparently being that they had protected Rūḥu-llah's murderers. But I.O. MS. 305 seems to have *jāwidān*, 'eternal,' which would mean that they were killed and also eternally disgraced as rebels. The Ma'āṣiru-l-umarā, iii, 13, has a different account of the manner of Rūḥu-llah's death. He was Fīdā'ī's elder brother.

615 The I.O. MSS. have Pīr Bahār and Chandra Kona, which latter may be the place in Midnapur.

it was arranged that he should finish his own affairs and start off quickly. The mansab of Khwāja 'Alī Beg Mīrzā, who had been appointed to the defence and administration of Ahmadnagar, was fixed at 5,000 personal and horse. An elephant apiece was given to Nūru-d-dīn Qulī, Khwājagī Ṭāhir, Sayyid Khān Muḥammad, Murtaẓā Khān, and Walī Beg. On the 17th the mansab of Ḥākim Beg was fixed, original and increase, at 1,000 personal and 200 horse. On the same day, after presenting Rāja Sūraj Mal with a dress of honour, an elephant, and a jewelled khapwa, and Taqī with a dress of honour, I gave them leave to proceed on duty to Kangra. When those who had been sent by my son of lofty fortune, Shāh Khurram, with the ambassadors of 'Ādil Khān and his offerings, arrived at Burhanpur, and my son's mind was completely satisfied with regard to the affairs of the Deccan, he prayed for the Subahdarship of Berar, Khandesh, and Ahmadnagar for the Commander-in-Chief, the Khankhanan, and sent his son Shāh-nawāz Khān, who is really Khankhanan junior, with 12,000 cavalry to hold possession of the conquered provinces. Every place and estate were put as jagirs into the hands of reliable men, and fitting arrangements were made for the government of the province. He left, out of the troops that were with him, 30,000 horse and 7,000 musketeer infantry, and took with him the remainder, amounting to 25,000 horse and 2,000 gunners, and set off to wait on me. On Thursday (Mubārak-shamba), the 20th[616] of the month of Mihr (Divine month), in the twelfth year from my accession, corresponding with the 11th Shawwāl, 1026 Hijra (12th October, 1617), after three watches and one ghari had passed, he entered the fort of Mandu auspiciously and joyfully, and had the honour of waiting on me. The duration of our separation was 11[617] months and 11

[616] Text 8th, but should be 20th. See p. 196, where the next Thursday is mentioned as the 27th. See Elliot, vi, 351.

[617] Text 15 months and 11 days, but it should be 11 months. Shāh Jahān left his father at Ajmir on the last day of Shawwāl, 1025, and he rejoined him on 11th Shawwāl of the following year.

days. After he had performed the dues of salutation and kissing the ground, I called him up into the jharokha, and with exceeding kindness and uncontrolled delight rose from my place and held him in the embrace of affection. In proportion as he strove to be humble and polite, I increased my favours and kindness to him and made him sit near me. He presented 1,000 ashrafis and 1,000 rupees as *nazar* and the same amount by way of alms. As the time did not allow of his presenting all his offerings, he now brought before me the elephant Sarnāk (?) (snake-head?), that was the chief of the elephants of 'Ādil K͟hān's offering, with a casket of precious stones. After this the bakhshis were ordered to arrange according to their mansabs the Amirs who had come with my son to pay their respects. The first who had the honour of audience was K͟hān Jahān. Sending for him above. I selected him for the honour of kissing my feet. He presented 1,000 muhrs and 1,000 rupees as nazr, and a casket filled with jewels and jewelled things as an offering (*pīs͟h-kas͟h*). What was accepted of his offering was worth 45,000 rupees. After this 'Abdu-llah K͟hān kissed the threshold, and presented 100 muhrs as nazr. Then Mahābat K͟hān had the honour of kissing the ground, and presented an offering of 100 muhrs and 1,000 rupees, with a parcel (*gaṭhṛī*)[618] of precious stones and jewelled vessels, the value of which was 124,000 rupees. Of these one ruby weighed 11 miskals; an European brought it last year to sell at Ajmir, and priced it at 200,000 rupees, but the jewellers valued it at 80,000 rupees. Consequently the bargain did not come off, and it was returned to him and he took it away. When he came to Burhanpur, Mahābat K͟hān bought it from him for 100,000 rupees. After this Rāja Bhāo Singh waited on me, presenting 1,000 rupees as nazr and some jewels and jewelled things as a *pīs͟h-kas͟h*. In the same manner Dārāb K͟hān, son of the Khan-khanan, Sardār K͟hān, brother of 'Abdu-llah K͟hān, S͟hajā'at K͟hān the Arab, Dayānat K͟hān, S͟hāh-bāz K͟hān, Mu'tamad K͟hān

---

[618] So in text, but I.O. MSS. have *kursī*, 'a chair or stool' (1.37).

bakhshi, Ūdā Rām,[619] who was one of the chief Amirs of Niẓāmu-l-mulk, and who came on the promise of my son Shāh Khurram and joined the ranks of the loyal, waited on me in the order of their mansabs. After this the Wakils of 'Ādil Khān had the honour of kissing the ground, and presented a letter from him. Before this, as a reward for the conquest of the Rānā, a mansab of 20,000 personal and 10,000 horse was conferred on my son of lofty fortune. When he had hastened to the capture of the Deccan he had obtained the title of Shah, and now, in reward for this distinguished service, I gave him a mansab of 30,000 personal and 20,000 horse, and bestowed on him the title of Shāh Jahān. An order was given that henceforth they should place a chair in the paradise-resembling assemblies near my throne for my son to sit upon. This was a special favour for my son, as it had never been the custom heretofore. A special dress of honour with a gold-embroidered *chārqab,* with collar, the end of the sleeves and the skirt decorated with pearls, worth 50,000 rupees, a jewelled sword with a jewelled *pardala* (belt), and a jewelled dagger were bestowed upon him. In his honour I myself came down from the jharokha and poured over his head a small tray of jewels and a tray of gold (coins).[620] Having called Sarnāk elephant to me, I saw without doubt that what had been heard in its praise and of its beauty was real. It stood all the tests in size, form, and beauty. Few elephants are to be seen of such beauty. As it appeared acceptable to me, I myself mounted (i.e. drove it) and took it into my private palace, and scattered a quantity of gold coins on its head, and ordered them to tie it up inside the royal palace. With regard to this I gave it the name of Nūr-bakht[621] (light of fortune). On Friday, the 24th, Rāja Bharjīv, Zamindar of Baglāṇa, came and waited on me. His name is Partāp; every Raja there has been of that place they call Bharjīv. He has about 1,500 horse in his pay (*mawājib-khwār*), and in time

[619] Text *būdand,* but Ūdā Rām is the only Dakhani officer mentioned.

[620] The MSS. have *zar-baft,* 'gold brocade.'

[621] In reference to his own name of Nūru-d-dīn.

of need he can bring into the field 3,000 horse. The province of Baglāṇa lies between Gujarat, Khandesh, and the Deccan. It has two strong forts, Sāler and Māler (Muler), and as Māler is in the midst of a populous country he lives there himself. The country of Baglāṇa has pleasant springs and running waters. The mangoes of that region are very sweet and large, and are gathered for nine months from the beginning of immaturity[622] until the end. It has many grapes, but not of the best kinds. The aforesaid Raja does not drop the thread of caution and prudence in dealing with the rulers of Gujarat, the Deccan, and Khandesh. He has never gone himself to see any of them, and if any of them has wished to stretch out his hand to possess his kingdom, he has remained undisturbed through the support of the others. After the provinces of Gujarat, the Deccan, and Khandesh came into the possession of the late king (Akbar), Bharjīv came to Burhanpur and had the honour of kissing his feet, and after being enrolled among his servants was raised to the mansab of 3,000. At this time, when Shāh Jahān went to Burhanpur, he brought eleven elephants as an offering. He came to Court in attendance on my son, and in accordance with his friendship and service was dignified with royal favours, and had presented to him a jewelled sword, an elephant, a horse, and dress of honour. After some days I conferred on him three rings of jacinth (*yāqūt*), diamond, and ruby. On Mubārak-shamba (Thursday), the 27th, Nūr-Jahān Begam prepared a feast of victory for my son Shāh Jahān, and conferred on him dresses of honour of great price, with a *nādirī* with embroidered flowers, adorned with rare pearls, a *sarpīch* (turban ornament) decorated with rare gems, a turban with a fringe of pearls, a waistbelt studded with pearls, a sword with jewelled *pardala* (belt), a *phūl kaṭāra* (dagger), a *sada* (?) of pearls, with two horses, one of which had a jewelled saddle, and a special elephant with two females. In the same way she gave his children and his ladies dresses of

[622] *Ghūragī*, 'u nripeness.'

honour, *tūquz* (nine pieces) of cloth with all sorts of gold ornaments, and to his chief servants as presents a horse, a dress of honour, and a jewelled dagger. The cost of this entertainment was about 300,000 rupees. Presenting on the same day a horse and dress of honour to 'Abdu-llah Khān and Sardār Khān, his brother, I gave them leave to go to the Sarkar of Kalpi, which had been given them in jagir, and also dismissed Shajā'at Khān to his jagir, which was in the Subah of Gujarat, with a dress of honour and an elephant. I dismissed Sayyid Ḥājī, who was a jagirdar of Behar, with a gift of a horse.

It was frequently reported to me that Khān Daurān had become old and weak, so as to be unfit for active duty, and the Subahs of Kabul and Bangash is a land of disturbance, and to subdue the Afghans required riding and active movement. Inasmuch as caution is the condition of rule, I appointed Mahābat Khān, Subahdar of Kabul and Bangash, giving him a dress of honour, and promoted Khān Daurān to the governorship of the province of Thatta. Ibrāhīm Khān Fatḥ-jang had sent as an offering from Behar forty-nine elephants; these were submitted to me. On this day they brought some *sōna-kela* (golden plantains, bananas) for me. I had never eaten such plantains before. In size they are one finger, and are very sweet and of good flavour; they have no resemblance to plantains of other descriptions, but are somewhat indigestible, so that from the two that I ate I experienced heaviness, whilst others say they can eat as many as seven or eight. Though plantains are really unfit to eat, yet of all the kinds this is the one fit to eat. This year, up to the 23rd of the month of Mihr, Muqarrab Khān sent Gujarat mangoes by post (*ḍāk-chaukī*).

On this date I heard that Muḥammad Rizā, ambassador of my brother Shāh 'Abbās, gave up the deposit of his life at Agra through the disease of *ishāl* (diarrhœa). I made the merchant Muḥammad Qāsim, who had come from my brother, his executor, and ordered that according to the will he should convey his goods and chattels to the Shah, so that he might grant them in his own presence to the heirs of the deceased. Elephants and dresses of honour were conferred on Sayyid Kabīr and Bakhtar Khān, Wakils of 'Ādil Khān. On Mubārak-shamba, the 13th Ābān, Jahāngīr Qulī Beg, Turkmān, who is dignified with the title of Jān-sipār Khān, came from the Deccan and waited on me. His father was included among the Amirs of Iran. He had come from Persia in the time of the late king Akbar, and having a mansab conferred on him was sent to the Deccan. He was brought up in that Subah. Although he had been appointed to a duty, yet as my son Shāh Jahān came at this time to pay his respects and represented his sincerity and devotion, I ordered that he should come post to Court and have the good fortune to wait upon me and then return. On this day I promoted Ūdā Rām[623] to the rank of 3,000 personal and 1,500 horse. He is a brahmin by caste, and was much relied on by 'Ambar. At the time when Shāh-nawāz Khān went against 'Ambar, Ādam Khān Ḥabshī, Jādū Rāy, Bābū Rāy Kāyath, Ūdā Rām, and some other Sardārs of Niẓāmu-l-mulk left him and came to Shāh-nawāz Khān. After 'Ambar's defeat they, by the persuasions of 'Ādil Khān and the deceit of 'Ambar, left the right road again and gave up their loyalty and service. 'Ambar took an oath on the Koran to Ādam Khān and put him off his guard, and, capturing him deceitfully, imprisoned him in the fort of Daulatabad, and at last killed him. Bābū Rāy Kāyath and Ūdā Rām came away and went to the borders of 'Ādil Khān's dominions, but he would not admit them into his territory. About that time Bābū Rāy Kāyath lost his life (lit. played away the coin of existence) by the deceit of his intimates, and 'Ambar sent a force against Ūdā Rām. He fought well and defeated 'Ambar's army. But afterwards, as he could not remain in that country, he threw himself on to the borders of the royal dominions, and, having got a promise, came with his family and dependants and entered the service of my

[623] The Ūdājī Rām of Ma'āṣiru-*l*-umarā, i, 142.

son Shāh Jahān. That son distinguished him with favours and kindnesses of all sorts, and made him hopeful by giving him a mansab of 3,000 personal and 1,000 horse, and brought him to Court. As he was a useful servant, I increased this by 500 horse. I also increased the mansab of Shāh-bāz Khān, who had one of 2,000 personal and 1,500 horse, by 500 more horse, and gave him the faujdarship of the Sarkar of Sārangpūr and a part of the Subah of Malwa. A special horse and elephant were given to Khān Jahān. On Mubārak-shamba (Thursday), the 10th of the month, my son Shāh Jahān produced his own offerings—jewels and jewelled things and fine cloths and other rare things. These were all laid out in the courtyard of the jharokha, and arranged together with the horses and elephants adorned with gold and silver trappings. In order to please him I came down from the jharokha and looked through them in detail. Among all these there was a fine ruby they had bought for my son at the port of Goa for 200,000 rupees; its weight was $19\frac{1}{2}$ tanks, or 17 miskals, and $5\frac{1}{2}$ surkhs. There was no ruby in my establishment over 12 tanks, and the jewellers agreed to this valuation. Another was a sapphire, among the offerings of 'Ādil Khān; it weighed 6 tanks and 7 surkhs and was valued at 100,000 rupees. I never before saw a sapphire of such a size and good colour. Another was the Chamkora diamond, also of 'Ādil Khān's; its weight was 1 tank and 6 surkhs, which they valued at 40,000 rupees. The name of Chamkoṛa is derived from this, that there is in the Deccan a plant called *sāg-i-chamkoṛa.*[624] At the time when Murtaẓā Niz̤āmu-l-mulk conquered Berar he had gone one day with his ladies round to look at the garden, when one of the women found the diamond in a chamkora vegetable, and took it to Niz̤āmu-l-mulk. From that day it became known as the

[624] *Jamkūra* is given in Forbes as the Dakhani word for a covering made of reeds or palm-leaves and used in rainy weather.

Chamkora diamond, and came into the possession of the present Ibrāhīm 'Ādil Khān during the interregnum (*fatarāt*) of Ahmadnagar. Another was an emerald, also among 'Ādil Khān's offerings. Although it is from a new mine, it is of such a beautiful colour and delicacy as I have never before seen. Again, there were two pearls, one of the weight of 64 surkhs, or 2 miskals and 11 surkhs, and it was valued at 25,000 rupees. The other weighed 16 surkhs, and was of exceeding roundness and fineness. It was valued at 12,000 rupees. Another was a diamond from the offerings of Quṭbu-l-mull, in weight 1 tank, and valued at 30,000 rupees. There were 150 elephants, out of which three had gold trappings, chains, etc., and nine had silver trappings. Though twenty[625] elephants were put into my private stud, five were very large and celebrated. The first, Nūr-bakht, which my son presented on the day of meeting, was worth 125,000 rupees. The second, Mahīpati,[626] from the offerings of 'Ādil Khān, was valued at 100,000 rupees; I gave it the name of Durjansāl. Another, also from his offerings, was Bakht-buland, and valued at 100,000 rupees; I called it Girān-bār. Another was Qaddūs Khān, and the fifth was Imām Riẓā. They were from the offerings of Quṭbu-l-mulk. Each of the two was valued at 100,000 rupees. Again, there were 100 Arab and Iraq horses, most of which were good horses. Of these, three had jewelled saddles. If the private offerings of my son and those of the rulers of the Deccan were to be written down in detail, it would be too long a business. What I accepted of his presents was worth 2,000,000 rupees. In addition to this he gave his (step-)mother,[627] Nūr-Jahān Begam, offerings worth 200,000 rupees, and 60,000 rupees to his other mothers and the Begams. Altogether my son's offerings came to 2,260,000 rupees, or 75,000 tumans of the currency of Iran or 6,780,000 current Tūrān-khānīs. Such offerings had never been made during this dynasty. I showed him much attention and

---

[625] The MS. has eight.

[626] In the MSS. the name seems to be Hansomat (swan-like ?).

[627] Text has *wālida-i-khūd*, 'his own mother.'

favour; in fact, he is a son who is worth grace and kindness. I am very pleased and satisfied with him. May God Almighty allow him to enjoy long life and prosperity!

As I had never in my life had any elephant-hunting, and had a great desire to see the province of Gujarat and to look on the salt sea, and my huntsmen had often gone and seen wild elephants and fixed on hunting-places, it occurred to me to travel through Ahmadabad and look on the sea, and having hunted elephants on my return, when it was hot and the season for hunting them, to go back to Agra. W th this intention I despatched to Agra Ḥaẓrat Maryamu-z-zamān (his mother) and the other Begams and people of the harem with the baggage and extra establishments, and betook myself to a tour in the Subah of Gujarat to hunt, with such as were indispensable with me. On thc cvc of Friday in the month of Ābān (precise date not given, but apparently the 10th), I marched auspiciously and happily from Mandu, and pitched on the bank of the tank of Nālchhā. In the morning I went out to hunt and killed a blue bull with my gun. On the eve of Saturday, Mahābat Khān was presented with a special horse and an elephant, and obtained leave to go to his Subah of Kabul and Bangash. At his request I conferred on Rashīd Khān a robe of honour, a horse, an elephant, and a jewelled dagger, and appointed him to assist him. I promoted Ibrāhīm Ḥusain to the post of bakhshi in the Deccan, and Mīrak Ḥusain to that of news-writer in the same Subah. Rāja Kalyān,[628] son of Rāja Toḍar Mal, had come from the Subah of Orissa; on account of some faults which had been attributed to him he had for some days been forbidden the honour of paying his respects. After enquiry his innocence appeared clear, and having given him a dress of honour and a horse, I appointed him to do duty together with Mahābat Khān in Bangash. On Monday I gave the Wakils of 'Ādil Khān jewelled turban fringes after the fashion of the Deccan, one of the value of 5,000 rupees and the other worth

[628] A repetition.

4,000 rupees. As Afẓal Khān and Rāy Rāyān had performed the duties of Wakils to my son Shāh Jahān in a becoming manner, I raised them both in mansab and honoured Rāy Rāyān with the title of Bikramājīt, which among Hindus is the highest title. In truth he is a servant worthy of patronage. On Saturday, the 12th, I went to hunt and shot two female nilgaw. As the hunting-ground was a long way from this halting-place, I on Monday marched $4\frac{1}{2}$ kos[629] and pitched at the village of Kaid Ḥasan. On Tuesday, the 15th, I killed three blue bulls, the larger one of which weighed 12 maunds. On this day Mīrzā Rustam escaped a great danger.[630] It seems that he had taken aim at a mark and fired his gun. Then he reloaded, and as his bullet was very flexible, he rested the gun on his chest and put the bullet between his teeth in order that he might contract it and put it right. By chance the match reached the pan, and his chest at the place where the gun was resting was burnt to the extent of the palm of the hand, and the grains of powder got into his skin and flesh and a wound was made, and he suffered much pain.[631]

On Sunday (?), the 16th,[632] four nilgaw were killed, three females and one *būkra*[633] nilgaw. On Mubārak-shamba (Thursday) I went to look round a hill valley in which there was a waterfall near the camp. At this season it had but little water,

---

[629] The MSS. have $3\frac{3}{4}$ kos.

[630] Text *khaṭa'*, 'fault,' but the MSS. show that the word is Motor is *khatar*, 'danger'.

[631] The passage is obscure, and the MSS. do not throw much light on it. Fortunately for the Mīrzā, there was no bullet in his gun. The word which I have translated by ' flexible ' is *rawān*. Perhaps the meaning is quite different. Possibly it is "he would fire a shot and then reload. As many of his bullets had been shot away, he put a pellet (*ghalulā*) into his mouth and was shaping it," etc.

[632] He has just spoken of Tuesday as the 15th ! And as Jahāngīr did not shoot on Sundays, Sunday must be a mistake for Wednesday. It is Wednesday in I.O. MS. 305.

[633] Perhaps *būkra* here means a male nilgaw; *būkra* means also a he-goat.

but as for two or three days they had dammed the watercourse and, about the time of my reaching the place, let it loose, it flowed over very well. Its height might be 20 *gaz*. It separates at the top of the hill and flows down. In this way it is a great boon (*ghanīmat*) on the road. Having enjoyed the usual cups on the edge of the stream and the shade of the hill, I came back to the camp at night. On this day the Zamindar of Jaitpur, whose offences I had forgiven at the request of my son Shāh Jahān, had the good fortune of kissing the threshold. On Friday, the 18th, a large blue bull and a bukra, and on Saturday, the 19th, two females, were killed. As my huntsmen represented that there was much game in the parganah of Ḥāṣilpūr, I left my large camp at this halting-place, and on Sunday, the 20th, and with some of my close attendants, hastened to Ḥāṣilpūr, a distance of 3 kos. Mīr Ḥusāmu-d-dīn, son of Mīr Jamālu-d-dīn Ḥusain Injū, who has the title of 'Aẓudu-d-daulah, was promoted to the mansab, original and increase, of 1,000 personal and 400 horse. I presented Yādgār Ḥusain Qūsh-begi and Yādgār Qūrchī, who had been appointed to do duty in Bangash, with an elephant each. On this day some Ḥusainī grapes without seeds arrived from Kabul; they were very fresh. The tongue of this suppliant at the throne of God fails in gratitude for the favours by which, notwithstanding a distance of three months, grapes from Kabul arrive quite fresh in the Deccan. On Monday, the 21st, three small blue bulls, on Tuesday, the 22nd, one blue bull and three cows, and on Kam-shamba (Wednesday), the 23rd, one cow, were killed. On Mubārak-shamba, the 24th, a feast of cups was held on the bank of the tank of Ḥāṣilpūr. Cups were presented to my son Shāh Jahān and some of the great Amirs and private servants. On Yusūf Khān, son of Ḥusain Khān (Tukriyah), who was of the houseborn ones worthy of patronage, was bestowed the mansab of 3,000 personal and 1,500 horse, original and increase, and he was dismissed to the faujdarship of Gonḍwāna, dignifying him with a gift of a dress of honour and an elephant. Rāy Bihārī Dās, the diwan of the Subah of the Deccan, had the good fortune to kiss the threshold. On Friday Jān-sipār Khān was exalted with a standard, presented with a horse and a dress of honour, and despatched to the Deccan. This day I made a remarkable shot with a gun. By chance there was inside the palace a *khirnī* tree (*Mimusops Kauki*). A *qurīsha*[634] (?) came and sat on a high branch, and I saw its breast in the midst of it. I fired at it and struck it in the middle of its breast; from where I stood to the top of the branch was 22 gaz. On Saturday, the 26th, marching about 2 kos, I pitched at the village of Kamālpūr. On this day I shot a blue bull.[635] Rustam Khān, who was one of the principal attendants of my son Shāh Jahān, and who had been appointed from Burhanpur with a body of the royal servants against the zamindars of Gonḍwāna, having taken a tribute of 110 elephants and 120,000 rupees, came this day to wait upon me. Zāhid, son of Shajā'at Khān, was given the mansab of 1,000 personal and 400 horse, original and increase. On Sunday, the 27th, I hunted with hawks and falcons. On Monday I killed a large blue bull and a bukra; the bull weighed 12 $\frac{1}{2}$ maunds. On Tuesday, the 29th, a blue bull was killed. Bahlūl Miyāna and Allah-yār came from service in Gonḍwāna, and had the good fortune to wait upon me. Bahlūl Khān is the son of Ḥasan Miyāna, and Miyāna is an Afghan tribe. In the commencement of his career Ḥasan was a servant of Ṣādiq Khān, but a servant who recognized the king (worthy of a king's service), and was at last included among the royal servants and died on service in the Deccan. After his death his sons were granted mansabs. He had eight sons, and two of them became famous as swordsmen. The elder brother in his youth gave up the deposit of his life. Bahlūl by degrees was promoted to the mansab of 1,000. At this time my son Shāh Jahān arrived at Burhanpur, and, finding him

---

[634] This is the same kind of bird that Nūr-Jahān is mentioned as having shot. Perhaps a green pigeon is meant.

[635] Text *nīla,* without the addition of *gaw*. The MSS. have *gor* or *chor,* a pheasant(?).

worthy of patronage, made him hopeful with a mansab of 1,500 personal and 1,000 horse. As he had not yet waited on me and was very desirous to kiss the threshold, I summoned him to Court. He is in truth a good Khāna-zāda (household-born one), inasmuch as his heart is adorned with the perfection of bravery and his exterior is not wanting in good appearance. The mansab my son Shāh Jahān had bespoken for him was granted at his request, and he was honoured with the title of Sar-buland Khān. Allah-yār Koka was also a brave youth and a servant worthy of patronage. Finding him fit and suitable for service in my presence, I sent for him to Court. On Kam-shamba (Wednesday), the 1st of the month of Āzar, I went out to hunt and shot a blue bull. On this day the Kashmir[636] reports were laid before me. One was that in the house of a certain silk-seller two girls were born with teeth, and with their backs as far as the waist joined together, but the heads, arms, and legs were separate; they lived a short time and died. On Mubārak-shamba, the 2nd, on the bank of a tank where my tents were, a feast of cups was held. Presenting Lashkar Khān with a dress of honour and an elephant, I promoted him to the duty of diwan of the Subah of the Deccan, and gave him the mansab of 2,500 personal and 1,500 horse, original and increase. To each of the Wakils of 'Ādil Khān two[637] *kaukab-i-ṭāli'* (horoscope star) muhrs, the weight of each of which was 500 ordinary muhrs, were given. I gave a horse and robe of honour to Sar-buland Khān. As fitting service and approved activity were manifest in Allah-yār Koka, I honoured him with the title of Himmat Khān and gave him a dress of honour. On Friday, the 3rd, I marched 4 1/4 kos and halted the royal standards in the parganah of Dikhtān.[638] On Saturday also I marched 4 1/4 kos and halted at the township of Dhār.

---

[636] Elliot, vi, 352.

[637] The 'two' is omitted in text.

[638] In Sarkār Māndū (Jarrett, ii, 207). Debi Prasad's Hindi version has *Daknā*.

Dhār is one of the old cities, and Rāja Bhoj, who was one of the great Rajas of Hindustan, lived in it. From his time 1,000[639] years have passed, and in the time of the Sultans of Malwa it was for a long time the capital. At the time when Sulṭān Muḥammad Tughluq was proceeding to the conquest of the Deccan, he built a fort of cut stone on the top of a ridge. Outside it is very showy and handsome, but inside the fort is devoid of buildings. I ordered them to measure its length, breadth, and height. The length inside the fort was 12 *ṭanāb,* 7 gaz; the breadth, 17 tanab, 13 gaz, and the breadth of the fort wall 19 1/2 gaz. Its height up to the battlements appeared to be 17 1/2 gaz. The length of the outer circuit (?) of the fort was 55 tanabs. 'Amīd Shāh Ghorī, who was called Dilāwar Khān, and who in the time of Sulṭān Muḥammad, son of Sultān Fīrūz, king of Delhi, had complete authority over the province of Malwa, built the Jāmi' mosque in the inhabitable part outside the fort, and opposite the gate of the mosque fixed a quadrangular iron column. When Sulṭān Bahādur of Gujarat took the province of Malwa into his own possession, he wished to transfer this column to Gujarat. The artificers did not take proper precautions when they lowered it, and it fell and broke into two pieces, one of them of 7 1/2 gaz and the other of 4 1/4 gaz. The column was 1 1/4 gaz round. As it was lying there useless, I ordered them to take the larger piece to Agra and put[640] it up in the courtyard of the mausoleum of H.M. Akbar, and to burn a lamp on the top of it at night. The aforesaid mosque has two gates. In front of the arch of one gate some sentences in prose have been carved on a stone tablet; their purport is that 'Amīd Shāh Ghorī founded this mosque in the

---

639 The MSS. have "more than 1,000." Raja Bhoj's date, according to Tod, is 567 A.D. (Jarrett, ii, 211).

640 This iron pillar is not now in existence at the mausoleum of Akbar (Note of Sayyid Ahmad). The pieces of the pillar are still lying at Dhār, outside the Lāt Musjid (I.G., new ed., xi, 295).

year 870,[641] and on the arch of the other gate a *qaṣīda* has been written, and these few couplets are from it—

"The lord of the age, the star of the sphere of glory, Centre of the people of the earth, sun of the zenith of perfection, Asylum and support of religious law, 'Amīd Shāh Dā'ūd,[642] In whose excellent qualities Ghor glories, Helper and protector of the Faith of the Prophet, Dilāwar Khān, Who has been chosen by the most mighty Lord (God), Founded the Jāmi' mosque in the city of Dhār, At a fortunate, auspicious time, on a day of happy omen.

The date of eight hundred and seven[643] had passed When the Court of hopes was completed by Fortune."

When Dilāwar Khān gave up the deposit of his life there was no king with full dominion over Hindustan, and it was a time of confusion. Hūshang, son of Dilāwar Khān, who was just and possessed of courage, seeing his opportunity, sat on the throne of sovereignty in Malwa. After his death through destiny the rule was transferred[644] to Maḥmūd Khaljī, son of Khān Jahān, who had been Vizier to Hūshang, and passed from him to his son Ghiyāṣu-d-dīn, and after him to Nāṣiru-d-dīn, son of Ghiyāsu-d-dīn, who gave his father poison and sat on the throne of infamy. From him it passed to his son Maḥmūd. Sulṭān Bahādur of Gujarat took from Maḥmūd the province of Malwa. The succession of kings of Malwa ended with the aforesaid Maḥmūd.

On Monday, the 6th, I went to hunt and shot a female nilgaw. Presenting an elephant to Mīrzā Sharafu-d-dīn Ḥusain Kāshgharī, I dismissed him to duty in the Subah of Bangash. A

---

641 The MSS. have 807, and this is correct, for Dilāwar conquered Malwa in 803 = 1400.

642 Probably this means that 'Amīd was the son of Dā'ūd.

643 Text 70, but should be 7. 807 = 1405.

644 A son of Hūshang, Muhammad Shāh, intervened.

present of a jewelled dagger, a muhr of 100 tolas, and 20,000 darbs was made to Ūdā Rām. On Tuesday, the 7th, I shot an alligator in the tank at Dhār. Though only the top of his snout was visible and the rest of his body was hidden in the water, I fired at a guess and hit him in his lungs and killed him with a single shot. An alligator is of the crocodile species and exists in most of the rivers of Hindustan, and grows very large. This one was not so very big. An alligator has been seen (by me) 8 gaz long and 1 gaz in breadth. On Sunday, marching 4 1/2 kos, I halted at Sa'dalpūr. In this village there is a stream over which Nāṣiru-d-dīn Khaljī built a bridge and erected buildings. It is a place like Kāliyāda, and both are his works. Although his building is not worthy of praise, yet as it has been built in the river-bed and they have made rivulets and reservoirs, it is somewhat remarkable. At night I ordered them to place lamps all round the canals and streams. On Mubārak-shamba (Thursday), the 9th, a feast of cups was held. On this day I made a present to my son Shāh Jahān of a ruby of one colour, weighing 9 tanks and 5 surkh, of the value of 125,000 rupees, with two pearls. This is the ruby which had been given to my father at the time of my birth by Ḥaẓrat Maryam-makānī, mother of H.M. Akbar, by way of present when my face was shown, and was for many years in his *sarpīch* (turban ornament). After him I also happily wore it in my sarpich. Apart from its value and delicacy, as it had come down as of auspicious augury to the everlasting State, it was bestowed on my son. Having raised Mubāriz Khān to a mansab of 1,500 personal and horse, I appointed him to the faujdarship of the province of Mewāt, distinguishing him with the present of a dress of honour, a sword, and an elephant. A sword was given to Himmat Khān, son of Rustam Khān. I gave Kamāl Khān, the huntsman, who is one of the old servants and is always present with me on hunting expeditions, the title of Shikār Khān (hunting-Khān). Appointing Ūdā Rām to service in the Subah of the Deccan, I conferred on him a dress of honour, an elephant, and Iraq horses (lit. wind-footed ones), and sent with him for the Commander-in-Chief, Khankhanan, the Ātāliq, a special gilt dagger (*zar-nishān*). On Friday, the 10th, I halted. On Saturday, the 11th, I marched $3\frac{3}{4}$ kos and halted at the village of Ḥalwat.[645] On Sunday, the 12th, marching 5 kos, I halted in the parganah[646] of Badnor. This parganah from the time of my father had been in the jagir of Kesho Dās Mārū,[647] and in fact had become a kind of *waṭan* (native country) to him. He had constructed gardens and buildings. Out of these one was a well (*bāolī*) (step-well probably) on the road, which appeared exceedingly pleasant and well made. It occurred to me that if a well had to be made anywhere on a roadside it should be built like this one. At least two such ought to be made.

On Monday, the 13th, I went to hunt and shot a blue bull. From the day on which the elephant Nūr-bakht was put into the special elephant stables, there was an order that he should be tied up in the public palace (court). Among animals elephants have the greatest liking for water; they delight to go into the water, notwithstanding the winter and the coldness of the air, and if there should be no water into which they can go, they will take it from a water-bag (*mashk*) with their trunks and pour it over their bodies. It occurred to me that however much an elephant delights in water, and it is suited to their temperament, yet in the winter the cold water must affect them. I accordingly ordered the water to be made lukewarm (as warm as milk) before they (the elephants) poured it into their trunks. On other days when they poured cold water over themselves they evidently shivered, but with warm water, on the contrary, they were delighted. This usage is entirely my own.

---

645 The MSS. have Jalot (as in the Hindi version).

646 Text, " the parganah aforesaid." But the MSS. have Badnor. See *infra*, p. 204 of text. (In this passage the Hindi version has *Madlor.*)

647 Blochmann, p. 502.

On Tuesday, the 14th, marching 6 kos, I halted at Sīlgaṛh (Sabalgaṛh?). On Wednesday, the 15th, crossing the Mahī River, a halt was made near Rāmgaṛh. A march of 6 kos was made on Thursday, the 16th, and a halt was made and a feast of cups held at a waterfall near the camp. Distinguishing Sar-buland Khān with a standard and giving him an elephant, I dismissed him to do duty in the Deccan. His mansab, original and increase, was fixed at 1,500 personal and 1,200 horse. Rāja Bhīm Narāyan, Zamindar of Gadeha, who had been promoted to the mansab of 1,000 horse, obtained leave to go to his jagir. Having raised Rāja Bharjīv, Zamindar of Baglāṇa, to the mansab of 4,000, I gave him leave to go to his native country, and an order was given that when he arrived there he should send to Court his eldest son, who was his successor, that he might do duty in my presence. I honoured Ḥājī Balūch, who was the chief of the huntsmen and was an active and old servant, with the title of Balūch Khān. On Friday, the 17th, marching 5 kos, I alighted at the village of Dhāvala. On Saturday, the 18th, which was the feast of Qurbān, after the Qurbān rites had been performed, marching $3\frac{1}{4}$ kos, I halted on the bank of the tank of the village of Nāgor.[648] On Sunday, the 19th, marching about 5 kos, the royal standards were erected on the bank of the tank of the village of Samriya. On Monday, the 20th, marching $4\frac{1}{4}$ kos, we alighted at the chief place of the Dohad[649] parganah. This parganah is on the boundary between Malwa and Gujarat. Until I passed Badnor the whole country was a jungle, with an abundance of trees and stony land. On Tuesday, the 21st, I halted. On Kam-shamba (Wednesday), the 22nd, marching $5\frac{1}{4}$ kos, I halted at the village of Ranyād (Renāv?). On Thursday, the 23rd, I halted and held a

[648] MSS. Bākor.

[649] Dāhūt in MSS. But Doḥad seems right, as it means two boundaries.

feast of cups on the bank of the village tank. On Friday, the 24th, marching $2\frac{1}{2}$ kos, the royal standards were hoisted at the village of Jālot. At this halt some jugglers from the Carnatic came and showed their tricks. One of them placed one end of an iron chain, $5\frac{1}{2}$ gaz in length and weighing 1 seer and 2 dams,[650] in his throat and slowly swallowed it with the aid of water. It was for a while in his stomach; after this he brought it up. On Saturday, the 25th, there was a halt. On Sunday, the 26th, marching 5 kos, I alighted at the village of Nīmdah. On Monday, the 27th, also marching 5 kos, I pitched on the bank of a tank. On Tuesday, the 28th, marching $3\frac{3}{4}$ kos, the royal standards alighted near the township of Sahrā[651] on the edge of a tank. The flower of the lotus, which in the Hindi language they call *kumudinī,* is of three colours—white, blue, and red. I had already seen the blue and white, but had never seen the red. In this tank red flowers were seen blooming. Without doubt it is an exquisite and delightful flower, as they have said—

"From redness and moistness it will melt away."[652]

The flower of the *kaṇwal*[653] is larger than the kumudini. Its flower is red. I have seen in Kashmir many kanwal with a hundred leaves (petals). It is certain that it opens during the day and becomes a bud at night. The kumudini, on the contrary, is a bud during the day and opens at night. The black bee, which the people of India call *bhauṇrā,* always sits on these flowers, and

---

650 The *dam* was also used as a weight, and was equal to 5 *tānk* or 1 *tola,* 8 *masha,* 7 *surkh* (Blochmann, p. 31).

651 Apparently Sahrā is the name of a town, and does not mean an open space here.

652 Perhaps the line refers to the bee, and means that the bee wishes to suck the moisture of the flower.

653 The MSS. have *gul-i-kūl,* 'the flower of the tank.' It seems to be a water-lily.

goes inside them to drink the juice that is in both of them. It often happens that the kanwal flower closes and the bee remains in it the whole night. In the same manner it remains in the kumudini flower. When the flower opens it comes out and flies away. As the black bee is a constant attendant on these flowers, the poets of India look on it as a lover of the flower, like the nightingale, and have put into verse sublime descriptions of it. Of these poets the chief was Tān Sen Kalāwant, who was without a rival in my father's service (in fact, there has been no singer like him in any time or age). In one of his compositions he has likened the face of a young man to the sun and the opening of his eyes to the expanding of the kanwal and the exit of the bee. In another place he has compared the side-glance of the beloved one to the motion of the kanwal when the bee alights on it.

At this place figs arrived from Ahmadabad. Although the figs of Burhanpur are sweet and well-grown, these figs are sweeter and with fewer seeds, and one may call them 5 per cent. better. On Kam-shamba, the 29th, and Mubārak-shamba, the 30th, we halted. At this stage Sar-faräz Khān came from Ahmadabad and had the good fortune to kiss the threshold. Out of his offerings a rosary of pearls, bought for 11,000 rupees, two elephants, two horses, two bullocks and a riding cart, and some pieces of Gujaratī cloth, were accepted, and the remainder presented to him. Sar-farāz Khān is a grandson of Muṣāḥib Beg, by which name he was called by Akbar after his grandfather, who was one of the Amirs of Humāyūn. In the beginning of my reign I increased his mansab and appointed him to the Subah of Gujarat. As he had an hereditary connection with the Court as a Khana-zada (one born in the house), he proved himself efficient in the Subah of Gujarat. Considering him worthy of patronage, I gave him the title of Sar-farāz Khān and raised him in the world, and his mansab has risen to 2,000 personal and 1,000 horse. On Friday, the 1st of Day, I marched 3 3/4 kos and halted on the bank of the tank of Jhasod.[654] At this stage Rāy Mān, captain of the Khidmatiya,[655] caught a *rohū* fish and brought it. As I am particularly partial to the flesh of fish, especially that of the rohu, which is the best kind of fish in Hindustan, and I had never, notwithstanding much enquiry, had one for eleven months from the time of crossing the pass of Ghātī Chand[656] until the present time, and now obtained it, I was greatly delighted. I presented a horse to Rāy Mān. Although the parganah of Dohad is reckoned as within the boundary of Gujarat, yet, in fact, it was from this stage that all things appeared different. The open plains and soil are of a different kind; the people are different and the language of another description. The jungle that appeared on the road has fruit-bearing trees, such as the mango and *khirnī* and tamarind, and the method of guarding the cultivated fields is with hedges of *zaqqūm*. The cultivators separate their fields with cactus, and leave a narrow road between them for coming and going. Since all this country has a sandy soil, when any movement takes place, so much dust rises that the faces of people are seen with difficulty, so that one should call Ahmadabad 'Gardābād'[657] (abode of dust). On Saturday, the 2nd, having marched $3\frac{3}{4}$ kos, I encamped on the bank of the Mahī. On Sunday, the 3rd, again after a march of $3\frac{3}{4}$ kos, I halted at the village of Bardala. At this stage a number of mansabdars who had been appointed to serve in Gujarat had the good fortune to kiss the threshold. Marching 5 kos on Monday, the 4th, the royal standards halted at Chitrasīmā, and the next day, Tuesday, after a march of 5 kos, in

---

654 Query "the tank of Yasodā," the foster-mother of Krishna ?

655 Blochmann, p. 252.

656 Jahāngīr crossed the Ghātī Chand or Chand, between Ajmere and Malwa, in the 11th year (see p. 172), but he does not speak of having had any rohu fish there. Perhaps the reference is to his halt at Rāmsar shortly before coming to Ghātī Chand. He got 104 rohu at Rāmsar. See p. 169.

657 Elliot, vi, 353.

parganah Mondā.[658] On this day three blue bulls were killed; one was larger than the others and weighed 13 maunds and 10 seers. On Wednesday, the 6th, I marched 6 kos and halted in parganah Naryād.[659] In passing through the town I scattered 1,500 rupees. On Thursday, the 7th, marching $6\frac{1}{2}$ kos, I halted in the parganah of Pitlād.[660] In the country of Gujarat there is no larger parganah than this; it has a revenue of 700,000 rupees, equal to 23,000 current tumans of Iraq. The population of the town (*qaṣba*), too, is dense. Whilst I passed through it I scattered 1,000 rupees. All my mind is bent upon this, that under any pretext the people of God may be benefited. As the chief way of riding among the people of this country is in carts, I also wished to travel in a cart. I sat for 2 kos in a cart, but was much troubled with the dust, and after this till the end of the stage rode on horseback. On the road Muqarrab Khān came from Ahmadabad, and had the good fortune to wait on me, and presented an offering of a pearl he had bought for 30,000 rupees. On Friday, the 8th, marching 6 1/2 kos, the place of the descent of prosperity was on the shore of the salt sea.

Cambay[661] is one of the old ports. According to the brahmins, several thousand years have passed since its foundation. In the beginning its name was Trimbāwatī, and Rāja Tryambak Kunwar had the government of the country. It would take too long to write in detail the circumstances of the aforesaid Raja as the brahmins relate it. In brief, when the turn to the government came round to Rāja Abhay Kumār,[662] who was one of his

---

658 Mondah of Jarrett, ii, 253.

659 Text Nīlāo. No such parganah is mentioned in the Āyīn; the two I.O. MSS. have Naryād.

660 Pitlād is mentioned in Bayley's Gujarat, p. 9, as having a very large revenue. It is the Patlād of Jarrett, ii, 253. Text wrongly has Nilāb. Possibly Bhīl is the parganah meant.

661 Elliot, vi, 353.

662 The I.O. MSS. have Abhay or Abhī Kār.

grandsons, by the decree of heaven a great calamity happened to this city. So much dust and earth were poured on it that all the houses and buildings were hidden, and the means of livelihood of many people was destroyed. Before the arrival of this calamity, an idol (*but*), which the Raja worshipped, came in a dream and announced this event. The Raja with his family embarked in a ship, and carried away the idol with them with a pillar it had behind it for a support. By chance the ship also was wrecked by a storm of misfortune. As there was left still a term of life for the Raja, that pillar bore the boat of his existence in safety to the shore, and he proposed to rebuild the city. He put up the pillar as a mark of repopulation and the coming together of the people. As in the Hindi language they call a pillar *istambh* and *khambh,* they called the city Istambhnagarī and Khambāwatī, and sometimes also Trimbāwatī, in connection with the Raja's name; Khambāwatī has by degrees and much use become Khambāyat (Cambay). This port is one of the largest ports[663] in Hindustan and is near a firth, which is one of the firths of the Sea of Oman. It has been estimated to be 7 kos in width, and nearly 40 kos in length. Ships cannot come inside the firth, but must cast anchor in the port of Gogā, which is a dependency[664] of Cambay and situated near the sea. Thence, putting their cargoes into *ghurābs*[665] (commonly called 'grabs') they bring them to the port of Cambay. In the same way, at the time of loading a ship they carry the cargo in ghurabs and put it in the ships. Before the arrival of the victorious host some ghurabs from European ports had come to Cambay to buy and sell, and were about to return. On Sunday, the 10th, they decorated them and showed them to me. Taking leave they went about their business. On Monday, the 11th, I myself went on board a ghurab for about a kos on the face of the water. On Tuesday, the 12th, I went out with cheetahs

---

663 Tiefenthaler, i, p. 380, etc., has an interesting notice of Cambay. He also gives a sketch of its bay (plate xxxii).

664 Now so silted up that no tolerably large vessel can approach it.

665 Abu-l-faẓl calls them *tāwarī* (Jarrett, ii, 241).

(*yūz*), and captured two[666] antelope. On Wednesday, the 13th, I went to see the tank of Tārangsar (Narangsar ?),[667] and passed through the streets and bazaar on the way, scattering nearly 5,000 rupees. In the time of H.M. Akbar (may Allah's lights be his testimony), Kalyān Rāy, the superintendent of the port, by His Majesty's order built a wall of brick and cement round the city, and many merchants came from various quarters and settled there, and built fine houses and employed themselves in gaining their livelihood under easy circumstances. Although its market is small, it is clean and full of people. In the time of the Sultans of Gujarat the customs of this port came to a large sum. Now in my reign it is ordered that they should not take more than one in forty. In other ports, calling it a tithe, they take one in ten or one in eight, and give all kinds of trouble to merchants and travellers. In Jeddah, which is the port of Mecca, they take one in four or even more. One may imagine from this what the customs of the ports of Gujarat must have come to in the time of the former rulers. God be praised that this suppliant at the throne of God obtained the grace to remit the whole of the customs dues of his dominions, which came to a countless sum, and the very name of customs (*tamghā*) has passed away from my empire. At this time an order was given that tankas[668] of gold and silver should be coined twice the weight of ordinary muhrs and rupees. The legend on the gold coin was on one side the words "Jahāngīr-shāhī, 1027" (1618), and on the reverse "Struck in Cambay in the 12th year of the reign." The legend for silver coins was on one side "Sikka, Jahāngīr-shāhī, 1027"; round it this hemistich, "King Jahāngīr of the conquering ray struck this"; and on the reverse, "Coined at Cambay in the 12th year of the reign," with this second hemistich round it—

---

666 I.O. MSS. have 'ten.'

667 *Tāl tārang*. Possibly *tārang* should read *tarang* (waves), and the meaning be that Jahāngīr went to see the famous bore in the Gulf of Cambay.

668 See Elliot, vi, 355, and note.

"When after the conquest of the Deccan he came to Gujarat from Māndū."

In no reign except mine have tankas been coined except of copper[669]; the gold and silver tankas are my invention. I ordered it to be called the Jahāngīrī coinage. On Mubārak-shamba (Thursday), the 14th, the offering of Amānat Khān, the superintendent (*mutaṣaddī*) of Cambay, was laid before me in the women's apartments. His mansab was fixed, original and increase, at 1,500 personal and 400 horse. Nūru-d-dīn Qulī was honoured with the mansab, original and increase, of 3,000 personal and 600 horse. On Friday, the 15th, mounted on the elephant Nūr-bakht, I made it run after a horse. It ran exceedingly well, and when it was stopped stood well. This is the third time that I myself have ridden it. On Saturday, the 16th, Rām Dās, son of Jay Singh, was promoted to the mansab, original and increase, of 1,500 personal and 700 horse. On Sunday, the 17th, an elephant each was given to Dārāb Khān, Amānat Khān, and Sayyid Bāyazīd Bārha. In these few days during which I was encamped on the shore of the salt sea, merchants, traders, indigent people, and other inhabitants of the port of Cambay having been summoned before me, I gave each according to his condition a dress of honour or a horse or travelling money or assistance in living. On this day, Sayyid Muḥammad, Ṣāḥib Sajjāda (Lord of the prayer carpet) of Shāh 'Ālam (a mosque near Ahmadabad), the sons of Shaikh Muḥammad Ghauṣ, Shaikh Ḥaidar, grandson of Miyān Wajīhu-d-dīn, and other Shaikhs living at Ahmadabad came to meet me and pay their respects. As my desire was to see the sea and the flow and ebb of the water, I halted for ten days, and on Tuesday, the 19th (Day, about 30th December, 1618), the royal standards started for Ahmadabad. The best description of fish procurable in this place, the name of which is *'arbīyat,*[670] was caught and

---

[669] In the text *aḥdī* occurs by mistake instead of *'ahdī*, and *man* instead of *mas.*,

[670] Or *'Arabī* (Arabian?).

frequently brought for me by the fishermen. Without doubt these fish are, as compared with other fish of this country, more delicious and better, but they are not of the flavour of the *rohū*. One might say as nine to ten or even eight to ten. Of the food which is peculiar to the people of Gujarat there is the *khichṛī* of *bājrā* (a mixture of split peas and millet boiled together); this they also call *la*z̲*ī*z̲*a*. It is a kind of split grain, which does not grow in any other country but Hindustan, and which in comparison with many other regions of India is more abundant in Gujarat; it is cheaper than most vegetables. As I had never eaten it, I ordered them to make some and bring it to me. It is not devoid of good flavour, and it suited me well. I ordered that on the days of abstinence, when I partake of dishes not made with flesh, they should frequently bring me this khichri. On the said Tuesday, having marched $6\frac{1}{4}$ kos, I halted at the village of Kosālā. On Wednesday, the 20th, I passed through the parganah of Bābrā[671] and halted on the bank of the river. This was a march of 6 kos. On Mubārak-s̲h̲amba, the 21st, I halted and held a feast of cups. In this river I caught many fish, and divided them among the servants who were present at the feast. On Friday, the 22nd, having moved on 4 kos, I pitched at the village of Bāṛīchā. On this road, walls came in sight from $2\frac{1}{2}$ to 3 *gaz* in length, and on enquiry it appeared that people had made them from the desire of spiritual reward. When a porter is tired on the road he places his burden on the wall and gains his breath a little, and lifting it up again with ease and without assistance from anyone proceeds towards his destination. This is one of the peculiar ideas of the people of Gujarat. The building of these walls pleased me greatly, and I ordered that in all large towns[672] they should make walls of this kind at the imperial expense. On Saturday, the 23rd,

---

[671] Mātar or Nātar in I.O. MSS.

[672] I.O. MS. 181 has "in all the cities of Upper India."

marching $4\frac{3}{4}$ kos, the camp was pitched at the Kānkriya tank. Quṭbu-d-dīn Muḥammad, grandson of Sulṭān Aḥmad, the founder of the city of Ahmadabad, made this tank, and placed round it steps of stone and cement. In the middle of the tank he constructed a little garden and some buildings. Between the bank of the tank and these buildings he had made a causeway, which was the way for entering and leaving Since this occurred a long time ago, most of the buildings had become dilapidated, and there was no place left fit to sit in. At the time when the host of prosperity was about to proceed towards Ahmadabad, Ṣafī Khān, bakhshi of Gujarat, repaired at the expense of government what was broken down and in ruins, and clearing out the little garden erected a new building in it. Certainly it is a place exceedingly enjoyable and pleasant. Its style pleased me. On the side where the causeway is, Niẓāmu-d-dīn Aḥmad,[673] who was for a while bakhshi of Gujarat in my father's time, had made a garden on the bank of the tank. At this time a representation was made to me that 'Abdu-llah Khān, in consequence of a dispute that he had with 'Ābid, son of Niẓāmu-d-dīn Aḥmad, cut down the trees of this garden. I also heard that during his government he, at a wine party, signed to a slave, and cut off the head of an unfortunate man who was not wanting in fun and jesting, merely because in a state of drunkenness he had uttered some improper expressions by way of a joke. On hearing these two reports, my sense of justice was shocked, and I ordered the Diwans to change one thousand of his two-horsed and three-horsed cavalry into one-horsed, and to deduct from his jagir the difference (of pay), which came to 7,000,000 dams.

As at this stage the tomb of Shāh 'Ālam was by the roadside, I recited the *fātiḥa* in passing by it. About 100,000 rupees had been spent in building this mausoleum. Shāh 'Ālam was the son

---

673 The historian.

of Quṭb 'Ālam, and their family goes back to Makhdūm-i-Jahāniyān[674] (a saint). The people of this country, high and low, have a wonderful belief in him, and they say that Shāh 'Ālam used to raise the dead. After he had raised several dead men, his father became aware of this and sent him a prohibition, saying it was presumption in him to meddle with the workshop of God, and was contrary to true obedience. It happened that Shāh 'Ālam had an attendant (female) who had no children, but at Shāh 'Ālam's prayer God Almighty bestowed a son on her. When he reached his 27th[675] year he died, and that slave came weeping and wailing into his presence, saying, "My son has died, and he was my only son; since God Almighty gave him to me by your favour, I am hopeful that through your prayer he may become alive." Shāh 'Ālam fell into thought for a time and went into his cell, and the attendant went to his son, who greatly loved her, and besought him to ask the Shah to make his son alive. The son, who was of tender years, went into his cell, and used much entreaty. Shāh 'Ālam said, "If you are content to give up your life for him, perhaps my petition may be accepted." He represented "I am perfectly contented with what may be your wish and the desire of God." Shāh 'Ālam took his son's hands, and lifting him up from the ground turned his face towards heaven and said, "O God, take this kid in place of that one." Instantaneously the boy surrendered his soul to God, and Shāh 'Ālam laid him down on his own bed and covered his face with a sheet, and coming out of the house said to that attendant, "Go home, and get news of thy son; perhaps he may have been in a trance and not have died." When she arrived at her house she saw her son alive. In short, in the country of Gujarat they say many things of this sort of Shāh 'Ālam. I myself asked Sayyid

---

674 A saint of Multan who died in 1384. See Beale, s.v. *Shaikh Jalāl*, and Jarrett, iii, 369.

675 So in text, but surely it should be " 8th or 7th" ? It appears from the Khazīnatu-l-aṣfiyā, ii, 71, that the attendant who lost the child was a female disciple, and that the child was young.

Muḥammad, who is lord of his prayer carpet (in charge of the mausoleum), and who is not wanting in excellence and reasonableness, what was the real state of the case. He said, "I have also heard the same from my father and grandfather, and it has come down in succession, and wisdom is from Allah." Although this affair is beyond the laws of understanding, yet, as it has attained great notoriety among men, it has been recorded as a strange occurrence. His departure from this perishable mansion to the eternal world took place in 880 (1475), in the time of the reign of Sulṭān Maḥmūd Bīgara, and the buildings of this mausoleum are the memorial of Tāj Khān Tariyānī,[676] who was one of the Amirs of Sulṭān Muzaffar, the son of Maḥmūd.

As an hour on Monday had been chosen for my entry into the city, on Sunday, the 24th, I halted. At this place some melons came from Kārīz, which is a town dependent on Herat, and it is certain that in Khurasan there are no melons better than those of Kārīz. Although this is at a distance of 1,400 kos, and kafilahs (caravans) take five months to come, they arrived very ripe and fresh. They brought so many that they sufficed for all the servants. Together with these there came oranges (*kauṇlā*) from Bengal, and though that place is 1,000 kos distant most of them arrived quite fresh. As this is a very delicate and pleasant fruit, runners bring by post as much as is necessary for private consumption, and pass it from hand to hand. My tongue fails me in giving thanks to Allah for this.

"Thankfulness for Thy favours is one of Thy favours."

On this day Amānat Khān presented two elephants' tusks; they were very large, one of them being 3 cubits 8 ṭ*assū* (finger-breadths) in length and 16 tassu in circumference; it weighed 3 maunds and 2 seers, or 24 1/2 Iraq maunds. On Monday, the 25th, after six gharis, I turned towards the city in pleasure and

[676] According to Bayley's Gujarat, p. 238, and Index, p. 515, the name is either Tāj Khān Tūrpāli or Narpāli.

prosperity at the propitious hour, and mounted the elephant Ṣūrat-gaj, a favourite elephant of mine, which is perfect in appearance and disposition. Although he was fractious (*mast*), I had confidence in my own riding and his pleasant paces (?).[677] Crowds of people, men and women, had assembled, and were waiting in the streets and bazars and at the gates and the walls. The city of Ahmadabad did not seem to me so worthy of praise as I had heard. Although they had made the main road of the bazar wide and spacious, they had not suited the shops to this breadth. Its buildings are all of wood and the pillars of the shops slender and mean (*zabūn*). The streets of the bazar were full of dust, and there was dust from the Kānkriyā tank up to the citadel, which in the dialect of the country they call Bhadar. I hastened along scattering money. The meaning of Bhadar is 'blessed' (*bhadra*). The houses of the Sultans of Gujarat, which were inside the Bhadar, have fallen into ruin within the last fifty or sixty years, and no trace of them is left. However, our servants who have been sent to the government of this country have erected buildings. When I was proceeding from Māndū to Ahmadabad, Muqarrab Khān had done up the old buildings and prepared other places for sitting that were necessary, such as a jharokha, a public audience hall, etc. As to-day was the auspicious day for the weighing of my son Shāh Jahān, I weighed him in the usual manner against gold and other things, and the 27th year from his blessed birth began in pleasure and enjoyment. I hope that the Giver of gifts will bestow him on this suppliant at His throne and let him enjoy life and prosperity. On the same day I gave the province of Gujarat in jagir to that son. From the fort of Māndū to the fort of Cambay, by the road we came, it is 124 kos, which were traversed in twenty-eight

---

[677] *Suwārī-i-khūd u khwush-jalū-i-ū*, "my own riding and his pleasant paces (?)." It does not seem likely that Jahāngīr would himself drive the elephant. The meaning here probably is that Jahāngīr trusted to his being on the elephant. *Khwush-jalū* is used lower down about another elephant, and seems to refer to the elephant's paces. See p. 214.

marches and thirty halts. I remained at Cambay for ten days; from that place to the city of Ahmadabad is 21 kos, which we traversed in five marches with two halts. Altogether, from Māndū to Cambay and from Cambay to Ahmadabad by the road we came is 145 kos, which we accomplished in two months and fifteen days; this was in thirty-three marches and forty-two halts.

On Tuesday, the 26th, I went to see the Jāmi' mosque, and gave with my own hand in alms to the fakirs who were present there about 500 rupees. This mosque was one of the memorials of Sulṭān Aḥmad, the founder of the city of Ahmadabad. It has three gates,[678] and on each side a bazar. Opposite the gate that looks towards the east is the mausoleum of the said Sulṭān Aḥmad. In that dome Sulṭān Aḥmad, his son Muḥammad, and his grandson Quṭbu-d-dīn are laid to rest. The length of the court of the mosque, excluding *maqṣūra* (the holy of holies), is 103[679] cubits, and its breadth 89 cubits. Round this they have made an *aywān* (portico), in breadth $4\frac{3}{4}$ cubits. The flooring of the court is of trimmed bricks, and the pillars of the portico of red stone. The maqsura contains 354[680] pillars, above which there is a dome. The length of the maqsura is 75 cubits, and its breadth 37 cubits. The flooring of the maqsura, the *mihrāb* (arch towards which the face is turned in prayer), and the pulpit are made of marble. On both sides of the main arch (*pīsh-ṭāq*) are two polished minarets of cut stone, containing three *āshyāna* (stories) beautifully shaped and decorated. On the right-hand side of the pulpit near the recess of the maqsura they have made a separate seat for the king. The space between the pillars has been covered in with a stone platform, and round this up to the roof of the

---

678 Or doors. The Iqbāl-nāma, 108, has "in front of each gate there is a bazar."

679 123 in Iqbāl-nāma.

680 350 in I.O. MSS.

maqsura they have put stone cages[681] (in which women sit so as not to be seen). The object of this was that when the king came to the Friday service or the 'Id he went up there with his intimates and courtiers, and performed his devotions. This in the dialect of the country they call the Mulūk-khāna (King's chamber). This practice and caution were on account of the crowding of the people. Truly this mosque is a very noble building.[682]

On Wednesday,[683] the 27th, I went to the monastery of Shaikh Wajīhu-d-dīn, which was near the palace, and the *fātiḥa* was read at the head of his shrine, which is in the court of the monastery. Ṣādiq Khān, who was one of the chief Amirs of my father, built this monastery. The Shaikh was a successor of Shaikh Muḥammad Ghauṣ,[684] but a successor against whom the teacher disputed. Wajīhu-d-dīn's loyalty to him is a clear proof[685] of the greatness of Shaikh Muḥammad Ghauṣ. Shaikh Wajīhu-d-dīn was adorned with visible excellencies and spiritual perfection. He dīed thirty years ago in this city (Ahmadabad), and after him Shaikh 'Abdu-llah, according to his father's will, took his place. He was a very ascetic dervish. When he died his son Shaikh Asadu-llah sat in his place, and also quickly went to the eternal world. After him his brother Shaikh Ḥaidar became lord of the prayer carpet, and is now alive, and is employed at the grave of his father and grandfather in the service of dervishes and in looking after their welfare. The traces of piety are evident on the

---

681 *Panjara-i-sang,* presumably lattice-work in stone.

682 See for dimensions of the mosque Bayley'a Gujarat, p. 92 and note, and the authorities there quoted.

683 Text wrongly has Sunday.

684 Muḥammad Ghauṣ was accused of heresy by some of the Gujāratī mullas. He was much respected by Humāyūn, and is buried at Gwalior.

685 Jahāngīr means that Wajīhu-d-dīn was a very learned man, and that his devotion to Muḥammad Ghauṣ, who was an ignorant man (*ummī*), shows what a great personality the latter was. Cf. Iqbāl-nāma, 169, and Ma'āṣiru-l-umarā, ii, 583, where we are told that Wajīhu-d-dīn thanked God that both his Prophet and his Pīr were ignorant.

forehead of his life. As it was the anniversary festival of Shaikh Wajīhu-d-dīn, 1,500 rupees were given to Shaikh Ḥaidar for the expenses of the anniversary, and I bestowed 1,500 rupees more on the band of fakirs who were present in the monastery, with my own hand in charity, and made a present of 500 rupees to the grandson (?) of Shaikh Wajīhu-d-dīn. In the same way I gave something for expenses, and land to each of his relatives and adherents according to his merit. I ordered Shaikh Ḥaidar to bring before me the body of dervishes and deserving people who were associated with him, in order that they might ask for money for expenses and for land. On Thursday, the 28th, I went to look round the Rustam - Khānbāṛī, and scattered 1,500 rupees on the road. They call a garden a *bāṛī* in the language of India. This is a garden that my brother Shāh Murād made in the name of his son Rustam. I made a Thursday entertainment in this garden, and gave cups to some of my private servants. At the end of the day I went to the little garden of the *ḥawālī* (mansion) of Shaikh Sikandar, which is situated in the neighbourhood of this garden, and which has exceedingly good figs. As picking the fruit with one's own hand gives it quite a different relish, and I had never before plucked figs with my own hand, their excellence in this respect was approved. Shaikh Sikandar[686] is by origin a Gujarati, and is not wanting in reasonableness, and has complete information about the Sultans of Gujarat. It is now eight or nine years since he has been employed among the servants (of the State). As my son Shāh Jahān had appointed to the government of Ahmadabad Rustam Khān, who is one of his chief officers, at his request I, in accordance with the association of his name, presented him with (the garden) Rustam-bāṛī. On this day Rāja Kalyān, zamindar of the province of Īḍar, had the good fortune to kiss my threshold, and presented an elephant and nine horses as an offering; I gave him back the elephant. He is one of the most considerable zamindars on the frontier of

[686] He wrote a history of Gujarat–the Mirāt-i-Sikandarī. Rieu, Cat., i, 287.

Gujarat, and his country is close to the hill-country of the Rānā. The Sultans of Gujarat constantly sent armies against the Raja of that place. Although some of them have professed obedience and presented offerings, for the most part none of them have come to see anyone personally. After the late king Akbar conquered Gujarat, the victorious army was sent to attack him. As he understood that his deliverance lay in obedience and submission, he agreed to serve and be loyal, and hastened to enjoy the good fortune of kissing the threshold. From that date he has been enrolled among the servants (of the State). He comes to see whoever is appointed to the government of Ahmadabad, and when work and service are necessary appears with a body of his men. On Saturday, the 1st of the month of Bahman, in the 12th year of my reign, Chandar Sen, who is one of the chief zamindars of this country, had the good fortune to kiss the threshold, and presented an offering of nine horses. On Sunday, the 2nd, I gave elephants to Rāja Kalyān, zamindar of Īḍar, to Sayyid Muṣṭafā, and Mīr Fāẓil. On Monday I went out hawking, and scattered nearly 500 rupees on the road. On this day pears came from Badakhshan. On Mubārak-shamba, the 6th, I went to see the "garden of victory" at the village of Sair-khaiz (Sarkhej), and scattered 1,500 rupees on the way. As the tomb of Shaikh Aḥmad Khaṭṭū[687] is on the road, I first went there and the *fātiḥa* was read. Khaṭṭū is the name of a town in the Sarkar of Nāgor, and was the birthplace of the Shaikh.[688] The Shaikh lived in the

---

[687] Blochmann, 507, note.

[688] "Shaikh Ahmad Khattū, who had the title of Jamālu-d-dīn, was born at Delhi of a noble family in 737 A.H. (1336-7). He was the disciple and successor of Bābā Islīāq (Isaac) Maghribī. His name was Naṣīru-d-dīn. By the jugglery of the heavens he was separated from his home in a storm, and after a while entered the service of Bābā Isḥāq Maghribī. He acquired from him spiritual and secular learning, and came to Gujarat in the time of Sulṭān Aḥmad. High and low accepted him, and paid him homage. Afterwards he travelled to Arabia and Persia, and made the acquaintance of many saints. He is buried at Sarkhech, near Ahmadabad." *Āyīn-i-Akbarī* (vol. ii, p. 220, of Bib. Ind., ed. Jarrett, iii, 371). See Bayley's Gujarat, p. 90, note, and Khazīnatu-l-aṣfiyā, ii, 314, and Blochmann, 507,

time of Sulṭān Aḥmad, who founded the city of Ahmadabad, and the latter had a great respect for him. The people of this country have a strange belief in him, and consider him one of the great saints. Every Friday night a great crowd of people, high and low, go to visit his shrine. Sulṭān Muḥammad, son of the aforesaid Sulṭān Aḥmad, built lofty buildings in the shape of mausoleums, mosques, and monasteries at the head of his tomb, and near his mausoleum on the south side made a large tank, and surrounded it with stone and lime (masonry). This building was completed in the time of Quṭbu-d-dīn, son of the aforesaid Muḥammad. The shrines of several of the Sultans of Gujarat are on the bank of the tank by the feet of the Shaikh. In that dome there have been laid at rest Sulṭān Maḥmūd Bīgara, Sulṭān Muẓaffar, his son, and Maḥmūd, the martyr, grandson of Sulṭān Muẓaffar, and who was the last of the Sultans of Gujarat. Bīgara, in the language of the people of Gujarat, signifies 'turned-up moustache,' and Sulṭān Maḥmūd had a large turned-up moustache; on this account they call him Bīgara. Near his (Shaikh Khaṭṭū's) tomb is the dome of his ladies.[689] Without doubt the mausoleum of the Shaikh is a very grand building and a beautiful place. It is estimated that 500,000 rupees were spent on it. God only knows what is true.

After performing this visitation I went to Fatḥ-bāgh (garden of victory). This garden is situated on the ground on which the Commander-in-Chief, Khānkhānān Ātāliq, fought with and defeated Nabū (Nannū? Nanhū ?), who gave himself the title of Muẓaffar Khān. On this account he called it Bāgh-i-fatḥ; the people of Gujarat call it Fatḥ-bāṛī. The details of this are that

---

note, where the reference to the Khazīna, 957, seems wrong. The story told in the Khazīna is that Shaikh Aḥmad belonged to the royal family of Delhi, and was, as a baby, blown out of his nurse's arms into the street during a storm.

689. Text *khawānīn*, 'khans,' but evidently this is a mistake for *khawātīn*, the plural of *khātūn*' a lady.

when, by means of the good fortune of the late king Akbar, the country of Gujarat was conquered, and Nabū fell into his hands, I'timād Khān represented that he was the son of a carter. As no son was left by Sulẓān Maḥmūd, and moreover there was no one of the descendants of the Sultans of Gujarat whom he could raise to the throne, he (I'timād) had accepted the most available course, and had made out that this was the son of Maḥmūd. He gave him the name of Sulṭān Muẓaffar, and raised him to the sovereignty. Men from necessity consented to this. As His Majesty considered the word of I'timād Khān of weight, he ignored Nabū, and for some time he did duty among the servants, and the king paid no attention to his case. In consequence of this he ran away from Fatḥpūr, and coming to Gujarat lived for some years under the protection of the zamindars. When Shihābu-d-dīn Aḥmad Khān was turned out from the government of Gujarat and I'timād Khān installed in his place, a body of the servants of Shihābu-d-dīn Khān, who were attached to Gujarat, separated from him, and remained at Ahmadabad in the hope of service with I'timād. After I'timād entered the city they had recourse to him, but had no good luck with him. They had not the face to go to Shihābu-d-dīn, and had no prospects in Ahmadabad. As they were without hope they thought their remedy lay in betaking themselves to Nabū, and in making him an excuse for disturbance. With this intent 600 or 700 horsemen from among them went to Nabū and carried him off along with Lonā Kāthī, under whose protection he was living, and proceeded to Ahmadabad. When he arrived near the city many wretched men on the look out for an occasion joined him, and nearly 1,000 horsemen, Mughals and Gujaratis, collected together. When I'timād Khān became aware of this he left his son Shīr Khān in the city, and hastened off in search of Shihāb Khān, who was proceeding towards the Court, in order that with his help he might quiet the disturbance. Many of the men had separated themselves from him, and he read on the faces of those who were left the signs of unfaithfulness, but

Shihābu-d-dīn, in company with I'timād Khān, turned his rein. It happened that before their arrival Nabū had entered the fort of Ahmadabad. Those who were loyal drew up their troops near the city, and the rebels came out of the fort and hastened to the battlefield. When the army of the rebels showed itself, those of the servants of Shihāb Khān who were left took the wrong road and joined the enemy. Shihāb Khān was defeated and hastened towards Paṭan (Pātan ?), which was in the possession of the royal servants. His retinue and camp were plundered, and Nabū, bestowing mansabs and titles on the rebels, went against Quṭbu-d-dīn Muḥammad Khān, who was in Baroda. The servants of the latter, like the servants of Shihāb Khān, took the road of faithlessness and chose separation, as is related in detail in the Akbar-nāma. In the end, after giving his word to Quṭbu-d-dīn Muḥammad, he sent him to martyrdom, and his goods and property, which were equal to the treasure of his courtesy and grandeur, were plundered. Nearly 45,000 horsemen collected round Nabū.

When this state of affairs was represented to H.M. Akbar he sent against him Mīrzā Khān, son of Bairām Khān, with a force of brave warriors. On the day when Mīrzā Khān arrived near the city, he drew up the ranks of good fortune. He had about 8,000 or 9,000 horse, and Nabū met him with 30,000, and drew up his host tainted with ruin. After prolonged fighting and slaughter the breeze of victory blew on the flag of the loyal, and Nabū, being defeated, fled in wretched plight. My father, in reward for this victory, gave Mīrzā Khān a mansab of 5,000, with the title of Khānkhānān and the government of the country of Gujarat. The garden that Khānkhānān made on the field of battle is situated on the bank of the River Sābarmatī. He founded lofty buildings along that eminence on the river, and made a strong wall of stone and cement round the garden. The garden contains 120 *jarīb* of land, and is a charming resort. It may have cost 200,000 rupees. It pleased me greatly. One may say that in the whole of Gujarat there is no garden like this. Arranging a Thursday feast,

I bestowed cups on my private servants, and remained there for the night. At the end of the day, on Friday, I entered the city, scattering about 1,000 rupees on the road. At this time the gardener represented that a servant of Muqarrab Khān had cut down some *champā* trees above the bench alongside the river. On hearing this I became angry, and went myself to enquire into the matter and to exact satisfaction. When it was established that this improper act had been committed by him, I ordered both his thumbs to be cut off as a warning to others. It was evident that Muqarrab Khān knew nothing of this affair, or otherwise he would have punished him there and then. On Tuesday, the 11th, the Kotwal of the city caught a thief and brought him. He had committed several thefts before, and each time they had cut off one of his members; once his right hand, the second time the thumb of his left hand, the third time his left ear, and fourth time they hamstringed him, and the last time his nose ; with all this he did not give up his business, and yesterday entered the house of a grass-seller in order to steal. By chance the owner of the house was on the look out and seized him. The thief wounded the grass-seller several times with a knife and killed him. In the uproar and confusion his relatives attacked the thief and caught him. I ordered them to hand over the thief to the relatives of the deceased, that they might retaliate on him.

"The lines of the face show the thought of your head (?)."

On Wednesday, the 12th, 3,000 rupees were handed over to ‘Aẓamat Khān and Mu‘taqad Khān, that they might go the next day to the tomb of Shaikh Aḥmad Khaṭṭū, and divide it among the fakirs and indigent people who had taken up their abode there. On Thursday, the 13th, I went to the lodging of my son Shāh Jahān, and held a Mubārak - shamba entertainment there, and distributed cups among my private servants. I gave my son the elephant Sundar Mathan,[690] which was superior to all my private elephants in speed and beauty and pleasant paces, and

---

690 I.O. MSS. have Sundar Sen.

competed with horses, and was the first among the elephants, and one much liked by King Akbar. My son Shāh Jahān had a great liking for him, and frequently asked him of me, and seeing no way out of it I gave it to him with its gold belongings of chains, etc., together with a female elephant. A present of 100,000 of darbs was given to the wakils of 'Ādil Khān. At this time it was represented[691] to me that Mukarram Khān, son of Mu'aẕẕam Khān, who was the governor of Orissa, had conquered the country of Khūrdā, and that the Raja of that place had fled and gone into the Rājmahendra. As he was a *khāna-zād* (houseborn one) and worthy of patronage, I ordered his mansab, original and increase, to be 3,000 personal and 2,000 horse, and honoured him with drums, a horse, and a dress of honour. Between the province of Orissa and Golconda there were two zamindars, one the Raja of Khūrdā and the second the Raja of Rājmahendra. The province of Khūrdā has come into the possession of the servants of the Court. After this it is the turn of the country of Rājmahendra. My hope in the grace of Allah is that the feet of my energy may advance farther. At this time a petition from Quṭbu-l-mulk reached my son Shāh Jahān to the effect that as the boundary of his territory had approached that of the King, and he owed service to this Court, he hoped an order would be issued to Mukarram Khān not to stretch out his hand, and to acquire possession of his country. It was a proof of Mukarram's valour and energy that such a one as Quṭbu-l-mulk should be apprehensive about his (Mukarram) becoming his neighbour.

On this day Ikrām Khān, son of Islām Khān, was appointed faujdar of Fatḥpūr and its neighbourhood, and presented with a dress of honour and an elephant; Chandar Sen, the zamindar of

---

691 See Elliot, vi, 355.

Haloẕ (Halwad ?),[692] was given a dress of honour, a horse, and an elephant. An elephant was also given to Lāchīn Qāqshāl. At the same time Muẕaffar,[693] son of Mīrzā Bāqī Tarkhān, had the honour of kissing the threshold. His mother was the daughter of Bārha (Bhārā), the zamindar of Kachh. When Mīrzā Bāqī died and the government of Thatta went to Mīrzā Jānī, Muẕaffar was apprehensive of Mīrzā Jānī, and he took refuge with the aforesaid zamindar. He had remained from his childhood until now in that country. Now that the fortunate retinue had reached Ahmadabad, he came and did homage. Though he had been reared among men of the wilds, and was unfamiliar with civilized ways and ceremonies, yet as his family had had the relations of service with our exalted dynasty from the times of Timur[694] —may God make his proof clear !—I considered it right to patronize him. For the present I gave him 2,000 rupees for expenses, and a dress of honour. A suitable rank will be given to him, and perhaps he will show himself efficient as a soldier.

On Thursday, the 20th, I went to the "Garden of Victory," and contemplated the red roses. One plot had bloomed well. There are not many red roses (*gul-i-surkh*) in this country, so it was pleasant to see so many here. The anemone[695] bed, too, was not bad, and the figs had ripened. I gathered some figs with my

---

692 This name is doubtful, for the MSS. have a different reading, apparently Namūd. There is a Halōd in Gujarat (Jarrett, ii, 242). See also Bayley's Gujarat, 439. Perhaps it is the Halol of the Indian Gazetteer.

693 The existence of this son of Bāqī Tarkhān does not seem to have been known to Abū-l-faẓl or to Blochmann. Nor is he mentioned in the Ma'āṡiru-l-umarā. See Jarrett, ii, 347, where only Payanda is spoken of as the son of Bāqī Khān, and Blochmann, p. 362. See also Ma'āṡiru-l-umarā, iii, 485, the biography of Mīrzā' Īsā Tarkhān. His name appears, however, in the pedigree of his house in the Tarkhān-nāma of Jamāl Shīrāzī.

694 The word *ṡānī* in *Ṣāḥib-qīrān-i-ṡānī* in text is a mistake.

695 *Shaqā'īq*, which perhaps means tulips. In Price's Jahangir, p. 115, there is much more said about the " Garden of Victory," and Jahāngīr's entertainment there by his wife Khairu-n-nisā, the daughter of the Khānkhānān.

own hands, and weighed the largest one. It came to $7\frac{1}{2}$ tolas. On this day there arrived 1,500 melons from Kārīz. The Khān ʻĀlam had sent them as a present. I gave a thousand of them to the servants in attendance, and five hundred to the women of the harem. I spent four days in this garden in enjoyment, and on Monday eve, the 24th, I came to the city. Some of the melons were given to the Shaikhs of Ahmadabad, and they were astonished to see how inferior were the Gujarat melons. They marvelled at the goodness of the Deity.

On Thursday, the 27th, I held a wine-feast in the Nagīna[696] garden, which is inside the palace grounds, and which one of the Gujarat Sultans had planted. I made my servants happy with flowing bowls. A pergola (*takhta*) of grapes had ripened in this garden, and I bade those who had been drinking to gather the bunches with their own hands and partake of them.

On Monday, the 1st of Isfandārmuz, I left Ahmadabad and marched towards Malwa. I scattered money on the road till we reached the bank of the Kānkriyā tank, where I halted for three days. On Thursday, the 4th, the presents of Muqarrab Khān were laid before me. There was nothing rare among them, nor anything that I took a fancy to, and so I felt ashamed. I gave them to my children to take into the harem. I accepted jewellery and decorated vessels and cloths to the value of a lakh, and gave him back the rest. Also about one hundred Kachhi horses were taken, but there was none of great excellence.

On Friday, the 5th, I marched 6 kos, and encamped on the bank of the Ahmadabad River. As my son Shāh Jahān was leaving Rustam Khān, one of his chief servants, in charge of the government of Gujarat, I, at my son's request, gave him a standard, drums, a dress of honour, and a decorated dagger. Up till now it had not been the custom in this dynasty to give to the

---

[696] Bagīna in text. Debi Prasad has *Bakīnā*.

prince's servants standards or drums. For instance, H.M. Akbar, with all his affection and graciousness to me, did not decide upon giving to my officers a title or a standard. But my consideration for this son is so unbounded that I would do anything to please him, and, in fact, he is an excellent son, and one adorned with every grace, and in his early youth has accomplished to my satisfaction, everything that he has set his hand to.

On this day Muqarrab Khān took leave to go to his home.

As the shrine of Quṭb 'Ālam, the father of Shāh 'Ālam Bukhāri, was in the village of Batoh,[697] and on my way, I went there and gave 500 rupees to the guardians. On Saturday, the 6th, I entered a boat on the Maḥmūdābād River and went a-fishing. On the bank is the tomb of Sayyid Mubārak Bukhārī. He was one of the leading officers of Gujarat, and his son Sayyid Mīrān erected this monument to him. It is a very lofty cupola, and there is a very strong wall of stone and lime round it. It must have cost more than two lakhs of rupees. None of the tombs of the Gujarat Sultans that I saw came up to one-tenth of it. Yet they were sovereigns, and Sayyid Mīrān was only a servant. Genius and the help of God have produced this result. A thousand blessings on a son who has made such a tomb for his father:[698]

"That there may remain a memorial of him upon earth."

On Sunday I halted and fished, and caught 400 fish. One of them had no scales, and is called the *sang-māhī*, 'the stone-fish.' Its belly was very large and swollen, so I ordered them to cut it open in my presence. Inside was a fish with scales which it had recently swallowed and which had as yet undergone no change.

---

[697] Banoh in text. See Bayley's Gujarat, p. 237 ; also Tiefenthaler, i, 377, who speaks of it as being 3 leagues south of Ahmadabad. See also Jarrett, ii, 240, n. 7.

[698] For Sayyid Mubārak and his son see Bayley's Gujarat. Sayyid Mubārak was the patron of the author of the Mirāt-i-Sikandarī. See loc. cit., p. 454.

I told them to weigh both fish. The stone-fish came to 6 1/2 seers and the other to nearly 2.

On Monday, the 8th, I marched 4 1/4 kos, and encamped in the village of Moda (Mahāondat). The inhabitants praised the rainy season of Gujarat. It happened that on the previous night and on this day before breakfast some rain fell, and the dust was laid. As this is a sandy country, it is certain that there would not be any dust in the rainy season, nor would there by any mud. The fields would be green and cheerful. At any rate, a specimen of the rainy season has been seen by me. On Tuesday I marched 5 1/2 kos, and halted at the village of Jarsīma (Jarīsamā).[699]

At this stage news came that Mān Singh Sewṛā had surrendered his soul to the lords of hell. The account of this in brief is that the Sewras[700] are a tribe of infidel Hindus who always go with their head and feet bare. One set of them root out their hair, their beards, and moustaches, while another set shave them. They do not wear sewn garments, and their central principle is that no living creature should be injured. The Banyans regard them as their *pīrs* and teachers, and even worship them. There are two sects of Sewras, one called Patā (Tapā) and the other Kanthal (Kartal). Mān Singh was the head of the latter, and Bāl Chand the head of the Patās.[701] Both of them used to attend upon H.M. Akbar. When he died and Khusrau fled and I pursued him, Rāy Singh Bhurṭiyā, zamindar of Bikanir, who had been made an Amīr by Akbar's kindness, asked Mān Singh what would be the duration of my reign and the chances of my success. That black-tongued fellow, who pretended to be skilled in astrology and the extraction of judgments, said to him that my reign would, at most, last for two years. The doting old idiot (Rāy Singh) relied upon this, and went off without leave to his home. Afterwards, when the

---

[699] It is the Chandsuma of Bayley's map.

[700] Jarrett, iii, 210 ; and Akbar-nāma, translation, i, 147, n. 2.

[701] This should be Tapā. See Addenda.

glorious God chose out this suppliant and I returned victorious to the capital, he came, ashamed and downcast, to Court. What happened to him in the end has been told in its proper place.[702] In fine, Mān Singh, in the course of three or four months, was struck with leprosy (*juẕām*), and his limbs fell off him till he was in such a state that death was by many degrees preferable to life. He was living at Bikanir, and now I remembered him and sent for him. On the road he, out of excessive fear, took poison, and surrendered his soul to the lords of hell. So long as the intentions of this suppliant at God's courts are just and right, it is sure that whoever devises evil against me will receive retribution according to his merits.

The sect of the Sewras exists in most of the cities of India, but is especially numerous in Gujarat. As the Banyans are the chief traders there, consequently the Sewras also are plentiful. Besides making idol-temples for them, they have built houses for them to dwell in and to worship in. In fact, these houses are the head-quarters of sedition. The Banyans send their wives and daughters to the Sewras, who have no shame or modesty. All kinds of strife and audacity are perpetrated by them. I therefore ordered that the Sewras should be expelled, and I circulated farmans to the effect that wherever there were Sewras in my empire they should be turned out.

On Wednesday, the 10th, I went out to hunt, and shot two nilgaw, one male and one female. On this day the son of Dilāwar Khān came from Pattan, which was his father's fief, and paid his respects. He presented a Kachhī horse. It was a very handsome animal, and pleasant to ride. Till I came to Gujarat no one had presented me with so fine a horse. Its value was 1,000 rupees.

---

702 LO. MS., instead of *khātimat-i-aḥkāl-i-ū*, has *chunānchih aḥwāl*, "as has been stated in its place." This is probably correct, as Jahāngīr has already referred to his death. See also the account of the 2nd year, where he speaks of Rāy Singh's going home without leave.

On Thursday, the 11th, I had a wine party on the bank of the tank, and bestowed many favours on those servants who had been appointed to the province, and then dismissed them. Among the promotions was that of Shajā'at Khān, the Arab, to the rank of 2,500 personal and 2,000 horse. I also gave him drums, a horse, and a robe of honour. Himmat Khān was raised to the rank of 1,500 with 800 horse, and had a robe of honour and an elephant. Kifāyat Khān, who was made Diwan of the province, received the rank of 1,200 with 300 horse. Safī Khān bakhshi received a horse and a robe of honour. Khwāja 'Āqil had the rank of 1,500 with 650 horse, and was made bakhshi of the Ahadis, and had the title of 'Āqil Khān. Thirty thousand darbs were given to the wakil of Quṭbu-l-Mulk, who had brought the tribute.

On this day my son Shāh Jahān presented pomegranates and quinces that had been sent to him from Farāh. I had never seen such large ones, and I ordered them to be weighed. The quince weighed 29 tolas 9 mashas and the pomegranate 40 1/2 tolas. On Friday, the 12th, I went a-hunting and shot two nilgaw, a male and a female. On Saturday, the 13th, I shot three nilgaw, two males and one female. On Sunday, the 14th, I gave Shaikh Ismā'īl, the son of Shaikh Muḥammad Ghauṣ, a robe of honour and 500 rupees. On Monday, the 15th, I went a-hunting and shot two female nilgaw. On Tuesday, the 16th, I again presented the Shaikhs of Gujarat, who were in attendance, with robes of honour and maintenance-lands. To each of them I gave a book from my special library, such as the Tafsīr-i-kashshāf,[703] the Tafsīr-i-Ḥusainī,[704] and the Rauẓatu-l-aḥbāb.[705] I wrote on the back of the books the day of my arrival in Gujarat and the day of presentation of the books.

---

[703] Perhaps an explanation of Zamakhshari's Commentary.

[704] A Persian commentary on the Koran (Rieu, p. 96).

[705] A life of Muhammad (Rieu, i, 147).

At the time that Ahmadabad was adorned by the setting up of the royal standards my employment by day and by night was the seeing of necessitous persons and the bestowing on them of money and land. I directed Shaikh Aḥmad the Ṣadr and some other tactful servants to bring before me dervishes and other needy persons. I also directed the sons of Shaikh Muhammad Ghauṣ, the grandson of Shaikh Wajīhu-d-dīn, and other leading Shaikhs to produce whatever persons they believed to be in want. Similarly I appointed some women to do the same thing in the harem. My sole endeavour was that as I a king had come to this country after many years, no single person should be excluded. God is my witness that I did not fall short in this task, and that I never took any rest from this duty. Although I have not been delighted with my visit to Ahmadabad, yet I have this satisfaction—that my coming has been the cause of benefit to a large number of poor people.

On Tuesday, the 16th, they caught Kaukab, the son of Qamar Khān. He had in Burhanpur put on a faqir's dress and gone off into the wilds. The brief account of his case is this :—He was the grandson of Mīr 'Abdu-l-Laṭīf, who was one of the Saifī Sayyids and was attached to this Court. Kaukab had been appointed to the Deccan army, and had spent some days with it in poverty and wretchedness. When for a long time he did not get promotion he suspected that I was unfavourable to him, and foolishly took the dress of asceticism and went off to the wilderness. In the course of six months he traversed the whole of the Deccan, including Daulatabad, Bidar, Bijapur, the Carnatic, and Golconda, and came to the port of Dābul.[706] From there he came by ship to the port of Gogā, and after visiting the ports of Surat, Broach, etc., he reached Ahmadabad. At this time Zāhid, a servant of Shāh Jahān, arrested him and brought him to Court. I ordered them to bring him before me heavily bound. When I saw him I said to him, "Considering the obligations of service of

[706] Dābhol (I.G., new ed., xi, 100).

your father and grandfather, and your position as a houseborn one, why have you behaved in such an inauspicious manner? " He replied that he could not tell a lie in the presence of his *qibla* and real teacher, and that the truth was that he had hoped for favours, but as he was unlucky he had left outward ties and gone into the wilderness of exile. As his words bore the marks of truth they made an impression on me, and I abandoned my harsh tone and asked him if in his misfortunes he had waited upon 'Ādil Khān, or Quṭbu-l-Mulk, or 'Ambar. He replied that though he had been unsuccessful at this Court and had remained thirsty in this boundless ocean of beneficence, he had never—God forbid that he should—approached with his lips other fountains. Might his head be cut off if it had bowed at this Court and then lowered itself at another ! From the time that he went into exile he had kept a diary showing what he had done, and by examining it it would be seen how he had conducted himself. These words of his increased my compassion for him, and I sent for his papers and read them. It appeared from them that he had encountered great hardship, and that he had spent much time on foot, and that he had suffered from want of food. On this account I felt kindly disposed towards him. Next day I sent for him and ordered them to remove the bonds from his arms and legs, and gave him a robe of honour, a horse, and 1,000 rupees for his expenses. I also increased his rank by one half, and showed him such kindness as he never had imagined. He repeated this verse—

"What I see, is it, O God, waking or in a trance ?
Do I behold myself in such comfort after such torture ?"

On Wednesday, the 17th, I marched 6 kos and halted at the village of Bārasīnor (Bālasīnor). It has already been mentioned that the plague had appeared in Kashmir. On this day a report of the chronicler of events arrived, stating that the plague had taken firm hold of the country and that many had died. The symptoms were that the first day there was headache and fever and much bleeding at the nose. On the second day the patient died. In the house where one person died all the inmates were carried off. Whoever went near the sick person or a dead body was affected in the same way. In one instance the dead body was thrown on the grass, and it chanced that a cow came and ate some of the grass. It died, and some dogs that had eaten its flesh also all died. Things had come to such a pass that from fear of death fathers would not approach their children, and children would not go near their fathers. A strange thing was that in the ward in which the disease began, a fire broke out and nearly 3,000 houses were burnt. During the height of the plague, one morning when the people of the city and environs got up, they saw circles on their doors. There were three large circles, and on the face of these (i.e. inside them) there were two circles of middle size and one small one. There were also other circles which did not contain any whiteness[707] (i.e. there were no inner circles). These figures were found on all the houses and even on the mosques. From the day when the fire took place and these circles appeared, they say there was a diminution of the plague. This has been recorded as it seems a strange affair. It certainly does not agree with the canons of reason, and my intellect cannot accept it. Wisdom is with God ! I trust that the Almighty will have mercy on his sinful slaves, and that they will be altogether freed from such calamity.

On Thursday, the 18th, I marched $2\frac{1}{2}$ kos and halted on the bank of the Mahī. On this day the Jām zamindar[708] had the good fortune to kiss the ground. He presented 50 horses, 100 muhrs, and 100 rupees. His name is Jassā, and Jām is his title. Whoever succeeds is called Jām. He is one of the chief zamindars of Gujarat, and, indeed, he is one of the noted rajas of India. His

---

[707] *Biyāẕ*. The meaning is not clear. Perhaps what is meant is that there was no writing, only the circles.

[708] Elliot, vi, 356.

country is close to the sea. He always maintains 5,000 or 6,000 horse, and in time of war can supply as many as 10,000 or 12,000. There are many horses in his country; Kachhī horses fetch as much as 2,000 rupees. I gave him a dress of honour.

On the same day Lachmī Narāyan, Raja of Kūch (Bihār), which adjoins Bengal, did homage and presented 500 muhrs. He received a dress of honour and an ornamented dagger.

Nawāzish Khān, son of Sa'īd Khān, who had been appointed to Jūnagaṛh, had the good fortune to pay his respects. On Friday, the 19th, I halted, and on Saturday, the 20th, I marched 3 3/4 kos and halted at the tank of Jhanūd. On Sunday I marched 4 1/2 kos and halted at the tank of Badarwālā. On this day there came the news of the death of 'Aẕamat Khān Gujarātī. On account of illness he had remained in Ahmadabad. He was a servant who knew one's disposition, and did good work. As he had thorough knowledge of the Deccan and Gujarat, I was grieved at his death. In the tank above mentioned I noticed a plant which at the approach of the finger or the end of a stick contracts its leaves. After a while it opens them out again. Its leaves resemble those of the tamarind, and it is called in Arabic *Shajaru-l-ḥayā,* 'the plant of modesty.' In Hindī it is called *Lajvantī. Lāj* means modesty. It is certainly not void of strangeness. They also call it *naghzak,* and say that it also grows on dry land.

On Monday, the 22nd, I halted. My scouts reported that there was a tiger in the neighbourhood which vexed wayfarers, and in the forest where it was they had seen a skull and some bones lying. After midday I went out to shoot it, and killed it with one discharge. Though it was a large tiger, I had killed several that were larger. Among them was a tiger which I killed in the fort of Māndū, and which was 8 1/2 maunds. This one weighed 7 1/2 maunds, or 1 maund less.

On Tuesday, the 23rd, I marched over $3\frac{1}{2}$ kos and alighted on the bank of the River Bāyab.[709] On Wednesday I marched nearly 6 kos and halted at the tank of Hamda.[710] On Thursday I ordered a halt and had a wine party, and gave cups to my special servants. I promoted Nawāzish Khān to the rank of 3,000 with 2,000 horse, which was an increase of 500 personal, and gave him a robe of honour and an elephant, and allowed him to go to his fief. Muḥammad Ḥusain Sabzak,[711] who had been sent to Balkh to buy horses, came to Court to-day and paid his respects. Of the horses he brought, one was piebald and was of fine shape and colour. I had never seen a piebald horse of this colour before. He had also brought other good roadsters. I therefore gave him the title of Tijāratī Khān.

On Friday, the 26th, I marched 5 1/4 kos and halted at the village of Jālod.[712] Rāja Lachmī Narāyan, the paternal uncle of the Raja of Kūch, to whom I had now given the territory of Kūch, was presented with a horse. On Saturday I marched 3 kos and halted at Boda.[713] On Sunday I marched 5 kos and set up the royal standards at Doḥad. It is on the borders of Malwa and Gujarat.

Pahluwān Bahā'u-d-dīn, the musketeer, brought a young monkey (*langūr*) with a goat, and represented that on the road one of his marksmen had seen the female langur with a young one in its arms on a tree. The cruel man had shot the mother, which on being struck had left the young one on a branch, and had herself dropped on the ground and died. Pahluwān Bahā'u-d-dīn had then come up and taken down the young one, and had put it beside the goat to be suckled. God had inspired the

---

709 MSS. seem to have Mānīb.

710 MSS. seem to have Nīmda.

711 The MSS. have Muḥammad Ḥusain Saudāgar (trader).

712 The Jhallod of Bayley's map.

713 MSS. have Ranūd

goat with affection for it, and it began to lick the monkey and to fondle it. In spite of difference of species she showed such love as if it had come out of her own womb. I told them to separate them, but the goat immediately began to lament, and the young langur also became much distressed. The affection of the monkey is not so remarkable, as it wanted to get milk, but the affection of the goat for it is remarkable. The langur is an animal belonging to the monkey tribe. But the hair of the monkey (*maimūn*) is yellowish and its face is red, while the hair of the langur is white and its face is black. Its tail, too, is twice as long as the maimun's. I have written these things on account of their strangeness. On Monday, the 29th, I halted and went to hunt nilgaw. I shot two, one male and one female. On Tuesday also, the 30th, I halted.

TABLE OF TRANSLITERATION

(Hamza) not represented at the beginning or end of a word;' in the middle of a word.

ب	b
پ	p
ت	t
ٹ	ṭ
ث	s̤
ج	j
چ	ch
ح	ḥ
خ	kh
د	d
ڈ	ḍ
ذ	z̲
ر	r
ڑ	ṛ
ز	z
ژ	żh
س	s
ش	sh
ص	ṣ
ض	ẓ
ط	t̤
ظ	z̤
ع	'
غ	gh
ف	f
ق	q
ک	k
گ	g
ل	l
م	m
ن	n

(m before ب and پ)

و	w

(v in Hindu names)

ہ	h

(not represented at the end of a word except when radical)

ی	y

Vowels – ـَ a. – ā. ـَى (alif maksūra) ā.

ـِ i. ـِی ī. e in some Hindu names. ـِیّ iyy; ī at the end of a word.

ـُ u. ـُو ū ; o in some Hindu names. ـُوّ uww; ū at the end of a word.

Diphthongs—ـَو au. ـَوّ aww. ـَی ai. ـَیّ ayy.

The 'Izāfat' is rendered by '-i-'.

The Persian copulative particle و is transliterated by 'u'.

The ل of the Arabic article is assimilated according to rule, the final vowel of the preceding word being preserved.

RULE OF TRANSLITERATION

ERRATA AND ADDENDA

Page 15, line 10. The figure 1 should be placed at Sulṭānun-nisā Begam.

p. 23, l. 10. *For* my *read* his. With reference to n. 2, p. 114, l. 9, shows that the father meant is Shāhrukh.

p. 33, l. 2 of verse. Solomon's greatness depended on the possession of a ring. When that was lost his power departed. See the story of its loss and recovery in Mīr Khwānd (Rehatsek's translation, pt. i, 100). Probably then the line should be rendered 'Call him the ring-wearing Solomon.'

p. 37, 1. 10, from foot. The words 'the news,' etc., are not a verse, and Naẓar-jīvī should be Naẓar Chūlī, i.e. the Naẓar who accompanied Humāyūn through the desert (*chūl*). See Akbar-nāma translation, i, 657, n. 3.

p. 37, l. 27. *For* near Lahore *read* a dependency of Lahore. Kalānūr is the Kalanaur of the maps, and is 15 miles west of Gurdāspūr (I.G., new ed., xiv, 297).

p. 42, note. *For* lithograph *read* text.

p. 44, l. 24. *For* Mīrzā *read* Mīrān.

p. 48, l. 16, and note 1. I.O. MSS. seem to have Tanam Bahādur. The reference to Ma'āṣiru-l-umarā is ii, 132. The name of Muẓaffar Gujarātī's son was Bahādur.

p. 52, n. 1. *For* Price, p. 5 *read* Price, p. 65. The Iqbāl-nāma and Khulāṣatu-t-tawārīkh say he was put in charge of Ihtimām Kotwāl.

p. 56, n. 2. It is Nīlera in I.O. MS. No. 181.

p. 58, l. 2. The meaning is that 'Ābidīn was the son of 'Abdu-llah Khān's spiritual adviser. 'Ābidīn is called 'Ābidī in Akbar-nāma, iii, 832. He came to India in 1013 (1604–5), and Akbar gave him the rank of 1,000 and 500 horse (iii, 834).

p. 63, l. 23. The MSS. seem to have Jaihāl.

p. 64, 1.14 Kilīn means 'daughter-in-law' in Turkī. Perhaps Kīlan here is a synonym for 'son-in-law.'

p. 64, l. 21. The words 'which in Hindustani is called *ballī*' are not in the I.O. MSS. I do not know the word *ballī* as meaning a pole. Perhaps it is a mistake for *laggī*.

p. 73, l. 3 from foot. Omit the words 'who is one of the khānazādas of the State.'

p. 76, l. 1. *For* and cash *read* in cash.

p. 77, n. 1. Delete question mark and the words 'near Multān.' Nandanpur, i.e. Nandana (I.G., xviii, 349), and Girjhāk are in the Jhelam district. The Rām Dās garden was some place near Lahore, where Jahāngīr took up his residence on the way to the hunting-ground. He spent 3 1/2 months in hunting.

p. 81, l. 3. *For* 'Abdu-r-Raḥīm *read* 'Abdu-r-Raḥmān.

p. 83, l. 3, from foot. Firishta in his account of Bābar says the Daulat Khān of that time was descended from the Daulat Khān who in 816 A.H. (1413–14) was Sultan of Delhi. See Elliot, iv, 45.

p. 86, l. 3 from foot. Jahāngīrpūr is mentioned in account of 15th year, p. 296, last line (text). It is the Shekhopura of the maps, and is 22 miles from Ḥāfi ẕ ābād and 18 miles west of Lahore. It was called Shaikhūpūra in allusion to Jahāngīr's pet name of Shaikhū Bābā, and also in honour of Shaikh Salīm. See Khulāṣa T. in account of Jahāngīr's reign. The I.G., xxii, 270, wrongly ascribes its origin to Dārā Shukūh. Mullā Ḥusain Kashmīrī, mentioned on p. 87, died in 1037 (1627–8), Rieu, ii, 7756. The minaret is still standing. See Eastwick's "Panjab Handbook," 200. Instead of 'the gravestone in the shape of an antelope' we should render, I think, 'a stone tomb with the figure of an antelope (engraved upon it).' The I.O. MSS. have Marrāj as the name of the antelope. Perhaps we should read Manorāj 'mind's lord.'

p. 95, l. 9. I.O. MSS. have *bahūr* as the name of the net.

p. 104, n. 1. Delete note. The *rang* is the ibex.

p. 110, n. 1. See J.A.S.B. for February, 1908, p. 39.

p. 111. The Iqbāl-nāma mentions in connection with the story of the mummified saint that many Sabzawār saints lived in Bāmiyān. See also Kāmgār Ḥusainī.

p. 113, l. 28. Delete word 'Georgians.' I.O. MS. No. 181 has ghurja.

p. 115, l. 30. Insert 'and' after 'sheep.'

p. 118, l. 32. *For* garden *read* gardens.

p. 125, l. 22. *For* £ *read* rupees.

p. 126, l. 28. *For* he died on the 29th *read* he died in his ninth decade (i.e. between 80 and 90). The Ma'ā ṣ̤iru-l-umarā, ii, 143, says he was 82 when he died.

p. 128, n. 1. The opinion expressed in this note is proved to be wrong by General Cunningham's Report, Arch. S., xiv, p. 58. The tombs are those of a musician and his pupil.

p. 132, l. 7. Delete *Sylvia olivacea.*

p. 135, l. 5. Apparently there were twelve balls, or at least objects, ten being as large as an orange, another being a citron, and the twelfth a *surkh*. So instead of 'one to a citron' we should read, perhaps, 'a citron and a *surkh*.'

p. 135, l. 8 from foot. *For* Ilf *read* Alf.

p. 139, l. 11. Delete the word 'Egyptian' and also n. 1. It appears from the Ghiyā ṣ̤ u-l-loghāt that a Qu ṭ bī ruby is a broad ruby suitable for a ring (signet?).

p. 144, l. 21. *For* Hamaẕānī *read* Hamadānī.

p. 146. According to Terry, Jahāndār was called Sultan Takht because born when Jahāngīr first sat on his throne.

p. 148, l. 23. Perhaps Yūzī = Yūz-bāshī, i.e. centurion. But I.O. 181 has not the word, only saying 'Shāh Beg Khān,' and No. 305 has Shāh Beg Khān Būrī (?).

p. 148, l. 24. The passage is wrongly translated. No elephant was presented to Salāmu-llah. The sentence should end on l. 9 after the word 'panther-keeper,' which word is probably a mistranslation. Then this new sentence should come, i.e. 'Salāmu-llah 'Arab, who is a young man of a distinguished Arabian family (*kih az jawānān-i-qarār-dāda-i-'Arab ast*) and related to Mubārak, the governor of Dizfūl, came to wait upon me on account of his being suspicious of the designs of Shāh 'Abbās (against himself).' 'I patronized him,' etc. (as on p. 148).

p. 148, n. 3, and p. 152, n. 1. Both notes are wrong. The place meant by Jahāngīr is Dizfūl, a town in the Khūzistān province of Persia, and Jūyza is evidently a copyist's error for Khūz or Khūza, another name for Khūzistān. Dizfūl is an ancient name, and according to Yāqūt, Barbier de Meynard's translation, p. 231, the proper spelling is Dizpūl, i.e. 'the Bridge of the Citadel,' the town being named after a famou bridge built over the river. For Khūz see B. de Meynard, 216.

p. 151, l. 1. Qabūlah was a town in the Bet Jālandhar Dū'āb.

p. 153, l. 9. It is 2,000 rupees in I.O. MSS.

p. 153, l. 14. It is not Qāchā Dakhanī in I.O. MSS., but I am not sure what the clause, as given by them, means. No. 181 seems to have *bafatāhāīgī* for 'assistance' (?). Two B.M. MSS. have apparently *bafatāhāī kapī,* but Add. 26, 215 has the Arabic *ḥa,* while Or. 3276 has the ordinary *h,* so that the words possibly mean 'the young of the monkey' (*kapī*).

p. 155, l. 30. Ḥusāmu-d-dīn was married to Abū-l-faẓl's sister, Blochmann, 441.

p. 157, l. 5. The word *rojh* in brackets is wrong. The MSS. have *qarā-quyragh* and *qarā-quyrāgh*. P. de Courteille gives *quyrūgh* as meaning a tail, so perhaps *qarā-qūyrūgh* means a black-tailed sheep or deer. See p. 122, l. 15, where the *qarā-qūyrūgh* is said to be the *chikāra.*

p. 159, n. 2. *For* Akbar's wives *read* Jahāngīr's wives.

p. 161, l. 21 seq. Is this the story referred to by Hawkins (Purchas), about Muqarrab having taken a Banian's daughter?

p. 166, note. *For* one-third of an inch *read* one and a third inches.

p. 183, l. 8. This is the annular eclipse entered in Dr. R. Schramm's Tables, Sewell's Indian Calendar, as having occurred on 5th December, 1610, which corresponds to 28th Ramaẓan, 1019.

p. 174, n. 3. Persian text, p. 309, l. 11, has the phrase *majrā girifta ātash dādand,* 'took aim and fired' (a cannon).

p. 176, l. 2, from foot. For Naẓīrī, see Rieu, ii, 807*b*, and Blochmann, 579. He died in 1622 (1613).

p. 179, l. 10. *For dhīk* (?) *read dhīk,* i.e. adjutant bird.

p. 179, l. 8. *Pātal* means 'red' or 'rose-coloured' in Sanskrit. Query 'red deer.'

p. 180, l. 2. Add year 1020.

p. 183, 1. 9 from foot. The passage is rather obscure, but the meaning seems to be that though formalities are not regarded by the wise, yet weak persons (*qāwāṣir,* which apparently is a plural of *qāṣir*), regard externals as the means of paying the dues of friendship (and so we must attend to them). Hence when at this auspicious time a province which had gone out of my ('Abbās's) possession has been settled by the exertions of angelic servants in accordance with the hopes of well-wishers, I ('Abbās) have returned to the capital, and have despatched Kamālu-d-dīn, etc.

p. 184, l. 32. *For* Khankhānān *read* Khān.

p. 184, l. 12. The I.O. MSS. have a different reading here. They say nothing about three ratis. What they say is, "At this time I had made some increase in the amounts of weights and measures. For instance, I added one-fourth (*siwā'ī*) to the weight of the muhrs and rupees." The *sih ratī* of text is a mistake for *siwā'ī.*

p. 184, l. 15 from foot. I.O. MSS. have 'Sunday in Ṣafar,' but they wrongly have 1022.

p. 197, l. 10 from foot. Both I.O. MSS. have 'Neknahar' instead of 'in the interior.'

p. 185, l. 31. *Or* Lohgar.

p. 192, l. 14. I do not think that the translation 'should not force Islam on anyone,' or the version in Elliot, vi, 325, 'Not to forcibly impose Musulman burdens on anyone,' gives the full force of the words *taklīf-i-Musulmānī bar kasī nakunand.* I think the reference clearly is to circumcision, and that the words *taklīf-i-Musalmānī* should be rendered 'the Muhammadan ceremonial,' This explains why the injunction comes in immediately after the prohibitions against blinding and mutilation. It has been said, and I believe with truth, that the members of the Delhi royal family never were circumcised. Probably one reason for this was that in many instances they had Hindu mothers. As pointed out in Elliot, the passage is omitted in the Iqbāl-nāma. It also does not occur in the version given in 'Alī Muḥammad's "History of Gujarat," vol. i, p. 200 of lithograph.

p. 201, verse. *For* red *read* a river.

p. 202. See picture of a turkey in Havell's "Indian Sculpture," pp. 214–15.

p. 205, l. 6. About Shāpūr see Ma'āsiru-l-umarā, i, 180.

p. 210, n. 1. *For* infra *read* supra, pp. 27 and 29, note.

p. 215, ll. 6 and 14. *For* Patna *read* Tatta.

p. 214, note. *For* brother *read* brother's son.

p. 217, l. 5. *For* Nihālpūr *substitute* Thālner as in the MSS. The news of the death seems to have reached Agra very quickly.

p. 217, l. 17. Insert the word 'and' before 'allowed.'

p. 220, l. 7. The word translated 'cranes' is *kārwānak,* and probably means 'a little crane.' In Blochmann, 63, *karwānak* is rendered by 'stone-curlew.'

p. 220, 1.4. The word seems to be *kunjishk,* 'sparrow,' in the MSS., but probably it should be *kunjak,* 'a curiosity, a rarity.'

p. 220, l. 14. It is Thursday, the 28th, in the MSS., and instead of 'night' we should read 'eve.' The English date corresponding to 28th Muḥarram is 10th March, 1613.

p. 222, l. 8. It is 1,000 in the MSS., and this is probably correct, though B.M. MS. 1645 has changed the word for 1,000 into one for 100. The ordinary *kaukab-i-ṭāli'* was 100 tolas in weight, see p. 11. At p. 406 two kaukab-i-tali's are mentioned of 500 tolas each. It is a mistake, I think, to regard the word muhr as always implying gold. The ordinary kaukab-i-tali' was of silver, and these large muhrs were no doubt also of silver. The note 1 to Elliot, vi, 355, is probably incorrect.

p. 222, l. 10. 'The feast went off well,' etc. The passage is obscure, but probably the translation should be 'There was a splendid assemblage (*majis shigufta gasht*), and after it was over I ordered that they should arrange an illumination.' The words in text, p. 110, l. 3, are *ḥukm kardam kih asbāb u āyin bār kunand*. The MSS. have *asbāb-i-āyīn rā*. No. 181 seems to have *bāz kunand,* and so has B.M. MS. 1645, but No. 305 has *bār kunand,* as in text. It may be that the meaning is that Jahāngīr told the servants they might appropriate the decorations, but I rather think the order was to make an illumination. It may also simply mean that he ordered the decorations to be taken down. *Bāz kunand* ordinarily means 'to open out,' *bār kunand* 'to load.'

p. 222, l. 13. Delete 'the' before Muqarrab.

p. 222, note. I.O. MSS: seem to have *zarīn,* 'golden' (?).

p. 226, l. 17. I.G., new ed., xvii, 309, speaks of a handsome mosque in Mairtha having been founded by Akbar, but probably it is this one of Shaikh Pīr. Perhaps Shaikh Pīr is the old beggar referred to in Roe's Journal.

p. 231, l. 3, from foot. For *chakrī* read *jhakkaṛ*. It was not necessarily a dust-storm.

p. 234, l. 1. The MSS. have Rūp instead of Rāwal, and so has Elliot, vi, 335. They have 'hill country of Mewāt,' as in text. They have Chitor, and not Jaipūr, as in Elliot, and they make (by error) Jahāngīr speak of the year as the 10th, instead of the 8th. Instead of 'have' at l. 12 we should read 'had,' and instead of 'from the Rāwal who was first known as Rāwal,' they have, as also has Elliot, 'Rahab, who was the first to take the title of Rānā.' Rahab is the Rahup of Tod, who says he came to the throne in 1201 A.D.

p. 236, ll. 25 and 11. I cannot find the word *pūlta-bāzī.* My friend, Mr. Irvine, suggests that we should read *paṭṭā bāzī. Paṭṭā* means a 'foil,' or 'wooden sword,' and *paṭṭā bāz* is given in Forbes as meaning a 'fencer.' *Palṭha mārnā* occurs in Forbes as meaning a 'peculiar posture.' The *yagānagī* of l. 11 should be *yakāngagi,* meaning 'one body,' or 'one limb,' and corresponds to the *yakhāth* of Blochmann, 252, both phrases meaning apparently 'that the fencer fights with one hand,' that is, 'without using a shield.'

p. 243, l. 5. This I'tiqād is the father of Mumtāz-maḥall, the wife of Shāh Jahān. He now became Āṣaf Khān, and apparently the title of I'tiqād was transferred to his younger brother (or cousin?) Shāhpūr, who was afterwards governor of Kashmir. See Ma'āṣir i, 180. The two previous Āṣaf Khāns of the family are Ghiyāṣu-d-dīn of Qazwīn (Blochmann, 433), and Mīrzā Ja'far Beg, who was Ghiyāṣu-d-dīn's nephew. The father of Nūr-Jahān was Ghiyāṣ Beg of Tīhran (Blochmann, 508). Blochmann, in his Table, 512, has not mentioned Shāhpūr, i.e. the I'tiqād who became governor of Kashmir.

p. 244, l. 11. *For* mother *read* mothers (i.e. stepmothers).

p. 244, l. 17. *For* nephews *read* nephew.

p. 259, l. 19. *For* named *read namad,* and it should be in italics.

p. 262, l. 3. The permission to beat his drums is explained by the Iqbāl-nāma, p. 79, where it is said that he was permitted to beat his drums in the capital, *dar pāy-i-takht.*

p. 262, l. 8 from foot. This eclipse is noted in Dr. Schram's Tables as occurring on 19th March, 1615.

p. 263, l. 16 from foot. Delete word 'Egyptian.'

p. 266, l. 17. *For* Frank *read* Venetian. *Kār-i-Wanadik,* as in MSS.

p. 268, l. 14. Chatūr, instead of Taḥayyur, in No. 305, and Bakhtar (?) in No. 181.

p. 272. According to the Iqbāl-nāma, 80, Kunwar Karan, son of Rānā Amar Singh, became an officer of Jahāngīr, receiving the rank of 5,000 personal and horse. He was the first of the direct royal line of his family to accept office.

p. 273, n. 2. No. 181 has Rasht.

p. 279, l. 24. According to Vullers' Dict., i, 482, a *tūlchạ* is 96 grains or about half a tola. The Ghīyāṣu-l-loghāt, however, says that *tūlcha* is merely the Persian form of the Hindustānī *tūlā.* According to the Burhān-iqāti' a tola is only 2 1/2 māsha in Upper India. Generally it is reckoned as 12 māsha. According to Sir Thomas Roe 2 1/2 tolas were equal to 1 ounce.

p. 295, MS. No. 181 has A.H. date 1025.

p. 299, l. 3. *For* several bits *read* some marten skins. See Tūzuk text, p. 308, l. 3 from foot, and Vullers' Dict. ii, 6. The MS. No. 181 has *ṣad dāna-i-kīsh,* 'one hundred marten skins.'

p. 299, l. 12. *For* transit dues *read* for keeping open the Pass (*rāh-dārī*).

p. 299, n. 2. The words in I.O. MSS. seem to be *īgāna begāna,* which is perhaps a mere jingle on the word *afghāna,* but may mean 'known, unknown.' Jahāngīr puns on the name Qadam, which means 'a foot, a pace.' The words occur again at p. 323.

p. 300, 1. 11, from foot. Probably *'āqirī* is, or is derived from, *'aqār,* which means a bird whose feathers were used for ornamentation. According to P. de Courteille, Turkī Dict., 384, *'aqār* is a heron.

p. 305, l. 9 from foot. *For* Shāh Shajā'at *read* Shāh Shujā'. He was Shāh Jahān's second son, and was born at Ajmir on the eve of Sunday, and on 11th Tīr.

Apparently this corresponds to 24th June, 1616, which is the date of birth mentioned by Sir Thomas Roe. Beale's date of 12th May is wrong.

p. 309, l. 7 from foot. Here the word *tūlcha* is used again, and apparently as meaning the same thing as *tola;* 6,514 tūlchas or tolas would be about 82 sīrs, or over 2 maunds, and about 12 stone. Next year Sir Thomas Roe saw Jahāngīr weighed, and he understood that his weight was 9,000 rupees. If so, his weight would appear to have considerably increased during the twelve months. Perhaps we should read 8,514, instead of 6,514 tūlchas. *Hasht* (8) and *shash* (6) are often confounded.

p. 317, l. 6 from foot. *For* times *read* days, the word *rūz* (days) having been omitted from the text.

p. 319, n. 1. Apparently we should read Toda. The difference between it and Nauda is, in Persian writing, only one dot. Toda is mentioned by Roe as the place where he overtook Jahāngīr, and the stages given by him come to 21 kos, counting from Rāmsar, and this agrees very nearly with Jahāngīr's stages from the same place.

p. 327, l. 3. The MS. No. 181 has the word *gaz* twice, and makes the *pahnā'ī,* or width, 175 1/2 *gaz* (yards).

p. 327, 1. 5, from foot. *For* Būlgharī *read* Pūlkharī.

p. 327, l. 18. Delete the words 'of Tīr.' The month was Bahman, corresponding to January-February, 1617, and 23rd Bahman would be about 1st February. In Sayyid Aḥmad's edition the word *Tīr* is a mistake for *nīz,* 'also,' the meaning being that the 23rd was a halt as well as the 22nd.

p. 328, l. 2. Ghaznīn Khān is mentioned by Finch under the name of Gidney Khān, and he is said to have been originally a Hindu. But this seems doubtful, as his father's name is given in the Mir'āt-i-Aḥmadī as Malik Khānjī Afghān. See also Bayley's "Gujarat," p. 15. Jālor is now in Jodhpūr. It is described by Finch.

p. 328, l. 2. This seems to be the case of matricide mentioned in Terry's "Voyage," p. 362, of ed. of 1777. His statement that it occurred at Aḥmadabad is presumably an oversight. Terry says the matricide was put to death by being bitten by two snakes. See also Irvine's "Manucci," iv, 422. Apparently the punishment recorded by Jahāngīr took place on the 4th February, for Sir Thomas Roe mentions that they reached Kāliyādaha, the next stage, on 6th February. The *bi* in *biyāsa* should be deleted. Jālaur, or Jalor, is in Jodhpūr (I.G., xiv, 29). It used to be in Ajmir. It is not quite clear if Terry was with Roe at Kāliyādaha, but if not he was with him at Ujjain. The execution may have taken place there.

p. 330, l. 23 'from the city of Ujjain,' etc., *read* 'to a rural spot near the city of Ujjain.'

p. 335, l. 20. *For* 128 1/4 cubits *read* 28 1/4 cubits. I.O. MS. 181 has 28 1/4 yards. The printed text of Sayyid Aḥmad has 128 1/4 cubits.

p. 337, l. 8 from foot. Delete (Bālchha?).

p. 347, l. 13 seq. This I'tiqād was the younger brother or perhaps cousin of Āṣaf Khān, the brother of Nūr-Jahān. He was also known as Shāhpūr. See Ma'ā ṣ iru-l-umarā, i, 180.

p. 349, n. 2. *Read* two diamonds.

p. 378, n. 3. Dīkhtān or Daikhtān seems right. It is so in both the I.O. MSS.

p. 378, l. 7 from foot. These muhrs were probably of silver, and were called muhrs because they were medals rather than coins. Dr. Kehr has given an account of a large muhr which is now apparently in Dresden. See also Richardson's Dict., article Sikka.

p. 379, l. 4. This is Jūna Khān, son of Ghīyā ṣ u-d-dīn Tughluq. He ascended the throne in 1325 under the title of Muḥammad bin Tughluq.

p. 379, l. 14. This is the prince known as Naṣīru-d-dīn. He ascended the throne as Muḥammad bin Fīrūz in 1387, and again in 1390.

p. 385, ll. 3 and 10, from foot. I.O. MSS. show that Sar-farāz should be Sarafrāz; apparently his present was 'seven bullock-carts' (*haft rās gāw bahal*) and not two bullocks.

p. 389, n. 2. Cancel note. Nārangsar seems right.

p. 389. The words are *dah bīst wazn muhr u rūpiya ma'mūl.* Elliot, p. 354, renders this 'ten and twenty times heavier than the current gold muhr and rupee.'

p. 390, l. 3. See n. 2 in Elliot, vi, 355. Apparently Jahāngīr means that he was the first person to coin double muhrs and double rupees. There is an account of tankas in the Bahār-i-'Ajam, 261, col 2, p. 421, n. 2. But it is 27 in I.O. MSS. 113, A *ṭassū* is more than a finger-breadth, it is the 1/24 of a *gaz* or yard, and should be about 1 1/3 inches.

p. 408. I am indebted to my friend Dr. Hoernle for the explanation of the names of the two sects of Sewras. They should be Tapā and Kharatara. Mān Singh's name in religion was Jīn-simha. See *Epigraphia Indica,* i, 37, and *Ind. Antiquary,* xi, 250. Mān Singh died at Mairtha (in Jodhpūr) according to the Jain books, in the beginning of 1618. The head of the Tapā sect in Jahāngīr's time was Vījayasena. There is an elaborate paper on the Jains of Gujarat and Marwar by Colonel Miles in the Transactions R.A.S., iii, pp. 335–71.

p. 412, l. 8. There is no previous reference to the outbreak of plague in Kashmir, though there is one to its occurrence in the Panjab. There is an interesting account of the plague in Khāfī Khān, i, 286–8, in which the description is carried down to the time of Aurangzīb.

INDEX

A

G

I

S

T